NATIONAL HUMAN RIGHTS INSTITUTIONS IN EUROPE

NATIONAL HUMAN RIGHTS INSTITUTIONS IN EUROPE

Comparative, European and International Perspectives

Jan Wouters
Katrien Meuwissen
(eds.)

intersentia
Cambridge – Antwerp – Portland

Intersentia Publishing Ltd.
Trinity House | Cambridge Business Park | Cowley Road
Cambridge | CB4 0WZ | United Kingdom
tel.: +44 1223 393 753 | email: mail@intersentia.co.uk

Distribution for the UK:
NBN International
Airport Business Centre, 10 Thornbury Road
Plymouth, PL6 7PP
United Kingdom
Tel: +44 1752 202 301 | Fax: +44 1752 202 331
Email: orders@nbninternational.com

Distribution for the USA and Canada:
International Specialized Book Services
920 NE 58th Ave Suite 300
Portland, OR 97213
USA
Tel.: +1 800 944 6190 (toll free)
Email: info@isbs.com

Distribution for Austria:
Neuer Wissenschaftlicher Verlag
Argentinierstraße 42/6
1040 Wien
Austria
Tel.: +43 1 535 61 03 24
Email: office@nwv.at

Distribution for other countries:
Intersentia Publishing nv
Groenstraat 31
2640 Mortsel
Belgium
Tel.: +32 3 680 15 50
Email: mail@intersentia.be

National Human Rights Institutions in Europe. Comparative, European and International Perspectives
Jan Wouters and Katrien Meuwissen (eds.)

ISBN 978-1-78068-114-6
D/2013/7849/65
NUR 820

British Library Cataloguing in Publication Data. A catalogue record for this book is available from the British Library.

EUROPEAN SCIENCE FOUNDATION
ESF Provides the COST Office through an EC contract

COST is supported by the EU RTD Framework programme

ACKNOWLEDGEMENTS

The editors of this book would like to thank the European Cooperation in Science and Technology (COST) for their financial support of COST Action IS0702, including the support for the organisation of a COST conference on NHRIs at the KU Leuven Centre for Global Governance Studies (April 2012), and the publication of this volume. Our appreciation goes especially out to Ms. Helga Baumschabl, who guided us through the COST administration. We also want to express our gratitude to Intersentia, the publisher of this book. We are thankful to all participants to the COST conference on NHRIs, specifically all members of COST Action IS0702 and Ms. Kirsten Roberts, who contributed to the elaboration of the COST Action IS0702 recommendations on NHRIs (Annex 1 to this book). We are much obliged to all authors for their kind cooperation throughout the "publication process": from delivering a presentation during the COST conference in Leuven to the finalisation of the contributions in this book.

COST: EUROPEAN COOPERATION IN SCIENCE AND TECHNOLOGY

COST – the acronym for European Cooperation in Science and Technology – is the oldest and widest European intergovernmental network for cooperation in research. Established by the Ministerial Conference in November 1971, COST is presently used by the scientific communities of 36 European countries to cooperate in common research projects supported by national funds. The funds provided by COST – less than 1% of the total value of the projects – support the COST cooperation networks (COST Actions) through which, with EUR 30 million per year, more than 30 000 European scientists are involved in research having a total value which exceeds EUR 2 billion per year. This is the financial worth of the European added value which COST achieves.

A "bottom up approach" (the initiative of launching a COST Action comes from the European scientists themselves), "à la carte participation" (only countries interested in the Action participate), "equality of access" (participation is open also to the scientific communities of countries not belonging to the European Union) and "flexible structure" (easy implementation and light management of the research initiatives) are the main characteristics of COST.

As precursor of advanced multidisciplinary research COST has a very important role for the realisation of the European Research Area (ERA) anticipating and complementing the activities of the Framework Programmes, constituting a "bridge" towards the scientific of emerging countries, increasing the mobility of researchers across Europe and fostering the establishment of "Networks of Excellence" in many key scientific domains such as: Biomedicine and Molecular Biosciences; Food and Agriculture; Forests, their Products and Services; Materials, Physical and Nanosciences; Chemistry and Molecular Sciences and Technologies; Earth System Science and Environmental Management; Information and Communication Technologies; Transport and Urban Development; Individuals, Societies, Cultures and Health. It covers basic and more applied research and also addresses issues of pre-normative nature or of societal importance.

Web: http://www.cost.eu

CONTENTS

PART I. COMPARATIVE PERSPECTIVES

LIST OF ABBREVIATIONS

ACP	African, Caribbean and Pacific countries
APF	Asia-Pacific Forum of National Human Rights Institutions
APT	Association for the Prevention against Torture
CAT	Convention against Torture and Other Cruel, Inhuman or Degrading Treatment or Punishment
CDDH	Council of Europe Steering Committee for Human Rights
CEDAW	Convention on the Elimination of All Forms of Discrimination against Women
CERD	Committee on the Elimination of Racial Discrimination
CEOOR	Centre for Equal Opportunities and Opposition to Racism (Belgium)
CHR	United Nations Commission on Human Rights
COSP	Conference of State Parties
COST	European Cooperation in Science and Technology
CPT	European Committee on the Prevention of Torture and Inhuman and Degrading Treatment or Punishment
CRC	Convention on the Rights of the Child
CRE	Commission for Racial Equality (United Kingdom)
CRPD	Convention on the Rights of Persons with Disabilities
CSOs	civil society organisations
CSP	country strategy paper
CSW	Commission on the Status of Women
DIHR	Danish Institute for Human Rights
DRC	Disability Rights Commission (United Kingdom)
DROI	Subcommittee on Human Rights of the European Parliament
DPA	Data Protection Authority
EaP	Eastern Partnership
ECOSOC	United Nations Economic and Social Council
ECHR	European Convention on Human Rights
ECtHR	European Court of Human Rights
ECJ	European Court of Justice
ECRI	European Commission against Racism and Intolerance
EDF	European Development Fund
EDPS	European Data Protection Supervisor
EEOC	Equal Employment Opportunity Commission (United States of America)

EHRC	Equality and Human Rights Commission (United Kingdom)
EIDHR	European Instrument for Democracy and Human Rights
EIGE	European Institute for Gender Equality
ENOC	European Network of Ombudsperson for Children
EOC	Equal Opportunities Commission (United Kingdom)
EQUINET	European Network for Equality Bodies
EU	European Union
FRA	European Union Agency for Fundamental Rights
HRC	United Nations Human Rights Council
HCHR	United Nations High Commissioner for Human Rights
IA	Impact Assessment
ICC	International Coordinating Committee of National Human Rights Institutions
ICC SCA	International Coordinating Committee of National Human Rights Institutions Sub- Committee on Accreditation
ICCPR	International Covenant on Civil and Political Rights
ICED	International Convention for the Protection of All Persons from Enforced Disappearance
ICERD	International Convention on the Elimination of All Forms of Racial Discrimination
ICESCR	International Covenant on Economic, Social and Cultural Rights
ICM	Inter-Committee Meeting of United Nations treaty body representatives
ICMW	International Convention on the Protection of the Rights of All Migrant Workers and Members of their Families
IHRC	Irish Human Rights Commission
IOI	International Ombudsman Institute
LGBT	lesbian, gay, bisexual and transgender
NEB	national equality body
NGO	non-governmental organisation
NHRI	national human rights institution
NHRS	national human rights structure
NIHR	Netherlands Institute for Human Rights
NIRMS	National Institutions and Regional Mechanisms Section of the UN Office of the High Commissioner for Human Rights
NJCM	Nederlands Juristen Comité voor Mensenrechten [Section of the International Commission of Jurists in the Netherlands]
NPM	national preventive mechanism under the Optional Protocol to the UN Convention against Torture and Other Cruel, Inhuman or Degrading Treatment or Punishment
OHCHR	United Nations Office for the High Commissioner of Human Rights

OPCAT	Optional Protocol to the UN Convention against Torture and Other Cruel, Inhuman or Degrading Treatment or Punishment
OSCE	Organization for Security and Cooperation in Europe
OSCE ODIHR	Organization for Security and Cooperation in Europe, Office for Democratic Institutions and Human Rights
Paris Principles	Principles Relating to the Status of National Institutions for the Promotion and Protection of Human Rights
RCT	Research Centre for Torture Victims (Denmark)
TAIEX	Technical Assistance and Information Exchange Instrument (European Commission)
TEU	Treaty on European Union
TFEU	Treaty on the Functioning of the European Union
UK	United Kingdom
UN	United Nations
UNDP	United Nations Development Programme
UN GA	United Nations General Assembly
UN CHR	United Nations Commission on Human Rights
UN HRC	United Nations Human Rights Council
UPR	universal periodic review
USA	United States of America

NATIONAL HUMAN RIGHTS INSTITUTIONS IN EUROPE: AN INTRODUCTION

Jan WOUTERS and Katrien MEUWISSEN

1. BACKGROUND AND FOCUS

This book constitutes a scientific output of COST Action IS0702, which has brought together a large number of European human rights experts on the theme of the European Union (EU) and United Nations (UN) human rights reform. On 16 April 2012, the Leuven Centre for Global Governance Studies organised an international conference under this COST Action on 'National Human Rights Institutions and the Promotion and Protection of Human Rights' in Leuven. This conference brought together prominent academic experts, civil society representatives and practitioners from the EU and the UN to discuss the challenges and opportunities which the increasing role of National Human Rights Institutions (NHRIs) raises for human rights promotion and protection at multiple levels: national, European and international. This book brings together the thoroughly re-worked and edited contributions to the conference.

The main objective of COST Action IS0702 was to increase and consolidate knowledge of the on-going processes of UN human rights reform in order to make policy-relevant recommendations for the EU in its work towards strengthening the protection of human rights worldwide. In view of the composition of the consortium (European human rights experts) and the finality of the Action (formulating recommendations towards the EU), this book does not cover NHRIs globally. Rather, it focuses on the functioning and role of NHRIs in Europe from a comparative, European and international perspective. Even here, choices needed to be made in terms of the case-studies of individual NHRIs (see *infra*, 3).

2. OBJECTIVES

This book aims to advance knowledge regarding the opportunities and challenges that accompany the increasing number and role of NHRIs in Europe established for the promotion and protection of human rights at national, European and international levels. It does so by bringing together contributions both from academics and practitioners at national, EU and international levels. The literature on NHRIs is in a nascent state and often focuses on specific issues, such as the proliferation of NHRIs,[1] aspects of their functioning,[2] their interaction with a particular human rights body,[3] or certain national,[4] regional[5] and international[6] dimensions.[7] This book contributes to the – rather scarce[8] – literature on NHRIs in Europe by offering a comprehensive multi-level approach: the functioning of NHRIs is analysed from a comparative, European and international perspective. Furthermore, the volume hopes to engender insights for practitioners, who are still developing their approach towards NHRIs. Particularly at a time when the EU is looking for a more coherent and strategic human rights policy,[9] this book intends to inform and further trigger the NHRI debate in Europe. In an annex, recommendations towards the EU are included that were elaborated at the end of COST Action IS0702. These recommendations were presented to, and discussed with EU policy-makers on 28 January 2013 at the Brussels Office of COST.

---

1 T. Pegram, 'Diffusion Across Political Systems: The Global Spread of National Human Rights Institutions', *Human Rights Quarterly*, vol. 32, no. 3, August 2010, pp. 729–760.

2 M. Brodie, 'Progressing Norm Socialisation: Why Membership Matters. The Impact of the Accreditation Process of the International Coordinating Committee of National Institutions for the Promotion and Protection of Human Rights', *Nordic Journal of International Law*, vol. 80, 2011, pp. 143–192.

3 G. de Beco, 'La Contribution des Institutions Nationales des Droits de l'Homme au Renforcement de l'Efficacité de la Cour Européenne des Droits de l'Homme', *Revue trimestrielle des droits de l'homme*, vol. 77, 2009, pp. 165–194.

4 C. J. Petersen, 'The Paris Principles and Human Rights Institutions: Is Hong Kong Slipping Further Away From the Mark?', *Hong Kong Law Journal*, vol. 33, no. 3, 2003, pp. 513–522; T. Thipanyane, 'Challenges Facing National Human Rights Institutions: a South-African Perspective', *African Legal Aid Quarterly*, vol. 32, 2009, pp. 14–26; C. Renshaw, A. Byrnes and A. Durbach, 'Implementing Human Rights in the Pacific Through National Human Rights Institutions: The Experience of Fiji', *Victoria University of Wellington Law Review*, vol. 40, no. 1, 2009, pp. 251–277.

5 B.R. Dinokopila, 'Beyond Paper-Based Affiliate Status: National Human Rights Institutions and the African Commission on Human and People's Rights', *African Human Rights Law Journal*, vol. 10, no. 4, 2010, pp. 26–52.

6 R. Carver, 'A New Answer to an Old Question: National Human Rights Institutions and the Domestication of International Law', *Human Rights Law Review*, vol. 10, no. 1, 2010, pp. 1–32.

7 Two more comprehensive academic publications on NHRIs are: R. Murray, *The Role of National Human Rights Institutions at the International and Regional Levels: the Experience of Africa*, Hart Publishing, 2007; R. Goodman and T. Pegram (eds.), *State Compliance and Social Change: Assessing National Human Rights Institutions*, Cambridge University Press, 2012.

8 Academic NHRI literature with a 'European' focus is scarce. See, for example, G. De Beco, 'National Human Rights Institutions in Europe', *Human Rights Law Review*, vol. 7, 2007, pp. 331–370. Extensive reports on NHRIs in Europe have been published recently by the European Agency for Fundamental Rights (FRA): FRA, *National Human Rights Institutions in EU Member States, Strengthening the Fundamental Rights Architecture in the EU*, Luxembourg, Publication Office of the European Union, 2010; FRA, *Handbook on the Establishment and Accreditation of National Human Rights Institutions in the European Union*, Luxembourg, Publication Office of the European Union, 2012.

9 Council of the European Union, 'EU Strategic Framework and Action Plan on Human Rights and Democracy', 11855/12, 25 June 2012.

2.1. NATIONAL HUMAN RIGHTS INSTITUTIONS IN A EUROPEAN CONTEXT

NHRIs are a rather new phenomenon in the international human rights arena. Since the 'International Workshop on National Institutions for the Promotion and Protection of Human Rights' in 1991, an international push for the establishment of national human rights institutions has started to materialise.[10] The 1991 Workshop culminated in the adoption of the international principles relating to the status of national institutions, the so-called 'Paris Principles',[11] which outline standards relating to the responsibilities, composition and working methods of NHRIs. Shortly after the Workshop, the UN Commission on Human Rights (in 1992)[12] and the UN General Assembly (in 1993)[13] formally adopted the Paris Principles.

Over the past twenty years, the number of NHRIs has grown exponentially, and today more than 100 NHRIs are spread over all continents.[14] The proliferation of NHRIs has been driven primarily by the UN, which promotes NHRIs that are in compliance with the Paris Principles as 'cornerstones' of the protection of human rights (see Part 3 of this book).[15] While the Paris Principles lay down internationally recognised standards for NHRIs, they simultaneously provide flexibility and recognise that 'it is the right of each state to choose the framework that is best suited to the particular needs at the national level'.[16] Indeed, as

---

10 This workshop was organised by the UN Secretary-General, at the request of the UN Commission on Human Rights. See: UN Commission on Human Rights, Resolution 1990/73 of 7 March 1990. For a short historical account, see OHCHR, *National Human Rights Institutions. History, Principles, Roles and Responsibilities*, New York/ Geneva, 2010.

11 There is surprisingly little literature about the Paris Principles. See: OHCHR, *National Human Rights Institutions. A Handbook on the Establishment and Strengthening of National Institutions for the Promotion and Protection of Human Rights*, New York/ Geneva, 1995; OHCHR, *National Human Rights Institutions. History, Principles, Roles and Responsibilities*, New York/ Geneva, 2010; M. Brodie, 'Progressing Norm Socialisation: Why Membership Matters. The Impact of the Accreditation Process of the International Coordinating Committee of National Institutions for the Promotion and Protection of Human Rights', *Nordic Journal of International Law*, vol. 80, 2011, pp. 143–192.

12 UN Commission on Human Rights, Resolution 1992/54 of 3 March 1992.

13 UN General Assembly, Resolution 48/134 of 20 December 1993.

14 For an overview of accredited NHRIs, see: ICC, Chart of the Status of National Institutions, Accreditation Status as of May 2012, available at http://nhri.ohchr.org/.

15 OHCHR, *National Human Rights Institutions: History, Principles, Roles and Responsibilities*, p. 13. See also P. Rosenblum, 'Tainted Origins and Uncertain Outcomes: Evaluating NHRIs', in R. Goodman and T. Pegram (eds.), *State Compliance and Social Change: Assessing National Human Rights Institutions*, pp. 297–323; G. Magazzeni, 'The Role of OHCHR in Promoting National Human Rights Institutions', in W. Benedek, C. Gregory, J. Kozma, M. Nowak, C. Strohal and E. Theuermann (eds.), *Global Standards-Local Action: 15 years Vienna World Conference on Human Rights*, Intersentia, 2009, pp. 169–176.

16 See UN General Assembly, 'Vienna Declaration and Programme of Action, UN Doc. A/CONF.157/23, 12 July 1993, part I, para. 36. See also OHCHR, *National Human Rights Institutions: History, Principles, Roles and Responsibilities*, p. 13–19.

Manfred Nowak's first chapter reveals, many variations of NHRIs exist as there are diverse geographic regions, political contexts and legal traditions.[17]

As indicated, this book especially presents insights into the emergence and activities of NHRIs in Europe. While the international promotion of Paris Principle compliant NHRIs does have an impact on the human rights scenery in Europe, the European human rights context entails a particular NHRI landscape in this region with its own specificities, challenges and opportunities.

2.2. EUROPEAN NHRIS AS MULTI-DIMENSIONAL HUMAN RIGHTS ACTORS

The worldwide drive towards the establishment of NHRIs is directly related to the potential role of NHRIs in transmitting and implementing international norms at the domestic level and in contributing human rights expertise to regional and global human rights fora. The Paris Principles indicate the 'bridge-building' role of NHRIs. Next to outlining the different responsibilities of NHRIs to promote and protect international human rights standards at the domestic level, the Paris Principles explicitly state that NHRIs should cooperate with international and regional human rights institutions, and suggest that NHRIs should contribute to international human rights reports of governments.[18] As indicated by the Paris Principles, at each of the levels of engagement, NHRIs need to establish working relations with a large variety of actors. The Paris Principles explicitly refer to the need for NHRIs to cooperate with UN organisations, regional institutions and other NHRIs.[19] More generally, they indicate that NHRIs should maintain consultations with 'other bodies, whether jurisdictional or otherwise, responsible for the promotion and protection of human rights'[20].

The present book aims to reveal and clarify the various dimensions that are relevant for the functioning of European NHRIs in a multi-layered human rights context. This is reflected in the structure of the book, which addresses European NHRIs from a comparative perspective (Part I), a European perspective (Part II) and an international perspective (Part III). In order to carry out their "bridge-building" function between the different layers of the human rights

17 OHCHR, *National Human Rights Institutions: History, Principles, Roles and Responsibilities*, p. 15, referring to International Council on Human Rights Policy and OHCHR, *Assessing the Effectiveness of National Human Rights Institutions*, 2005.

18 Principles relating to the status of national institutions (further: Paris Principles), para. 3-e.

19 Paris Principles, competence and responsibilities, art. 3, (e): 'To cooperate with the United Nations and any other organization in the United Nations system, the regional institutions and the national institutions of other countries that are competent in the areas of the promotion and protection of human rights'.

20 Paris Principles, methods of operation, (f): 'Maintain consultation with the other bodies, whether jurisdictional or otherwise, responsible for the promotion and protection of human rights (in particular ombudsmen, mediators and similar institutions)'.

system, European NHRIs simultaneously engage with a wide variety of actors and mechanisms at different policy levels. European NHRIs need to operate on the continent with the largest variety and density of human rights protection mechanisms, from the EU to the Council of Europe, the Organisation for Security and Cooperation in Europe (OSCE) and the UN. The multi-layered engagement of European NHRIs depends on many context-specific factors, practices and rules. For example, the cooperation of the Danish Institute for Human Rights (DIHR) with the European Court of Human Rights (ECtHR) is contingent on a variety of elements such as the capacity of DIHR, its prioritisation of roles and national mandate, as well as the rules of procedure and practices of the ECtHR.[21]

3. STRUCTURE

Flowing from the above focus and objectives the book is divided into three parts, each concentrating on the functioning of NHRIs from a different perspective: a comparative (Part I), European (Part II) and international perspective (Part III).

Preceding these three parts, the book starts with a **first chapter** by **Manfred Nowak.** Nowak paints the contours of the NHRI landscape by comparing the present number, types, status and functions of NHRIs at the global level, in Europe and in the EU. His survey indicates that regional preferences can be identified regarding the types of NHRIs that are established by governments throughout the world. While states in Africa, Asia and the Pacific clearly prefer the commission (or advisory council) type, most Latin-American states show a preference for the Spanish ombuds-institution type. Compared to the three other regions, Europe is characterised by greater diversity. In Europe, all types of NHRIs can be found including commissions, ombuds-institutions and institutes with a research focus. Nowak notes that a high level of fragmentation exists in the domestic human rights architecture of many European states. He calls upon the EU to request its Member States to create fully independent, professional and pluralistic NHRIs with a strong preference for national human rights commissions with an over-arching mandate, including the examination of individual complaints. In order to avoid fragmentation and a lack of synergies, Nowak indicates that specialised human rights bodies, such as equal treatment commissions and national preventive mechanisms, might be placed under the umbrella of national human rights commissions.

[21] For more information on the functioning of DIHR, see: C. Badse, Chapter two in this volume. For more information on the opportunities for NHRI engagement with the European Court of Human Rights, see A. Buyse, Chapter 8 in this volume.

Part I of the book takes a **comparative approach** in the analysis of selected European NHRIs. It contains four chapters of which each address the functioning of a specific European NHRI and thereby illustrate the considerable diversity of NHRIs throughout Europe. The four case-studies were selected on the basis of regional and institutional differentiation and the expertise available with members of the COST consortium.[22] Generally, three different types of NHRIs can be discerned: human rights commissions, ombudsmen and institutes.[23] All of these NHRIs comply to a more or less extent with the Paris Principles. Accordingly, it was deemed to be of great value to examine, in the first place, the Danish Institute for Human Rights, one of the oldest and most active NHRIs operating in a progressive national human rights context; in the second place, the Polish Human Rights Ombudsman, an NHRI of a different type that operates in the Eastern European context; and last but not least the Dutch and Belgian cases, which reflect the difficulties that go together with the establishment of a new NHRI on the basis of a pre-existing national equality body (NEB).

In the second chapter, the Danish Institute for Human Rights (DIHR) is discussed by **Christopher Badse**, a senior legal advisor of the DIHR. The DIHR is the classic example of an institute-type NHRI, with a focus on delivering evidence-based advice to government. It undertakes a wide variety of human rights related activities and cooperates intensively with civil society and international human rights mechanisms. However, it does not have a mandate to address individual complaints. While only ten years ago the Danish Institute was threatened with closure, new legislation adopted in 2012 further strengthened its independent mandate and administration and enhanced the funding for the different tasks of the Institute. DIHR combines its functioning as a broadly mandated NHRI with various special mandates deriving from EU Directives and

22 Also because of its multi-level approach (comparative, European and international dimensions), this volume does not contain case-studies on all European NHRIs. Thus, a number of well-established NHRIs within the EU, such as the French *Commission nationale consultative des droits de l'homme* (http://www.cncdh.fr/en), the Spanish *Defensor del Pueblo* (http://www.defensordelpueblo.es/en/index.html) and the *Deutsches Institut für Menschenrechte* (http://www.institut-fuer-menschenrechte.de/en/home.html) are not the subject of a case-study, although they are included in the overview of the NHRI landscape provided in Manfred Nowak's Chapter 1. The same applies for European NHRIs outside the EU, such as the Centre for Human Rights in Norway or the Commissioner for Human Rights in the Russian Federation. An extensive comparative study on European NHRIs is non-existent today. For a full overview of NHRIs in EU Member States, see: FRA, *National Human Rights Institutions in EU Member States, Strengthening the fundamental rights architecture in the EU*, Luxembourg, Publication Office of the European Union, 2010. For more information on NHRIs in the wider Europe, we can refer to: G. Kucsko-Stadlmayer (ed.), *European Ombudsman-Institutions*, Springer Wien/ New York, 2008; L. Adler, 'National Human Rights Institutions in the OSCE Area: Taking Stock of an Innovative Concept', *OSCE Yearbook*, 2011, pp. 379–391; R. Carver, 'National Human Rights Institutions in Central and Eastern Europe: The Ombudsman as Agent of International Law', in R. Goodman and T. Pegram (eds.), *State Compliance and Social Change: Assessing National Human Rights Institutions*, 2012, pp. 181–209.

23 See M. Nowak, Chapter 1 in this volume.

the UN Convention on the Rights of Persons with Disabilities. Badse identifies the prioritisation of tasks as a continuous challenge for the Danish Institute.

In chapter three, **Aleksandra Gliszczyńska-Grabias** and **Katarzyna Sękowska-Kozłowska** elucidate the functioning of the Polish 'Commissioner for Citizens' Rights'. As an NHRI of the ombudsman-type, the Polish Ombudsman is a single-person body (supported by an office) with the key competence to serve as a complaint body. The Ombudsman is actively involved in human rights promotion and education in Poland and in the wider Eastern European region. While the Ombudsman actively cooperates with European human rights procedures, the authors observe that his engagement with UN mechanisms is underdeveloped. Despite the various strengths of the Ombudsman – described as a 'key entity of human rights protection in Poland'- the authors conclude that a major obstacle for his effective functioning is insufficient funding. While specific mandates of the Ombudsman are adding up (serving as the national preventive mechanism under the Optional Protocol to the Convention Against Torture since 2008, and operating as equality body under EU law since 2011), his financial resources are at the same time decreasing.

Chapters four and five exemplify that there is an increasingly high pressure on EU Member States –even if they have a decent human rights record – to establish an NHRI in compliance with the Paris Principles.

In chapter four, **Yvonne Donders** and **Marjolijn Olde Monnikhof** assess the establishment of the Netherlands Institute for Human Rights (NIHR), which opened its doors in October 2012. The authors find that the prior existence of several national bodies dealing with human rights was one of the factors slowing down the process of the establishment of an NHRI in the Netherlands. After wide consultations, the Dutch government opted for the establishment of an NHRI through seeking junction with one of the existing national institutions, the Dutch Equal Treatment Commission. Donders and Olde Monnikhof discuss the main opportunities and challenges for the Netherlands Institute. Special attention is paid to the delicate reorganisation of an institute with a specific equal treatment mandate into an NHRI with a broad human rights mandate. The authors conclude that 'perhaps the most crucial challenge for the new institute is to find a way to fulfil all its tasks [...], in particular in relation to the relatively modest budget allocated to the NIHR'.

In chapter five, **Jogchum Vrielink and Stefan Sottiaux** examine the 'national institutions' landscape in Belgium. Belgium is one of the EU Member States which does not have a Paris Principle compliant NHRI. Its Centre for Equal Opportunities and Opposition to Racism is only accredited with a B-status. In the Belgian federal system, both federal and federated governments have important powers in the human rights domain, resulting in the creation of a number of specialised human rights institutions by each of the (federal and federated) governments. The authors critically assess the current impetus in Belgium to centralise the various federated equality bodies into a single inter-federal equality body, and subsequently expand the inter-federal equality body and turn it into an NHRI with a broad human rights mandate. On the basis of comparative research, the authors point out advantages and disadvantages of centralising human rights institutes, and aim to counterbalance the 'one-sided nature of the debate in Belgium today, which seems to be focused exclusively on centralisation, integration, and expansion'.

Part II of this book comprises four contributions that concentrate on various **European dimensions** of the functioning of NHRIs. The chapters pay attention to *horizontal* cooperation between European NHRIs among themselves (chapter six) and between NHRIs and data protection agencies (chapter seven). Moreover, there is extensive attention for *vertical* cooperation of NHRIs with European human rights mechanisms in the context of the OSCE (chapter six), the Council of Europe – especially the ECtHR – (chapters six and eight), and the EU (chapters six and nine).

In chapter six **Bruce Adamson**, a legal officer at the Scottish Human Rights Commission and the Coordinator of the European Group for NHRIs, spells out the scope for strengthened cooperation and performance of European NHRIs towards European human rights institutions. Adamson notes that, despite having the largest number and most diverse NHRIs in Europe, the European Group of NHRIs is one of the least developed regional coordination groups in the world. At the same time, however, the European Group of NHRIs has to operate within the most advanced regional human rights structure, which requires NHRIs to engage with a broad range of bodies, including the OSCE, Council of Europe and the EU. This chapter provides an overview of the interaction between European NHRIs and the various European human rights mechanisms. While opportunities for interaction are increasing in various respects, the engagement between the regional mechanisms and NHRIs is inconsistent and the resources of European NHRIs are insufficient. A variety of findings lead the author to conclude that European NHRIs and regional institutions need to explore new modalities of engagement in a more strategic sense. In these times of financial austerity, Adamson especially highlights that European NHRIs and their European counterparts must stand together to oppose cuts that would put the human rights framework at risk.

In a following chapter, **Peter J. Hustinx**, the European Data Protection Supervisor, analyses a typically European type of national human rights body with a specific mandate: national data protection authorities (DPAs). DPAs find their origin in Council of Europe rules,[24] and are now strongly anchored in EU law. The chapter examines the discrepancies and deficiencies of the – highly diverse – European DPA scenery. It points to the further harmonisation that would be introduced through the newly proposed EU legal framework for data

[24] Council of Europe, Convention for the Protection of Individuals with regard to Automatic Processing of Personal Data, Strasbourg, 28.I.1981.

protection. The new legal framework incorporates the requirement – set by case-law of the Court of Justice of the EU – of DPAs' complete independence, enhances the enforcement powers of DPAs and encourages EU-wide cooperation between DPAs on cross-border and common issues. Hustinx concludes that the requirements of the new proposals will not greatly affect the relationship between DPAs and NHRIs, which should continue to 'develop and structure mutual relationships to their best common benefit'.

Chapter eight explains how NHRIs can function as the 'ears and arms' of the ECtHR. **Antoine Buyse** describes how NHRIs can support and cooperate with the ECtHR in three distinct stages of the Court's proceedings. Firstly, while they cannot lodge complaints, Buyse indicates that NHRIs have an important preventative and information-channelling function before a complaint reaches the Court. Secondly, the chapter shows how NHRIs can intervene during proceedings as *amici curiae* by 'contextualising a case for the Court in a broader perspective than an individual applicant *could* ever do and from a more independent perspective than the defendant State *would* ever do'. Thirdly, the chapter shows how NHRIs can play a role after a judgment has been delivered and when it comes to implementation. Buyse argues that NHRIs can be extremely useful partners for the Court, a factor which may contribute to solving some of the challenges the latter faces.

Chapter nine sheds light on the potential role for NHRIs to foster a more effective human rights architecture in the EU. **Wouters, Barros and Meuwissen** find that there is scope for NHRIs to become more important partners of the EU in the implementation and further development of its fundamental rights architecture. Throughout the chapter, different issue areas are addressed, ranging from the potential role of NHRIs in the process of EU law-making to the possible relevance of NHRIs in the field of EU development cooperation. While the constitutional and institutional innovations introduced by the Lisbon Treaty offer momentum for enhanced EU-NHRI cooperation, the authors observe that NHRIs are not structurally integrated in the EU human rights working culture yet. They encourage both EU institutions and European NHRIs to consistently consider mutual cooperation and to identify common priorities, while recognising each other's strengths and weaknesses.

Finally, **Part III** zooms into the third layer of the NHRI scenery and provides international perspectives on the functioning of national institutions. This part addresses both the horizontal interaction among NHRIs themselves (chapters ten and eleven) and the vertical interaction between NHRIs and UN human rights mechanisms (chapters ten and twelve).

In chapter 10, **Kirsten Roberts** identifies Paris Principles-compliant NHRIs as *sui generis* actors occupying a 'fourth space' in the international human rights framework, as they are neither state representatives, non-governmental organisations (NGOs) nor international organisations. The author illustrates how NHRIs engage with UN human rights mechanisms, such as the UN Human Rights Council, the UN General Assembly and the UN treaty procedures. Specific attention is paid to the role of the International Coordinating Committee of national human rights institutions (ICC), which promotes and supports the international engagement of NHRIs. Roberts indicates how NHRIs – despite their shortcomings – can provide added value to the international human rights system. The author calls for more critical attention for NHRI effectiveness to help understand how NHRIs can positively develop and increase their contribution to the promotion and protection of human rights.

In chapter eleven, **Gauthier de Beco** examines the assessment of NHRI compliance with the Paris Principles as carried out by the ICC Sub-Committee on Accreditation (SCA). The author highlights the important consequences for NHRIs of SCA accreditation, as the latter determines the position of NHRIs in international human rights forums and strengthens the legitimacy of NHRIs at home. This chapter outlines the international standards contained in the Paris Principles and describes how the SCA determines whether NHRIs are deemed to be compliant with the Paris Principles or not. De Beco indicates that the ICC has shown great willingness to strengthen its accreditation procedure. However, besides identifying advantages of the SCA peer review, he points out several shortcomings of the current accreditation process. De Beco suggests how the accreditation process might be further strengthened and questions whether the Paris Principles should continue to be the only benchmark against which NHRIs are measured.

In chapter twelve **Katrien Meuwissen** analyses the extent to which the role of NHRIs as "bridge-builders" between the national and international layers of human rights promotion and protection is integrated in the institutional frameworks of the UN Human Rights Council and the UN treaty bodies. Even if the participation of NHRIs in international procedures is rather low and while their impact on human rights compliance is not clear, they have acquired a privileged position in the UN human rights procedures. The chapter shows that the approach of the UN human rights mechanisms towards NHRIs is still evolving, both in terms of identifying their position and role in UN procedures as with regard to defining which NHRIs can participate in the UN procedures.

In a final chapter, **Jan Jarab**, the Regional Representative for Europe of the UN High Commissioner for Human Rights, outlines OHCHR's perspectives on the need for NHRIs in Europe and the world. He highlights the reasons for creating NHRIs based on international law and argues that NHRIs should be created in both 'immature' and 'mature' democratic systems. The author specifically points to the relevance of NHRIs in the evolving human rights context of the 21st century and notes that NHRIs can play an important role for the protection of 'groups of people at risk', such as children, migrants or disabled people. The author expresses the hope of OHCHR that 'in 10 to 15 years, it will be an exception not to have an

A-status NHRI in Europe, and that the majority of States worldwide will have at least some kind of NHRI, if not always one of A-status'.

At the end of the book, **concluding remarks** wrap up the common threads and main findings and sketch lines for the development of further research.

NATIONAL HUMAN RIGHTS INSTITUTIONS IN EUROPE: COMPARATIVE, EUROPEAN AND INTERNATIONAL PERSPECTIVES

Manfred NOWAK[1]

1. WHAT ARE NATIONAL HUMAN RIGHTS INSTITUTIONS (NHRIs)?

NHRIs are non-judicial bodies which play an increasingly important role in the human rights architecture at the national level. Traditionally, many governments in Western states were of the opinion that legally binding judgments by domestic courts (ordinary or special courts, in particular constitutional courts) on individual complaints of alleged victims of human rights violations provided sufficient protection of human rights. NHRIs were regarded by such governments as important only for countries with a weak judiciary as a substitute for effective judicial human rights protection. This traditional view usually corresponded to a narrow understanding of human rights as entailing merely negative state obligations of non-interference. But gradually the awareness is developing that international human rights law encompasses a broad variety of positive and negative state obligations to respect, protect and fulfil civil, political, economic, social and cultural rights.[2] In order to be fully compliant with their respective obligations under a variety of international and regional human rights treaties, states should develop national action plans and strategies with respective targets and benchmarks. This requires a specific knowledge and expertise regarding international human rights standards, theories and practice, which national ministries are not usually endowed with. Some states reacted to this challenge by establishing specific human rights ministries. But soon it became clear that it was more effective to entrust independent national institutions with the politically sensitive task of promoting human rights, advising the executive and

---

1 Prof. Dr. Manfred Nowak, Professor of International Law and Human Rights, University of Vienna; Director of Ludwig Boltzmann Institute of Human Rights.

2 See, for example, M. Nowak, *Introduction to the International Human Rights Regime,* Leiden/Boston, Martinus Nijhoff Publishers, 2003, p. 48 et seq.

legislative branch and monitoring compliance with international standards. In addition, NHRIs conduct research on various human rights issues, carry out a wide range of awareness-raising and human rights education activities, review the human rights compatibility of draft legislation, publish annual reports about the legal and factual human rights situation in their respective countries, initiate preventive measures, carry out preventive visits to places of detention etc. Some NHRIs also examine individual human rights complaints by non-judicial means. As independent bodies with a pluralistic composition, NHRIs constitute an important link between governments and civil society on the one hand, and between the international and the domestic level on the other.

2. WHAT ARE THE PARIS PRINCIPLES?[3]

In principle, the idea of NHRIs is as old as the idea of international human rights.[4] But it was only in the 1980s and early 1990s that this idea was taken up by an increasing number of states. At an International Workshop on National Institutions for the Promotion and Protection of Human Rights, held in Paris from 7 to 9 October 1991, principles relating to the status of national institutions were defined which later became known as the "Paris Principles". They were recognised by the UN Commission on Human Rights already during the following session.[5] At the Vienna World Conference on Human Rights in June 1993, states reaffirmed the 'important and constructive role played by national institutions for the promotion and protection of human rights, in particular in their advisory capacity to the competent authorities, their role in remedying human rights violations, in the dissemination of human rights information, and education in human rights'.[6] Consequently, the World Conference explicitly encouraged the establishment and strengthening of NHRIs in accordance with the Paris

---

3 See also: G. De Beco, 'Assessment of the Paris Principles and the ICC Sub-Committee on Accreditation', Chapter 11 in this volume.

4 Already as early as 1946, the United Nations was promoting the establishment of some form of human rights entity at the national level. See, for example, ECOSOC Resolution 2/9 of 21 June 1946, para. 5, ECOSOC Resolution 772(XXX) of 25 July 1960 and ECOSOC Resolution 888(XXXIV) of 24 July 1962. See in this respect also the comprehensive comparative study by the EU Fundamental Rights Agency (FRA): 'National Human Rights Institutions in the EU Member States: Strengthening the Fundamental Rights Architecture in the EU', Vienna, Publication Office of the European Union, 2010, p. 16. See also: B.G. Ramcharan, 'The Role of Regional, National and Local Institutions: Future Perspectives' in B.G. Ramacharan (ed.), *Human Rights: Thirty Years after the Universal Declaration: Commemorative Volume on the Occasion of the Thirtieth Anniversary of the Universal Declaration of Human Rights*, Leiden, Boston, Martinus Nijhoff, 1979, 274 p.; B. Burdekin & J. Naum, *National Human Rights Institutions in the Asia Pacific Region*, Leiden, Boston, Martinus Nijhoff Publishers, 2007, p. 5.

5 UN CHR Resolution 1992/54 of 3 March 1992.

6 Vienna Declaration and Programme of Action, *UN Doc.* A/CONF.157/23 of 12 July 1993, para. 36.

Principles, which were shortly thereafter formally adopted by the General Assembly in December 1993.[7]

According to the Paris Principles, any NHRI shall be given as broad a mandate as possible, which shall be clearly set forth in a constitutional or legislative text, specifying its composition and its sphere of competence aimed at promoting and protecting human rights. NHRIs must be independent from their governments and not be subject to financial control which might affect their independence. Members shall be appointed or elected by an official act which shall establish the specific duration of the mandate and which shall afford all necessary guarantees to ensure the pluralistic representation of the social forces of civil society, including non-governmental organisations, professional organisations, universities, religious communities and parliament. Although the mandate of NHRIs shall be as broad as possible, the examination of individual complaints in a quasi-judicial procedure is not a requirement for NHRIs, but merely an optional additional function.

3. WHICH TYPES OF NHRIs EXIST IN THE WORLD?

In an attempt to provide a typology of existing NHRIs, Valentin Aichele distinguished four different types of NHRIs: commissions (the "British model"), advisory committees (the "French model"), ombuds-institutions (the "Swedish/ Spanish model") and research institutes (the "Danish model").[8] But since there are no clear criteria distinguishing commissions from advisory committees, I prefer to refer only to the following three types of NHRIs:

- *commissions* are multi-member bodies, typical for Commonwealth countries and countries in the African and Asia-Pacific regions. Whereas national human rights commissions in Commonwealth countries often are also entrusted with examining individual human rights complaints, the advisory committees in Francophone countries lack such powers and are restricted to a mere advisory role.
- *ombuds-institutions* are usually single-member bodies, appointed by parliament with oversight of the administration. The idea of the Ombudsman originated in Sweden and is typical for Latin America (Defensor del Pueblo,

7 UN GA Resolution 48/134 of 20 December 1993.

8 V. Aichele, 'Nationale Menschenrechtsinstitutionen in Europa', Deutsches Institut für Menschenrechte, Berlin 2004, available at http://www.institut-fuer-menschenrechte.de/uploads/tx_commerce/studie_nationale_menschenrechtsinstitutionen_in_europa.pdf; V. Aichele, *Nationale Menschenrechtsinstitutionen: ein Beitrag zur nationalen Implementierung von Menschenrechten*, Frankfurt am Main, Peter Lang, 2003, 225 p.

Procuradoría de los Derechos Humanos) and parts of Europe (Nordic countries, Spain, Portugal, Central and Eastern Europe).
- *institutes* are human rights research institutes and documentation centres focusing on evidence based advice. They exist primarily in Europe (Danish model, EU Fundamental Rights Agency).

4. HOW ARE NHRIs ACCREDITED?[9]

There is a need to register NHRIs and to assess whether they fulfil the Paris Principles. But it would not be a good idea to entrust this important and highly sensitive task to governments or to UN bodies with state members, such as the Human Rights Council. Consequently, NHRIs opted for a self-accreditation procedure through peer review. They established an *International Coordination Committee* (ICC) with legal personality independent of its members with the aim of promoting and strengthening NHRIs in accordance with the Paris Principles and providing leadership in this regard.[10] Only NHRIs that fully comply with the Paris Principles are members of the ICC and enjoy certain rights, such as voting rights in the international and regional conferences of NHRIs[11] and full participation rights in international fora such as the UN Human Rights Council.[12]

In order to determine membership, i.e. full compliance with the Paris Principles, the ICC established the *Sub-Committee on Accreditation* (SCA) and entrusted it with the accreditation procedure. The SCA is composed of four members, namely one representative of each of the four regional groupings (Africa, the Americas, Asia-Pacific and Europe). The SCA meets twice a year to review and analyse applications for accreditation, periodic re-accreditation and special reviews.[13] The accreditation procedure is supported by the National Institutions Unit in the Office of the UN High Commissioner for Human Rights in Geneva. In 2008, the accreditation process was improved by introducing an appeal procedure to the ICC, greater transparency, more rigorous preparation before accreditation sessions and more focused recommendations provided to NHRIs in order to ensure their compliance with the Paris Principles.[14] The ICC and its SCA accredit NHRIs with one of the following status:

---

9 See also: G. De Beco, 'Assessment of the Paris Principles and the ICC Sub-Committee on Accreditation', Chapter 11 in this volume.

10 See Article 5 of the ICC Statute of 30 July 2008, available at http://www.nhri.net.

11 *Ibidem*, Article 38.

12 UN HRC Resolution 5/1 of 18 June 2007, 'Institution-building package of the United Nations Human Rights Council', Annex, part VII (Rules of Procedure), rule 7(b). The participation and speaking rights of NHRIs were strengthened as a result of the Human Rights Council Review Process 2011: see UN HRC Resolution 16/21 of 25 March 2011, para. 28 and para. 22, a).

13 Articles 15 and 16 of the ICC Statute, note 7.

14 See, e.g. the Guidelines for Accreditation & Re-Accreditation of National Human Rights Institutions to the International Coordination Committee of National Human Rights Institutions of 4 June 2009, available at http:/www.nhri.net.

- *Status A*: fully in compliance with the Paris Principles: voting member in ICC, full participation and speaking rights in UN Human Rights Council and other international bodies
- *Status B*: not fully in compliance with Paris Principles: observers in open meetings of ICC without voting rights, observers without right to speak in UN Human Rights Council
- *Status C*: not in compliance with the Paris Principles: may participate as observers in meetings or workshops of the ICC
- *Not accredited*: no rights

5. HOW MANY NHRIs EXIST WORLDWIDE? (AS OF FEBRUARY 2013)

According to the website of the ICC, there are presently 103 NHRIs, more than two third of which (69) enjoy status A and are, therefore, in full compliance with the Paris Principles.[15] According to the four regions, the accreditations status of NHRIs is as follows:

- *Status A*: 69 NHRIs, of which 18 in Africa, 15 in the Americas, 15 in Asia and the Pacific, and 21 in Europe
- *Status B*: 24 NHRIs, of which 6 in Africa, 1 in the Americas, 3 in Asia and the Pacific, 3 in Central Asia, and 11 in Europe
- *Status C*: 10 NHRIs, of which 2 in Africa, 3 in the Americas, 2 in Asia and the Pacific, and 3 in Europe
- *Suspended Institutions*: one in Africa (Niger) and one in Asia and the Pacific (Fiji)
- *Institutions whose accreditation has lapsed due to non-submission of information*: one in Africa (Burkina Faso), and one in Europe (Slovakia)

It is interesting to note that the *three types of accreditation status are fairly equally divided among the four different regions*. Only with respect to status B, Europe has a significantly higher number of NHRIs than the other regions. This illustrates that there are quite many non-judicial institutions for the protection of human rights in Europe, above all anti-discrimination bodies, but they are not fully in compliance with the Paris Principles.

With respect to the three, respectively four, different *types of NHRIs* outlined above, one can, however, identify *clear regional preferences*. While states in Africa, Asia and the Pacific clearly prefer the commission (or advisory council) type,

[15] ICC, Chart of the Status of National Institutions, Accreditation Status as of February 2013, available at http://nhri.ohchr.org/. See also the Report and Recommendations of the SCA Session of 26–30 March 2012, available at the same website since 1 June 2012.

most Latin-American states show a preference for the Spanish ombuds-institution type. Of the 18 NHRIs with status A in *Africa*, a total of 14 (Cameroon, Ghana, Kenya, Malawi, Mauritania, Mauritius, Nigeria, Rwanda, Sierra Leone, South Africa, Tanzania, Togo, Uganda and Zambia) follow the British model of national commissions and three (Egypt, Morocco and Senegal) the French model of advisory councils, whereas only one country (Namibia) designated an ombuds-institution as NHRI. The same picture emerges in the *Asia and Pacific region*: of the 15 NHRIs with status A, not less than 12 are national commissions (Afghanistan, Australia, India, Indonesia, Malaysia, Mongolia, Nepal, New Zealand, Occupied Palestine Territory, the Philippines, Republic of Korea and Thailand), and only one each follow the advisory committee type (Qatar), the ombuds-type (Timor Leste) and the institute-type (Jordan). On the other hand, out of 15 NHRIs with status A in *the Americas*, not less than 12 (Argentina, Bolivia, Colombia, Costa Rica, Ecuador, El Salvador, Guatemala, Nicaragua, Panama, Paraguay, Peru and Venezuela) follow the Spanish ombuds-type model (Defensor del Pueblo, Defensoría de los Habitantes, Procuradoría de los Derechos Humanos etc.), while only in Canada and Mexico a national commission was established and in Chile an institution-type NHRI exists. Compared to the three other regions, Europe shows much more variety.

6. WHERE HAVE NHRIs BEEN ESTABLISHED IN EUROPE AND IN THE EU? (AS OF FEBRUARY 2013)

Within the 47 Council of Europe member states, there are presently 21 NHRIs with status A in 19 countries, since in the United Kingdom, there are three fully recognised NHRIs (in England, Scotland and Northern Ireland). In addition, there are 11 status B NHRIs in ten countries (two in Bulgaria) and three status C NHRIs in two countries (two in Switzerland). The B-status of the National Centre for Human Rights in Slovakia has lapsed, due to non-submission of documentation to the ICC.[16] This means that 15 of the 47 member states have not yet established any NHRI.

Within the 27 EU member states, the percentage of countries that have established NHRIs is not much higher. There is a total of 12 NHRIs with status A in 10 countries, namely Denmark, France, Germany, Greece, Ireland, Luxembourg, Poland, Portugal, Spain and the United Kingdom (with 3 fully recognised NHRIs). Apart from Italy, all big EU member states, therefore, have NHRIs in full compliance with the Paris Principles. In addition, there are presently 8 NHRIs with status B in the following 7 countries: Austria, Belgium, Bulgaria (2 NHRIs),

16 ICC SCA, 'Report and Recommendations of the Session of the Sub-Committee on Accreditation (SCA)', Geneva, 26–30 March 2012, p. 28, para. 3.8.

Hungary, the Netherlands, Slovenia and Sweden. While the B-status NHRI of Slovakia has lapsed. Finally, there is 1 NHRI with status C in Romania. This means that only 19 of the 27 EU member states have a NHRI, whereas no such institution has been established so far in Cyprus, the Czech Republic, Estonia, Finland, Italy, Latvia, Lithuania and Malta. This does not mean, however, that no non-judicial institution with human rights implementation functions would exist in these states. But these institutions, for whatever reason, have so far not requested accreditation by the SCA of the ICC. These institutions include, e.g., the National Institute for the Protection of Human Rights (ETHNOPAD) in Cyprus, the Public Defender of Rights/Ombudsman in the Czech Republic, the Estonian Institute of Human Rights, the Parliamentary Ombudsman and the Advisory Board on Human Rights in Finland and various ombuds-institutions in Latvia, Lithuania and Malta. But even in countries with an accredited NHRI, there exist many other non-judicial human rights bodies that have not requested accreditation, such as the Human Rights Advisory Board and various equal treatment commissions in Austria.[17]

The reasons for the comparably high number of NHRIs in EU member states, which have only been accredited with status B or C, are manifold. Partly, the respective institutions have only a very limited mandate, such as the Equal Treatment Commissions in Belgium, Bulgaria and the Netherlands[18] and the Swedish Equality Ombudsman, which is the result of a recent merger of four different ombuds-institutions. In most cases, a certain lack of independence seems to have been the reason for not being regarded as fully compliant with the Paris Principles. Typical examples are the ombuds-institutions in Austria, Bulgaria, Hungary and Slovenia as well as the human rights centres in Slovakia and Romania. Finally, most ombuds-institutions consist only of one single individual ("ombudsman") and, therefore, also have problems to comply with the pluralism requirement of the Paris Principles.

7. WHICH TYPES OF NHRIs WITH STATUS A CAN BE FOUND IN EUROPE AND IN THE EU?

The British model of *national commissions* exists only in the United Kingdom (British Equality and Human Rights Commission, Northern Ireland Human Rights Commission, Scottish Human Rights Commission) and in Ireland (Irish Human Rights Commission). The French model of *advisory councils/commissions/committees* was applied in France (Commission Nationale Consultative des Droits

[17] See FRA, loc. cit. *supra* note 4.

[18] The recently established 'Netherlands Institute for Human Rights' has been established in order to comply with the Paris Principles, but has not yet been accredited by the ICC. For more information on this institution, see Y. Donners & M. Olde Monnikhof, chapter 4 in this volume.

de l'Homme), Luxembourg (Commission Consultative des Droits de l'Homme du Grand-Duché de Luxembourg) and Greece (National Commission for Human Rights) although the Greek Commission illustrates that the difference between the British and the French models is only marginal.[19] The Swedish/Spanish model of *ombuds-type institutions* was followed in Poland (Commissioner for Civil Rights Protection), Portugal (Provedor de Justiça) and Spain (El Defensor del Pueblo). Finally, the Danish model of *research institutes* was realised in Denmark (Danish Institute for Human Rights) and Germany (Deutsches Institut für Menschenrechte).

It follows that half of the 10 EU member states with fully accredited NHRIs have multi-member (advisory) commissions (UK, Ireland, France, Greece and Luxembourg) whereas three prefer one-member ombuds-institutions (Poland, Portugal and Spain) and two opted for research institutes (Denmark and Germany). If one looks beyond the 27 EU member states and includes also the other 20 member states of the Council of Europe, i.e. primarily states from the former Yugoslavia and the former Soviet Union, the ombuds-model seems to be the most favoured one. Out of 19 European countries with status A NHRIs, not less than 12 were opting for an ombuds-type institution (Albania, Armenia, Azerbaijan, Bosnia and Herzegovina, Croatia, Georgia, Poland, Portugal, Russia, Serbia, Spain and the Ukraine), two for a research institute (Denmark and Germany), and the five EU member states cited above (France, Greece, Ireland, Luxembourg and the UK) for a national commission or an advisory council. The ombuds-type institutions derive from the original Scandinavian model, are usually single-member bodies elected by parliament with a particular focus on dealing with complaints of maladministration. As single-member institutions, they encounter difficulties with regard to the pluralism requirement.[20] They have to secure pluralism in other ways, such as through governing bodies. The same holds true for research institutes.

8. WHICH TYPES OF NHRIs WITH STATUS B CAN BE FOUND IN EUROPE AND IN THE EU?

By far the highest number of NHRIs with status B, i.e. not fully in compliance with the Paris Principles, can be found in Europe: a total of 11 NHRIs in ten countries, including seven EU member states. Most of them are *ombuds-type institutions in six countries,* including four EU member states: Austria, Bulgaria, Hungary, Macedonia, Moldova and Slovenia. The Human Rights Centre of Moldova fulfils a double role as research institute and ombuds-institution. During its most recent session in March 2012, the SCA decided that the status B of the Slovakian

[19] See in this respect also FRA, loc. cit., *supra* note 4, p. 24, figure 4 and notes 138–139.

[20] FRA, loc. cit. *supra* note 4, p.28.

National Centre for Human Rights has lapsed and recommended that it seeks again accreditation in accordance with article 10 of the ICC Statute.[21] There are various reasons for these ombuds-institutions not being in full compliance with the Paris Principles, above all lack of independence and pluralism or lack of a clear human rights mandate. As of 1 July 2012, the Austrian Ombudsman Board (Volksanwaltschaft), a collegial organ of three members, has also assumed the function of a national preventive mechanism (NPM) in accordance with the Optional Protocol to the UN Convention against Torture (OPCAT). This has clearly strengthened its human rights mandate. Since the three members are politicians nominated by the three largest political parties in Parliament, it still lacks, however, the independence required for a status A accreditation, which was confirmed by the SCA in 2011. In November 2012, the Norwegian Centre for Human Rights was downgraded from status A to status B.

The other four NHRIs with status B in Europe (all EU member states) are *equality bodies* which lack a broad human rights mandate required for status A institutions: The Centre for Equal Opportunities and Opposition to Racism in Belgium, the Commission for Protection against Discrimination of the Republic of Bulgaria, the Equal Treatment Commission of the Netherlands, and the Equality Ombudsman of Sweden. There are current initiatives to upgrade the equality bodies in Belgium and the Netherlands to NHRIs with a broad human rights mandate in full compliance with the Paris Principles.[22] Sweden had an ombuds-institution enjoying A status since 1999, but this was lost during a reform in 2008 that merged the four specialised ombudsmen represented in the ICC into one new institution, the Equality Ombudsman of Sweden.[23]

9. WHY SHOULD STATES ESTABLISH NHRIs?

There is no legal obligation for states to establish NHRIs. But the *political pressure by the United Nations and regional organisations* to supplement the judicial implementation of human rights through professional and independent non-judicial NHRIs is certainly on the increase. In addition to the political recommendations in the Vienna Declaration and Programme of Action, the Paris Principles and other resolutions of the UN General Assembly, the former Commission on Human Rights and its successor, the Human Rights Council, legally binding *human rights treaties* also require states parties to set up

21 ICC SCA, 'Report and Recommendations of the Session of the Sub-Committee on Accreditation (SCA)', Geneva, 26–30 March 2012, p. 28, para. 3.8.

22 See Y. Donners & M. Olde Monnikhof, 'The Newly Established Netherlands Institute for Human Rights: Integrating Human Rights and Equal Treatment', Chapter 4 in this volume; J. Vrielink & S. Sottiaux, 'Federalism, Equality Bodies and NHRIs: A Critical Analysis of the Belgian Debate on Equality Bodies and NHRIs', Chapter 5 in this volume.

23 FRA, loc. cit. *supra* note 4, p. 27.

non-judicial bodies for the domestic implementation of international human rights obligations. The first such provision is contained in Article 14(2) of the *International Convention on the Elimination of All Forms of Racial Discrimination* (ICERD) of 1965 in relation to the optional individual complaints procedure. It encourages any state party which accepts the individual complaints procedure before the Racial Discrimination Committee of the UN to 'establish or indicate a body within its national legal order which shall be competent to receive and consider petitions from individuals and groups of individuals within its jurisdiction who claim to be victims of a violation of any of the rights set forth in this Convention and who have exhausted other available local remedies'. This domestic racial discrimination body shall keep a register of all petitions received from alleged victims after they have exhausted all domestic judicial remedies. The ICERD, therefore, envisages a system of non-judicial mediation after exhaustion of judicial remedies but before the Racial Discrimination Committee of the UN is officially seized with the matter. NHRIs with the power to deal with individual complaints, such as national equality and human rights commissions would certainly be well qualified to fulfil this function. Article 2(3) of *the International Covenant on Civil and Political Rights* (ICCPR) requires states parties to ensure that alleged victims of human rights violations have an effective remedy before competent judicial, administrative or legislative authorities, 'or by any other competent authority provided for by the legal system of the state'. Similar provisions can also be found in various other human rights treaties, and UN treaty monitoring bodies regularly call upon states parties to establish NHRIs for a more professional implementation of their respective treaty obligations.[24]

More recent UN human rights treaties even oblige states parties to designate or establish non-judicial domestic bodies with specific implementation and monitoring tasks. Articles 3 and 17 to 23 of the *Optional Protocol to the Convention against Torture* of 2002 (OPCAT) require each state party to 'set up, designate or maintain at the domestic level one or several visiting bodies for the prevention of torture and other cruel, inhuman or degrading treatment or punishment', called "national preventive mechanisms" (NPMs). These NPMs shall carry out unannounced visits to all places of detention and conduct private interviews with detainees, victims and witnesses of torture and other forms of ill-treatment. They shall be independent commissions with a pluralistic composition representing a variety of professions. According to Article 18(4) OPCAT, states parties shall give due consideration to the Paris Principles when establishing NPMs. This means that states shall either designate existing NHRIs with the task of NPMs or establish new visiting commissions with the same requirements of independence

[24] See, for example, ICESCR Committee, Draft General Comment No. 10: 'the role of national human rights institutions in the protection of economic, social and cultural rights', *UN Doc.* E/C.12/1998/25, 10 December 1998. See also K. Meuwissen, 'NHRI Participation in United Nations Human Rights Procedures: International Promotion versus Institutional Consolidation', Chapter 12 in this volume.

and pluralism.[25] In reality, many states parties to OPCAT have entrusted NHRIs with the task of NPMs.[26]

Article 33(2) of the *UN Convention on the Rights of Persons with Disabilities* of 2006 (CRPD) requires each state party to 'maintain, strengthen, designate or establish within the state party, a framework, including one or more independent mechanisms, as appropriate, to promote, protect and monitor implementation of the present Convention'. When designating or establishing such a mechanism, states parties shall take into account the Paris Principles. Again, states with independent NHRIs tend to entrust these institutions with this specific task rather than establishing a new monitoring mechanism in relation to the CRPD.

Finally, the *Human Rights Council* as the highest political human rights body of the United Nations has decided to provide NHRIs which fully comply with the Paris Principles (status A) with the right to participate and speak in all its sessions.[27] During its 2011 review, the Human Rights Council further strengthened the role of NHRIs during the universal periodic review of their respective states.[28] NHRIs are also important counter-parts for special procedures of the Human Rights Council. During my mandate as UN Special Rapporteur on Torture, I carried out fact-finding missions to 18 countries in all world regions. Wherever independent and professional NHRIs existed, they were an important source of information and played an essential role in ensuring the domestic implementation of my recommendations.

In addition to the United Nations, various regional organisations encouraged their member states to establish NHRIs. At the level of the *Council of Europe*, e.g., the Committee of Ministers and the European Commission against Racism and Intolerance (ECRI) repeatedly called upon European governments to establish independent and professional NHRIs.[29] In the area of *European Union* law,

---

25 See M. Nowak & E. McArthur, *The United Nations Convention against Torture – A Commentary*, Oxford, Oxford University Press, 2008, p. 1071 et seq.

26 See Association for the Prevention of Torture (APT), Global Status of ratifications, signatures and NPM designations of the Optional Protocol to the UN Convention against Torture, February 2012, available at http://www.apt.ch/npm/OPCAT0212.pdf.

27 HRC Resolution 5/1 of 18 June 2007, Annex VII (Rules of procedure), rule 7. See, for example, J. Lynch, 'Fifteen Years after Vienna: The Role of National Human Rights Institutions', and G. Magazzeni, 'The Role of OHCHR in Promoting National Human Rights Institutions', in W. Benedek, C. Gregory, J. Kozma, M. Nowak, Ch. Strohal, E. Theuermann (eds.), *Global Standards – Local Action: 15 Years Vienna World Conference on Human Rights*, Wien/Graz 2009, p. 155 et seq. and p. 169 et seq. See also K. Roberts, 'The Role and Functioning of the International Coordinating Committee of National Human Rights Institutions in International Human Rights Bodies', Chapter 10 in this volume; K. Meuwissen, 'NHRI Participation in United Nations Human Rights Procedures: International Promotion versus Institutional Consolidation', Chapter 12 in this volume.

28 HRC Resolution 16/21 of 25 March 2011, para. 28.

29 Council of Europe, Recommendation No. R (97) 14 of the Committee of Ministers to Member States on the Establishment of Independent National Human Rights Institutions for the Promotion and Protection of Human Rights, 30 September 1997; ECRI, General Policy Recommendation N°2: Specialised Bodies to Combat Racism, Xenophobia, Antisemitism and

certain EU directives require the establishment of monitoring mechanisms, such as the Racial Equality Directive of June 2000, which envisages the creation of one or more bodies for the promotion of equal treatment of all persons without discrimination on the grounds of racial or ethnic origin and which explicitly foresees that such bodies 'may form part of agencies charged at national level with the defence of human rights'.[30] Similar provisions can be found in the Gender Equality Directives[31] and the Data Protection Directive.[32] In the founding Regulation for the Fundamental Rights Agency (FRA) of 2007, the Council of the European Union explicitly refers to the Paris Principles and requires members of its management board appointed by member states to be independent persons 'having high level responsibilities in an independent national human rights institution or other public or private sector organisation'.[33] In exercising its various functions, the FRA shall closely cooperate with NHRIs, a process that underlines the importance given by the European Union to NHRIs as essential elements of the new human rights architecture in the European Union.[34] In fact, the FRA may itself be regarded as a "NHRI" at the level of the European Union.[35]

10. WHICH CONCLUSIONS CAN BE DRAWN FROM THIS COMPARATIVE SURVEY?

This short survey of the present number, types, status and functions of NHRIs on the global level, in Europe and in the European Union clearly illustrates the increasing role of NHRIs as part of the national human rights architecture and of the fundamental rights architecture in the EU. In more than half of the 193 member states of the United Nations NHRIs have been created, and in more than

Intolerance at National Level, 13 June 1997; Thomas Hammarberg, Commissioner for Human Rights, Recommendation on Systematic Work for Implementing Human Rights at the National Level, CommDH(2009)3, Strasbourg, 18 February 2009. See also B. Adamson, 'NHRIs and Their European Counterparts: Scope for Strengthened Cooperation and Performance towards European Human Rights Actors', Chapter 6 in this volume.

30 Council Directive 2000/43/EC of 29 June 2000 implementing the principle of equal treatment between persons irrespective of racial or ethnic origin, *OJ L* 180, Art. 13. See also FRA, loc. cit. *supra* note 4, p. 14.

31 Council Directive 2004/113/EC of 13 December 2004 implementing the principle of equal treatment between men and women in the access to and supply of goods and services, *OJ L* 373/37, Art. 12; Directive 2006/54/EC of the European Parliament and of the Council of 5 July 2006 on the implementation of the principle of equal opportunities and equal treatment of men and women in matters of employment and occupation, *OJ L* 204/23, Art. 20.

32 Directive 1995/46/EC of the European Parliament and of the Council of 24 October 1995, *OJ L* 281/31, Art. 28.

33 Council Regulation (EC) No. 168/2007 of 15 February 2007 establishing a European Union Agency for Fundamental Rights, Art. 12(1)(a).

34 See FRA, loc. cit. *supra* note 4, p. 7.

35 See COST Action IS0702 Recommendations on NHRI, Recommendation 12, taken up in annex 1 to this volume. For further considerations on FRA as "the EU's NHRI", see: J. Wouters, K. Meuwissen and A. Barros, Chapter 9 in this volume at 2.1.

one third of all states, these NHRIs have been accredited with status A, which means that they are considered to be in full compliance with the requirements of the Paris Principles, such as a broad human rights mandate, professionalism, independence and pluralism. Out of the 47 member states of the Council of Europe, 32 have established NHRIs, and in 19 of them these NHRIs enjoy status A. Within the 27 member states of the European Union, the situation is similar: there are NHRIs in 19 states, but only in 10 states are these institutions in full compliance with the Paris Principles.

In Africa, Asia and the Pacific region, as well as in North America, most NHRIs follow the British or Commonwealth model of multi-member national human rights commissions, including well-known and highly professional commissions in countries such as Australia, New Zealand, India, the Philippines, Indonesia, South Africa, Nigeria, Uganda, Kenya, Ghana, Mexico and Canada. Some countries in Francophone Africa and the Arab world, such as Senegal, Morocco or Egypt, prefer the French model of advisory councils or committees, which have more consultative and promoting rather than protective functions. On the other hand, most countries in Latin America follow the Swedish/Spanish model of having entrusted ombuds-institutions with the task of NHRIs.

In Europe, we find all types of NHRIs, including national commissions in the UK and Ireland, advisory commissions in France, Greece and Luxembourg, research institutes in Denmark, Norway and Germany, as well as ombuds-institutions in Poland, Portugal, Spain and many successor states of the former Yugoslavia and the former Soviet Union. At the same time, we find a high level of fragmentation in the non-judicial domestic human rights architecture of many European states. Rather than establishing a professional NHRI with a broad mandate, many governments reacted to the respective EU directives and UN human rights treaties by establishing a variety of equal treatment commissions, anti-racism advocates, special ombuds-institutions for children, persons with disabilities and patients, data protection commissions, national preventive mechanisms and similar specialised human rights monitoring and advisory bodies. Most of these specialised bodies are under-resourced, under-staffed and suffer from a lack of cooperation and coordination with other human rights bodies. In order to make better use of scarce resources and synergy effects, it would be highly recommendable to join forces and convert these different bodies into NHRIs with an over-arching mandate.

In general, multi-member national human rights commissions seem to comply better with the minimum standards of the Paris Principles than single-member ombuds-institutions and human rights research institutes. First of all, the requirement of pluralism, which includes a fair representation of various stakeholders of civil society (NGOs, professional organisations, universities, religious organisations etc.), can be much easier realised in a multi-member commission than in a single-member institution. Secondly, ombudsmen are usually high-level personalities elected by parliament who often lack the necessary distance and independence from the political establishment. The high political profile of such individuals might be beneficial for addressing professional shortcomings in the bureaucracy ("maladministration"). But effective monitoring of human rights is a politically much more sensitive task which requires a particularly high level of professionalism and independence from all branches of government, including the legislative power. Finally, human rights research institutes seem to be better qualified in supporting NHRIs with the necessary research expertise and human rights education skills rather than fulfilling the various other tasks of NHRIs themselves. In realising these shortcomings, the Norwegian Institute of Human Rights recently proposed that its function as a NHRI should be replaced by a national human rights commission with the institute continuing in a supporting role in the field of research, documentation and training.

The entry into force of the Lisbon Treaty, the legally binding status of the EU Charter of Fundamental Rights and the EU accession to the European Convention on Human Rights create a situation of increased importance of human rights in the European Union, both in its internal and external policies. It would be desirable for a well-functioning human rights architecture in Europe that the EU requests from all its member states to create fully independent, professional and pluralistic NHRIs with a strong preference for national human rights commissions with an over-arching mandate, including the examination of individual complaints. In order to avoid fragmentation and a lack of synergy, specialised human rights bodies, such as equal treatment commissions and national preventive mechanisms, might be put under the umbrella of national human rights commissions.

PART I
COMPARATIVE PERSPECTIVES

THE DANISH EXPERIENCE: THE DANISH INSTITUTE FOR HUMAN RIGHTS

Christoffer BADSE[1]

1. INTRODUCTION

Since the establishment of the *Institut for Menneskerettigheder – Danmarks Nationale Menneskerettighedsinstitution* (The Danish Institute for Human Rights (DIHR)) 25 years ago, the context has changed dramatically, sometimes for the better and sometimes for the worse. Decisive years for the DIHR have been its establishment in 1987, the near closing down of the institution in 2002, and the adoption of a new act and significant strengthening of the institution in 2012, including increased and desperately-needed funding. Along the way have come different special mandates and tasks based on EU directives or with origins in the ever-expanding human rights regime. Since its first years, international partnership programmes have been a significant part of DIHR's work. These programmes have been carried out in close cooperation with the Danish Ministry of Foreign Affairs and with other donors, and they have been expanding over the years.[2] Along with institutional growth and new mandate areas, issues have arisen regarding how the institution has been perceived, both internally and externally. Is the DIHR an international consultant agency? Is it a research institution? A civil society organisation? A national equality body on gender and ethnicity?

1 Senior Legal Advisor, Head of Monitoring, Danish Institute for Human Rights. The contents of this chapter are the sole responsibility of the author and do not necessarily represent the views of the DIHR. Please note that the chapter will focus on domestically related issues and mandates, even though a large part of DIHR's work is related to international projects and programs.

2 The Danish Ministry of Foreign Affairs and DIHR have entered into a multi-annual co-operation agreement in support of the DIHR's international programmes, which in 2011 constituted 25.7% of the DIHR's annual budget. The DIHR also received funding from other sources. The international programmes cover countries such as China, West Africa, Afghanistan, Rwanda and Ethiopia. They deal with topics such as access to justice for poor people, HIV/AIDS, strengthening civil society and reducing violence against women. In addition, the DIHR also carries out consultancy work in the field of human rights and business, which also has an increasing national focus eg. the development of the DK national baseline study on implementation of the UN Guiding Principles on Business and Human Rights is in the process of being drafted and there is an increased focus on Greenlandic issues especially in mining projects (autumn 2012).

A specific UN convention monitoring entity? Or can the brand of being a national human rights institution sum it all up in an elegant umbrella concept and convey the message to the society as well to the staff of the institution?

This chapter will attempt to provide an overview of the history and background of the DIHR, its current situation, as well as the challenges and best practices we have learned from 25 years of human rights work.[3]

2. BACKGROUND AND HISTORY

DIHR is the Danish national human rights institution. Its objective is to function in accordance with the UN Paris Principles. This set of principles can be used as a tool for benchmarking in relation to accountability, independency and impact as well as providing an outlet for discussing further improvements when the periodic re-accreditation of the institution occurs.[4] DIHR is the principal organisation in Denmark for monitoring and advising on human rights. In respect to typology of NHRIs, the DIHR can be categorised as an "institute", with a focus on evidence-based advice.[5] In 2007, the DIHR was re-accredited as an A-Status NHRI, confirming its compliance with the UN Paris Principles.[6] Some further improvements were suggested, and it was noted that only 9% of the budget of the NHRI came from the Danish State. The Sub-Committee on Accreditation (SCA) stressed the importance of ensuring adequate funding in a sustainable manner to address core domestic responsibilities and activities.[7] DIHR was once

[3] Please note that the facts referred to in this chapter have largely already been published in the Statement of Compliance with the Paris Principles, the re-accreditation of the Institute for Human Rights – Denmark's National Human Rights Institution – Revised Edition, September 2012.

[4] Principles relating to the Status of National Institutions, adopted by the UN General Assembly, Resolution 48/134 of 20 December 1993, *UN Doc.* A/RES/48/134, Annex.

[5] For more information on the typology of NHRIs, see M. Nowak, 'National Human Rights Institutions in Europe: Comparative, European and International Perspectives', Chapter 1 in this volume.

[6] A-status is the term given to NHRIs that are considered by the Sub-Committee on Accreditation of the International Coordinating Committee of National Human Rights Institutions (ICC) to be in compliance with the Paris Principles. For more information on the accreditation procedure, see G. De Beco, 'Assessment of the Paris Principles and the ICC Sub-Committee on Accreditation', Chapter 11 in this volume.

[7] ICC, 'Report and Recommendations of the Sub-Committee on Accreditation', Geneva, 22 to 26 October 2007: 'Recommendation: The Sub-Committee recommends that the Danish Institute be accredited status A. The Sub-Committee notes the following:
'1) While appreciating the international engagement of the NHRI, the Sub-Committee notes that 9% of the budget of the NHRI comes from the State and stresses the importance of ensuring adequate funding in a sustainable manner to address core domestic responsibilities and activities.
2) It refers to the General Observation on "Ensuring Pluralism" in the composition of the governing bodies.
3) It notes the importance for the Danish Institution on Human Rights to have a legal mandate to issue reports or be accountable for its activities to the Parliament.

again re-accredited as an A-Status NHRI in 2012. Under the latest review SCA recommended among other minor points that an independent and objective process should be established in case of dismissal of board members, since the new act did not address this issue. In the answer DIHR agreed that a provision on dismissal could be entered into the act e.g. in case of criminal conviction of a board member. DIHR stated that board members are appointed in their personal capacity and are appointed for a renewable period of 4 years. It was suggested that in a case of dismissal by the board, a board member could take the case to the ordinary courts.[8]

The DIHR was established in 1987 as the "Danish Centre for Human Rights" by a Parliamentary decision.[9] Hence, in the first 15 years of its existence, the legal basis of the DIHR was weaker than that of an act, even though there was no practical difference to its everyday activities. The DIHR's status as the national human rights institution was acknowledged and confirmed in 2002 by the adoption of the "Act governing the Establishment of the Danish Centre for International Studies and Human Rights".[10] Due to the new act, the institution was restructured in 2002 and a major organisational change was implemented. A common administration with the Danish Institute for International Studies (DIIS) was established, along with two governing boards; one "centre board" to oversee financial and administrative matters and one "institute board" to oversee substantive matters. The entity was called The Danish Centre for International Studies and Human Rights (DCISM). According to the wording of the act, the DCISM was established with the aim of strengthening research, analysis, and information activities in Denmark concerning international affairs, i.e. the fields of foreign affairs, security and development policy; conflict; holocaust; genocide and political mass murder; and human rights in Denmark and abroad. The Centre established as of January 2003 consisted of two independent institutes:

1. The Danish Institute for International Studies, DIIS, incorporating the activities of the former Danish Institute of International Affairs (DUPI), the Centre for Development Research (CDR), the Copenhagen Peace Research Institute (COPRI), and a special section for the activities of the Danish Centre for Holocaust and Genocide Studies (DCHF).
2. The Danish Institute for Human Rights (DIHR), incorporating the activities of the former Danish Centre for Human Rights (DCHR) and parts of the Board for Ethnic Equality (NEL).

---

4) It refers to the General Observation on the "Selection and appointment of the governing body", in particular sub-paragraphs b), c), and d).'

8 Letter from ICC Sub-Committee on Accreditation to DIHR dated 3 December 2012 on the recommendations that the ICC Sub-Committee on Accreditation (SCA) made regarding the accreditation of DIHR, which was considered at the SCA's session in Geneva from 19–23 November 2012 and appendix 4.1 (reply from DIHR).

9 Parliamentary Decision (B71) of 5 May 1987.

10 See Act No. 411 of 6 June 2002.

The Danish Centre for Human Rights was renamed *Institut for Menneskerettigheder*, which in the English translation by the institution itself has become *the Danish Institute for Human Rights*[11] (DIHR). Moreover, the structure of the Danish Institute was changed in 2002, as the administration of the DIHR was shared with that of the Danish Institute for International Studies. The work of the Danish Centre for Human Rights was carried on – now with a strengthened legislative mandate.

The background and context of the new legislation was not as benign as what might appear from reading the letter of the law. On the 11th January 2002, the Danish government (a liberal/conservative government supported by the Danish People's Party, which had come into power in 2001) published a list of more than 100 centres, councils and boards that were planned to be closed down, merged or reduced with respect to funding or mandate. The DIHR was on this list. The rationale was to save money and to limit what the government perceived to be "arbiters of taste" i.e. experts or researchers of more independent nature than the staff in the ministries. These experts had often expressed a different opinion when a potential conflict emerged between the government's political initiatives, administrative regulations or legislation and the implementation of Denmark's human rights obligations. The statements and analysis put forward by the independent experts, especially if they made headlines in the media, had led to serious annoyance among some political parties, opinion makers and other legal experts. This group of politicians and commentators perceived the expert opinions of DIHR staff as being politically motivated, as unsound or as incorrect applications of Denmark's human rights obligations. The atmosphere and political focus during 2002 was to a high degree oriented towards a restrictive migration, asylum and family-reunification policy. The issue of ethnic minorities, social welfare and integration was the number one priority and concern among the voters and the political parties. This development in Denmark was a little ahead of most of the rest of Europe, where heightened public concern towards immigrants followed some years later. The criticism was that DIHR had at times warned of potential human rights abuses when, according to the critics of DIHR, the government could have conducted an even more restrictive migration policy without infringing on Denmark's human rights obligations. However, it was harder for the critics to support the accusations with hard evidence when the research and reports of the DIHR were scrutinised. When the plans to close down the DIHR were made known, many colleagues, friends and supporters of the DIHR from other national human rights institutions, research institutions and the international community raised their concern in letters and other forms of communication. In Parliament, among politicians and even among some

[11] Even though a more precise translation would be Institute for Human Rights, it would not be very informative.

ministers, there existed hesitation towards the plan to close down the DIHR. The international work and good reputation of the DIHR and capacity building among fellow institutions, as well as the involvement of the staff and the director in high profile international and regional work definitely helped to attract international attention and played a significant part in the survival of the DIHR. In the end, the Danish politicians had a change of heart, and the DIHR survived. Other institutions of Danish political and cultural life were not so lucky, however. The financial support of stakeholder organisations was cut. For example, the Danish Board for Ethnic Equal Treatment (*Nævnet for Etnisk Ligestilling*)[12] was closed down (and their staff transferred to the DIHR). Also, as the sub-committee on re-accreditation noted in 2007, the new, somewhat cumbersome administrative structure and the division of the budget between the institutes in DCISM deriving from the Finance Act created budgetary challenges for the DIHR in the years that followed.[13]

In 2003, the DIHR became the designated national equality body for the promotion of equal treatment and effective protection against discrimination on grounds of racial or ethnic origin, as set out in Article 13 of the EU Council Directive 2000/43/EC on Equal Treatment Irrespective of Race and Ethnic Origin. As part of implementing the mandate, the DIHR established the Complaints Committee for Ethnic Equal Treatment (*Klagekomiteen for Etnisk Ligebehandling*) in 2003, with the rationale that the complaints-handling mechanism should be placed within a special unit and not combined with initiatives that were of a proactive nature or oriented toward victim-support. The Committee reviewed individual complaints (based on ethnicity or race) and expressed its opinion as to whether the prohibition of discrimination had been violated.[14] The Complaints Committee could recommend that assessed victims of discrimination should be granted free legal aid in accordance with the Danish Administration of Justice Act. After amending the Act on Prohibition against Discrimination in respect of employment,[15] the Institute was also given the mandate to hear cases on discrimination on the grounds of race or ethnic origin in the labour market. In 2009, the mandate to deal with individual complaints on grounds of race and ethnicity, a mandate that the DIHR had held for over five years, was transferred to a newly established public body (with no organisational attachment to the DIHR), the Board for Equal Treatment (*Ligebehandlingsnævnet*), which began operation on 1 January 2009.[16] The DIHR, however, retained its status as a national equality body in relation to article 13 of the EU Council Directive 2000/43/EC. Earmarked

12 Originally established in 1993, yet the most recent act of the Board on Ethnic Equal Treatment is Act no. 408 of 10 June 1997.

13 The DIHR compiled two reports containing the material, some in Danish and some in English, documenting the debate of the planned closure of the DIHR: *Hvidbog 1 and Hvidbog 2 – Debatten om det Danske Center for Menneskerettigheder 2001–2003.*

14 Act no. 374 of 28 May 2003 and Consolidated Act no. 31 of 12 January 2005.

15 Act no. 40 of 30 March 2004.

16 Act no. 387 of 27 May 2008 with further amendments.

funding for this specific mandate was – and remains – allocated to the DIHR. Thus, the DIHR cannot deal with individual complaints anymore and has no quasi-jurisdictional competences. However, the DIHR continues to assist and inform victims of discrimination based on race and ethnicity.

In 2011 the DIHR was also appointed as the National Equality Body (NEB) with respect to gender discrimination under Article 12 of EU Directive 2004/113/EC and Article 20 of EU Directive 2006/54/EC. In addition, a Parliamentary decision in 2010 laid down the framework for Denmark's compliance with Article 33(2) of the UN Convention on the Rights of Persons with Disabilities (CRPD) on promoting, protecting and monitoring the implementation of the Convention, awarding DIHR the mandate to enforce this Convention. During the consideration of the placement of the Article 33 CRPD mandate, decisive emphasis was put on the fact that the DIHR was an independent NHRI. Earmarked additional funding was allocated for these two new tasks. Budgetary constraints on NHRI core funding and earmarked funding for special mandates or consultancy work has often dictated strategic priorities and movement towards areas of available funding. Therefore, the experience of DIHR on the national scene should be seen as having been driven by the special mandates. Luckily – in reality – the most prevailing human rights issues and earmarked funding for special mandates often find common ground by the fact that many serious issues needing to be addressed fall within the purview of a NHRI. It seems that the 2012 Act addresses this imbalance in funding (*infra* section 4.2).

3. THE 2012 ACT: STRENGTHENED INDEPENDENCE AND CLEAR MANDATE AS A "NHRI"

3.1. THE 2012 ACT IN DENMARK

On 29 May 2012, the new Act on the Institute for Human Rights – Denmark's National Human Rights Institution was adopted.[17] The Government declared that the act 'seeks to strengthen and clarify the role of the Danish Institute for Human Rights as Denmark's national human rights institution.' The Act seeks to respect and implement the Paris Principles that are mentioned twice in the Act and 56 times in the commentaries to the Act. The new Act of 2012 entered into force on 1 January 2013.

The introductory provision to the Act expressly refers to the Paris Principles, and the words "Denmark's National Human Rights Institution" and the full name

17 Bill on the Danish Institute for Human Rights – Denmark's National Human Rights Institution, section 5(2). L 154 Forslag til lov om Institut for Menneskerettigheder – Danmarks Nationale Menneskerettighedsinstitution § 5, stk. 2.

of the DIHR are mentioned in the title of the Act. In line with the previous 2002 act, the mandate of the DIHR takes as its point of departure, the human rights recognised at any given time by the international community, especially those rights laid down in the United Nations Universal Declaration, the Conventions adopted by the United Nations and the Council of Europe, and the civil rights contained in the Danish Constitution. The 2012 Act states that the Institute shall work to strengthen research and information relating to human rights in times of peace and during armed conflict. The Act broadens the references to international human rights to cover the Charter on Fundamental Rights of the European Union as well as the human dimension of the OSCE. Moreover, the 2012 Act inserts a new provision on the monitoring and reporting role of DIHR, which is an increasingly important function of DIHR (*infra* section 5.1). Another highlight of the 2012 Act is the explicit reference to the 'freedom to conduct independent research' of the Danish Institute, underscoring independency, both at institutional and individual level (*infra* section 5.2).

In addition, the Bill and the explanations to the Bill expressly refer to the comments made during the 2007 review by the SCA. The Bill and its explanations seek to address the SCA recommendations, thereby seeking to enhance the compliance of the DIHR with the Paris Principles. In the brief to the bill, the DIHR recommended that its role could be strengthened by an obligation to submit a mandatory annual report to parliament on the human rights situation in Denmark (in line with Sub-Committee on Accreditation's recommendation). Furthermore, in 2007, the SCA stressed the importance of adequate sustainable funding to address core domestic responsibilities and activities, which is addressed in the bill with the increased funding (*infra* section 4.2).

Regarding the structure of the DIHR, the new act of 2012 amends provisions on the composition of the DIHR board: additional representatives from national universities, in addition to members of organisations from the specialised mandate areas (gender and disability as well as ethnicity) are now included. Finally, according to the new act, a new Council will be established following a public announcement in order to ensure that it is better rooted in civil society (*infra* section 6.1). The Council of Human Rights (*Rådet for Menneskerettigheder*) is a forum for discussing the overall principles guiding the activities of the DIHR. The Council for Human Rights is composed in a manner reflecting the views of interested volunteer organisations, relevant public authorities, researchers with an interest in human rights issues, and other individuals and groups particularly interested, including ethnic minorities. Six members of the 13-member board are appointed by the Council. According to the Act, the board adopts guidelines for membership of the Council in accordance with the UN Paris Principles for NHRIs. According to the Act the Council for Human Rights can propose new activities before the board. Only civil society members of the Council have a right to vote in Council meetings.

The new legislation, especially the additional funding and independent administration, has generated a significant strengthening of the work of the DIHR as an independent, self-governing institution within the public administration, as well as being a national human rights institution and national equality body at the same time.

3.2. NORTH-ATLANTIC DIMENSION OF THE 2012 ACT

The DIHR does not automatically have jurisdiction in all parts of the Danish Realm when the 2012 Act on the institution enters into force. The Act of 2002 mandates DIHR to function as an NHRI with respect to Greenland, but with the abolition of the 2002 Act, a new Royal Decree needs to be adopted in order for the new Act to enter into force in Greenland. The mandate under the former Act did cover Greenland (since 2005).[18] Hence, it is expected that the new Act will be brought into force in Greenland. Initiatives by the DIHR have so far been scarce due to limited funding regarding the functioning of the DIHR as an NHRI in Greenland.[19] For the new Act, the Government of Greenland has expressed its wish that the mandate of the DIHR in Greenland be renewed, and the DIHR is positive about this possibility and considers Greenland a priority. However, no additional or earmarked funding beside the increase in the DIHR's core funding has been allocated for this work in the new legislation or in the Act of Finance (contrary to the NEB, special mandates and the disability mandate). The current expectation is that the Act of 2012 will enter into force in Greenland. Therefore, on 15 November 2012, the Greenlandic Parliament adopted an Act[20] establishing a Council for Human Rights in Greenland, consisting of Greenlandic stakeholders (14 NGOs and four public bodies) with the aim of providing knowledge and creating ownership and anchoring. One of the tasks of this new Council is to assist in the independent monitoring and reporting of the implementation of human rights in Greenland. Another task is to appoint a member to the Board of the DIHR. The DIHR can participate in the Greenland Council meetings but cannot vote. It is assumed that the DIHR will provide technical assistance and human rights expertise to this Council. The budget for the Council is 900,000 DKK (app. 120,000 €) for expenses such as translation, travel and meeting costs.

---

18 Act no. 411 of 6 June 2002 Establishing the Danish Center for International Studies and Human Rights was brought into force in Greenland by Royal Decree no. 414 of 30 May 2005.

19 Greenland is not a member of the European Union. Hence, the equality mandates and funding earmarked for national equality body work based on EU directives is not technically applicable in a Greenlandic context. Also, there might be limitations to programmes normally initiated internationally, since Greenland is part of the Danish Realm.

20 Act (Inatsisartutlov) of 2012 (not yet numbered) on the Greenlandic Council for Human Rights (*om Grønlands Råd for Menneskerettigheder*).

In relation to the special mandate on monitoring the implementation of the UN Disability Convention according to article 33 (2) of the CRPD and Greenland, it appears that the DIHR will be mandated to take on this task by the Greenlandic government and parliament, within the funding already allocated to the DIHR.

The DIHR's mandate does not cover the Faroe Islands, which is also a part of the Danish Realm with self-governance and parliament. However, the mandate may be extended to cover this part of Denmark by Royal Decree. While this expansion of the mandate to cover the Faroe Islands is possible, it is not likely to be implemented in the foreseeable future, since no debate has been conducted in the Faroe Islands on the need and wish for an NHRI. The 2002 Act never took effect in the Faroe Islands. The same challenges in monitoring the implementation of human rights in a Faroese context exist to some extent (but on a smaller and less complex scale) as in the Greenlandic context described above. The fact that part of the Danish Realm is not covered by a mandate of a National Human Rights Institution could be an issue regarding the full implementation of the UN Paris Principles, since there is no independent monitoring of human rights issues in the context of the Faroe Islands.

4. INSTITUTIONAL STRUCTURE AND BUDGET

4.1. INSTITUTIONAL STRUCTURE AND ADMINISTRATION

Under the Act from 2002, the DIHR is part of the Danish Centre for International Studies and Human Rights (DCISM) and thus shares administrative infrastructure with another organisation. The common administration covers accounting, reception, IT services, human resources administration, canteen and internal support functions and services. According to the Act of 2012, the DIHR will acquire its own administration and institutional structure, which is therefore described below.

4.1.1. The Board

The DIHR is governed by a board of directors appointed in their personal capacity and fully independent of Government and Parliament who decide all important questions regarding the professional field of work, the economy and the administration of the institute.[21]

[21] According to the new Act of 2012 Section 3 and 4, The board comprises 13 members designated from the Danish Human Rights Council (6), the Rector of the University of Copenhagen (1), the Rector of Aarhus University (1), the Rector of the University of Southern Denmark (1), the Rector of Aalborg University (1), The Danish Conference of Rectors under Universities Denmark (2), and by the employees of the Institute (1).

The board members can be remunerated pursuant to general rules under Danish law. Currently, no member receives remuneration, although for a number of years, it has been the practice that the chairperson of the board be remunerated. The new Act of 2012 strengthens the pluralism of the board of DIHR by requiring representation of persons from ethnic organisations, disability organisations and gender equality organisations, just as the Council shall have a broader linkage to the surrounding society. With the new Act planned to enter into force in Greenland, the Greenlandic Council for Human Rights will also be able to appoint a member of the Board.

4.1.2. The Council

According to the current guidelines adopted by the council, membership applications are processed by a membership committee composed of the chairmanship of the council and the chairman of the board. The committee forwards its recommendation to the council, which then makes its own decision. The new Act of 2012 changes the governance of the council. The Act stipulates that the board shall establish the council following a public hearing. The board will now reform the council in accordance with the guidelines specified in the new Act. The new Act of 2012 states as follows in Section 5:

> 'Following a public hearing, the board sets up the Human Rights Council, which shall be composed so that it reflects prevailing views among civil society organisations working with human rights. Specially affected public authorities can also be admitted as members of the Council. The board establishes the details regulating membership of the Council in accordance with the UN Paris Principles for national human rights institutions.'

The current Council has approximately 80 members representing civil society organisations, political parties represented in Parliament as well as public institutions and universities. The current chairmanship of the council is composed of a representative of Denmark's Disability Organisation (DPOD) and a representative of the Rehabilitation and Research Center for Torture Victims (RCT) (*DIGNITY – Dansk Institut Mod Tortur*). The council meets twice a year. The new Act of 2012 requires the establishment of a new council by the board of directors. The reasons for amending the council's composition are described in the Bill of 2012 as follows:

> 'It is considered important to spread the knowledge of and ensure a wide national support to the work of the National Human Rights Institution and to ensure cooperation and synergy between the work of the institution and of other actors promoting human rights. It is foreseen that an increased public attention of the council, its work and composition of the council can contribute to this purpose. It

is therefore suggested that the board, after a public hearing, appoint a new Human Rights Council. It is suggested that the board, by public advertisement, encourage both current members of the Council to actively renew their membership and other interested civil society organisations and affected authorities to apply for a membership of the council to make sure that the council is permanently represented by those civil society organisations and authorities that are actively involved in the promotion of human rights. In this connection, the board will lay down more specific conditions that are in accordance with the UN Paris Principles relating to National Human Rights Institutions regarding a membership of the council.[...].'

4.1.3. *Daily Management*

Following a public call, the board appoints a director to be in charge of the daily management of the professional, economic and administrative affairs of the institute. The director is in practice responsible for all matters relating to the operation of DIHR under the strategic guidance of the board. The Act of 2012 stipulates that the position of director should be for a specified period. The current director, Dr. Jonas Christoffersen, was appointed with effect from 1 January 2009.[22] The director is supported by a small management secretariat. The management group of DIHR consists of the executive director, the two deputy directors and the director for financial and administrative affairs.

4.1.4. *International Area and National Area, Administration and Communication*

The work of the DIHR is divided into an international area, a national area and a department of administration directed by two deputy directors and a director for administrative matters, with overall responsibility in her particular field referring to the executive director. The National Area is divided into a Monitoring Team, an Education Department and a Research Department as well as an Equality Department, consisting of all the special mandates (race, gender and disability). Each area is divided into departments, units and teams depending on the number of staff. The International Area is divided into a Rule of Law Department, Civil Society Department and Human Rights & Business Department. There is also a Communication Department. The staff of DIHR (as of autumn 2012) totals 128 (41 male and 87 female). The DIHR has one office in the central part of Copenhagen, but no regional presence.

22 The other directors of the institution have been: Mr. Morten Kjærum who took up his post as Executive Director of the Institute for Human Rights on January 1, 2003 – March 2008. From 1991–2002 Morten Kjærum served as Executive Director of the Danish Centre for Human Rights. From 1987–1991 Mr. Lars Adam Rehof served as Executive Director of the Danish Centre for Human Rights.

4.2. BUDGET

The Act of 2012 strengthens the administrative independence of the DIHR by adding the word 'independent' to the text of the Act and by deleting the requirement that the DIHR follow the guidelines of the Ministry of Foreign Affairs in relation to the preparation of its budget and accounts. The DIHR is officially classified as an independent state institution within the public administration, which means that even though the institute has to report to the Ministry of Foreign Affairs on matters regarding the Finance Act, the DIHR has the freedom to choose which strategic areas to focus on in the budget.

The core funding of the DIHR is based on the Danish Finance Act, which is budgeted for a three-year period. Each year, Parliament has to approve the national budget (the Finance Act), which determines the annual funding. The DIHR's core funding covers core activities within monitoring, research and education. In addition, there is a separate core funding for the activities within the special mandates on equal treatment. The DIHR also receives government funding from the Ministry of Foreign Affairs to cover multiannual framework agreement for international programmes. The funding under the agreement is also incorporated in the Finance Act. During the period 2004–2012, the core funding of DIHR under the Finance Act increased from DKK 16.8 million in 2004 (approx. EUR 2.25 million) to DKK 38 million in 2012 (approx. EUR 5.10 million). This increase in budget is obviously significant. In addition, during the period 2004–2010, the DIHR received an additional annual allocation of DKK 6 million (approx. EUR 0.8 million) from the Finance Act for earmarked equal treatment work in the field of ethnic discrimination. Since 2011, the DIHR has received an additional DKK 6 million (approx. EUR 0.8 million) earmarked for gender discrimination, and DKK 4.5 million (approx. EUR 0.60 million) earmarked for monitoring the implementation of the CRPD. In 2012, approximately 55 per cent of the DIHR budget comes from the Finance Act. The annual reports of DIHR describe the figures in more detail.[23]

5. SUBSTANTIVE FUNCTIONS OF THE DIHR

5.1. MONITORING FUNCTIONS

The 2012 Act explains that: 'according to the Paris Principles, a national institution shall be able to monitor the implementation of human rights inter alia by examining any legislation and administrative provision in force, including provisions relating to judicial organisations, just as national institutions must

---

23 Annual Reports of the Danish Institute for Human Rights (DIHR) available at http://www.humanrights.dk/publications/annual+reports.

be able to examine bills and proposals to ensure that these provisions are in accordance with human rights (Paris Principles section 4, 3 (a) (i))'.[24] DIHR exercises its monitoring function in different ways. It considers the monitoring of legislative developments a cornerstone of its monitoring work, and trained legal staff are allocated to fulfil this task, drafting legal briefs assessing the extent to which proposed legislation is in compliance with Denmark's international human rights obligations. The monitoring team receives requests by the central administration and identifies any researcher from the research department or an expert within the special mandates (ethnicity, gender, disability) with specific knowledge to draft the legal brief. If no such expert is available, the legal brief will be drafted by the legal monitoring team. Depending on the importance of the topics as well as an assessment of political sensitivities, the executive director will sign the brief. Otherwise, it will be signed by the expert, the researcher or the jurists in the legal monitoring team (*infra* section 5.2). Much of the academic research (*infra* section 5.4), as well as the annual Status Report and other reports on human rights issues, both national and international (*infra* sections 5.3 and 6.3) are all part of the monitoring work.

The concrete monitoring of the implementation of human rights obligations in a regional setting (e.g. in the municipalities), and especially in Greenland, continues to be a challenge in terms of resources. Steps are being taken, however, to make a fundamental mapping of Greenlandic human rights issues, which has not been done before. Special challenges in the Greenlandic context seem to be: large scale mining projects and human rights and business issues; discrimination; language issues; conditions in detention facilities as well as social conditions, domestic violence and issues regarding the rights of the child. Since Denmark has a public administration, which to a large extent publishes relevant information on the internet via public web pages, desk monitoring of the human rights situation can be carried out. The DIHR's monitoring work often relies on surveys and statistics provided by other organisations or institutions, including ministries and other government agencies as well as universities, independent research organisations and civil society organisations.

5.1.1. Review of Legislative and Administrative Regulation

The Danish central administration makes use of the option to involve expert organisations through consultations – including in connection with legislative proposals, which might have a human rights impact. The DIHR receives draft bills deemed relevant in a human rights context, normally before the bill is presented in parliament, to ensure the parliament has an independent assessment of the impact of the future law on Denmark's human rights obligations. Most

[24] Section 1, subsection 1, No. 1 of the 2012 Act.

consultation requests are related to a bill amending existing Danish legislation or establishing new law. The DIHR will conduct a legal analysis and a human rights assessment of the compatibility of the draft legislation with international obligations in the form of a brief. If human rights implications are found, the DIHR will raise these issues in the legal brief and forward it to the requesting ministry. It appears that in the near future, the DIHR will receive an increase in requests for legal briefs for the Greenlandic Government (*Naalakkersuisut*), since the mandate will be expanded and cooperation between stakeholders in Greenland and the DIHR has been prioritised by management, and some additional funding has allowed for this work to some extent.

As part of its mandate, the DIHR may also conduct *ex officio* analyses of draft laws. This is done mainly in the form of reports containing substantive analyses of draft laws as well as recommendations. Briefs may also be sent *ex officio* if no official request (meaning a letter or e-mail sent directly to the DIHR with a request) has been forwarded to the Institute.

The DIHR submits approximately 80 legal briefs to Parliament annually. Recent examples where legal briefs by the DIHR have entailed a positive change in legislation in accordance with recommendations by the DIHR can be illustrated as follows:

- After the extension of preventive detention by the Parliament,[25] the DIHR warned that the detention of people not guilty of any disturbance – or of being concretely involved in such activity – would create a chilling effect on the fundamental right of freedom to peaceful assembly.[26] The Danish courts have had rulings[27] and the Parliamentary Ombudsman, in the OPCAT report[28] of the office, has found reason to express criticism of the conduct by police and referred to international human right standards.

[25] Prior to the Climate Summit in Copenhagen, the Parliament, fearing widespread disturbances at the climate demonstrations, introduced extended preventive detention.

[26] DIHR Legal Brief of 3 November 2009.

[27] Copenhagen District Court of 16 December 2010, BS 4B-333/2010 (not published) found that the conditions for the arrest of some of the detainees amounted to degrading treatment and therefore constituted a violation of ECHR article 3. The detainees received compensation. The case was appealed to Denmark's Eastern High Court, which upheld the judgment on 11 November 2011. Weekly Law Review (*Ugeskrift for Retsvæsen*) U.2012.1439Ø. The Courts found the illegal detention of demonstrators to be a violation of ECHR article 5(1) since the detention had not be in accordance with the Act on Police Service (*Politiloven*) and furthermore to be a violation of ECHR article 10 and 11, however the courts did not find the compensation should be increased beyond what was already awarded for the article 5 violation.

[28] The Parliamentary Ombudsman expressed criticism of the placement of the detainees on the cold winter ground for 3–4 hours and concluded that it constituted degrading treatment. See: *OPCAT-Undersøgelse af Københavns Politis Behandling af anholdte /tilbageholdte under klimatopmødet i December 2009*. Report of 20 December 2010.

- A brief on the practical use of incorrect registration of stateless persons resulted in new rules for the registration of statelessness and a new formula for the application of passports.[29]
- Briefs on the amendment of the Act on the age of criminal responsibility resulted in the change in the age of criminal responsibility from 14 to 15.[30]

It is obvious that an indicator of impact cannot only be succeeding in changing and amending legislation. That would be to set the bar too high. Sometimes, the input of the DIHR has a direct impact, while on other occasions the DIHR joins with other human rights stakeholders to have an impact on policies and legislation. Moreover, arguments may at times be taken over by political parties without explicit reference to where the input came from, making it hard to measure the impact. At other times, the DIHR provides input that results in discussions in Parliament or in the media.[31] The political reality and majority is not always and not only driven by the desire to uphold human rights standards. Therefore, the success is to a large extent dependent on the goodwill in the political system combined with a high level of organisational credibility among key stakeholders.

5.1.2. National Reporting[32]

From 1999 to 2011, the national reporting work of DIHR was anchored in an annual report compiling human rights relevant material, thus given an indication of the present situation of the human rights in Denmark. Main issues were highlighted in the foreword. The title of the publication was *Menneskeret i Danmark – Status* followed by the year the publication dealt with. The annual report described the concluding observations, country reports, international judgments, individual decisions as well as national court cases and administrative decisions and

[29] On 4 October 2011, DIHR sent a memorandum on the registration of statelessness to the Danish Immigration Service. This memorandum and some improvements planned by the Danish Immigration Service were discussed by the Danish Immigration Service and DIHR. Afterwards, a new form was uploaded for individuals seeking to revise their personal data registered by the Danish Immigration Service and to obtain a new passport application form with a focus on statelessness to www.nyidanmark.dk, the website of the Danish Immigration Service, on 25 October 2011. Source: DIHR Annual Report 2011.

[30] Concerns about the lowering of the age of criminal responsibility from 15 to 14, See: DIHR, Legal Brief dated 19 February 2010. Comments on the reintroduction of an age of criminal responsibility from 14 to 15, See: DIHR, Legal Brief dated 2 December 2011.

[31] To mention a few examples: direct reference to a statement by the DIHR in the Proposal for Parliamentary Decision of 31 March 2011 on the establishment of a transit room for homeless people with foreign background (*Forslag til folketingsbeslutning om etablering af transitrum for udenlandske hjemløse*), a proposal that was not adopted. Also, assessments made in February 2009 in relation to the impact of ECtHR judgment S. and Marper v UK, which was deemed relevant for amending Danish limits for acquitted persons to be kept in police DNA registers. The Ministry of Justice concurred, and amendments were adopted.

[32] For international reporting (parallel reports and reporting in the Universal Periodic Review Process, etc.) see below section 6.3 on Cooperation with The United Nations and Other International Actors.

other material deemed relevant for a particular year. The reporting focused on developments each year but did not follow up on earlier reports and did not contain a detailed overview of the prevailing and accumulated human rights challenges in Denmark. Hence, it was mainly a compilation, describing and summarising published human rights material within a particular year. In the Fundamental Rights Agency's report on National Human Rights Institutions, the annual status report of the DIHR was highlighted as a "good practice". According to the FRA, the DIHR's report on the human rights situation in Denmark is commendable: 'It explains legislative proposals and examines critiques of Denmark issued by UN treaty bodies and the ECtHR. In this way, awareness of the human rights situation in Denmark is raised in a manner accessible to broader society, and the connection with the international human rights system is emphasised.'[33] Until 2009, the report was presented to the standing legal committee of Parliament, but due to its limited effect, the DIHR has revised its strategy in terms of reporting and decided to develop a new status report.

In 2011, the process of producing the new status report was launched, and it was published for the first time at the 25th Anniversary of the DIHR, in May 2012. Internally, the status report acts as a strategic tool for compiling the expertise of the Institute into a single publication and identifying pressing issues where a prioritised effort could be initiated by DIHR if no other stakeholders are willing to take on a leading role. The status report therefore plays a vital role in the development of the house strategy, the identification of priority areas, the launching of specific reports and analysis as well as the provision of input to concrete plans of action and follow-up initiatives.

The new status report[34] is structured in thematic chapters[35] covering the most pressing human rights issues. It provides an overview of the international framework and contains a description of the domestic context. This information leads up to a list of recommendations for improving human rights implementation in particularly problematic areas in Denmark. Recommendations are oriented towards executive, legislative, implementing powers and institutions at central and regional levels. Where there is a lack of information and statistics, this is also noted. Hence, the recommendations are formulated in a structured way, indicating the level of seriousness of the issue at hand. The report has been published in a new design and format that makes the summary available in hard copy (the only part of the report to be so), while the chapters and complete analysis are available

33 EU Fundamental Rights Agency, 'National Human Rights Institutions in the EU Member States: Strengthening the Fundamental Rights Architecture in the EU', Vienna, Publication Office of the European Union, 2010, p. 40.

34 The Danish Institute for Human Rights – Denmark's National Human Rights Institution, 'Human Rights in Denmark Status – May 2012, A summary', 2012.

35 The report contains thematic chapters and recommendations on the implementation of human rights, asylum, children, data protection, deprivation of liberty, disability, gender, human trafficking, race and ethnic origin, citizenship, education, deportation and extradition and freedom of expression.

online in chapter files[36] for easy reference and access to issues of interest. The report is a dynamic document, which will gradually be expanded to include more thematic chapters and will be revised and updated on an on-going basis.

The new Act of 2012 contains a reporting obligation for the DIHR. With respect to this obligation, a fully developed and updated report will be submitted to Parliament annually, commencing in 2013. Hence, in the future, the DIHR will report annually to Parliament (probably in the autumn of each year) on the operations of the Institute and on the development of human rights in Denmark. The DIHR is currently in the process of establishing a system of follow-up measures on the recommendations of the report to ensure that DIHR can continuously monitor improvements or deterioration in a particular situation.

The first status report which was presented in May 2012 contains 232 recommendations. The recommendation which drew the most attention from the public, the media and the international community was that DIHR, considering the impact on the freedom of expression, recommended the abolition of the prohibition against blasphemy as stipulated in the existing Danish criminal code. This was a shift in approach compared to the year 2006, when DIHR legal briefs on the matter contained a more moderated approach, balancing freedom of expression vis-a-vis the mocking of minorities. The stronger stance of DIHR on the issue can be framed in light of trends on the issue in international human rights law since 2006.[37] Another recommendation highlighted by the DIHR was the need for a more systematic approach to the implementation of international human rights. This was the focus in the UPR individual stakeholder report submitted by DIHR and elaborated upon in the status report. In the status report, the DIHR recommends that the government should prepare a national action plan for human rights; establish a permanent inter-ministerial committee to coordinate the implementation of the action plan and follow up on international human rights recommendations; develop national human rights indicators; and undertake an annual parliamentary evaluation of the country's human rights situation.

5.2. RESEARCH, EDUCATION AND INFORMATION

The mandate for the DIHR's research activities is to carry out independent and self-supporting research in the field of human rights. This mandate is vested

[36] The Status Report is available at www.menneskeret.dk/status (in Danish only). The Summary of the report is available in Danish and English.

[37] This was prior to the UN resolutions attempting to introduce the prohibition against blasphemy as a protection in human rights law with an obligation to criminalise such expressions and for instance prior to the UN General Comment no. 34 of the UN Human Rights Committee on the interpretation of the right to freedom of expression as stipulated in article 19 of the ICCPR.

in the Act, where one of the mandates is to perform, promote and co-ordinate independent research and communicate research about international topics.

The DIHR undertakes not only practical research and analysis but also academic research aimed at national and international research journals, articles and other publications. Besides contributing to the general monitoring functions, in recent years the academic research has covered and had significant impact on the effective implementation of human rights obligations in a national context, such as the right to citizenship, rights of children of imprisoned parents, human rights and counter-terrorism, economic and social rights, the rights of refugees and aliens in Danish society and human rights compliance of Danish troops in Iraq and Afghanistan.

Quite a few research products can be highlighted. One which was particularly successful recently, in the fall of 2012, is a research study, book publication and related activities aimed at creating better conditions for children of imprisoned parents through a rights-based approach. This effort led to a new agreement on prisons and probation, and a significant allocation (approx. EUR 1.8 million) to improve conditions for children of imprisoned parents and their possibilities to maintain contact and family life.[38]

The DIHR also conducts substantive analyses *ex officio* on issues deemed relevant from a human rights perspective. The reports are aimed at politicians and the media. Such analyses are published in a series of *Udredninger* (analyses)[39], which have so far dealt with the following topics: family reunification in Denmark (2004); Danish strategy on equal treatment and DIHR (2005); persons with disabilities in Denmark (2005); special measures towards mentally ill criminal offenders (2006); effective protection against discrimination (2007); rejected asylum seekers and other foreigners (2009); discrimination based on union membership (2009); hate crimes in Denmark (2011); ethnic profiling in Denmark (2011); self-determination and guardianship (2012); and ethnic diversity in the police force (2012).

As regards education, DIHR offers courses, seminars and workshops on specific and general human rights issues aimed at both national and international audiences. DIHR's national education activities are mainly targeted at schoolteachers and students, law enforcement and justice sector actors, civil society activists and civil servants.

Regarding communication, the DIHR maintains websites and publishes newspaper articles, writes blogs and provides features, background information and interviews to a large variety of media. As a state institution, the DIHR is obliged to provide access to information under the Public Administration Act when requested to do so by the media or other actors. Since the DIHR has a special

38 An overview of publications is available at: http://www.menneskeret.dk/udgivelser/tema/tema+om+f%C3%A6ngsel/b%C3%B8rn+af+f%C3%A6ngslede/publikationer.

39 The reports are available for download at: http://menneskeret.dk/udgivelser/udredninger. English summaries are found in the back of each publication.

mandate regarding disability, there is obviously a focus to prioritise a policy of accessibility, meaning that publications must be as accessible as possible. Finally, the DIHR participates in key public events as part of public awareness-raising on human rights and anti-discrimination issues.[40]

6. DIHR INTERACTION WITH OTHER ACTORS ACTIVE IN THE FIELD OF HUMAN RIGHTS

6.1. RELATIONSHIPS WITH CIVIL SOCIETY

The DIHR is mandated to coordinate and assist civil society organisations working in the field of human rights. The Danish Council on Human Rights is part of the structure of the DIHR and provides an institutional link between DIHR and civil society.

Currently, the Council convenes on a biannual basis. During these meetings, exchange of information between DIHR and members of the Council takes place on the main activities undertaken during the previous six months, and the DIHR presents plans for major upcoming activities. Moreover, the Council has engaged in thematic debates on selected human rights issues of common interest.

In recent years, the DIHR has increased its focus on including civil society in its work relating to international reporting. A publication on suggestions for initiatives was produced, especially with the Danish UPR (universal periodic review) process in mind.[41]

In addition, common follow-up initiatives have been initiated in relation to the United Nations reporting processes under the seven core international human rights treaties that Denmark has ratified (out of nine).[42] These follow-up initiatives provide a systematic method for input of NHRIs and civil society relating to the various stages of the reporting and follow-up cycles. Approximately one year after publication of the Concluding Observations from the CERD[43] and CRC committees,[44] the DIHR in cooperation with civil society organisations, invited country rapporteurs from the treaty bodies to Denmark to meet with stakeholders

40 In recent years, the DIHR has participated in *Folkemødet på Bornholm* inspired by the Swedish event *Almedalsveckan*, a large public event where politicians, the media and the general public participate in discussions on topics of general interest and where the DIHR invites people to discuss human rights and discrimination issues.

41 See: 'Universal Periodic Review – First Cycle, Reporting Methodologies from the Position of the State, Civil Society and National Human Rights Institutions,' 2nd ed, 2012 The Danish Institute for Human Rights, distributed by the International Coordinating Committee of National Institutions for the Promotion and Protection of Human Rights.

42 CERD, ICCPR, ICESCR, CEDAW, CAT, CRC and CRPD. Denmark has not ratified CMW and CED. Moreover, Denmark has not ratified CRC Optional Protocol 3 and CESCR Optional Protocol.

43 See: *UN Doc.* CERD/C/DNK/CO/18-19 of 20 September 2010.

44 See: *UN Doc.* CRC/C/DNK/CO/4 of 7 April 2011.

and the general public and to discuss the concerns and recommendations that had been put forward. During 2011, collaboration with civil society took place in relation to reporting to the Human Rights Committee under the ICCPR. Some members of the Council submitted input to the Human Rights Committee's 'List of Issues' pertaining to Denmark's examination, and some did it on their own accord.[45] The process that took place in the Danish Human Rights Council was guided and coordinated by the DIHR.

Moreover, it is a well-established working method at DIHR to invite civil society organisations as well as other stakeholders to exchange knowledge and coordinate efforts as part of various projects and interventions. A few examples of this type of cooperation are described below:

- Since 1991, the Coalition on the Convention on the Rights of the Child has assembled 16 NGOs working with children's issues and rights in Denmark. The National Council for Children *(Børnerådet)* and DIHR are members of the group, even if neither organisation is an NGO. The objective of the coalition is to strengthen awareness of the Convention in order to promote its implementation in Danish legislation and practice. The DIHR has acted as an adviser to the Coalition on international reporting procedures. Most recently, the DIHR advised the Coalition on its Supplementary NGO Report submitted in relation to the examination of the Danish government's periodic report to the UN Committee on the Rights of the Child.[46] While the NGOs submitted a joint parallel report to CRC, the DIHR and the National Council for Children submitted separate parallel reports to the CRC, due to their special mandates and status.[47]
- In 2006, the DIHR initiated a dialogue process to improve the rights of children of imprisoned parents. Together with representatives from the police, prison

[45] See e.g. LOIPR Procedure – List of Issues Prior to Reporting, Submission by the Inuit Circumpolar Council, 5 August 2011; List of Issues Prior to Reporting & an Assessment of the Implementation of the International Covenant on Civil and Political Rights Jointly Reported by Women's Council in Denmark, Rehabilitation and Research Centre for Torture Victims (Denmark), Save the Children, Denmark, 19 August 2011; Denmark Reporting for The UN Committee of Human Rights 2011 from Refugees Welcome/The Committee for Underground Refugees (NGO); Joint submission by Disabled People's Organisations – Denmark (DPOD), European Disability Forum (EDF) & the International Disability Alliance (IDA) on the List of Issues prior to reporting for Denmark, Country Report Task Force, Human Rights Committee, 103rd Session.

[46] Supplementary NGO Report – to the Danish Government's 4th periodic report submitted to the UN Committee on the Rights of the Child. Joint submission by the NGOs participating in the Coalition on the Convention on the Rights of the Child. Danish version May 2009. English translation June 2010.

[47] Danish National Council for Children, Report to the United Nations Committee on the Rights of the Child, Supplementary Report to Denmark's 4th Periodic Report, 2010; Danish Institute for Human Rights, Parallel Report July 2010 to the UN Committee on the Rights of the Child on the 4th Periodic Report by the Government of Denmark on the Implementation of the Rights of the Child, 2010.

and social authorities, informal talks included representatives of prisoners, former inmates, imprisoned parents, as well as childrens' organisations. The different interest groups provided input to a DIHR research project with the objective of securing the best interests of children of imprisoned parents. The dialogue with stakeholders, combined with enhanced political attention to the topic, resulted in a joint endeavour to develop guidelines for the treatment of children and their imprisoned parents.

- The Anti-Trafficking Network is an informal group of organisations and individuals working with issues related to trafficking of women in prostitution. The Network convenes quarterly. The DIHR, in particular, has taken on a role in drafting input on behalf of the network to the government's action plan against trafficking in human beings. In 2009 and 2010, the DIHR, in cooperation with the network, hosted two events to highlight the European Union's Anti-Trafficking Day.
- In 2011, the DIHR held a seminar for researchers and specialists at Danish universities and other academic institutions in order to launch a Human Rights Research Platform. The purpose of the platform is to facilitate exchange of information on current activities of interest to academics working with human rights or related issues, to further common discussions through seminars and conferences and to explore possibilities to establish joint programmes for human rights scholars.
- The Danish Council for Human Rights, in April 2003, established the Equal Treatment Committee (*Ligebehandlingsudvalget*), the aim of which is to draft a Danish equal treatment strategy and to assist and provide input to DIHR regarding the national work on promoting equal treatment and prevent discrimination. The Committee consists of members of the Danish Human Rights Council who have special knowledge or experience in working with equal treatment related to age, disability, gender, race and ethnicity, religion and faith, as well as sexual orientation. DIHR acts as secretariat for the Committee. The Committee has provided valuable input to the reports published by the DIHR as a national equality body (NEB) according to the EU Directives.[48]
- DIHR cooperates with civil society pursuant to Article 33 of the CRPD. The DIHR has been appointed to promote, protect and monitor the implementation of the Convention. According to Article 33(3) CRPD, civil society – and particularly persons with disabilities and their representative organisations – must be involved and participate fully in the monitoring process. The DIHR has conducted roundtable meetings on the UN Convention with around 30 Danish disability organisations and held meetings with

---

48 See e.g. the Report Equal Treatment – Status and future perspectives (*Ligebehandling – Status og fremtidsperspektiver*), report no. 2 DIHR 2005 and Efficient Protection against Discrimination – Legal and Practical Initiatives (*Effektiv beskyttelse mod discrimination – om retlige og faktiske tiltag*) report no. 5 DIHR, 2007.

the leading organisations, including the Danish Disability Council (an independent advisory council set up by the Danish Government), and the umbrella organisation Disabled Peoples' Organisations Denmark (*Danske Handicaporganisationer*)[49], e.g. in regard to the creation of a homepage about the Convention[50] as well as a project about political participation for persons with disabilities.

6.2. RELATIONSHIP WITH OTHER NATIONAL BODIES

Obviously, the DIHR has an interest in a strong, effective national human rights protection system and thus provides assistance, where possible, considering the resources available. In Denmark, the core national human rights structures with a legislative foundation can be narrowed down to the Parliamentary Ombudsman, the Danish National Council for Children and the Data Protection Agency.

The DIHR cooperates with the Ombudsman in several ways. A Parliamentary decision of 2010 laid down the framework for Denmark's compliance with Article 33(2) of the UN Convention on the Rights of Persons with Disabilities on promoting, protecting and monitoring the implementation of the Convention.[51] The DIHR was assigned to promote, protect and monitor the implementation of the Convention, in close dialogue with disability organisations. The Parliamentary Ombudsman contributes to monitoring and protecting human rights in the disability area through his current work of monitoring developments in equal treatment.[52] The DIHR meets with the Danish Disability Council and the Parliamentary Ombudsman every six months to discuss progress and developments in the implementation of the Disability Convention and to coordinate efforts.

In 2004, Denmark ratified the Optional Protocol to the UN Convention against Torture (OPCAT). The National Prevention Mechanism (NPM) required under Article 3 of OPCAT was subsequently established as part of the Ombudsman functions in 2007. In Denmark, the NPM is not regulated by law but by Parliamentary decision.[53] The Danish Parliament decided that the Danish Ombudsman should be appointed as the Danish NPM and that the Ombudsman could utilise the expertise of the Danish Rehabilitation and Research Centre for Torture Victims (RCT) and DIHR. The NPM is currently organised with a working group handling the inspections, which consists of staff from the Ombudsman's

[49] DPOD is an NGO-umbrella organization for 32 national member organisations representing more than 320.000 people with disabilities in Denmark.

[50] Available at www.handicapkonvention.dk (in Danish only).

[51] No. B 15 of 4 November 2010.

[52] No. B 43 of 2 April 1993.

[53] No. B 129 of 19 February 2004. See more here (in English): http://en.ombudsmanden.dk/opcat/.

office, RCT and sometimes DIHR. In addition, there is a so-called OPCAT Council that meets annually or twice yearly to discuss the overall strategy and inspection plan of the NPM. The Council consists of the Ombudsman, DIHR and RCT. With respect to Greenland, DIHR has entered into a cooperation agreement with the Greenlandic Ombudsman (*Inatsisartut Ombudsmandiat*) with a view to supporting her work. The DIHR participated in an inspection carried out in Greenland in 2012.

The DIHR has provided input when a Children's Office was established at an integrated part of the Parliamentary Ombudsman office in 2012 on the basis of a recommendation from the UN Committee on the Rights of the Child.[54] The Children's Office was established with the purpose of enhancing the protection of the rights of the child according to the UN Convention on the Rights of the Child. The Children's Office therefore visits locations where children are placed away from home and has launched a specific child-friendly webpage to receive individual complaints from children.[55] The DIHR will continue to cooperate and monitor the efforts and work of the designated office and will provide technical assistance if needed.

Regarding interaction with other national human rights structures, the DIHR has regular meetings with representatives from the Danish National Council for Children[56] discussing for example follow-up initiatives within the area of the rights of the child. More rarely, the DIHR meets with the Data Protection Agency. However, their expertise is used and they are consulted often, when DIHR receives a request for a legal brief in the area of data protection.

The experience with the universal periodic review process on Denmark resulted in the development of methodologies on reporting for state, civil society and national human rights institutions.[57]

---

54 Act no. 568 of 18. June 2012.

55 See http://boernekontoret.ombudsmanden.dk/ (in Danish only).

56 The National Council for Children is an independent national institution for children. The National Council for Children is politically independent and acts on its own decisions. In administrative terms, the Council is linked to the Danish Ministry of Social Affairs and Integration, while the Children's Office at the Parliamentary Ombudsman works with individual complaints handling and visits places where children are placed.

57 The Danish Institute for Human Rights, Universal Periodic Review First Cycle, Reporting Methodologies from the Position of the State, Civil Society and National Human Rights Institutions, Disseminated Through the International Coordinating Committee of National Institutions for the Promotion and Protection of Human Rights (ICC), 2nd edition, 2011.

6.3. COOPERATION WITH THE UNITED NATIONS AND OTHER INTERNATIONAL ACTORS[58]

6.3.1. *The Universal Periodic Review (UPR)*

DIHR was engaged in different stages of the process leading up to the universal periodic review of Denmark, which took place in May 2011.[59] Besides assisting the Danish government during the UPR preparations and establishing a secretariat for a joint NGO stakeholder report, the DIHR engaged in the UPR process as an independent stakeholder.

In November 2010, the DIHR drafted and submitted a stakeholder report for the Danish UPR process.[60] The report focused on human rights structures in Denmark and included recommendations for improvement of such structures. The report contained mainly general human rights recommendations not normally covered by the scope of the UN treaty bodies, including human rights and business issues.

In April 2011, a month before the UPR interactive dialogue of Denmark, the DIHR published an additional report containing a broad list of recommendations within various categories.[61] In the report, the DIHR had gathered the recommendations considered to be most relevant in Denmark at the time. While the recommendations were based primarily on stakeholder reports to the Danish UPR and on the OHCHR compilation, new recommendations were also included. The aim of the report was to provide an overview of relevant human rights issues in Denmark to States participating in the Universal Periodic Review of Denmark. Each recommendation was formulated in a way that could be directly applied when drafting recommendations to the Danish government. The report was disseminated widely to embassies and country missions in Denmark and Geneva. Furthermore, representatives from DIHR were available to meet with country representatives in Geneva prior to the examination of Denmark.

During the UPR of Denmark in May 2011, DIHR facilitated a side event in Geneva concerning the human rights situation in Denmark and the most

---

58 For more information on NHRI interaction with the UN, see also K. Roberts, 'The Role and Functioning of the International Coordinating Committee of National Human Rights Institutions in International Human Rights Bodies', Chapter 10 in this volume; K. Meuwissen, 'NHRI Participation in United Nations Human Rights Procedures: International Promotion Versus Institutional Consolidation', Chapter 12 in this volume.

59 The Danish Institute for Human Rights, Universal Periodic Review First Cycle, Reporting Methodologies from the Position of the State, Civil society and National Human Rights Institutions, Disseminated through the International Coordinating Committee of National Institutions for the Promotion and Protection of Human Rights (ICC), 2nd edition 2011.

60 Danish Institute for Human Rights, Individual Stakeholder Report of November 2010 to the Universal Periodic Review of Denmark, 11th Session of the Working Group of the Human Rights Council, 2 May 2011.

61 Danish Institute for Human Rights, Universal Periodic Review of Denmark 2011, Selected Human Rights Concerns and Suggestions for Recommendations.

essential DIHR recommendations to Denmark. DIHR staff was present during the review and was available for consultations with the Danish government after the review. DIHR furthermore facilitated a live public broadcast of the review in Copenhagen.

Shortly after the interactive dialogue, DIHR published a report in Danish and English containing all the written recommendations made to Denmark.[62] In the report, the recommendations are ordered and categorised, making them more accessible to the general public. The purpose of the report was to strengthen the Danish debate on the recommendations by making the recommendations easily accessible.

When the Danish government had submitted its replies to the recommendations to Denmark, DIHR compiled a final UPR outcome report in Danish.[63] The report lists all the recommendations, the replies from the Danish government and a response from DIHR to the Danish replies. The report furthermore outlines the DIHR's views on how the recommendations could be implemented.

In December 2011, the DIHR facilitated a UPR hearing during which the Danish UPR recommendations were discussed. At the hearing, the Danish minister of foreign affairs discussed the UPR recommendations and answered questions from the participants. In addition, the DIHR has facilitated follow-up meetings with the Ministry of Foreign Affairs, foreign representations and civil society representatives and held public meetings.

After the UPR process, the Danish Parliamentary Ombudsman received additional funding and an expanded mandate: the Ombudsman's mandate was extended with a Children's Office, the mission of which was to improve children's access to the Ombudsman, and the Ombudsman obtained the possibility to inspect centres where children are placed. The extension of the Ombudsman's mandate partly results from the international recommendations made to Denmark in the context of the UPR (and the treaty body recommendations: see *infra* section 6.6.2), but it is also due to lobbying from civil society and the DIHR and a dramatic rise in the number of cases where child abuse has been discovered.

Another interesting result of the UPR process can be noted in the political programme (*regeringsgrundlag*) for the present governmental period of the new government that was formed on 3 October 2011. The new government is a coalition of the Social Democrats *(Socialdemokraterne)*, the Social Liberals *(Radikale Venstre)* and the Socialist People's Party *(Socialistisk Folkeparti)*. The new government programme contains several suggestions for amendments relevant

[62] The Danish Institute for Human Rights, 'The Universal Periodic Review of Denmark 2011 Compiled Recommendations from UN Human Rights Council' (English Version), 2011; Danish Institute for Human Rights, 'Den Universelle Periodiske Bedømmelse af Danmark 2011 Sammenskrevne anbefalinger fra FN's Menneskerettighedsråd' (Danish Version).

[63] The Danish Institute for Human Rights, '*Den Universelle Periodiske Bedømmelse af Danmark 2011, Institut for Menneskerettigheders vurdering af Danmarks Besvarelse af Anbefalinger fra FN's Menneskerettighedsråd*', 2011 (in Danish only).

to human rights, such as the aim to ratify the optional protocol to the CRPD on individual communications; the strengthening of the DIHR's administrative independence and resources; as well as several amendments in the area of asylum, family reunification and related policy areas. While it is difficult to measure the exact impact of the UPR on the new governmental programme,[64] one cannot rule out that the UPR process has had a significant effect on the programme, both regarding the placement and status of topics of human rights relevance in the new programme, as well as regarding the highlighting and awareness-raising that DIHR was in fact a NHRI operating on a somewhat limited budget. This example also indicates that political reality and context play a huge role for the implementation of human rights recommendations of a "soft law" nature and for the possibilities and success of a National Human Rights Institution.

Another output of the efforts of DIHR was that the UPR process - and especially the aspect of having concrete "soft law" recommendations and the response of the State in writing for each and every recommendation - opened the way toward a more structured follow-up, since DIHR could assess the answers of the government and highlight any discrepancies in the interpretations by government representatives and those of the DIHR. This approach and the inclusion of proactive recommendations for improved implementation of human rights obligations was adapted in the new Status Report, launched in May 2012 (*supra*, section 5.1.2).

6.3.2. Interaction with the UN Treaty Body System

The DIHR systematically participates in the reporting process of the UN treaty body system, mainly by submitting individual NHRI parallel reports wherein selected concerns are raised and concrete recommendations suggested. The aim is to provide independent human rights input and to provide an independent source of information on the human rights situation in Denmark in order to assist the treaty body system in publishing relevant, high quality recommendations in its Concluding Observations to Denmark. The drafting and submission of parallel reports, being present in person either at the pre-session or at the examination of Denmark's report and presenting the DIHR's views on the human rights situation in Denmark are all priorities for DIHR.

During the last two years, DIHR has submitted individual parallel reports (including reports prior to the drafting of the "list of issues") to the Committee of the Rights of the Child (2010), the Committee for the Elimination of Racial Discrimination (2010) as well as to the Human Rights Committee (2011). DIHR singles out topics to be described in its submission based on general relevance, as well as the DIHR's own expertise and the special mandates of DIHR

64 No reference is made to reports and recommendations by the DIHR or by other stakeholders in the governmental programme.

regarding disability, ethnicity and gender. DIHR submits parallel reports under the reporting procedures of all UN human rights core conventions ratified by Denmark.[65] Furthermore, DIHR participates during the treaty body examination of Denmark to the extent possible and takes initiatives to follow up on the UN treaty body recommendations.

As regards the CERD, DIHR submitted a parallel report to the UN CERD Committee in 2010. The Director of DIHR participated in the examination of Denmark and presented a statement to the Committee during the examination. As a follow-up to the CERD recommendations, the DIHR facilitated a meeting in Denmark between the country rapporteur of CERD and representatives from the Danish government. The objective of the meeting was to discuss and elaborate on the recommendations to Denmark. Afterwards, the UN rapporteur participated in a hearing with Danish members of Parliament from various political parties. The presentation by the country rapporteur and the subsequent discussion before parliamentarians was organised by a Danish NGO.

As regards CRC, DIHR representatives were present in January 2011 during the CRC examination of Denmark together with a group of civil society representatives. As a member of a Danish coalition on the Convention on the Rights of the Child,[66] the DIHR has participated in the follow-up to the CRC recommendations to Denmark since February 2011. The coalition has participated in follow-up meetings with the Ministry of Social Affairs and Integration concerning the recommendations and the possible initiatives to implement the recommendations. Furthermore, in February 2012, the coalition organised a visit to Denmark by a country rapporteur of the CRC. During the visit, the CRC member met with the Minister of Social Affairs and Integration, a representative from the Ministry of Children and Education, the Parliamentary Ombudsman and with civil society organisations. Furthermore, the CRC member met with a group of Danish children and participated in a public meeting concerning child rights in Denmark and the CRC recommendations. Prior to the visit, the DIHR

---

65 Denmark has ratified the following seven of the nine UN core human rights instruments and protocols (unless otherwise stated): CERD, ICCPR, ICESCR, CEDAW, CAT, CRC and CRPD. Denmark has not ratified CMW and CED. Denmark has not ratified CRC OP 3 and CESCR OP.

66 The Coalition Group meets on a regular basis to coordinate the work aiming at better implementation of the UN Convention on the Rights of the Child in Denmark; e.g. to submit parallel reports to the UN Committee on the Rights of the Child and conduct follow-up procedures. The Coalition consists of Amnesty International, Børnerådet (National Council for Children), Børnesagens Fællesråd (The Joint Council for Child Issues), Børns Vilkår (Children's Welfare in Denmark), Dansk Ungdoms Fællesråd (Danish Youth Council), Danske Handicaporganisationer (Disabled Peoples Organisations Denmark), Det Danske Spejderkorps (The Danish Guide and Scout Association); DUI – Leg & Virke; Foreningen Grønlandske Børn, Institut for Menneskerettigheder (The Danish Institute for Human Rights), Red Barnet (Save the Children); Red Barnet Ungdom (Save the Children -Youth); Ungdommens Røde Kors (Red Cross -Youth) and UNICEF Danmark (UNICEF Denmark).

drafted a briefing paper on the latest developments concerning child rights in Denmark.[67]

In August 2011, the DIHR submitted input to the UN Human Rights Committee on issues to be included on the Danish list of issues prior to reporting to the UN International Covenant on Civil and Political Rights (ICCPR)[68] and in November 2012 a similar report was submitted to the UN Committee of Economic, Social and Cultural Rights (ICESCR).[69] The work of submitting *both* a report to the list of issues and an ordinary parallel report can give rise to some concern in terms of resources, since it is in fact a doubling of the workload in relation to treaty body reporting.

6.3.3. Visit by Delegations

The DIHR meets with relevant delegations visiting Denmark whenever possible. The DIHR always seeks to contribute to a discussion on the human rights situation in Denmark and to provide delegations with required information. In 2008, the UN Special Rapporteur on torture visited Denmark. In preparation for the visit, the DIHR drafted a briefing paper to assist the Special Rapporteur. The DIHR has also met with Council of Europe delegations, for instance from the European Commission against Racism and Intolerance (ECRI) and a Committee of Experts of the European Charter for Regional or Minority Languages as well as the Council of Europe's Commissioner for Human Rights.

6.3.4. Reporting to International Networks and Agencies

Over the years, the DIHR has provided input on developments in the human rights situation in Denmark, communicating with various international networks, often on consultancy basis. Among these networks the following can be cited: FRA-NET Research Network; the FRA-Lex Network; European Network of Experts on Fundamental Rights; European Network of Legal Experts in the Non-discrimination Field (on the grounds of Race or Ethnic Origin, Age, Disability, Religion or Belief and Sexual Orientation); and EQUINET, the European Network of Equality Bodies. The benefit of drafting and submitting these reports is that these reports provide information and transparency on ongoing developments in human rights in the country while providing factual evidence based on which international stakeholders can decide to take action, launch initiatives or make further inquiries of the domestic authorities.

---

67 Not published.

68 Available at www.ccprcentre.org/country/denmark/ and www2.ohchr.org/english/bodies/hrc/docs/ngos/DIHR_Denmark103.pdf.

69 Not publicly available.

7. CONCLUSION: CHALLENGES AND BEST PRACTICES OF THE DIHR

On 29 May 2012, a new Act on the Institute for Human Rights – Denmark's National Human Rights Institution was adopted by Parliament. The new Act which has entered into force on 1 January 2013, strengthens the Institute's mandate and independence. The DIHR's mandate under the new Act has been drafted with a view to implementing the Paris Principles on NHRIs in a more explicit way than the former Act. The DIHR is also mandated to act as a NEB in the fields of gender and ethnic discrimination as well as being a monitoring entity under the CRPD. The DIHR is vested with the competence to monitor, report, advise, conduct analysis and research, promote coordination with civil society, implement education, manage information, ensure library facilities and contribute to the implementation of human rights, both domestically as well as internationally. New funding that is not earmarked to the special mandates is ensured for giving greater priority to the main human rights challenges confronting the Danish society. These challenges still need to be addressed more fully. Continuous work needs to be done in terms of synergy in relation to the various mandates, an increased involvement of civil society, the development of follow-up and implementation procedures and regarding issues related to the territorial limitations of the mandate. Other avenues to consider are a more proactive effort in the area of amicus curiae or support for concrete domestic cases relevant for developing human rights jurisprudence. Quasi-judicial powers or power to access various sites of human rights relevance is not on the table in the foreseeable future inasmuch as other statutory bodies fulfil that role. As the DIHR has no mandate to investigate specific complaints or incidents, it leaves this task to other institutions established for this purpose, such as the Parliamentary Ombudsman, the Data Protection Agency, the Independent Police Complaints Authority and the Equality Board. However, the DIHR may access documentation, facilities and individuals in order to obtain relevant information for general reports and analysis.

The DIHR is an institution with several different mandates; some are derived from EU directives, such as the national equality body mandates on race, ethnicity and gender. Others are found in UN principles and conventions. Taken together with the professional interest and self-identification of the staff, as well as the funding of the salary of a particular employee on either the special mandate funding or the "core-funding" for the NHRI, there exists an inherent risk of clashes in terms of priorities. Take for example the name of the institution: Danish Institute for Human Rights – Denmark's National Human Rights Institution. The name does not refer to DIHR as also being a national equality body. This probably results in a lack of visibility – or at least a concern about lack of visibility – of the special mandates. Will the special mandates be prioritised, or will they just be absorbed in the general human rights work? What about victims of discrimination? Do they know that they can approach the DIHR for support or advice? An extra effort in the everyday work has to be made so as to ensure visibility of the special mandate. This is done, for example, in those specific chapters of the status report which cover the special mandates automatically. The DIHR needs to show stakeholders who take interest in the special mandates how the earmarked funding is being administrated, that it has been mainstreamed into all areas of the institution and that it is visible in the products.

Internally, there is also a question of who should support whom, since core funded staff cannot avoid working on discrimination issues as an inherent component of all human rights documents, just as staff working on a special mandate cannot avoid working on general human rights issues – and to some extent are expected to do so. Should the resources for working on a specific topic come out of core-funding or from the special mandate funding? The special CRPD mandate lies somewhat in the middle, since the rights of disabled people is not solely an issue of discrimination, although there might be a tendency to treat it as such.

The knowledge and orientation of staff towards specific sources of law is another matter. Especially gender issues are strongly oriented towards EU legislation, while race and ethnicity have a strong presence in both EU Anti-Discrimination Directives and in the core treaties of the UN. Staff members working with disability orient themselves mostly towards the CRPD. It is also a matter of staff expertise, where the issue is one of being either a specialist or a human rights generalist. The human rights generalist has to some extent come under pressure in relation to the growing numbers of human rights treaties and due to the EU becoming a more active stakeholder in the field – especially with the introduction of the EU Charter of Fundamental Rights. But there is definitely a need for jurists and other experts who are able to deal with a very broad knowledge and have flexibility in their approach so they can address the variety of issues surfacing the national human rights agenda. Hence, there exists a capacity issue as to whether staff will be able to operate and keep themselves updated with legal developments taking place at bodies in the United Nations, the Council of Europe, the European Union as well as the domestic legal setting. The solution, obviously, is more stringent prioritisation in strategy plans and action plans as well as allowing time for training and education of staff. A final issue to take into consideration is whether the assessment of a particular topic will vary according to the eye of the beholder, since many human rights issues inherently encompass competing interests. One's field of expertise and professional background will obviously have some degree of influence on the assessment of human rights.

Perhaps due to the discussion on the closure of the DIHR in 2002, the Institute in the last decade has been very keen on being precise in its analyses and explicit when there is a concern, a soft law recommendation, or an issue of potential or even direct human rights violation. This is obviously an important aspect in reports and legal briefs and in the DIHR's advice to Parliament. A challenge here is to predict the ever-evolving human rights catalogue and the dynamic interpretation of human rights obligations as interpreted both by regional human rights courts and regional and international committees, as well as balancing the interpretation concerning vulnerable groups protected by the special mandates. This must be done without being accused of being politically biased by some opinion makers. To avoid criticism entirely, one would have to take the minimum interpretation and most conservative approach to international human rights obligations, an approach, which would allow for the broadest political manoeuvrability possible and would therefore be more appreciated. However, it seems that there is a growing understanding of the role of a NHRI and its advisory function. This has been a slow and evolving process, but it is going in the right direction. Hence, a Danish minister has stated: 'the [Danish Institute for Human Rights] in general delivers solid work substantiated by research, even though the Government may not always agree in all the conclusions. The Institute is independent, which is a strength. I would have had much greater concerns if the Institute agreed with the Government all the time.'[70]

One of the benefits when encountering resistance or even hostility is that the professionalism, expertise and argumentation of the institution has to be of the highest possible standard. It sharpens the senses of the institution. To communicate complex legal human rights issues in a precise manner and still be able to convey the message to ordinary people and journalists is definitely a challenge. Training NHRI staff in communication skills is needed, and both our partners and interlocutors appreciate this training when interacting with us. The expert should be clear and precise as to whether there is a risk of violating Denmark's human rights obligations or whether it is "just" a softer recommendation to improve or promote the implementation of human rights principles or values which the Government has the option of following or not. When one speaks of the political impact of human rights, and when human rights to a larger extent are supported by one part of the Parliament and not the other, there can be a risk that the NHRI will be perceived as politically biased. The solution is to always have the courage to focus on the critical dialogue and to address the most grave human rights challenges regardless of the support or lack thereof from the Government, while maintaining a constructive relationship with the Parliament and a high degree of relevance in the public eye.

---

70 Quote from the Minister for Foreign Affairs, Lene Espersen. In a Parliamenaty debate, the Danish Parliament discussed the role of DIHR based on a motion put forward on 15 March 2011 (B 84 *Forslag til folketingsbeslutning om ændring af arbejdskommissoriet for Institut for Menneskerettigheder*). The motion limiting the DIHR mandate had been proposed due to criticism by certain politicians about concerns raised and activities initiated by DIHR leadership and experts, mainly related to integration and migration issues. The motion was not adopted, and the debate reflected general political support for the DIHR. Quotation taken from the DIHR Annual Report 2011.

The lessons learned from the UPR process have drawn more attention to concrete recommendations and to the follow-up procedures, especially in receiving a clear opinion from the Government on whether they intend to follow the recommendation and the reasoning behind a possible rejection of a recommendation. This method has been imbedded in the new status report of DIHR and will continue to be developed with the aim of creating public and systematised political ownership with the adequate structural support, thus enhancing human rights protection and promotion.

One can conclude by saying that 25 years after the entity now called the DIHR was established, it is now finally an authentic and fully recognised national human rights institution, with a more balanced funding allocation between different tasks. Despite all the inherent challenges that might flow from being designated as a national human rights institution with special mandates, it appears evident that the foundation for fulfilling this role is in place.

NHRI IN POLAND: AS GOOD AS IT GETS?

Aleksandra Gliszczyńska-Grabias[1] and
Katarzyna Sękowska-Kozłowska[2]

The role of a national human rights institution in Poland is performed by The Commissioner for Citizens' Rights (The Ombudsman), a body established in 1987. Undoubtedly, the 25-year history of this body contributes to its stability, positive image and institutional memory. Its mandate and independence are firmly secured in constitutional provisions. However, does this mean that the Ombudsman acting as a NHRI fulfils all expectations connected to this role? The granting of A-status to this body indicates that it fully meets the requirements established by the Paris Principles. Despite this, there are still some problems to resolve and challenges to undertake. This chapter aims to examine the status, mandate and practice of the Polish Ombudsman and to analyse its strengths and weaknesses.

1. INTRODUCTION

Rzecznik Praw Obywatelskich (in English: The Commissioner for Citizens' Rights – further: The Ombudsman[3]) was established by the law of the 15th of July

---

1 The author holds a M.A. in European Legal Studies and works as a Researcher at the Poznan Human Rights Centre of the Institute of Legal Studies of the Polish Academy of Sciences. She has completed her Ph.D. thesis at the Institute of Legal Studies of the Polish Academy of Sciences. Contact: aggrabias@gmail.com.

2 The author holds a Ph.D. from the Institute of Legal Studies of the Polish Academy of Sciences and works as a senior researcher at the Poznan Human Rights Centre of the Institute of Legal Studies of the Polish Academy of Sciences. Contact: kasiaseko@interia.pl.

3 Some terminology issues demand clarification. The name "The Commissioner for Citizens' Rights" is a literal translation of the Polish name *Rzecznik Praw Obywatelskich* used *inter alia* in the official English translation of the Polish Constitution (http://www.trybunal.gov.pl/eng/index.htm). In some publications this name is translated also as "The Commissioner for Civil Rights" (see for example: EU Fundamental Rights Agency (FRA), 'National Human Rights Institutions in the EU Member States: Strengthening the Fundamental Rights Architecture in the EU', Vienna, Publication Office of the European Union, 2010, p.28). The documents produced by the Office of the Ombudsman however use the term "The Human Rights Defender" (http://www.rpo.gov.pl/index.php?s=3). In order to simplify and avoid confusion, this chapter uses "The Ombudsman".

1987.[4] The institution was inspired by the Swedish Ombudsman. The establishment of such a body under the communist regime may be recognised as a move towards democratic transition.[5] On the other hand, some argue that this institution was established by the then state authorities to serve as a façade of legality, with an aim to influence and control its activity.[6] Nevertheless, since 1989 the Ombudsman was able to perform its functions in a democratic environment. At the same time it played an important role in the process of increasing the human rights standards, for example by promoting Poland's accession to the international human rights treaties, particularly those offering the right to individual complaint such as the European Convention on Human Rights (accession in 1993) and to the Optional Protocol to the International Covenant on Civil and Political Rights (accession in 1991)[7]. In the past 25 years the Ombudsman's role in a democratic society was reinforced by the development of its mandate and practice. As a typical single-person body, it also profited from the image of persons holding this office who were usually outstanding legal experts.[8]

2. STATUS

In 1999 the Polish Ombudsman was granted A-status by the International Coordinating Committee of National Institutions for the Promotion and Protection of Human Rights (ICC)[9]. This means that that the institution has been recognised as fully compliant with the Principles Relating to the Status of National Institutions (The Paris Principles) adopted by the General Assembly in 1993.[10] Furthermore, it belongs to a narrow group of 12 NHRIs from the

---

4 The English translation of the Ombudsman Act is published on its home page: http://www.rpo.gov.pl/index.php?md=8537&s=3.

5 In the same decade other institutions that form important control mechanisms were also established in Poland: The Chief Administrative Court (1980), The Tribunal of State (1982), The Constitutional Tribunal (1985).

6 M. Zubik, 'Rzecznik Praw Obywatelskich (po 20 latach istnienia urzędu)' [The office of the Commissioner for Civil Rights Protection (after twenty years of its existence], *Państwo i Prawo* No. 11, 2008, p. 3.

7 It is worthwhile to mention that the core UN human rights treaties were ratified by Poland before 1989: International Convention on the Elimination of all Forms of Racial Discrimination in 1968, International Covenant on Civil and Political Rights and International Covenant on Economic, Social and Cultural Rights in 1977, Convention on the Elimination of All Forms of Discrimination against Women in 1980.

8 This function was performed by Prof. Ewa Łętowska (1987–1992), Prof. Tadeusz Zieliński (1992–1996), Prof. Adam Zieliński (1996–2000), Prof. Andrzej Zoll (2000–2006), Dr. Janusz Kochanowski (2006–2010) and Prof. Irena Lipowicz (since 2010 to present).

9 The A-status was re-granted after the revision in 2007, see Report of the ICC Sub-Committee on Accreditation (SCA), Geneva, 22 to 26 October 2007 (the ICC SCA reports are only available on the ICC website from 2006 onwards, see: http://nhri.ohchr.org/EN/AboutUs/ICCAccreditation/Pages/SCA-Reports.aspx).

10 UN GA Resolution 48/134 of 20 December 1993, Annex.

EU countries which gained A-status,[11] which must be viewed as a remarkable achievement of an institution which was created in an environment so unfriendly to human rights and the historical period in which the very concept of NHRI was still to be developed.[12] Shaped as an Ombudsman, the Polish NHRI is rather atypical, as such bodies are usually designed as commissions or institutes.[13] As will be indicated in this chapter, this atypical structure may be seen both as a strength and an obstacle in performing the role of the NHRI.

The following section examines legal guarantees securing the status of the Ombudsman from the perspective of its independence and pluralism, which arise from the fundamental requirements formulated by the Paris Principles.

2.1. INDEPENDENCE

There are several elements that play a crucial role in assuring independence of the NHRI. These are foremost: legal autonomy, guarantees concerning the appointment and dismissal procedures, immunity and the budget.

2.1.1. Legal Autonomy

The Institution of the Polish Ombudsman is based on a solid legal foundation as it was established by the Ombudsman Act in 1987.[14] This law constitutes a legal framework for its functioning by determining its mandate. Moreover, the status of the Ombudsman is secured by the Constitution of 1997 which contains the most fundamental guarantees of its independence.

According to Article 210 of the Constitution, the Ombudsman 'shall be independent in his activities, independent of other state organs and shall be accountable only to the Sejm[15] in accordance with principles specified by statute'. The Constitutional Tribunal, acting on a motion of the Ombudsman, decided in a 2010 judgement that the provisions of the Ombudsman Act which entitled the Speaker of the Sejm to provide the Office of the Ombudsman with the statute were

---

11 For an extensive analysis of the different types of NHRIs in Europe, see M. Nowak, 'National Human Rights Institutions in Europe: Comparative, European and International Perspectives', Chapter 1 in this volume.

12 Even though the idea of NHRI dates back to 1946, a breakthrough was achieved in 1991 when the Paris Principles were defined at the first International Workshop on National Institutions for the Promotion and Protection of Human Rights. See: G. de Beco, 'National Human Rights Institutions in Europe', *Human Rights Law Review*, vol. 7, 2007, pp. 333–335. See also: M. Nowak, 'National Human Rights Institutions in Europe: Comparative, European and International Perspectives', Chapter 1 in this volume.

13 Institution of the Ombudsman is typical for the former socialist countries and Latin America countries. Other Ombudsman bodies in the EU granted with A-status are the Spanish and Portuguese NHRIs. See also: M. Nowak, Chapter 1 in this volume.

14 See *supra*, note 4.

15 Sejm is the lower chamber of the Parliament.

not in compliance with the principle of independence of the Ombudsman set forth in the Constitution.[16] Moreover, the Speaker of the Sejm is no longer entitled to appoint the deputies of the Ombudsman.[17] Accordingly, the Ombudsman is granted full autonomy in performing its duties. The only legal constraint is the rule of accountability to the Sejm. This means first and foremost that the Sejm decides on the appointment and dismissal of the Ombudsman and that it may waive his/her immunity (see *infra* section 2.1.3). The Ombudsman is also obliged to annually inform the Parliament about his/her activities.[18] The annual reports of the Ombudsman are a significant source of information on the state of human rights in Poland.

2.1.2. Appointment and Dismissal

Provisions concerning appointment and dismissal of the Ombudsman constitute crucial safeguards of its independence. According to Article 209 para. 1 of the Constitution, the Ombudsman is appointed by the Sejm, with the consent of the Senate[19] for a period of five years. The Ombudsman is appointed on the motion expressed by the Speaker of the Sejm or by a group of 35 deputies.[20] Thus, the appointment of the NHRI in Poland is fully independent from the executive power. Naturally the appointment of a particular person to this office is to a certain extent linked to politics, as is reflected by the fact that the elected candidate is usually supported by the ruling party. The tenure of the Ombudsman is however independent from the term of the Parliament which lasts four years. This means that usually the Ombudsman operates before and after parliamentary elections. According to Article 5 para. 2 of the Ombudsman Act, there is a possibility to be re-elected once. This may be estimated as some threat to the independence of this office, since a person standing for re-election may avoid raising issues uncomfortable to the ruling party and feel the temptation to conform to its expectations. From this point of view, probably a six or seven-year term, without a possibility of re-election, would be a better safeguard of the independence of this office.[21] So far not a single person holding this office stood for re-election, which may point to a purely theoretical nature of this consideration.

A provision crucial to preserving the independence of the Ombudsman from external pressures, particularly of a political nature, is provided by Article 209 para. 2 and 3 of the Constitution. It states that the Ombudsman shall not hold any other post, except for a professorship in an institute of higher education, nor perform any other professional activities. She or he shall not belong to a political

[16] Constitutional Tribunal, Judgment K35/09 of 19 October 2010.
[17] *Ibidem*.
[18] Article 212 of the Constitution of Poland.
[19] The Senate is the upper chamber of the Parliament.
[20] Article 3 para. 1 of the Ombudsman Act.
[21] M. Zubik, loc. cit. *supra* note 6, p. 6.

party, a trade union or perform other public activities incompatible with the dignity of the office. Other conditions for the eligibility are very general, since the law only requires that the Ombudsman be 'a Polish citizen with outstanding legal knowledge, professional experience and high prestige due to the individual's moral values and social sensitivity'[22]. Hitherto the qualifications of the persons holding this office have not been disputed since they were usually eminent scholars and recognised legal experts.

Legal requirements concerning the dismissal procedure guarantee stability of the office. The Ombudsman may be discharged by the Sejm prior to the end of his/her term of office only in four cases.[23] These instances are if: 1) the Ombudsman has refused to perform his/her functions; 2) he or she has become permanently incapable to perform the office due to medically certified ailment, disability or decline of strength; 3) his/her lustration statement was assessed by court to be untruthful;[24] 4) he or she acts against the oath.[25] The Sejm takes the resolution on discharging the Ombudsman upon the motion of the Speaker of the Sejm or a group of at least 35 deputies. The resolution is required to be carried by a majority of at least three-fifths of the votes with at least half the regular number of deputies present.[26] This qualified majority prevents the abuse of the dismissal procedure, which has never been initiated so far.

2.1.3. Immunity

According to Article 211 of the Constitution, the Ombudsman shall not be held criminally responsible nor deprived of liberty without prior consent granted by the Sejm. He/she shall be neither detained nor arrested, except in cases when he/she has been apprehended in the commission of an offence and in which his/her detention is necessary for securing the proper course of proceedings. The Speaker

---

22 Article 2 of the Ombudsman Act.

23 Article 7 para. 1 and 2 of the Ombudsman Act.

24 According to the Lustration Act of 2006, a person holding the office of the Ombudsman is required to submit a lustration statement concerning cooperation with the secret police in 1944–1990.

25 According to Article 4 of the Ombudsman Act, prior to assumption of duties, the Ombudsman makes the following oath before the Sejm 'I solemnly swear that in performing the duties entrusted to me as the Human Rights Defender I shall keep faith with the Constitution of the Republic of Poland, safeguard the liberties and rights of the human being and the citizen, being guided by the Law and the principles of community life and social justice. I pledge to perform the duties entrusted to me impartially, with the greatest of diligence and care, to safeguard the dignity of the office and to keep the State and office matters in strict confidence.'(The oath may be taken with the closing epithet 'So help me God'.). In the opinion of J. Świeca "acting against the oath" means for instance: repeating actions leading to constraint of human rights and freedoms, persistent inaction in cases clearly demanding activity of the Ombudsman or demonstrating lack of impartiality, for example by engaging in politics. See: J. Świeca, *Ustawa o Rzeczniku Praw Obywatelskich. Komentarz* [*The Ombudsman Act. A Commentary*], C.H. Beck, 2010, p. 89.

26 Article 7 para. 3 and 4 of the Ombudsman Act.

of the Sejm shall be notified forthwith of any such detention and may order an immediate release of the person detained. Thereby, the Ombudsman belongs to the narrow group of the public officials[27] equipped with immunity, which aims to guarantee their independence and autonomy.

2.1.4. Budget

In line with the Paris Principles, the financial autonomy is an important safeguard of a NHRI's independence.[28] The Polish NHRI's activity is financed from state resources[29] and the budget of the Ombudsman is fully at his/her disposal. Unfortunately, the funds granted to this institution are insufficient. Irena Lipowicz, the current Ombudsman, warned the Parliament in 2010 that proper performance of her duties is seriously endangered by the lack of sufficient funding. As she stated: 'it is obvious that financial independence of the Human Rights Defender, which is questionable in the situation of imposing new tasks without securing adequate funds, is [...] one of the elements of the constitutional principle of the Defender's independence.'[30] New tasks imposed on the Ombudsman in recent years include: the mandate of the national preventive mechanism (NPM) established by the Optional Protocol to the Convention against Torture and other Cruel, Inhuman or Degrading Treatment or Punishment – the OPCAT (since 2008) and the mandate of the equality body set up under European law[31] (since 2011). The Ombudsman will be also charged with monitoring implementation of the Convention on the Rights of Persons with Disabilities due to Poland's accession to this treaty in 2012. In spite of this considerable extension of the Ombudsman's mandate, the level of its funding has not increased, which hindered the Office of the Ombudsman from employing additional staff.[32] On the contrary, the budget has been reduced. Compared to 2009 the budget for 2010 was reduced by PLN 1.3 million (around EUR 300,000), i.e. almost reducing the entire amount allocated for the NPM in 2009, which ultimately led to the reduction of the visits

---

27 In general, the immunity of the Ombudsman is similar to the immunity granted to judges.

28 Paris Principles, para. 2: 'The national institution shall have an infrastructure which is suited to the smooth conduct of its activities, in particular adequate funding. The purpose of this funding should be to enable it to have its own staff and premises, in order to be independent of the Government and not be subject to financial control which might affect its independence'.

29 The budget of the Ombudsman is determined by the Parliament in the State Budget Act.

30 Human Rights Defender Bulletin. Sources 2011, No. 2, p. 14, http://www.rpo.gov.pl/index.php?md=9058&s=3.

31 Namely: Council Directive 2000/43/EC of 29 June 2000 implementing the principle of equal treatment between persons irrespective of racial or ethnic origin; Council Directive 2004/113/EC of 13 December 2004 implementing the principle of equal treatment between men and women in the access to and supply of goods and services; Directive 2006/54/EC of the European Parliament and of the Council of 5 July 2006 on the implementation of the principle of equal opportunities and equal treatment of men and women in matters of employment and occupation (recast).

32 For the past several years the number of the staff of the Ombudsman Office has not changed significantly. In 2010 the Office employed 267 persons, loc. cit. *supra* note 30, p. 70.

in detention centres.[33] Similarly, duties linked to the mandate of the equality body are not secured by additional resources, thus making the commitment of the state to counteract discrimination seriously questionable.[34] This issue was pointed out in 2012 during the second cycle of the Human Rights Council's universal periodic review, when Poland was recommended to ensure that the Office of the Ombudsman is sufficiently resourced to carry out anti-discrimination functions.[35]

2.2. PLURALISM

Securing pluralism, as required by the Paris Principles,[36] by a single-person body such as the Ombudsman presents a serious challenge. There are two elements that seem to be critical in this regard: the procedure of appointment and the way of performing the mandate.

As the report of the EU Fundamental Rights Agency on NHRI states, in the case of the Polish Ombudsman, pluralist representation of the society may be achieved to a certain extent through the possibility of submission of the candidate proposal by minority parties.[37] Indeed, since the law requires that the candidate be nominated by the group of 35 deputies, opposition parties may easily nominate their candidate. Of course in reality a candidate of a ruling party has a greater chance to be appointed. A matter that raises serious concerns is a lack of public consultations in the context of the selection of the Ombudsman. The selection of a candidate is usually an entirely internal decision of a party and the public does not have a chance to participate in the whole process. It is therefore highly advisable to reinforce the visibility and transparency of the procedure. Some steps in this respect were initiated in 2010 by non-governmental organisations

---

33 Visiting places of detention is the principle task of the NPM. In 2010 representatives of the Ombudsman visited 80 detention centres whereas the whole number of detention centres in Poland following the provision of the OPCAT is 1800, *ibidem*, p. 11.

34 It is worth to underline that Poland is seriously lagging behind in this area since it is the last EU Member State to establish the equality body under the EU Directives.

35 Report of the Working Group on the Universal Periodic Review. Poland, *UN Doc.* A/HRC/21/14, 6 July 2012, para 27.

36 Paris Principles, para. 3: 'The composition of the national institution and the appointment of its members, whether by means of an election or otherwise, shall be established in accordance with a procedure which affords all necessary guarantees to ensure the pluralist representation of the social forces (of civilian society) involved in the protection and promotion of human rights, particularly by powers which will enable effective cooperation to be established with, or through the presence of, representatives of: (a) Non-governmental organizations responsible for human rights and efforts to combat racial discrimination, trade unions, concerned social and professional organizations, for example, associations of lawyers, doctors, journalists and eminent scientists; (b) Trends in philosophical or religious thought; (c) Universities and qualified experts; (d) Parliament; (e) Government departments (if these are included, their representatives should participate in the deliberations only in an advisory capacity).'.

37 FRA, 'National Human Rights Institutions in the EU Member States: Strengthening the Fundamental Rights Architecture in the EU', Vienna, Publication Office of the European Union, 2010, p. 32.

which organised public hearings of the candidates within the framework of civic monitoring of candidates for public offices.[38]

Obviously, the Ombudsman does not perform his/her duties alone since he/she is supported by the Office. According to article 20 para. 3 of the Ombudsman Act he/she may also appoint up to three deputies.[39] Nevertheless, unlike NHRIs that have a shape of commissions or institutes, the body itself consists of a single person. Therefore, the issue of cooperation with civil society seems to be extremely important. Currently, the Ombudsman is supported by the Social Council which consists of distinguished representatives of civil society.[40] NGOs are also invited to three expert committees that focus on present priorities of the Ombudsman: the Expert Committee on Elderly People, the Expert Committee on People with Disabilities, and the Expert Committee on Migrants. Thus, it can be observed that the non-governmental sector is invited to counsel and cooperate with the Ombudsman and can play a crucial role in supporting pluralism of this institution. The issue of cooperation of the Ombudsman with NGOs will be developed further below in this chapter (*infra* section 3.4).

3. MANDATE

The Polish Ombudsman has been granted a mandate with a broad scope. The comprehensive character of the mandate is additionally strengthened by the Ombudsman's entitlement to take measures on his/ her own initiative in all areas covered by the mandate.[41]

The Ombudsman safeguards all human rights and freedoms specified in the Polish Constitution and other legal acts, notwithstanding the fact that there are other designated bodies responsible for specific areas of safeguarding rights and freedoms of individuals, including the Commissioner for Children's Rights and the Inspector General for the Protection of Personal Data. The concentration of so many thematic fields within the mandate of the Ombudsman results both in its current status as a key entity of human rights protection in Poland, and in the society's perception of the Ombudsman's Office as an institution responsible for

---

38 Institute for Law and Society (INPRIS), 'OMX: Civic Monitoring of Candidates for Public Offices', available at: http://www.inpris.pl/en/projects/omx-monitoring-eng/.

39 In practice, the Ombudsman usually appoints two deputies. When reassessing the status of the Polish NHRI in 2007, the ICC noted with concern that the position of the deputy Ombudsman remained vacant. See: ICC, Report and Recommendations of the Sub-Committee on Accreditation, 22–26 October 2007, para. 3.10, 1), available at: http://nhri.ohchr.org/EN/AboutUs/ICCAccreditation/Documents/2007_October%20SCA%20Report.pdf.

40 For more information on the Social Council, see *infra* section 3.4.

41 Article 9 para. 3 of the Ombudsman Act.

protecting citizens' rights in general and for intervening in individual cases of human rights violations.[42]

One of the consequences of Poland's ratification of the Optional Protocol to the UN Convention against Torture and Other Cruel, Inhuman, or Degrading Treatment or Punishment has been an obligation to establish a national preventive mechanism (NPM).[43] Since 2008 the Ombudsman serves as the Polish NPM and the decision to entrust him/her with its tasks flows inter alia from the premise that this is an institution acting independently from other state authorities.[44] The Ombudsman undertakes all responsibilities and activities assigned to this function: '[...] the national preventive mechanisms have the power to regularly examine the treatment of the persons deprived of their liberty in places of detention, with a view to strengthening, if necessary, their protection against torture and other cruel, inhuman or degrading treatment or punishment. They are entitled to make recommendations to the relevant authorities with the aim of improving the treatment and the conditions of the persons deprived of their liberty and to prevent torture and other cruel, inhuman or degrading treatment or punishment. Besides, the mechanisms submit proposals and observations concerning existing or draft legislation'.[45]

Since 2011 the Ombudsman performs yet another highly significant function. Based on the provisions of the Act of 3 December 2010 on the implementation of some regulations of the European Union regarding equal treatment, it serves as the equality body. Additional tasks linked to this function which the Ombudsman has been charged with include:[46]

- Safeguarding the observation and implementation of the obligation of equal treatment;
- Providing legal support and advice to the victims of discriminatory treatment;
- Drafting independent reports and recommendations concerning discrimination and unequal-related issues;
- Cooperating with the representatives of the civil society engaged with the problem of safeguarding equal treatment for all.

---

42 J. Arcimowicz, *Rzecznik Praw Obywatelskich. Aktor sceny publicznej* [The Ombudsman. The Actor of the Public Scene], Trio, 2003, p. 171.

43 The Protocol was adopted by the General Assembly of the United Nations in New York on 18 December 2002. The President of the Republic of Poland ratified the Protocol on 2 September 2005 pursuant to the Act of 8 July 2005 on the ratification of the OPCAT. The Protocol came into force on 22nd of June 2006 in the Republic of Poland.

44 The basic information on the character of the NPM and Ombudsman's responsibilities assigned to this function, are available at the website of the Ombudsman: http://www.rpo.gov.pl/pliki/12538758330.pdf.

45 *Ibidem.*

46 The full list of the Ombudsman's tasks concerning his/her equality body's function are listed at: http://www.rpo.gov.pl/index.php?md=9183&s=3.

If an individual becomes a victim of the violation of the principles of equal treatment and non-discrimination on the part of state authorities, the Ombudsman is entitled to apply to another control body for examination of the case if he/she establishes that the principle of equal treatment has been violated and to require from the competent authorities the elimination of violation and to subsequently monitor the implementation of his/her recommendations. Additionally, the Ombudsman may require the initiation of preparatory proceedings and participate in ongoing civil or administrative proceedings.

Simultaneously, the Ombudsman has a limited power to act in individual cases of discrimination, where the discriminatory treatment is contributed to by a private entity. Although the Ombudsman examines facts described in the complaint he/she receives, the only way to receive an effective outcome is to indicate legal measures to which a victim is entitled. Thus, as one of the representatives of the Ombudsman's office stated, the Ombudsman lacks the legal power and entitlement to intervene in cases where, for example, the owner of the private restaurant or pub denies persons belonging to particular ethnic or national groups the right to enter his property.[47] However, the Ombudsman tries to by-pass this limitation through informing the competent state representatives.

One should particularly note that as an equality body the Ombudsman does not have a legislative initiative, although he/she can turn to competent authorities with a request to undertake legislative initiatives and issue or amend legal acts in order to fully implement the principles of equal treatment for all.

3.1. KEY-COMPETENCE: A COMPLAINT BODY

Dealing with cases of human rights violation by the public authorities is the principal task of the Ombudsman. It differs significantly from other NHRIs which focus on counselling, research, promotion or education on human rights. The Paris Principles do not require the NHRI to be mandated to deal with individual complaints and only a few NHRIs in the EU are equipped with such power.[48] From this perspective, the mandate of the Polish Ombudsman may be estimated as its significant strength, since it has been granted a unique overview on the condition of human rights in the country and is vested with the authority to counteract their violations.

How does the Ombudsman act as a complaint body? According to Article 1 para. 3 of the Ombudsman Act, 'in cases involving protection of the rights and

47 E. Siedlecka, *Dyskryminacja ma się niestety dobrze* [Discrimination is, unfortunately, fine], 2011, http://wyborcza.pl/1,75478,10797587,Dyskryminacja_ma_sie__niestety__dobrze.html #ixzz1wLX7Mutk.

48 FRA, 'National Human Rights Institutions in the EU Member States: Strengthening the Fundamental Rights Architecture in the EU', Vienna, Publication Office of the European Union, 2010, pp. 38–39.

liberties of the human being and of the citizen, the Defender shall investigate whether, due to any action or abstaining on the part of organs, organisations or institutions responsible for the observance and implementation of those rights and liberties, the law and principles of community life and social justice have been infringed'. The mandate of the Ombudsman to consider individual complaints is very broad, since it is entitled to investigate alleged violations of all human rights and freedoms set forth in the Constitution and other legal acts, including international treaties. It may receive complaints from all individuals and their organisations. The whole procedure is easy-accessible: there is no charge or formal requirements concerning submission of complaints.[49] The complaints can be submitted in writing, orally – in the Office of the Ombudsman[50], or via e-mail. There is also phone advising.

At the first stage the Ombudsman decides if he/she handles the case or not. He/she may also instruct the applicant as to the action the person is entitled to take or can convey the case to the relevant body. What are the venues of reaction if the Ombudsman handles a case? There are numerous proceedings at his/her disposal. In brief, he/she can: refer to the relevant body or its superior body asking for explanations and give recommendations in case of identifying human rights violations; demand to initiate civil, penal or administrative proceedings; join civil, penal or administrative proceedings; lodge cassation or extraordinary appeal.[51]

The mandate of the Polish Ombudsman seems to be very broad, even in comparison with other Ombudsman institutions. Particularly the entitlement to participate in legal proceedings is unusual.[52] Unfortunately this opportunity is very rarely used. For instance, in 2010 the Ombudsman joined judicial and administrative proceedings only in a few cases.[53] Thus, its activity in this area may be intensified. On the other hand, as presented in the next section, the Ombudsman is very active in the field of systemic problems and law improvement, which may indicate that it tends to prioritise the cases of general interest. The numbers prove that it enjoys much trust as a complaint body. In 2010 the Ombudsman examined about 34,000 complaints, among which it referred around 35% for further proceedings.[54] Within this group, the most numerous were cases concerning penal law (21,7%), executive penal law (20%) and public administration, health care and foreigner rights protection (15,6%)[55]. Among cases completed in 2010, the outcome expected by the applicant and the Ombudsman

[49] A complaint cannot be anonymous (Article 10 of the Ombudsman Act).

[50] Apart from the headquarter in Warsaw, there are three offices of the local representatives of the Ombudsman in various regions of the country, as well as numerous information points.

[51] All procedures are described in detailed manner in Articles 11–18 of the Ombudsman Act.

[52] See: G. Kucsko-Stadlmayer (ed.), *European Ombudsman-Institutions. A Comparative Legal Analysis Regarding the Multifaceted Realisation of an Idea*, Springer, 2008, pp. 505–521.

[53] Human Rights Defender Bulletin. Sources 2011, No. 2, p. 63.

[54] *Ibidem*, p. 64.

[55] *Ibidem*, p. 65.

was achieved in 17,4% of the cases.[56] This raises serious doubts about the efficacy of the Ombudsman as a complaint mechanism.

3.2. IMPACT ON A LEGISLATIVE PROCESS

The Ombudsman has at his/her disposal several instruments that facilitate his/her influence on the law-making process. Owing to his/her expertise in human rights and their implementation – gained primarily during examination of individual complaints – the Ombudsman may play an important role in shaping national politics in this area. Thus the Ombudsman may not only act on reported human rights violations but also play a role in preventing the occurrence of future violations.

The Ombudsman may refer general petitions concerning specific problems to the competent state authorities e.g. ministries. These petitions may concern enforcement of human rights as well as proposals for legal amendment. The authorities addressed by the Ombudsman are not legally obliged to act on such petitions, but they are required to state their position. Therefore, general petitions may serve as an important tool used by the public to monitor the implementation of human rights. This tool is actively used by the Ombudsman. In 2010 there were 293 general petitions lodged to the various state authorities, among which 95 petitions called for a legislative initiative, which points towards a high degree of legislative dysfunction.[57] For instance, in a general petition addressed to the Ministry of Justice, the Ombudsman indicated that the law stipulating an obligatory retirement age of 70 years for notaries constituted discrimination based on age in comparison to other legal professionals who were free to decide on their retirement.[58]Another notable example is the petition to the Speaker of the Sejm (and the whole Sejm itself) concerning the fact that election law did not respect the right to vote of persons with disabilities and elderly people.[59]

Another important instrument that enables the Ombudsman to influence the law is the mandate to lodge an application to the Constitutional Tribunal to verify normative acts with regard to their compliance with the Constitution. In 2010 the Ombudsman lodged 10 applications. They concerned *inter alia* the right to privacy of prisoners[60] and property rights of persons who were evicted due to construction of the public roads.[61] Apart from the motion for constitutional review, the Ombudsman may also take part in proceedings before the Constitutional

56 *Ibidem*, p. 66.
57 *Ibidem*, p. 9.
58 *Ibidem*, p. 17.
59 *Ibidem*, p. 21.
60 *Ibidem*, p. 33: the Ombudsman questioned the legal regulation according to which health services to convicts should be provided in the presence of an officer not from the medical profession, further if there were no risk to the safety of the person providing medical services.
61 *Ibidem*, p. 46.

Tribunal initiated by the constitutional complaint lodged by an individual claiming that his/her rights were violated by unconstitutional regulations. In 2010 the Ombudsman decided to support 10 constitutional complaints.[62]

Apart from the abovementioned procedures, the Ombudsman may also take advantage of his/her position in order to promote international human rights standards in Poland. For instance, the current Ombudsman was making a significant effort in encouraging the ratification by Poland of the UN Convention on the Rights of Persons with Disabilities.

3.3. INTERNATIONAL COOPERATION

The Polish Ombudsman is visibly involved at the various arenas of international cooperation in the field of human rights protection, although not all of them are treated with sufficient attention.

Its flagship international involvement concerns the Eastern Partnership (EaP).[63] Within its framework, the Ombudsman developed a cooperation project with the main objectives including:

- Reinforcing the capacity of the Ombudsman institutions in the EaP countries to participate in building and developing a democratic state which respects the individual's rights and freedoms;
- Providing the conditions for the full realisation of the right to access to the court in the EaP countries through the improvement of the functioning of the judicial systems;
- Supporting non-governmental organisations in their contribution to the development of civil society in the EaP countries;
- Improving the functioning of the civil service through promotion and sharing of good practices in administration;
- Supporting and securing freedom of speech, in particular in the area of the media.

62 *Ibidem*, p. 9.

63 The Eastern Partnership (EaP) is a European Union initiative directed at six countries of Eastern Europe and the South Caucasus: Armenia, Azerbaijan, Belarus, Georgia, Moldova and Ukraine. The EaP was launched by the 27 EU member states and the six partner countries at a summit in Prague on 7 May 2009. The initiative aims at tightening the relationship between the EU and the Eastern partners by deepening their political co-operation and economic integration. The EaP neither promises nor precludes the prospect of EU membership to the partner states. It offers deeper integration with the EU structures by encouraging and supporting them in their political, institutional and economic reforms based on EU standards, as well as facilitating trade and increasing mobility between the EU and the partner states. For more details see http://www.easternpartnership.org/content/eastern-partnership-glance.

The Ombudsman's project, designed for the period of 2009–2013, has been until now accomplished through such initiatives as: organisation of a series of workshops and trainings on human rights protection, monitoring the situation of prisoners in countries within the project, as well as implementing proper mechanisms to prevent torture.

The project consists also of the analysis of the regulations in national law of EaP countries paying special attention to the extent to which those regulations meet the European standards of protection applied to the rights of individuals. Moreover, it has been accompanied by specialised analysis and expert reports, such as the analytical report on the human rights protection in the EaP countries from the perspective and assessment of the UN treaty bodies or the analysis 'Supporting Ombudsman Cooperation in the Eastern Partnership Countries'.[64]

The Polish Ombudsman has signed agreements on cooperation with the Ombudspersons of other states (among others from the Russian Federation and Ukraine), and signed a Memorandum of Understanding between the Commissioner for Civil Rights Protection and the European Regional Bureau of the United Nations Development Programme on the implementation of the program designed to support democracy, governance and participation.[65] However, it is regrettable that no agreement has been concluded between the Polish Ombudsman and any of the leading European National Human Rights Institutions. Close and active cooperation of this kind would be undoubtedly beneficial to all partners.

Moreover, regular meetings of the Ombudsmen of the Visegrad Group[66] countries have been held regularly since 2004. At the meetings, the Ombudsmen discuss the legal challenges they face in their work and strengthen their practical cooperation. As the Visegard Group consists of countries that all have undergone the transformation from an oppressive regime to democracy, their experiences help to find common solutions to existing problems.

Another primary sphere of the Polish Ombudsman's active involvement regarding international cooperation takes place in the framework of its functioning as a National Preventive Mechanism. The representatives of the Ombudsman's Office participate *inter alia* in the activities of the European National Preventive Mechanisms for the Prevention of Torture as well as in the various thematic seminars, such as the meeting in March 2011 in Geneva on the issue of monitoring

---

64 All reports are available at the web page of the Ombudsman: http://www.rpo.gov.pl/index.php?md=8143&s=1.

65 A full list of the agreements and memorandums signed by now is available at: http://www.rpo.gov.pl/index.php?md=8589&s=3.

66 According to the information provided by the organization itself: 'The Visegrad Group reflects the efforts of the countries of the Central European region to work together in a number of fields of common interest within the all-European integration. The Czech Republic, Hungary, Poland and Slovakia have always been part of a single civilisation sharing cultural and intellectual values and common roots in diverse religious traditions, which they wish to preserve and further strengthen'. For more details see: http://www.visegradgroup.eu/.

the procedures of deportations.[67] The Ombudsman is involved in the cooperation with other NPMs, and it helps to establish new NPMs, e.g. in Ukraine in 2011.

At the same time there is a perceptible under-representation of the Ombudsman's Office at the stage of the international human rights monitoring procedures. It seems that the recommendation issued in 2007 by the International Coordinating Committee of National Institutions for the Promotion of Human Rights, encouraging the Polish Ombudsman to engage with the regional and international human rights system and in particular with the UN Human Rights Council and the UN treaty bodies, has not been implemented to a satisfactory extent. During the monitoring procedures concerning Poland at the UN treaty bodies level between 2005–2010, the Ombudsman's Office was present only in 2010, when its representatives participated in the 2010 session of the UN Human Rights Committee examining the Polish report. Moreover, the Ombudsman didn't participate in the universal periodic review (UPR) concerning Poland in 2008: neither as NHRI nor as one of the stakeholders. Rather, the Ombudsman was one of the institutions which were involved in the preparation of the state report. Following the review of the work and functioning of the Human Rights Council and the adoption of new regulations,[68] the modalities of the UPR process for the second cycle have changed in certain respects, including the fact that NHRIs with A status will have a dedicated section in the summary of other stakeholders' information. Nevertheless, in 2012, during the second cycle of the UPR, the Polish Ombudsman has once again not provided information included in the stakeholders' report.

The Ombudsman met with the representatives of the UN Special Procedures during the country visit of the Special Rapporteurs in Poland (including the Special Rapporteur on the adverse effects of the movement and dumping of toxic and dangerous products and wastes on the enjoyment of human rights in 2011 and the Special Rapporteur on trafficking in persons especially women and children in 2010), providing them with information concerning their special interest areas.[69]

At the European level, with reference to the European system of human rights protection, the involvement of the Ombudsman seems more visible and takes place inter alia in the form of information provided to the Council of Europe Human Rights Commissioner or the EU Fundamental Rights Agency in relation

67 All international activities undertaken within the Framework of the NPM are included in the information available at the Ombudsman's web page: http://www.rpo.gov.pl/index.php?md=7747&s=3.

68 UN HRC Resolution 16/21, *UN Doc.* A/HRC/RES/16/21, 25 March 2011; UN HRC Decision, *UN Doc.* A/HRC/DEC/17/119, 17 June 2011.

69 See annual activities reports of the Polish Ombudsman available at: http://www.rpo.gov.pl/index.php?md=1121&s=1. The limited number of summary reports are also available in English: http://www.rpo.gov.pl/index.php?md=8573&s=3.

to their work on country-specific issues concerning Poland.[70] What should be emphasised is the fact that the Ombudsman is well informed and aware of the recent European developments and monitoring procedures concerning Poland and reacts to the findings and results of the European institutions competent in the area of human rights.[71]

3.4. COOPERATION WITH CIVIL SOCIETY

The cooperation with civil society is a statute-based obligation of the Polish Ombudsman, explicitly expressed in the Ombudsman Act, which in article 17a stipulates that the Ombudsman 'collaborates with associations, civic movements or other good-will societies for the protection of the liberties and rights of a human and a citizen'. Currently, with the growing importance of the role that the civil society plays in almost all areas of social and public life, this obligation of the Ombudsman gains importance. At the same time, it is worth noticing that already the first Polish Ombudsman had laid the foundations for the Ombudsman's relations with civil society.[72] It seems that as a result of this long-term well-established relationship, there are only rarely publicly articulated negative opinions of NGOs concerning the Ombudsman.

At the practical level the obligation to cooperate with civil society is being fulfilled through the Ombudsman cooperating with NGOs on both a formal and informal basis, with the aim to protect human rights in a more effective way. The Ombudsman directs his/her invitation to all stakeholders listed in the above mentioned provision of the Ombudsman Act to provide information on individual cases they intervene in and on more general issues: structural problems demanding the Ombudsman's reaction, as well as information on the conditions and barriers for the functioning of NGOs in Poland. As a result, the Ombudsman also stays involved in the process of building up and strengthening of the civil society in Poland.

Since December 2010, the cooperation with representatives of civil society continues to be strengthened by the activities of the Social Council to the Ombudsman. The Social Council is tasked with supporting the Ombudsman in performing his/her statutory tasks, as well as maintaining contacts with public authorities and with other entities, in particular NGOs. It consists of well-known

---

70 See for example the report provided by the Ombudsman to the EU Fundamental Rights Agency concerning discrimination on the grounds of sexual orientation in Poland, drafted from the perspective of the Ombudsman activities, http://www.rpo.gov.pl/pliki/12103268680.pdf.

71 See for example the statement of the Ombudsman issued after the adoption of the Fundamental Right's Agency report on racism and xenophobia in relation to Poland, http://www.rpo.gov.pl/pliki/1189690116.pdf.

72 Y. Finkel, 'Defending Rights, Promoting Democracy: The Institution of Ombudsman in Poland, Russia and Bulgaria', 2006, available at: www.ef.huji.ac.il/publications/finkel.pdf.

representatives of the civil society, including highly recognised, distinguished public figures.

The cooperation with NGOs is also to be noticed within the framework of the Ombudsman functioning as a national preventive mechanism. In this regard, the Ombudsman conducts broad consultations with NGOs on the process of implementation by Poland of the provisions of the Optional Protocol to the UN Convention against Torture and Other Cruel, Inhuman, or Degrading Treatment or Punishment.[73]

Praise should be given to the Ombudsman's consultations with the representatives of civil society on highly important but politically and socially sensitive issues, such as the recent Anti-Counterfeiting Trade Agreement (ACTA) controversy. The Ombudsman reacted promptly to the large public protests in Poland conducted by the opponents of the treaty, who claim that it adversely affects fundamental rights including freedom of expression and privacy.[74] In this particular case the Ombudsman acted as a spokesman of the protesters, issuing official letters to the government representatives and posing questions based on the doubts and arguments of the anti-ACTA movement. Moreover, a series of consultations co-organised by the Ombudsman took place at the largest Polish universities. Thus the decision of the Polish government to "suspend" the process of ACTA ratification should be contributed also to the position of the Ombudsman.[75]

3.5. PROMOTION AND EDUCATION ON HUMAN RIGHTS

Promotion and education of human rights can be considered an important, but not the core element of the Ombudsman's activities, although it is true that the educational role of this institution was of crucial importance in the first years of its existence. The first Polish Ombudsman Professor Ewa Łętowska undertook the challenge of introducing to the Polish society and the political representatives, after a long era under Communist regime, the basic knowledge of the rule of law, democracy and human rights. It must be underscored that she considered placing the education of Polish society on the above issues as one of the highest priorities of her ombudsmanship.

Notwithstanding the fact that the situation has since evolved, promotion and education are undoubtedly still regarded as the most socially tangible aspects

[73] The consultations continue from April 2008. Information on the consultative process are available at: http://www.rpo.gov.pl/index.php?md=6093&s=1.

[74] G. Mezzofiore, 'Act against Acta: Demonstrators Protest against Poland Signing', International Business Times, 25 January 2012, available at: http://www.ibtimes.co.uk/articles/287236/20120125/act-against-acta-demonstrators-protest-poland-signing.html.

[75] A. Trudelle, 'Polish government asks European Parliament not to sign ACTA', Warsaw Business Journal, 17 February 2012, available at: http://www.wbj.pl/article-58076-polish-government-asks-european-parliament-not-to-sign-acta.html.

of the Ombudsman presence. In particular the regular and publicly presented standpoints of the Ombudsman, including annual reports to the Parliament, should be regarded as a useful tool of promoting a human rights-oriented legal culture. Moreover, the various publications authored by the Ombudsman definitely serve as helpful and informative tools, which can be used by individuals seeking legal advice. In the previous years the Ombudsman has also developed two educational programs: "Learn your rights" and "The Legal Daily", both designed to deliver a wide range of information concerning individual rights and freedoms, as well as information on proposed legal acts, legislative initiatives, amendments, etc.

The Ombudsman regularly meets with the media, informing them on the latest initiatives of the Office and the results achieved. Press articles, TV and radio interviews, as well as press conferences of the Ombudsman contribute to the already well-established tradition, started by Professor Łętowska, of close cooperation with the media.[76] The Ombudsman also meets with representatives of governmental agencies, promoting the inclusion of human rights perspectives in all fields of their activities.

Through the Eastern Partnership the Ombudsman has a chance to promote the implementation of human rights standards among beneficiary states of the Partnership, often facing serious problems with respecting human rights. One of the most useful tools of such promotion, as well as of the education on human rights, are the consultative meetings and exchange visits of the representatives of the governments, Ombudsmen Offices and other human rights stakeholders coming from the beneficiary states. The "soft" instruments such as the meetings and talks often proved to be more effective and fruitful than treaty-based legally binding obligations.[77]

The promotion of human rights can also be observed through the particular interventions of the Ombudsman on a case-by-case basis, both at the national and international level. Two interventions may serve as examples here. The first one concerned the problem of participation of persons with disabilities in the parliamentary elections and was accompanied by the Ombudsman's promotion of the UN Convention on the Rights of Persons with Disabilities.[78] The second intervention, taken at the international level, was an official appeal of the Ombudsman directed to the Ambassador of the Republic of China to Poland, in

---

76 On the attitude of the previous Polish Ombudsmen towards the media see: Y. Finkel, 'Defending Rights, Promoting Democracy: The Institution of Ombudsman in Poland, Russia and Bulgaria', 2006, available at: www.ef.huji.ac.il/publications/finkel.pdf.

77 See for example the report from the project on cooperation between the Ombudsmen within the framework of EP 'Partnership for Human Rights – Poland and Azerbaijan 2011', http://www.rpo.gov.pl/pliki/13382056590.pdf, available in Polish and Russian.

78 In 2011 the Polish Ombudsman issued a special informative booklet "Elections for all", where the state's obligations towards persons with disabilities regarding official, state elections are discussed.

which the urgent request to respect all human rights of the people of Tibet by the Chinese government was expressed.[79]

At the same time there is a further need of wider inclusion of promotion of human rights as part of the Ombudsman mandate, along with human rights education. This has been explicitly stated in one of the recommendations issued in 2007 by the International Coordinating Committee of National Human Rights Institutions directed to Poland.[80] The analysis of the reports of activities undertaken by the current Ombudsman proves that the ICC recommendations are being implemented.

3.6. RESEARCH ON HUMAN RIGHTS

The Polish Ombudsman has not been designed as a research institution, and it lacks statute-based competences in the field of conducting research. Thus there is no separate research department within the structure of its Office. However, for the purpose of the Ombudsman's activities, some research must obviously be conducted. The primary source of information analysed and examined by the Ombudsman are the individual complaints received, conclusions from the visitations within the framework of NPM and other internal sources of the Ombudsman. In three particular thematic fields, namely: rights of the elderly, rights of persons with disabilities and migrants' rights, expertise and in-depth research is conducted by Expert Committees, permanently serving the Ombudsman with recommendations on different issues, such as amendments in the legislation and changes in the process of its implementation.[81] These three thematic fields belong to the list of priority issues of the present Ombudsman. Focusing the attention on this limited number of problem areas can contribute to their more effective counteracting. However, it seems that broadening the scope of these thematic areas with the aim of providing the Ombudsman with precise information would be a desirable decision, as there emerge more and more issues within the human rights protection framework which demand the reaction of the Ombudsman Office and often require it to take a public position on those issues. Taking into account the number of daily interventions of the Ombudsman, the

[79] The appeal was issued in 2007 at the occasion of the 20th anniversary of the Ombudsman Office in Poland, http://www.rpo.gov.pl/pliki/12112065370.pdf.

[80] International Coordinating Committee Of National Institutions For The Promotion And Protection Of Human Rights, Geneva 22 to 26 October 2007, Report and Recommendations of the Sub-Committee on Accreditation, http:/nhri.ohchr.org/EN/ICC/ICCAcreditation/Documents/2007_October%20SCA%20Report.pdf.

[81] For more information on the Expert Commissions supporting the work of the Ombudsman, see: http://www.rpo.gov.pl/index.php?md=9186&s=3.

gathering of exact information and extending the research-based knowledge are indispensable.[82]

The results of the research conducted within the Ombudsman Office are regularly presented in the form of various types of publications: analysis, reports and advisory booklets concerning particular priority issues, such as rights of persons with disabilities, effectiveness of combating hate crimes and situation of persons in different types of detention institutions. They are available free of charge on the Ombudsman's website. Moreover, the Ombudsman him or herself and other members of the Office actively take part in numerous domestic and international scientific conferences, expert seminars and workshops, presenting not only Ombudsman's activities, but also the conclusions of their analysis and research. Importantly, this visible presence of the Ombudsman both in the scientific circles and in the society as a whole has always been an important element of building up the position and image of the Ombudsman as an institution which remains involved in matters important to the society. The Polish Ombudsman has certainly never been an unidentified office, unknown to the public.[83]

One of the most recent examples of the Ombudsman research is the report entitled: 'The principle of equal treatment – law and practice. Counteracting hate crimes motivated by the racial, ethnic and national origin. Analysis and recommendations'.[84] The report, devoted to one of the most problematic and alarming problems in the field of fighting discrimination and hate towards minorities in Poland, was presented in a conference organised by the Ombudsman, featuring experts, researchers and NGO representatives active in the thematic field of the report. The report provided a valuable contribution to the conference, particularly due to the included recommendations.

4. CONCLUSION

The attempt to assess the institution of the Polish Ombudsman needs to include pointing out its strengths and weaknesses, as they all influence the effectiveness of its functioning.

---

82 During the first quarter of 2012 the Ombudsman presented its position on particular problems within the thematic areas of its mandate 88 times. See the quarterly information on the activities of the Ombudsman available at: http://www.rpo.gov.pl/index.php?md=10086&s=1.

83 The surveys carried out in the previous years indicate that the Ombudsman is one of the best recognised and trustworthy institutions in Poland. According to the results of the public opinion survey from the time period of 2002–2008, 62% of Poles trust the Ombudsman. See: http://www.aglomeracja.holdikom.com.pl/LinkClick.aspx?fileticket=1e0Qw9Q6dO8%3D&tabid=329 (in Polish).

84 See: http://www.rpo.gov.pl/index.php?md=980&strona=18743&s=1; available in Polish at: http://www.rpo.gov.pl/sites/default/files/Biuletyn_Rzecznika_Praw_Obywatelskich_2012_nr_4_0.pdf.

Undoubtedly one of the strongest points of the Polish Ombudsman is its positive, well-established image built throughout the 25 years of its history. In this context, its stable institutional framework is accompanied by the equally important influence of the personalities of individuals holding the office, as they draw from a large scope of autonomy in deciding on their priorities and interventions.[85]

Another strength of this institution lies in its firm legal guarantees of stability and independence. It is in fact an independent institution, free from the political influences on its current activities.

The broad mandate of the Ombudsman is yet another element which appears advantageous. The comprehensive character of the mandate, which covers all rights and freedoms guaranteed in the Polish Constitution and other legal acts, allows for the better fulfillment of the Ombudsman's tasks.

Finally, the Polish Ombudsman deserves praise for its readiness to take up difficult and sensitive issues, such as safeguarding LGBT rights, addressing excessive instruments of state control over the citizens or the support for anti-hate speech laws. The willingness to solve the most acute social and legal problems proves that the Ombudsman understands well the role and responsibility entrusted to him/her.

Notwithstanding all those positive aspects, the Ombudsman faces problems and challenges which prevent us from considering this office as a role model of a national human rights institution. One of the major obstacles concerns the insufficient funding and human resources, especially in the context of the Ombudsman acting as the NPM and equality body. However, the safeguarding of these financial needs does not depend on the Ombudsman, since it is the Parliament who decides on the Ombudsman's budget.[86]

At the same time the Ombudsman should react to remaining problematic points, such as the issue of guaranteeing pluralism. Functioning as a single-person body, the Ombudsman has a special duty to maintain the pluralism of his/her office, through the conducting of wide consultations for example with the representatives of the civil society and advisory bodies, such as the Social Council at the Ombudsman's Office. Strengthening cooperation with international human rights bodies is yet another point to be considered. The Ombudsman should definitely become more involved within the UN human rights protection system, among others by submitting separate reports for the purpose of the UN Human Rights Council's universal periodic review.

---

85 Report of the Institute of Public Affairs on the Polish Ombudsman, 2010, p. 161, available at: http://www.isp.org.pl/uploads/filemanager/RPO.PDF.

86 The recommendations issued in this respect by the experts of the Institute of Public Affairs include the idea of creating the institution for the purpose of the NPM. Report of the Institute of Public Affairs on the Polish Ombudsman, 2010, p. 164, available at: http://www.isp.org.pl/uploads/filemanager/RPO.PDF (in Polish).

To conclude, it should be stated that due to the well-established institutional guarantees, strong mandate and active involvement in many fields of concern, the general assessment of the Polish Ombudsman acting as the NHRI must be positive and approving. There still are, however, some problematic issues which need to be resolved, as well as challenges which need to be tackled.

THE NEWLY ESTABLISHED NETHERLANDS INSTITUTE FOR HUMAN RIGHTS: INTEGRATING HUMAN RIGHTS AND EQUAL TREATMENT

Yvonne DONDERS[1] and Marjolijn OLDE MONNIKHOF[2]

1. INTRODUCTION

In October 2012, the Netherlands Institute for Human Rights (NIHR) – the Dutch national human rights institution opened its doors. The law setting up the NIHR (in Dutch *College voor de Rechten van de Mens*) was approved by the Dutch House of Representatives on 19 April 2011 and by the Dutch Senate on 22 November 2011. The entry into force of this law in 2012 and the start of the NIHR form the happy conclusion of a long and challenging process.

For a long time, Dutch human rights organisations and parliamentarians have pleaded for the establishment of a national human rights institution. They emphasised that the Netherlands, while promoting the importance of human rights all over the world, was one of the few countries that did not have a human rights institute at national level. It was not that the Netherlands lacked national institutions dealing with the promotion and protection of human rights. In fact, the existence of several national bodies dealing with human rights, including the Ombudsman, the Equal Treatment Commission and the Dutch Data Protection Authority, was one of the factors slowing down the process of the establishment of a national human rights institution. The debate on whether or not such a national institute was needed centred around questions concerning the form the new national human rights institution should take and the role it should play in

1 Yvonne Donders is Professor International Human Rights and Executive Director of the Amsterdam Center for International Law at the University of Amsterdam. From March 2011 to September 2012 she was assigned for one day a week to the Dutch Equal Treatment Commission as project manager of the new Netherlands Institute for Human Rights.

2 Marjolijn Olde Monnikhof is Head of the Policy Department of the Netherlands Institute for Human Rights (former Dutch Equal Treatment Commission) and Project Manager of the establishment of the Netherlands Institute for Human Rights.

the promotion and protection of human rights, including its additional value to existing human rights institutions.

The Dutch government did not support the creation of an all-new institute; instead they sought to join existing institutions. After the exploration of different options, it was decided that the Dutch Equal Treatment Commission (in Dutch *Commissie Gelijke Behandeling*) would be absorbed into the new national human rights institution.

The process of drafting the law establishing the NIHR including the integration of the Equal Treatment Commission brought several issues to the fore. These varied from the form of the NHRI (should it be an institute, a bureau, or a commission) and its name (institute for human rights and equal treatment or institute for human rights), to its mandate and tasks (for instance, the possibility of the NHRI to pay on site visits or to initiate legal proceedings). After the law was adopted and the mandate established, the Dutch Equal Treatment Commission started an interesting but challenging process of change, both in terms of practice and content.

The NIHR will fulfil the watchdog function in the field of human rights in the Netherlands. It has a broad mandate to promote and protect human rights through monitoring, advice, research and information. In this contribution, we analyse and elaborate the main opportunities and challenges for the new organisation from three dimensions. First we analyse its tasks, including reporting at national and international level, conducting research, and dealing with individual complaints on equal treatment. Second, the prioritisation of human rights topics to be addressed, bearing in mind their quantity and diversity, and the relationship between equal treatment and human rights. Third we examine its institutional structure and cooperation with Ministries, other human rights bodies and civil society organisations. Before addressing these issues, however an outline is provided of the history and establishment of the NIHR.

2. HISTORY

The Netherlands has always underlined the importance of human rights at national as well as at international level. The Netherlands has been actively involved in human rights promotion and protection within the United Nations, the Council of Europe, the European Union and other international organisations. It has always supported international and national non-governmental organisations promoting and protecting human rights. In 1993, the Dutch government endorsed the UN-resolution with 'Principles relating to the Status of National

Institutions' (the Paris Principles)[3], as well as the 'Resolution on Co-operation between National Human Rights Institutions of Member States and between them and the Council of Europe'.[4] Both these documents encourage member states to create a national human rights institution to promote the observance of human rights. With the acceptance of both documents, the Dutch government affirmed the importance of national human rights institutions.

Bearing in mind this active role it was rather strange and surprising that The Netherlands was one of the (European) countries that did not have a national human rights institution.[5] It had several human rights bodies, including the Ombudsman, Dutch Data Protection Authority and the Equal Treatment Commission having a B-status under the Paris Principles, but not a fully-fledged national human rights institution with A-status under the Paris Principles.[6]

The first real step towards establishing a Dutch human rights institution was taken by the Dutch Section of the International Commission of Jurists (NJCM). In 1999 they organised a symposium on the desirability and the organisation of a national human rights institution in The Netherlands. As a follow-up measure, a member of the House of Representatives formally requested the government to take a position on the establishment of such an institution. The Minister of Foreign affairs replied that such an establishment was the responsibility of civil society. It was only after publication of the congress-proceedings and repeated requests by members of the House of Representatives, that the Minister of Justice and the Minister of the Interior undertook to draft legislation regulating the establishment of a national human rights institution.[7]

The creation of national human rights institutions also appeared regularly in various international fora. At the EU level the European Parliament urged Member States to establish human rights institutes that could function as partner for the yet-to-be established EU Fundamental Rights Agency.[8] In 2005–2007, during the Dutch campaign to obtain a seat in the UN Human Rights Council, the Dutch Minister of Foreign Affairs declared publicly the intention of the Dutch government to set up a national human rights institution.

---

3 Principles relating to the Status of National Institutions, adopted by UN General Assembly Resolution 48/134 of 20 December 1993, *UN Doc.* A/RES/48/134, Annex.

4 Council of Europe, Committee of Ministers, Resolution (97) 11 on co-operation between national human rights institutions of member states and between them and the Council of Europe (adopted by the Committee of Ministers on 30 September 1997 at the 602nd meeting of the Ministers' deputies).

5 For an extensive overview of the different types of national human rights institutions in Europe and the world, see M. Nowak, 'National Human Rights Institutions in Europe: Comparative, European and International Perspectives', Chapter 1 in this volume.

6 For more information on the accreditation of national human rights institutions according to their compliance with the Paris Principles, see G. de Beco, 'Assessment of the Paris Principles and the ICC Sub-Committee on Accreditation', Chapter 11 in this volume.

7 Parliamentary Papers II 2001/2002, 28 000 VI, no. 38.

8 Report on promotion and protection of fundamental rights: the role of national and European institutions, including the Fundamental Rights Agency (2005/2007(INI), 15 May 2005; European Parliament, Resolution A6-0144/2005, 26 May 2005.

In the period from 2005 to 2007 a 'consortium' composed of the Ombudsman, the Data Protection Agency, the Equal Treatment Commission and the Netherlands Institute of Human Rights at Utrecht University (better known by its Dutch abbreviation SIM), published a number of reports on a possible blueprint for a human rights institution. In April 2007 the consortium presented its summary report to the Minister of the Interior containing recommendations for the setting up of a new institution while maintaining the existing human rights infrastructure.[9]

The government's reaction to the report, including the reaction to a motion by the House of Representatives pressing for the speedy establishment of a human rights institution, was forwarded to the House of Representatives in July 2008.[10] The government proposed that the new institution should form part of the same organisation as the Ombudsman. The House of Representatives asked the government to re-examine the integration of the new organisation in existing institutions.[11] After further analysis the government proposed in July 2009[12] that the Equal Treatment Commission should be merged with the new institution.[13]

The government gave several reasons for merging the Equal Treatment Commission with the newly established institution. In terms of content, it argued that the principle of equality is not only an independent human right but also a key element of all other human rights. The integration of equal treatment tasks of the Equal Treatment Commission within the new Institute would create synergy. This would benefit the vertical (between citizens and the state) and the horizontal (between private parties) effect of the rights concerned. Furthermore, the activities to promote awareness of human rights and the right to equal treatment would be mutually reinforcing. The institute would expand the scope of international reporting, education and information programmes, no longer limited to equal treatment legislation but encompassing all human rights, thereby creating a broader and more coherent picture. A more practical reason to integrate the Equal Treatment Commission into the new institute was to keep with the government policy not to expand the number of government bodies. The government also referred to the practice in other countries where human rights

---

9 The report was called '*Mensenrechten verbinden en verplichten – Een national instituut voor de rechten van de mens ook voor Nederland*' [human rights connect and oblige – a national human rights institution also for The Netherlands], published in April 2007. See, also, Explanatory Memorandum to the Netherlands Institute for Human Rights Act, Parliamentary Papers II, 2009–2010, 32 467 Appendix 2 to ref. nr. 2011-2000054729, pp. 3–4.

10 Parliamentary Papers II 2006/2007, 30 800 V, no. 29; Parliamentary Papers II 2007/2008, 31 200 VI, no. 75.

11 Parliamentary Papers II 2008/2009, 31 700 VII, no. 52.

12 Parliamentary Papers II 2008/2009, 31 700 VII, no. 95.

13 Explanatory Memorandum to the Netherlands Institute for Human Rights Act, Parliamentary Papers II, 2009–2010, 32 467 Appendix 2 to ref. nr. 2011–2000054729, p. 4.

institutions and equal treatment counterparts were successfully integrated, such as the British Equality and Human Rights Commission.[14]

3. LEGAL PROCESS

The legal process of drafting the Bill setting up the NIHR took four years (2007–2011). From the beginning it was clear that the legislator wanted to set up an institute with the legal mandate that would fulfil the criteria set out in the Paris Principles and that would obtain the A Status.[15]

The Paris Principles require *inter alia* that the institution should be fully independent; free of government control.[16] The government, however, realised that the institute could not be completely separated from government as the legislator defines its mandate and tasks for instance. In addition, the government allocates the budget and sets the conditions for funding. The government also plays a role in appointing the members of the institution. The members and alternate members of the NIHR are appointed by Royal Decree at the recommendation of the Minister of Security and Justice. The advisory council of the NIHR advises the Minister of Security and Justice on the recommendation, focusing on the need for an expert and independent institute and of the wish to ensure diversity in its membership.[17]

The Paris Principles prescribe that the national human rights institution should have a basis in public law and have a broad mandate, including all human rights.[18] On the basis of this statutory mandate, the institute should be able to freely determine its own priorities, including investigation of human rights violations, monitoring observance of human rights, providing law and policy advice, as well as information to a broad public. The Paris Principles also set out requirements for pluralism: the organisation should ensure the pluralist representation of the sectors of society involved in the protection and promotion of human rights.[19] The Principles leave it to the national authorities to choose the most suitable structure for the institute, provided that it meets the specified criteria and conditions.

In preparing the draft Bill, the government extensively consulted with human rights institutions and NGOs. The draft Bill was also formally commented upon by the Council of State.[20] In addition, the UN Office of the High Commissioner for Human Rights (OHCHR) advised the Equal Treatment Commission informally

---

14 Explanatory Memorandum to the Netherlands Institute for Human Rights Act, Parliamentary Papers II, 2009–2010, 32 467 Appendix 2 to ref. nr. 2011–2000054729, p. 13–14.
15 Parliamentary Papers II 2007/2008, 31 200 VI, no. 75.
16 Paris Principles, 'Composition and guarantees of independence and pluralism'.
17 Explanatory Memorandum to the Netherlands Institute for Human Rights Act, Parliamentary Papers II, 2009–2010, 32 467 Appendix 2 to ref. nr. 2011–2000054729, p. 6.
18 Paris Principles, 'Competence and responsibilities'.
19 Paris Principles, 'Composition and guarantees of independence and pluralism'.
20 *Advies Raad van State* [Advice Council of State], No. WO4.10.0131/1, The Hague, 16 June 2010.

and confidentially in mid-June 2010 on the Bill's compliance with the Paris Principles.[21] The State of The Netherlands also requested the OHCHR for advice at the end of August 2010.[22]

Main points of concern for the NGOs, which were also addressed by the OHCHR, were the name of the organisation, the budget and its mandate and tasks.[23] The Council of State pointed out that the initial name 'Board for Human Rights and Equal Treatment' ('*College voor Mensenrechten en Gelijke Behandeling*') was confusing. It preferred the Dutch translation for National Human Rights Institution, '*Nationaal Instituut voor de Rechten van de Mens*'.[24] NGOs found the name to be unappealing and largely unrecognisable both in The Netherlands and abroad. Alternatives proposed were 'institute' or 'commission'. Some organisations also argued that only 'human rights' and not also 'equal treatment' should be mentioned in the name. As a result of these reactions, the government decided that, for the sake of international recognition, the new organisation would bear the English name 'Netherlands Institute for Human Rights'. The Dutch name would however continue to be '*College*' (Board). The government found that the term 'board' ('*college*'), unlike 'institute' ('*instituut*'), would cover both the body itself as well as the staff.[25]

As regards the budget, the Council of State, most NGOs, as well as members of Parliament, indicated that the proposed budget would be insufficient to enable the NIHR to achieve all its aims. The total budget of the NIHR will consist of the budget of the Equal Treatment Commission plus 900,000 Euros for each of the first three years of its existence. From the fourth year onwards, the budget will be permanently increased by 800,000 Euros.

Another point of concern was the distinction and balance between human rights and equal treatment duties. At various places in the draft Bill, both equal treatment and human rights were mentioned, in this order. The Council of State maintained that this could create the impression that the NIHR would mainly deal with equal treatment issues, which would not correspond to the intended profile.[26] The final Bill no longer lists the specific duty of ensuring equal treatment

---

21 Office of the High Commissioner for Human Rights – National Institutions and Regional Mechanisms Section, Confidential legal advice on the draft law of the Commission for Human Rights and Equal Treatment (CHRET) of The Netherlands, June 2010, available at: www.mensenrechten.nl.

22 Office of the High Commissioner for Human Rights – National Institutions and Regional Mechanisms Section, Second Legal advice on the "Draft Law Proposing the Netherlands Institute for Human Rights", 15 October 2010, available at: www.mensenrechten.nl.

23 The points made by NGOs and the OHCHR are reflected in the Explanatory Memorandum to the Netherlands Institute for Human Rights Act, Parliamentary Papers II, 2009–2010, 32 467 Appendix 2 to ref. nr. 2011–2000054729, pp. 22–24.

24 *Advies Raad van State* [Advice Council of State], No. WO4.10.0131/1, The Hague, 16 June 2010, p. 3.

25 Explanatory Memorandum to the Netherlands Institute for Human Rights Act, Parliamentary Papers II, 2009–2010, 32 467 Appendix 2 to ref. nr. 2011–2000054729, pp. 22–24.

26 *Advies Raad van State* [Advice Council of State], No. WO4.10.0131/1, The Hague, 16 June 2010, p. 3.

first and refers in the mandate only to human rights, on the assumption that human rights include equal treatment.

As regards the mandate, several NGOs recommended that the existing duty of hearing complaints about equal treatment legislation should be extended to all human rights. The Paris Principles provide that a national human rights institution may be authorised to hear and consider complaints and petitions concerning individual situations.[27] The government had however in response to the consortium report in 2007, already decided that the human rights institution would not be given the responsibility of hearing individual complaints. It kept this position, mainly to avoid overlap with the specific duties of the Ombudsman, who monitors the compatibility of government actions with human rights. The final Bill therefore does not include the responsibility to hear individual complaints in relation to all human rights, but only those related to equal treatment laws.[28]

The OHCHR emphasised the importance of the independence of the Institute; its recommendation to include a specific provision on the Institute's independence was implemented (current Section 4 of the Bill). The recommendation also led to the change in the Bill that members of the Board would not be appointed by the Minister of Security and Justice, but by Royal Decree, on the recommendation of the Minister and after advice from the advisory council of the NIHR (Section 16 of the Bill). The OHCHR also recommended that the financial autonomy of the Institute would be explicitly included in the Bill.[29] The government, however, while stressing that the Institute would control its own finances, chose to include that the Ministry of Security and Justice bears the costs of establishing the Institute and approves its annual budget.[30]

The draft Bill was discussed in the House of Representatives in March and April 2011.[31] There was broad support for the establishment of the NIHR and most members stressed the importance of having such an Institute. During the deliberations, similar points as outlined above were discussed. First, the specific role of the Institute was discussed, in particular the added value of the NIHR to Dutch organisations already active in the field of human rights. Second, debate took place on the issue of the relationship between equal treatment and human rights.

---

27 Paris Principles, 'Additional principles concerning the status of commissions with quasi-jurisdictional competence'.

28 Explanatory Memorandum to the Netherlands Institute for Human Rights Act, Parliamentary Papers II, 2009–2010, 32 467 Appendix 2 to ref. nr. 2011–2000054729, p. 26. The fact that equal treatment cases may also involve broader human rights issues is further discussed *infra*, section 6.

29 Office of the High Commissioner for Human Rights – National Institutions and Regional Mechanisms Section, Second Legal advice on the "Draft Law Proposing the Netherlands Institute for Human Rights", 15 October 2010, p. 1 and 5, available at: www.mensenrechten.nl.

30 Explanatory Memorandum to the Netherlands Institute for Human Rights Act, Parliamentary Papers II, 2009–2010, 32 467 Appendix 2 to ref. nr. 2011–2000054729, pp. 14–15.

31 *Stenografisch verslag Tweede Kamer* [Stenographic Report House of Representatives], '*College voor de Rechten van de Mens*' [Netherlands Institute for Human Rights], 32467, 30 March 2011, TK 67 and 12 April 2011, TK 72.

It was argued that the integration of the Equal Treatment Commission into the NIHR and the fact that a large part of the budget of the NIHR will be spent on the tasks of the former Equal Treatment Commission might suggest a prioritisation to some extent of human rights. This idea might be strengthened by the fact that equal treatment and non-discrimination are explicitly mentioned in the Bill and the other human rights are not. Third, questions were raised whether the assigned budget would be sufficient to enable the NIHR to realise its goals and mandate. Fourth, the expertise and competence of board members and staff were points of discussion. Members and staff of the Equal Treatment Commission would be converted as members and staff of the NIHR. Bearing in mind the relatively small budget for appointing new board members and staff, questions were raised about whether the NIHR would have sufficient knowledge and expertise in the broad field of human rights, in particular in relation to international and European law. Fifth, different methods of appointment of the Board members were considered, including appointment by the House of Representatives itself, to ensure their independence. Sixth, several specific competences of the NIHR were discussed, such as the competence to initiate legal proceedings on all human rights, not to be used frequently, but as *ultimum remedium*. It was also discussed whether the NIHR should have the competence to conduct on-site visits and obtain access to all places, apart from dwellings without the consent of the occupant. In the final Bill the first specific competence was not included, while the second was. Finally, the House of Representatives discussed the (public) support for the NIHR in the current social-political climate. Some members expressed the concern that the NIHR might be considered a "left-wing, multicultural cuddle club".

The Bill was finally supported by all members of the House of Representatives, except for the members of the Party for Freedom (PVV).[32]

The draft Bill was discussed in the Senate in November 2011.[33] In the Senate there was also broad support for the Bill and the establishment of the NIHR. During the deliberations similar points to those raised in the House of Representatives were discussed, including the added value of the institute, the prioritisation of human rights and the competence to initiate legal proceedings. Much attention was devoted to the institutional embedding in the Equal Treatment Commission. It was emphasised that the focus of the NIHR should not be on equal treatment only. Although the principle of equality is of special importance within the catalogue of human rights, shown by the fact that it is mentioned in the Bill, the Senate considered that the NIHR should work on all human rights.

32 The Party for Freedom was established in 2005 by its chairman Geert Wilders. From October 2010 to April 2012 the PVV supported the Dutch minority cabinet composed of the People's Party for Freedom and Democracy (VVD) and the Christian Democratic Appeal (CDA).

33 *Stenografisch verslag Tweede Kamer* [Stenographic Report House of Representatives], '*College voor de Rechten van de Mens*' [Netherlands Institute for Human Rights], 32467, 15 November 2011, EK 7.

The Senate further stressed the importance of the NIHR fulfilling the criteria laid down in international standards, in particular the Paris Principles. The members wanted to be reassured that the way the NIHR would be financed – via the budget of the Ministry of Security and Justice – would not be an obstacle for the NIHR to obtain the A status. The appointment procedure of the members of the Board was also discussed, as some Senate members expressed concern that the proposed procedure would not guarantee absolute independence.

The Senate also discussed the limited budget of the NIHR in relation to its broad mandate and tasks. In this regard, the importance of the two-year evaluation was emphasised. An evaluation of the activities and functioning of the NIHR will be carried out two years after its establishment. Depending on the results, the Government will decide on the funding requirements for the subsequent period.

All parties voted in favour of the Bill, except for the Party for Freedom (PVV), which voted against and the Reformed Political Party (SGP), which was absent.[34]

4. MANDATE AND TASKS

The NIHR has a broad mandate in accordance with the Paris Principles. The object of the NIHR is described in the Bill as '[...] to protect human rights, including the right to equal treatment, in The Netherlands, to increase awareness of these rights and to promote their observance'.[35] According to the explanatory memorandum, the NIHR will promote and protect all human rights in The Netherlands, as they are enshrined in the Constitution as well as in international and European treaties and directives, as well as soft law instruments such as declarations and guidelines. It is emphasised that the scope of the mandate includes both classic fundamental rights as well as social rights, although '[...] the Institute will not concern itself with all rights to the same extent'[36]. It is up to the NIHR to decide on its work and activities and therefore set priorities.[37]

According to Section 3 of the Bill, the NIHR has the following statutory duties, which include the statutory duties formerly assigned to the Equal Treatment Commission:

- conducting investigations into the protection of human rights, including investigating matters relating to equal treatment and communicating its findings;

---

34 Parliamentary Papers I 2011–2012, 8, no.3.

35 Amended Bill, *Establishment of the Netherlands Institute for Human Rights* (Netherlands Institute for Human Rights Act), 19 April 2011, Section 1(3).

36 Explanatory Memorandum to the Netherlands Institute for Human Rights Act, Parliamentary Papers II, 2009–2010, 32 467 Appendix 2 to ref. nr.2011–2000054729, p.8.

37 *Ibidem*, pp. 7–8. These priorities are laid down in the Strategic Plan adopted by the NIHR, which is discussed in Section 5.

- reporting on and making recommendations about human rights;
- advising on Acts, Bills, orders in council, draft orders in council, ministerial orders and drafts of ministerial orders that relate directly or indirectly to human rights;
- providing information on and encouraging and coordinating education about human rights;
- encouraging research into the protection of human rights;
- cooperating on a systematic basis with civil society organisations and with national, European and other international institutions engaged in the protection of one or more human rights, for example by organising activities in partnership with civil society organisations;
- pressing for the ratification, implementation and observance of human rights treaties and for the withdrawal of reservations to such treaties;
- pressing for the implementation and observance of binding resolutions of international organisations on human rights;
- pressing for observance of European or international recommendations on human rights.[38]

5. CREATING AND DEVELOPING THE NIHR

Awaiting the adoption and entry into force of the Bill, the Minister of Security and Justice gave permission to the Equal Treatment Commission to start preparing for the new organisation. The Equal Treatment Commission formed a project team that prepared the transformation towards the NIHR, including the extension of the content area of work, as well as the adjustment of the internal structure and organisation. External experts were also hired with knowledge and expertise in the broad field of national and international human rights, as well as in the field of communication. The Ministry of Security and Justice actively supported this preparation process with a transition budget. The fact that this process started at the same time as the Bill was being negotiated meant that although preparations were carried out, the process could still be stopped or changed following the debate in Parliament.

5.1. DEVELOPING A STRATEGIC PLAN

It was decided that the NIHR would need a strategic plan, in which it would formulate its priorities and activities for the first three years. The mandate of the NIHR contains a number of different tasks, including the broad promotion of

[38] Explanatory Memorandum to the Netherlands Institute for Human Rights Act, Parliamentary Papers II, 2009–2010, 32 467 Appendix 2 to ref. nr. 2011-2000054729, pp. 8–9.

human rights, policy and legislation advice and human rights education. Moreover, it includes all human rights, which raises a large amount of possible issues to be addressed. In order to make proper and weighted choices in prioritising topics and deciding on the best course of action, a broad stakeholders' consultation was held and a comprehensive investigative research was conducted in parallel.

5.1.1. Stakeholders' Consultation

The project team spoke with more than 150 persons, representing all different stakeholders, including NGOs and civil society organisations, academic institutions, universities and schools, ministries, government institutions and the Parliament, employers and employees organisations, specific profession groups, etc. These persons were broadly asked what they expected from the NIHR, which tasks they found most important, which human rights issues they proposed as priorities for the NIHR and how they considered cooperation between the NIHR and their respective organisation. The picture that emerged from these consultations was colourful in many ways. There was broad support for the establishment of the NIHR and most people indicated the importance of having such an Institute. They all expressed readiness to cooperate with the NIHR. However, questions relating to the tasks and topics led to a wide variety of answers. Broadly speaking, representatives of NGOs and non-state actors preferred an active role of the NIHR and emphasised the importance of ensuring that the NIHR would not become a government institute. Representatives of the Ministries and government institutions cautioned against a too-strong activist role and stressed the need for cooperation with the government and parliament while remaining independent.

The majority of the stakeholders agreed on the core values of the NIHR: it has to be courageous, independent, competent and authoritative. To build such a position, it was emphasised that the NIHR should work on a solid basis, including well substantiated positioning and argumentation within the societal debate. Its policies should not be overly 'incidental' or ad hoc. Stakeholders also called upon the NIHR to be recognisable, visible and relevant for society, whereby it should have an open and transparent attitude towards civil society and a low threshold for the general public.

As regards the mandate and tasks, there were differences of opinion among the different stakeholders. There was broad consensus that the main task of the NIHR is to monitor whether and how the government implements (international) human rights standards and norms in law and policy and how these work out in practice. There was also agreement on the role of the NIHR in clarifying and elaborating human rights norms, placing them in a broader perspective. Much less agreement existed among stakeholders about the question which tasks should receive priority. Some stakeholders emphasised that the NIHR should focus on advice on laws and policies. Others found that the main tasks of the NIHR are information and education, thereby empowering the general public. Finally, some stakeholders found that the investigative task of the NIHR is most important.

Stakeholders were also asked about the positioning of the NIHR. The choice for the prioritisation of subject matters would strongly determine the position of the NIHR in the political and public debate. On the issue of building legitimacy and authority, many stakeholders expressed their concern that the NIHR could be considered a 'left-wing, multicultural club'. Some even advised that it may be best in the first period to avoid politically sensitive issues, such as migration, asylum and discrimination on the basis of race. Interestingly, while these stakeholders advised against putting such issues prominently on the agenda of the NIHR, at the same time they indicated that these issues were very important from a human rights perspective. Stakeholders also took a different position on whether or not the NIHR should include an equal treatment topic on its agenda during the first period. On the one hand it was emphasised that the NIHR should show that it is a new, competent institute in the broad field of human rights, and not an Equal Treatment Commission 'Plus'. On the other hand it was argued that non-discrimination and equal treatment remain important topics in The Netherlands, in relation to which much can still be improved. Moreover, the Institute has much experience in this field and still has to properly fulfil the tasks of the former Equal Treatment Commission.

As regards the human rights topics to be given priority, the stakeholders proposed a broad variety of topics, often related to the specific topic they were themselves dealing with. There was broad agreement that the NIHR should promote the ratification of the Convention on Rights of Persons with Disabilities (CRPD). Topics that were mentioned frequently concerned migration and human rights, for instance issues related to family reunion, integration, asylum and rights of undocumented persons. Also frequently mentioned were topics concerning detention, such as the regimentation of conditions of detention and placing asylum seekers in detention. Topics relating to security, terrorism and privacy were also mentioned.

The stakeholders' proposals, although rather diverse, helped the new organisation to determine its position and to choose the topics to be placed on the agenda. Other important input for this process came from the investigative studies that were conducted.

5.1.2. Investigative Research

Broad investigative research was conducted from different dimensions on current human rights issues in The Netherlands.[39] A report was drafted on the recommendations and jurisprudence of international supervisory bodies

[39] The investigative research paper was meant for internal use only, but its outcomes can be found at: www.mensenrechtenkwesties.nl.

concerning The Netherlands. An overview and analysis was provided on the concluding observations and recommendations by the UN treaty bodies on The Netherlands over the last five years, as well as the cases against The Netherlands before the UN Human Rights Committee and the European Court of Human Rights. Moreover, it was studied how the Dutch government responded to and dealt with these recommendations and the outcomes of these cases. Also, a study was done on the most important human rights related jurisprudence of the three highest legal institutions in The Netherlands – the Supreme Court, the Administrative Jurisdiction Division of the Council of State and the Central Appeals Tribunal – in order to identify the main human rights issues dealt with by these three institutions.

Another analysis was done on which human rights topics figured prominently in the Dutch media. Since an overall and broad research was impossible, a timeframe of three months was picked during which four national newspapers were extensively analysed and an overview was given of human rights issues reported and discussed.

From these studies, a list of 102 topics was drawn up representing important human rights issues in The Netherlands. This long list of topics was narrowed down into a shortlist of 14 issues; elderly care; labour exploitation; poverty, in particular on the BES islands in the Caribbean;[40] measures taken in the fight against terrorism; child abuse; human trafficking; several issues related to migration and asylum, such as family reunion; detention; human rights education; and the political and societal climate in relation to human rights. On these issues, more extensive research was done and so-called issue papers were drafted.[41] These issue papers contained a short outline of the issue at hand, the legal human rights framework of this issue, an overview of other stakeholders dealing with the issue, and the potential tasks and activities of the NIHR. The issue papers facilitated the members of the Commission to make informed choices on the prioritisation of issues and topics.

5.1.3. The Balancing Framework

In order to facilitate the decision making process on the prioritisation of topics, a balancing framework was developed to weigh the different issues. This framework also allowed for a transparent justification of the choices made. It contained criteria for the determination of which topics were to be placed on the list of priorities and which courses of action were to be undertaken. The clusters of criteria were the following: seriousness, added value, broad human rights perspective, awareness raising, founded opinion, and result. Questions included,

40 The three 'BES' islands are: Bonaire; Sint Eustatius and Saba.

41 The issue papers were meant for internal use only, but some of the content can be found at: www.mensenrechten.nl.

for instance: to what extent is the issue covered by one or more (international) human rights provisions; what is the seriousness of the issue; is there potential added value of the action of the NIHR; to what extent can the issue be embedded in a broader human rights perspective; does the issue contribute to increased awareness on human rights; is it possible to form a founded opinion on the topic; and is there sufficient result to be expected. A default criterion was included in the form of a final check whether for some reason it would be necessary to diverge from the above-mentioned criteria.

5.1.4. Vision, Mission and Strategy

The above described process and actions lead to the translation of the mandate into a vision, mission and strategic aims for the NIHR. These were laid down in a strategic plan, on which a large stakeholders consultation was held end of June 2012. This strategic plan was adopted by the full Board of the NIHR, including the new members, in the fall of 2012.[42]

The mission of the NIHR is formulated as follows:

> 'The Netherlands Institute for Human Rights protects human rights in The Netherlands, increases awareness of these rights and promotes their observance in practice, policy and law-making.'

The vision of the NIHR is:

> 'The NIHR courageously strives to improve the human rights situation in The Netherlands in order to fulfil the requirements of a society:
> - where human rights are guaranteed for all who are in The Netherlands or within the sphere of influence of The Netherlands;
> - with a culture of respect for human rights;
> - in which people can develop themselves freely and in accordance with their potential, not hindered by prejudices and discrimination;'

Five strategic aims have been formulated:

1. Human rights are (being) preserved in policy, law and rule making;
2. Violations of human rights by the government and third parties are prevented or corrected;
3. All persons in The Netherlands understand their rights and those of others and are capable to enjoy them in practice;

42 The Strategic Plan is available at: www.mensenrechten.nl: http://www.mensenrechten.nl/sites/all/themes/cgb/other/2012-10-01%20-%20Strategisch%20plan%20College%20voor%20de%20Rechten%20van%20de%20Mens.pdf.

4. Government, Parliament, organisations and individuals actively take responsibility in the area of human rights;
5. The Netherlands Institute for Human Rights develops into an institute playing a leading role in the area of human rights in The Netherlands.

The following topics were chosen as priorities for the NIHR for the first three years: elderly care and human rights; migration and human rights; and discrimination in the area of access to labour for young people, the elderly, persons with disabilities and minorities from non-western origin. These issues on which the NIHR will act proactively will serve as flagships in the first phase. Evidently, other human rights issues will also be dealt with. Human rights education, in particular training of professionals, will be one of the prominent activities of the NIHR.

5.2. DEVELOPING THE ORGANISATION

Apart from the elaboration of the content of the strategic plan, the organisation itself needed to be changed. The Bill prescribes that the members of the Equal Treatment Commission form the Board of the NIHR, complemented by three new members. The staff of the Equal Treatment Commission, which was broadly divided into a policy and a legal department, would in principle be retained. Bearing in mind that the playing field of the NIHR is much larger in terms of human rights issues, laws and procedures, the organisation undertook a complex process of education and training. All staff received weekly additional training on human rights, varying from international and European human rights law and monitoring mechanisms to specific topics such as economic, social and cultural rights, business and human rights and human rights indicators. Apart from these content courses, staff from other NHRIs in Europe was invited to share their experiences and knowledge. Particular attention was given to institutes which had developed along similar lines as the Dutch situation, integrating an Equal Treatment Commission in an NHRI, such as in the United Kingdom.

In the meantime, several positioning activities were undertaken. The website on the newly to be established institute was built (www.naareenmensenrechteninstituut.nl). The Netherlands further underwent the Universal Periodic Review in 2012 and the NIHR, in the formal form of the Equal Treatment Commission, facilitated the stakeholders report.[43] Furthermore, an empirical study on 'how people in The Netherlands feel about human rights' was

---

43 The report as submitted to the Office of the High Commissioner for Human Rights is available at: www.mensenrechten.nl, under 'publications'.
For the OHCHR stakeholders report used for the UPR, which is a compilation of all stakeholders' submissions, see UN HRC, 'Summary prepared by the Office of the High Commissioner for Human Rights in accordance with paragraph 5 of the annex to Human Rights Council resolution 16/21- The Netherlands', *UN Doc.* A/HRC/WG.6/13/NLD/3, 12 March 2012.

conducted.[44] Questionnaires were distributed among a representative selection (n=1082) of the Dutch population. Participants were between 18 and 70 years old and were selected from an online panel of research bureau *Motivaction*. The main purpose of the study was to gain insight in the population's experience with human rights. It appeared from the study that Dutch people consider discrimination and unfair treatment as the main violations of human rights in The Netherlands. Freedom of expression appeared to be the human right people were most familiar with. Almost one out of five Dutch persons indicated that they thought human rights violations often take place in The Netherlands. One out of ten persons indicated to be themselves victims of human rights violations. A large majority of respondents (85%) indicated that they found monitoring of compliance with human rights very important. The establishment of the NIHR was considered (very) useful by 65%, while 12% did not find it useful (at all).

The study furthermore showed that when people think about human rights, they broadly think about equal opportunities for all (16%), Amnesty International (15%), and freedom of expression (11%). One third of the respondents did not have a direct association with human rights. The top three of situations that Dutch people recognise as human rights violations are: sexual abuse (89%), violence against homosexuals (88%) and violence against elderly persons in institutions of care (84%). Almost all respondents found that something had to be done against these violations (resp. 94%, 89% and 93%). Two thirds of the respondents found that issues in relation to asylum seekers should be tackled. A large majority further found that action should be taken against violations in relation to labour, such as unequal pay for women (72%). Attention for human rights in education (82%) and for professionals was also widely supported.

6. CHALLENGES AND OPPORTUNITIES

Looking back on a process of two years in which institutional and organisational changes have taken place and the field of work has been extended, it can be concluded that the process of building a new human rights institute that has to emerge out of an already existing equal treatment commission renders opportunities as well as challenges.

The most obvious and practical advantage was that there already existed a functioning organisation. This meant that the practical and operational infrastructure that is needed for the new institute to run normally (such as a building, a financial department, human resource management, etc.) was already in place. This infrastructure was financed by the budget of the Equal

44 *Nederland en Mensenrechten* [Human Rights in The Netherlands], Amsterdam, 7 December 2011, available at: www.mensenrechten.nl, under 'publications'.

Treatment Commission. Consequently, the extra budget allocated to the NIHR to prepare for its broader human rights tasks could be spent on content related activities, such as research and training on the broad range of human rights topics and the preparation of human rights communication tools, as well as on selecting new board members and additional staff with the needed broader human rights knowledge and expertise.

Another practical advantage that came with the integration of the Equal Treatment Commission with the NIHR was that a lot of experience and expertise with some of the tasks that the new institute would have to perform was already present. Staff members of the Equal Treatment Commission were already equipped for performing tasks such as conducting empirical research, reporting to UN treaty bodies, advising on legislation, and information and promotion activities. Although these tasks used to be carried out within the sphere of equal treatment, the new organisation will profit from the existing skills that come with the experience in conducting these types of tasks.

The Equal Treatment Commission furthermore had wide experience in operating independently and in taking position in a social and political climate in which public support for the *raison d'être* of the organisation was not always apparent. In 2006–2007 the Equal Treatment Commission itself was subject of heated debate, when it had decided on several cases concerning men and women who refused to shake hands with other men or women for religious reasons and therefore did not get a certain job or were not allowed access to educational institutions.[45] The Commission concluded in these cases that there was (indirect) discrimination on the basis of religion, because there was no reasonable and objective justification for the distinction made. It argued in some cases that shaking hands was not a necessary functional criterion and in others that other possible forms of greeting should have been explored. The public debate that followed not only concerned disagreement with the opinions themselves, but involved questioning the capabilities and proper functioning of the Equal Treatment Commission itself. During this period the Equal Treatment Commission learned that remaining silent and waiting for the debate to blow over was not a good strategy. It was further agreed among the organisation

[45] In 2006–2007 the Equal Treatment Commission dealt with several cases concerning the shaking of hands, including: *Case No. 2006-202*, which concerned a municipality that refused a person's application for the job of client manager because he refused to shake hands with women; *Case No. 2006-51*, which concerned a woman who, because of her religion, refused physical contact with persons of the other sex, including shaking hands, and was refused access to education as teaching assistant; and *Case No. 2006-220*, which concerned an Islamic employee who was suspended because she refused to shake hands with men. The Commission concluded that these cases involved indirect discrimination on the basis of religion as regards the refusal to shake hands, because there was no reasonable and objective justification for such distinction. More recent cases include *Case No. 2011-7*, which concerned a student who was refused access to ICT education because he refused to shake hands with women; and *Case No. 2011-139*, which concerned a Muslim student who was suspended from his internship at a school, because he refused to shake hands with his fellow female teachers.

that the Equal Treatment Commission, and this will in our view be the same for the NIHR, should not avoid addressing a topic because it is controversial or unpopular. Instead, the NIHR should resolutely engage with all human rights issues that are present in The Netherlands and put them on the political agenda and in the public debate.

Another lesson learned was that it is essential for an organisation like the Equal Treatment Commission, and again for the NIHR alike, to cooperate closely with its stakeholders and to be in constant contact not only with friends of the organisation, but also with critics. The Equal Treatment Commission has always functioned as a liaison between the Government and civil society organisations and this experience has allowed the NIHR to build a stakeholders' network quickly and become a focal point in the existing human rights infrastructure in The Netherlands. As outlined above, the stakeholders have formed an important group of cooperation and advice in the transition phase towards the NIHR.

A more content related advantage of the integration process is that the Equal Treatment Commission had much experience with human rights in horizontal relations. Many of the individual cases dealt with by the Commission concerned the horizontal sphere, for instance between employers and employees. This experience will be very helpful for the NIHR. The NIHR will, apart from vertical issues between individuals and the government, also deal with several important human rights issues that emerge in situations of horizontal relations, for example in private health care institutions or in the case of the domestic violence. The NIHR will also work to improve the human rights situation between private actors.

A final positive point in the preparation process was that since the new organisation was set up from within the existing setting of the Equal Treatment Commission, it could work and develop itself in the shade, away from the public eye. This meant that the organisation was not yet bombarded with questions and did not need to respond yet to current developments or issues, causing energy to be spent on reaction instead of creation. The project team could sometimes organise a try out or a pilot study without running the risk of being immediately scrutinised for negative outcomes. The NIHR therefore had a head start in October 2012.

At the same time, there are also downsides to building a human rights institute on the foundations of an Equal Treatment Commission, which can be summarised as "the law of the handicap of a head-start". The fact that a similar organisation already existed has on certain occasions also slowed down the process. Despite all the similarities with the new institute, there are also differences; the much broader mandate and new tasks for instance. This implied changes to some extent in the manner in which the staff carried out their work so far. Such organisational change, although interesting from a change management perspective, is not an easy process. A few specific challenges faced during the transition process in relation to the mandate of the NIHR can be highlighted.

An important challenge was to find a proper balance for the new organisation between human rights and equal treatment. Fact is that there exists an imbalance in the budget. The Equal Treatment Commission that will transform into the NIHR has an annual budget of a little over five million Euros. For the broader mandate and new tasks regarding human rights of the NIHR an amount of 800,000 Euros is added on an annual basis. The Bill establishing the NIHR states that commissioners and staff of the Equal Treatment Commission will automatically become respectively members of the Board and staff of the NIHR. Consequently the majority of the staff of the NIHR originates from the equal treatment side.

Understandably, this raises questions about a proper balance of work between human rights and equal treatment and concern was expressed that the NIHR would be no more than an Equal Treatment Commission *Plus*. It was feared that the new institute would disproportionally focus its attention on equal treatment. The political discussions about the hierarchy between fundamental rights, as described above, also showed this concern for imbalance. It was argued that if a conflict would arise between the principle of equal treatment and other fundamental rights, the NIHR, as former Equal Treatment Commission, might act upon the notion that equal treatment would prevail unless the legislator determined otherwise.[46]

Although such concerns are understandable, it should be noted that the Equal Treatment Commission has always advocated the position that equal treatment and human rights should be integrated and that the NIHR would *not* be an Equal Treatment Commission *Plus*. The starting point has always been the added value of embedding equal treatment in the broader perspective of human rights. This implies that all tasks, except for the individual cases on equal treatment, will be fully and holistically integrated within the new institute. The treatment of individual cases will be organised in a separate department and formally concern equal treatment issues only. However, although these cases are reviewed on the basis of the law on equal treatment, it was determined that they will, where appropriate, be placed in a broader human rights framework. This broader approach is in fact not new. Although formally it has always been possible, in 2011 the Equal Treatment Commission for the first time explicitly considered whether it had the competence to involve in its opinions the question whether human rights other than mere equal treatment were violated.[47] This opinion by

---

46 See, among others, A. Terlouw, '*De CGB en de algemene mensenrechtentoets*' [The Equal Treatment Commission and the general human rights examination], *NJCM-Bulletin*, vol. 36, nr. 6/7, 2011.

47 Commission on Equal Treatment, Case No. 2011-69, 28 April 2011, *Reed Business BV.* In this case the Commission decided that Reed Business B.V. did not discriminate on the basis of political opinion by not providing a man access to the forum on the website of Elsevier.

the Commission was publicly debated. The debate not so much concerned the question as to whether the Commission was competent to apply other human rights norms, but more as to the type of cases in which the Commission should do this, how the Commission should balance equal treatment and other human rights, and how it could interpret the latter.

It can indeed be argued that when the NIHR as former Equal Treatment Commission applies broader human rights norms in its opinions, it should be able to assess the precise content and state obligations of such norms, as also developed by international supervisory bodies. This requires additional knowledge and expertise. At the same time, involving, where appropriate, other human rights in the individual cases is, in our view, a logic consequence of the human rights mandate of the NIHR. The NIHR is embedded in a broader constitutional judicial system, of which equal treatment legislation is only one part. The NIHR can in its opinions on individual cases not be totally blind to the link with other human rights and the possible friction between equal treatment and other human rights, or else it would soon lose its credibility.

As indicated above, concerns have been raised about the broader human rights expertise of the Commissioners and staff of the Equal Treatment Commission. This was the reason why the current staff was intensively trained in the broad field of human rights at the national and international level so that they would be able to perform their tasks adequately when the NIHR opened. Moreover, new board members were selected with the necessary human rights expertise. All this, of course, does not mean that in October 2012 the NIHR will be at the ultimate level of knowledge and expertise. This will certainly take more time. In the period 2012 through 2014 new staff and new board members shall be appointed. In addition, the training of staff will continue in the coming years.

Another major challenge for the NIHR will be the balancing of different tasks. For instance, the NIHR on the one hand gives opinions about equal treatment in individual cases, based on the facts of a specific case. On the other hand it gives advice and recommendations on legislation or conducts independent research on more general or abstract issues. These might be perceived as different from the opinions in individual cases. This is, however, not new. As indicated above, the Equal Treatment Commission already has a lot of experience in combining these different tasks and it has generally not led to major problems. Although the broadening of the human rights field may increase the perceived difference, no major problems are to be expected.

Another important challenge is the accessibility and the distinctive character of the new institute, which requires a lot of information and communication. For instance, persons wanting to submit cases on equal treatment need to be informed that they can no longer go to the Equal Treatment Commission but must instead

---

The editorial freedom of Reed Business B.V. was given preference on the basis of the direct application of Article 10 of the European Convention on Human Rights.

submit their case to the NIHR. Also, the general public has to be informed about what the NIHR can do for it and, perhaps just as important, what it cannot do or is not competent to do. After all, the NIHR cannot deal with individual cases concerning all human rights and cannot initiate legal proceedings. This is why a solid and visible front office has been set up to which individuals can turn with all their questions. In the first months of the NIHR this front office shall provide a lot of information about the goals and tasks of the new institute and will refer people to other organisations when necessary. Furthermore, a new and clarifying website is set up to serve this purpose.[48]

Finally, perhaps the most crucial challenge for the new institute is to find a way to fulfil all its tasks and to do justice to the large number and diversity of relevant human rights issues in The Netherlands, in particular in relation to the relatively modest budget allocated to the NIHR. There simply are not enough resources to do everything at the same time, which means that the budget will determine which activities will be possible. The transition process allowed the NIHR to get a good overview of the relevant human rights issues in The Netherlands. Still, it will be a constant challenge to operate within the broad human rights perspective, to be able to focus on several selected issues, to ensure that they receive sufficient attention, and at the same time to adequately react to new developments. The decision framework will certainly help in this process in the future and the established relations with stakeholders will be crucial, as the NIHR can turn to them for input, assistance and cooperation.

Is all of this in the end sufficient for an effective and successful NIHR? We will have to wait and see. After two years the adequacy of the budget will be evaluated. But the finances will not be the only point of evaluation. The NIHR has ambitions, plans and intentions that will be evaluated too. Expectations are high. It has very important tasks ahead. The Netherlands deserve an outstanding NIHR that works with governmental and non-governmental partners to advance human rights for all.

48 See: http://www.mensenrechten.nl/.

FEDERALISM, EQUALITY BODIES AND NHRIs: A CRITICAL ANALYSIS OF THE BELGIAN DEBATE ON EQUALITY BODIES AND NHRIs

Jogchum VRIELINK[1] and Stefan SOTTIAUX[2]

1. INTRODUCTION

'There can be only one!' This tagline from the cult action film *Highlander*[3] – depicting immortal warriors, only one of which can survive for some mystical reason – aptly describes the tenor of the Belgian debate concerning human rights institutions.

Belgium is a 'federal state, composed of communities and regions', as Article 1 of the Constitution proclaims. Legislative and executive powers are not the sole preserve of the federal level, but are shared – by way of exclusive powers along a number of subject matters – with the communities and the regions. The three communities[4] are competent for issues related to culture, education and certain social issues. The three regions[5] were historically inspired by aspirations of economic autonomy, and hold important powers in that field. The federal level, for its part, retains powers in areas such as foreign affairs, justice, finance and social security.

Importantly, in the Belgian federal system, legislation in the field of human rights is not an enumerated power, exclusively attributed to a single level of government. All federated levels hold important regulatory and enforcement powers in this domain. In order to determine which level of government has

---

1 Jogchum Vrielink is a postdoctoral researcher, University of Leuven. Contact: jogchum.vrielink@law.kuleuven.be. This chapter is based on research funded by the Flemish Ministry within the framework of the third Policy Research Centre Program (2012–2015).

2 Stefan Sottiaux is professor of constitutional law, University of Leuven. Contact: Stefan.sottiaux@law.kuleuven.be.

3 1986, directed by Russell Mulcahy, and starring Christopher Lambert and Sean Connery. The initial movie inspired a franchise including two sequels (1991 and 1994), a television spin-off, and an upcoming remake.

4 The Flemish Community, the French Community and the German speaking Community.

5 The Flemish Region, the Brussels Capital Region and the Walloon Region.

competence in any given situation or context, a link must always be established with a specific (enumerated or ancillary) power.[6] The federal level, for instance, is competent in most matters of employment, while virtually all aspects of education fall under the competence of the communities.

As a result, both the federal level and the communities and regions created a number of (specialised or thematic) human rights institutions. At the federal level there are the equality bodies (i.e. the Centre for Equal Opportunities and Opposition to Racism (CEOOR) and the Institute for the Equality of Women and Men), the Federal Ombudsman, the National Commission for the Rights of the Child, the Commission for the Protection of Private Life, and the High Council of Justice. At the level of the Flemish Community and the Flemish Region, mention can be made of the Flemish Ombudsman Service and the Commissioner's Office for Children's Rights. The French Community has an Ombudswoman and the Delegate General for the Rights of the Child. Finally, the Walloon Region has its own Ombudsman as well.

Recent political debate concerning these institutions focused on two issues. The first is that the current bodies do not amount to a full implementation of all international obligations incumbent upon Belgium. More specifically, most levels of government have yet to assign or create equality bodies in the sense of the EU gender and racial equality directives.[7] In this regard, there has been a predominant and virtually unquestioned consensus to arrive at one single institution, responsible for the enforcement of the combined body of discrimination legislation of both the federal and the federated levels. This body would be an 'interfederal' institution, created through a cooperation agreement between the federal state and the various regions and communities, and jointly run and financed by all entities. The main option, within this scenario, consisted in the transformation of the existing federal equality body – the CEOOR – into an inter-federal body. The CEOOR itself, summarised the arguments in favour of this solution as follows:

---

6 See S. Van Drooghenbroeck and J. Velaers, 'La répartition des compétences dans la lutte contre la discrimination' [The division of powers in the fight against discrimination], in C. Bayart, S. Sottiaux and S. Van Drooghenbroeck (eds.), *De nieuwe federale antidiscriminatiewetten* [The new federal anti-discrimination laws], Bruges, die Keure, 2008, pp. 101–129; J. Vanpraet, *De latente staatshervorming. De bevoegdheidsverdeling in de rechtspraak van het Grondwettelijk Hof en de adviespraktijk van de Raad van State* [The latent state reform. The division of powers in the case-law of the Constitutional Court and the advisory opinions of the Council of State], Bruges, die Keure, 2011, pp. 250–253.

7 Council Directive 2000/43/EC of 29 June 2000 implementing the principle of equal treatment between persons irrespective of racial or ethnic origin (Racial Equality Directive), Art. 13; Council Directive 2004/113/EC of 13 December 2004 implementing the principle of equal treatment between men and women in the access to and supply of goods and services, Art. 12; Directive 2006/54/EC of the European Parliament and of the Council of 5 July 2006 on the implementation of the principle of equal opportunities and equal treatment of men and women in matters of employment and occupation (recast), Art. 20.

> '[It will] provide every citizen of the country with one single contact point for reporting discrimination or violations of the fundamental rights of aliens. Opting for a single institution provides each resident with the guarantee of the highest quality treatment of his questions, in the national language of their choice. An interfederal Centre will benefit the international positions of each of our governments, and of course be much less costly than if each government were to establish its own separate institution.'[8]

A second issue in the political debate concerns the fact that the current institutions do not include a National Human Rights Institution (NHRI) that is in full compliance with the Paris Principles.[9] The creation of a Belgian NHRI with an A-status,[10] has been on the agenda for several years. In its 2003 declaration to Parliament, the federal government stated that it would establish a Commission on Human Rights.[11] To this aim, a working group was set up in the Office of the Prime Minister. This working group consulted civil society representatives,[12] and it led to several human rights NGOs submitting a proposal for the establishment of a Belgian Commission for Fundamental Rights.[13] However, in the declarations to Parliament of the successive governments after the elections of June 2007, this proposal was never again mentioned.[14] Subsequent governments also failed to undertake further action.[15]

---

8 CEOOR, 'Het Centrum in 2011. Jaarverslag Algemene werking 2011' [The Centre in 2011. Annual Report 2011], Brussels, 2012, p. 7.

9 Nor do they together make up a composite body that can be considered as a NHRI. Principles relating to the Status of National Institutions, Adopted by UN General Assembly Resolution 48/134 of 20 December 1993, *UN Doc.* A/RES/48/134, Annex.

10 A-status NHRIs are NHRIs that are considered to be in compliance with the Paris Principles according to the accreditation of the International Coordinating Committee of National Human Rights Institutions (ICC). For a further analysis of the ICC accreditation, see G. de Beco, 'Assessment of the Paris Principles and the ICC Sub-Committee on Accreditation', Chapter 11 in this volume.

11 Government declaration, Parliamentary Documents, House of Representatives, extraord. session 2003, no. 51-20/1, p. 77. See also the government agreement of 2003 (Government Verhofstadt II).

12 Reply of G. Verhofstadt (Prime Minister) to H. Vautmans, Parliamentary Reports, House of Representatives, Commissions, 2006–07, no. 51-1195, 7 February 2007, p. 2.

13 The proposal provided for the creation of a national commission via a "cooperation agreement" between the federal State and the federated entities, which entailed that the agreement would have had to be adopted by the parliamentary assemblies and governments of the federal State, the Flemish Community, the Flemish Region, the French Community, the Walloon Region, the German speaking Community, the Region of Brussels-Capital, the French Community Commission of Brussels and the Common Community Commission of Brussels. The Commission would be composed of eleven members, all elected by the federal Senate, eight of which would be nominated by the federal government and the community and the regional governments, and the remaining three by the human rights NGOs.

14 See reply of the Minister of Justice to the written question of C. Nyssens, Parliamentary Questions and Answers, House of Representatives, 2007–08, no. 52-11, pp. 1757–1759.

15 The federal government agreement of 2011 did renew the federal government's commitments.

The issue re-emerged during the discussion about the "interfederalisation" of the CEOOR. According to the federal government, the mandate of the CEOOR could be expanded at the occasion of its "interfederalisation", thereby turning it into a full-fledged (and "interfederal") NHRI. Proponents of this approach point to the fact that the CEOOR was already accorded a B-status by the ICC, and that the EU non-discrimination directives explicitly allow for equality bodies to 'form part of agencies charged at national level with the defence of human rights or the safeguard of individuals' rights'.[16] Moreover, the CEOOR itself repeatedly expressed its wish to become a general NHRI.[17] It sees its "interfederalisation" as a mere "interim step", albeit a necessary one, 'in order to establish a general national human rights institution, in the near future [...]'.[18]

This chapter critically assesses the drive towards both federal and thematic centralisation within the landscape of Belgian human rights agencies. Is a single, 'interfederal' equality body really the only viable option, as its proponents would have us believe? (Section 2) And should the activities of this body also be expanded to those of a full-fledged NHRI? (Section 3) In short: can there really 'be only one', or are there perhaps reasons to be cautious about such a development?[19]

2. AN "INTERFEDERAL" INSTITUTION VS FEDERATED INSTITUTIONS

Turning the existing, federal equality body into an "interfederal" institution was considered the obvious solution to the lack of equality bodies at the region and community levels. Looking at this solution from a comparative point of view leads to a number of striking conclusions.

As mentioned in the introduction, in the Belgian federal system, each level of government is not only competent for legislating in its proper domain, but also for the *enforcement* of the legislation it adopts. A first important observation is that in *other* human rights-related fields, this has resulted in the creation of separate institutions at the various governmental levels (cf. *supra*, section 1). For instance,

16 Art. 13.1 Racial Equality Directive; Art. 12.1 Gender Goods and Services Directive; Art. 20.1 Gender Employment Equality Directive.

17 See i.a. CEOOR, '*Memorandum ter attentie van de formateur*', Brussels, 2011, p. 3; CEOOR, '*Het Centrum in 2011. Jaarverslag Algemene werking 2011*' [The Centre in 2011. Annual Report 2011], Brussels, 2012, p. 7; CEOOR, '*Discriminatie. Diversiteit. Jaarverslag 2011*' [Discrimination. Diversity. Annual Report 2011], Brussels, 2012, p. 41 and p. 127.

18 CEOOR, '*Het Centrum in 2011. Jaarverslag Algemene werking 2011*' [The Centre in 2011. Annual Report 2011], Brussels, 2012, p. 7.

19 This chapter is based on research by the authors commissioned by the Flemish government: S. Sottiaux and J. Vrielink, *'Institutionalisering' van gelijkheid en mensenrechten. Gelijkheidsorganen en mensenrechteninstellingen in Vlaanderen en België* ['Institutionalisation' of equality and human rights. Equality bodies and human rights institutions in Flanders and Belgium], Antwerp/Cambridge, Intersentia, 2012, xii + 163 p.

there are ombudsmen at the federal level and at the level of the regions and the communities. And in addition to a children's rights body at the federal level there are Flemish and French Community bodies as well. This raises the question as to why this should be different in the context of non-discrimination and equality.

Furthermore, a comparative analysis of other federal and regionalised countries demonstrates that none of them opt for a single "interfederal" equality body. This is the case both within and outside the European context. Countries as diverse as the United States, Canada, Australia, Germany, Italy, Spain and the United Kingdom, have all established equality (or human rights) bodies at multiple levels of government.[20] Moreover, even non-federal States – such as the Netherlands and France – tend to partially decentralise the enforcement of discrimination law by means of provincial, municipal or local institutions.

What are the benefits and disadvantages of having multiple equality bodies within federal States, and – more generally – of a centralised versus a decentralised enforcement of discrimination legislation?

From the outset, it should be noted that research (and empirical research in particular) on this topic is scarce. In most federal States virtually no political or academic debate exists about this issue. Rather, and in stark contrast to the Belgian approach, the coexistence of federal and state agencies is simply regarded as a logical consequence of the federal state structure and the division of powers.

The only exception to this lack of research is the United States of America, where there have been attempts to empirically investigate the combined functioning of federal, state and local equality bodies. However, given the USA's different system of division of powers, the relevance of this research for Belgium is limited. Nevertheless, it seems interesting to briefly discuss this research. Unlike in Belgium, non-discrimination and equal opportunities are largely shared competences in the USA. In the area of enforcement this has led to an advanced form of cooperative federalism. The enforcement of federal anti-discrimination laws is partially left to state and local (municipal) equality bodies. To this end, the federal agencies (like the Equal Employment Opportunity Commission (EEOC))[21] conclude cooperation agreements with their local partners. Empirical research on the enforcement of the federal Civil Rights Act in the housing market, has demonstrated the advantages and efficacy of this model.[22] It turns out that the local and state equality bodies boast better results, and that they are able to function

[20] See extensively S. Sottiaux and J. Vrielink, *ibidem.*, chapter IV.

[21] For more information on the EEOC, see: http://www.eeoc.gov/.

[22] See, for example, L.R. Dodge, 'Intergovernmental relations and the administrative enforcement of equal employment opportunity laws', *Public Administration Review*, vol. 57, 1997, pp. 431–440; C.M. Lamb and E.M. Wilk, 'Civil rights, federalism, and the administrative process: favourable outcomes by federal, state, and local agencies in housing discrimination complaints', *Public Administration Review*, 2010, pp. 412–421; E.M. Wilk and C.H. Lamb, 'Federalism, efficiency, and civil rights enforcement', *Political Research Quarterly*, 2011, vol. 64, pp. 392–404.

more efficiently than their federal level counterparts. Especially mediation and arriving at settlements tends to consume more time on the federal level than on the state and local levels.[23] Furthermore, this research reveals that there are no significant differences between northern and southern States, and between States with a Democratic governor and those with a Republican governor.[24] The studies resulted in the recommendation that the federal government should delegate more powers and responsibilities to state and local authorities in the enforcement of federal legislation.[25]

Apart from this American research, little empirical evidence exists of the advantages and disadvantages of a centralised as opposed to a decentralised approach to the organisation and operation of equality bodies. However, this does not imply that nothing sensible can be said about this subject. In the remainder of this section, we will list a number of pros and cons concerning the coexistence of equality bodies on both the federal and the state (and local) level, drawing not only on the legal literature but also on arguments derived from the general theory of federalism, regulation and governance.[26]

2.1. INNOVATION, AUTONOMY AND POLICY RESPONSIVENESS

> 'It is one of the happy accidents of the federal system that a single courageous State may, if the citizens choose, serve as a laboratory, and try novel social and economic experiments without risk to the rest of the country.'[27]

These are the famous words of US Supreme Court Justice Brandeis, which capture one of the beneficial effects of a federal system: States may function as 'laboratories of democracy', and can experiment with novel forms of regulation and policy. The literature on federalism and anti-discrimination policies frequently employs this image.[28] Several authors suggest that federalism allows and encourages the various levels of government to develop new means to tackle discrimination. This applies both to the content of the norms (e.g. new grounds of discrimination or affirmative action obligations), and to the sanctions and enforcement by independent bodies (e.g. new powers). As one author notes: 'State agencies provide a unique forum

23 *Ibidem*, p. 393.

24 L.R. Dodge, loc. cit. *supra* note 22, p. 436.

25 E.M. Wilk and C.H. Lamb, 'Federalism, efficiency, and civil rights enforcement', *Political Research Quarterly*, vol. 64, 2011, p. 402.

26 For a useful overview, see O. Lobel, 'The renew deal: the fall of regulation and the rise of governance in contemporary legal thought', *Minnesota Law Review*, vol. 89, 2004, p. 342.

27 *New York Ice Co. v. Lieberman*, 285 U.S. 262, 311 (1932) (Brandeis, J., dissenting).

28 S.L. Buhai, 'In the meantime: state protection of disability civil rights', *Loyola of Los Angeles Law Review*, vol. 37, 2004, p. 1065.

where new and creative approaches can be designed to eliminate discrimination and meet the needs of the particular State.'[29]

The next point is closely connected to this. Enforcement of discrimination law by means of independent bodies follows naturally from the power to legislate in these domains: it is a logical consequence of a federal system with autonomous regions that the legislation and policies within those areas may vary. When politically independent polities have a diverging approach concerning equal opportunities policies and when they entertain different priorities in this regard, it may also lead them to have different expectations of equality bodies. This is the case not only for the body's duties, tasks and powers, but also for the budget allocated to it. Not every level of government will necessarily be prepared to invest the same amount of budgetary resources to finance equality bodies. Indeed, in practice, discrimination legislation and, as a corollary of this, the powers and tasks of the various equality bodies, not only vary from country to country, but also within one and the same country.[30]

What does this imply for the Belgian debate on one or more enforcement agencies? Firstly, it would seem that the option of a single ("inter")federal agency may fail to benefit from one of the advantages offered by having multiple bodies: healthy competition, leading to novel and innovative approaches and means. Furthermore, as a practical matter, opting for a single body will be especially difficult in a context of asymmetric regulation and policies. If norms and policies are more or less similar across the federal and state levels, "interfederal" cooperation will be more feasible. In situations in which norms and policies diverge, however, governments will have different expectations regarding enforcement bodies (e.g. in terms of deployment of resources, staff qualifications, policy priorities, etc.).

As far as the traditional anti-discrimination legislation is concerned, there exists – to date – a considerable degree of symmetry in Belgium. The main Flemish non-discrimination statute, for instance, was inspired in part by the federal legislation, which was in turn strongly influenced by the European non-discrimination directives. However, it is not clear that this situation will remain so in the future: several recent legislative initiatives indicate that the federal legislator is increasingly relying on penal measures.[31] In the Flemish region

29 P.J. Tierney, 'Separate but equal – An analysis of state civil rights law enforcement and is interaction with federal law', *Notre Dame Lawyer*, vol. 49, 1973, p. 140. See also E.M. Wilk and C.H. Lamn, 'Federalism, efficiency, and civil rights enforcement', *Political Research Quarterly*, vol. 64, 2011, p. 402.

30 The latter is illustrated, for instance, by Canada (the Ontario Pay Equity Act) and the United Kingdom (where the Northern Irish institution is charged with specific tasks, that other (national) equality and human rights institutions do not possess).

31 Something which already was the case concerning racial and ethnic hate speech and discrimination, concerning which the federal legislation contains several additional criminal provisions (and the majority of cases in which the federal equality body undertakes legal action, is based on these provisions), compared to the Flemish legislation (which relies almost exclusively on civil provisions). Currently, legislative bills have been submitted on the federal

and community, the criminal law approach to non-discrimination is traditionally perceived as ineffective, and is regarded with suspicion. Moreover, in certain areas, policies and legislation already clearly diverge today. Examples include several pro-active measures of achieving substantive equality (e.g. setting target quotas, requiring equality plans, and employing the open method of coordination) and the establishment of a system of low-threshold, local complaints offices. All these measures are developed to a much greater extent in Flanders.

2.2. FOCUS AND SUBSIDIARITY

A second set of arguments in the debate about centralisation versus decentralisation of equality bodies relates to focus and subsidiarity. Regional or local equality bodies are often said to be better able to attune their work to specific regional and local problems.[32] Several reasons are cited for this: decentralised agencies have superior access to information about regional and local problems, and are better able to develop partnerships with regional and local governments and civil society.[33] Regional and local equality bodies also tend to be more open to policies that focus on specific local and regional issues. For national bodies it is less obvious to devote scarce resources to investigating local and regional problems.[34]

It is precisely this concern about local focus and subsidiarity that leads even *non-federal* States – particularly those experienced in dealing with discrimination – to decentralise their enforcement agencies. In the Netherlands, for instance, the government has allocated substantial funds for the establishment of municipal or regional equality bodies, alongside the national Equal Treatment Commission, thus establishing a network covering the entire country.[35] The *travaux préparatoires* of the act commissioning these institutions shows that the

level, seeking to expand the existing criminal provisions to include all protected grounds (e.g. sex, sexual orientation, religion, political conviction, physical characteristics, wealth, civil status, nationality, etc.). The federal equality body supports and actively advocates this development: Jdw, "CGKR: 'Lid zijn van homohatende groepen moet strafbaar worden' [CEOOR: 'Being a member of anti-gay groups should become a criminal offense'], *Gazet van Antwerpen*, 29 June 2012.

32 See e.g. N.M. Modesitt, 'Reinventing the EEOC', *SMU Law Review*, vol. 63, 2010, p. 1257; E.M.H. Schill, 'Local enforcement of laws prohibiting discrimination in housing: the New York City human rights commission', *Fordham Urban Law Journal*, vol. 23, 1996, pp. 1027–1028; J.P. Witherspoon, 'Civil rights policy in the federal system: proposals for a better use of administrative process', *Yale Law Journal*, vol. 74, 1965, p. 1205 and following.

33 See e.g. E.M.H. Schill, loc. cit *supra* note 32, pp. 1027–1028.

34 *Ibidem*.

35 Explanatory Memorandum, Parliamentary Papers II 2007/2008, 31 349, no. 3, p. 7. Since October 2012, the Equal Treatment Commission has been assimilated in the Netherlands Institute for Human Rights. For an extensive analysis, see Y. Donders and M.O. Monnikhof, 'The newly established Netherlands Institute for Human Rights: integrating human rights and equal treatment', Chapter 4 in this volume.

intent of the Dutch legislature was to enable a locally customised approach to tackling discrimination:

> 'Discrimination manifests itself in the immediate social environment of people: in one's district or neighbourhood, at work, where people do sports or spend their leisure time, et cetera. [...] The purpose of this bill is to provide the means for citizens to receive assistance in their immediate vicinity if they are discriminated against. [...] Easy accessibility is an absolute precondition here, since filing a complaint for discrimination is often already a big step for victims of discrimination.'[36]

Moreover many national bodies have adopted the practice of opening offices in other major cities besides the head office.[37] This decentralised approach is welcomed by international bodies like the European Commission against Racism and Intolerance (ECRI).[38]

2.3. DOUBLE PROTECTION AND BUDGETARY ISSUES

A recurring argument in the literature on federalism and fundamental rights is that federal States can serve to provide double protection for fundamental rights; both the federal government and the States can take measures to safeguard and enforce rights. This argument goes back to the Federalist No. 51 of James Madison.[39]

Specifically with regard to discrimination legislation and enforcement agencies, it has been pointed out that problems at one level of government may be compensated by another level.[40] Thus, leadership issues, budgetary problems due to financial cutbacks, or problems caused by a backlog in the treatment of cases by a federal equality body, may be counterbalanced by increased reliance on the State bodies, and vice versa. As Tierney observes with respect to the situation in the USA:

> 'Certainly the present case backlog at the federal level indicates that the need exists for state agencies to participate in the civil rights field. Experience has shown there

36 Explanatory Memorandum, Parliamentary Papers II 2007/2008, no. 3, pp. 1–2.

37 See the overview in J. Hatchard, 'The inter-relationship between Commonwealth human rights commissions and other national human rights institutions', 2003, available at: http://www.britishcouncil.org/john_hathchard_inter_relation.pdf, p. 41.

38 Principle 6 of General Policy Recommendation No. 2 on equality bodies reads as follows: 'Specialised bodies should consider, where appropriate, setting up local offices in order to increase their accessibility and to improve the effectiveness of their education and training functions'. See: ECRI, General Policy Recommendation No. 2 of 13 June 1997, CRI(97)36.

39 See, for example, E. Katz and G.A. Tarr, 'Introduction', in E. Katz and G.A. Tarr (eds.), *Federalism and rights*, Lanham, Rowman & Littlefield Publishers, 1996, xiv.

40 This argument is most relevant however in federal systems based on concurrent powers rather than exclusive ones.

is sufficient discrimination to support the existence of civil rights agencies at all levels, federal, state and local'.[41]

Furthermore, the literature shows that insufficient financial means for and overburdening of equality bodies may not only be the result of cutbacks, but can also result from expanding the mandate of these institutions without increasing their budget.[42] Expanding the scope of equality laws – for instance by including new protected grounds or by extending the legislations' reach – can result in a 'net' reduction of the budget for those grounds or contexts that were already protected. Experiences suggest that in such situations the new competences tend to suffer from a lack of attention, as institutions are generally prone to a significant degree of inertia, and are predisposed to (remain) focus(ed) on pre-existing tasks and competences. This risk should be taken into account in case the mandate of the current federal CEOOR is extended due to its "interfederalisation".

2.4. ACCOUNTABILITY AND INDEPENDENCE

The independence of equality bodies should be ensured. However, *absolute* independence – in the sense of no oversight whatsoever – is both impossible and undesirable: as public institutions, funded by the State, equality bodies should always be held publicly and democratically accountable for the use of their resources, most obviously by means of parliamentary control.[43]

The literature on federalism indicates that it will generally be much easier for regional or local authorities to organise effective democratic checks and balances vis-à-vis a regional or local equality body.[44] The democratic control that regional parliaments can exercise vis-à-vis federal or 'interfederal' agencies is necessarily limited. However, at the same time this can be viewed as a potential drawback or danger of decentralisation. Local or regional bodies run a greater risk of coming under pressure of or being influenced by local policy-makers or by local public opinion, which may endanger their independence.[45]

---

41 P.J. Tierney, loc. cit. *supra* note 29, p. 140.

42 See, for example, H.B. Clifford, 'Discrimination and the efficiency of an equal opportunity agency', *Policy Studies Journal*, vol. 15, 1986, p. 17; L.R. Dodge, loc. cit. *supra* note 22, p. 433; R.B. Howe and D. Johnson, *Restraining equality: human rights commissions in Canada*, Toronto, University of Toronto Press, 2000.

43 G. Moon, 'Chapter eight. Enforcement bodies', in D. Schiek, L. Waddington and M. Bell (eds.), *Cases, materials and texts on national, supranational and international non-discrimination law*, Oxford, Hart, 2007, p. 954. Also compare, in the context of independence versus democratic control of privacy commissions in relation to EU law: ECJ, *Commission v. Germany*, C-518/07, 9 March 2010.

44 A.E.D. Howard, 'Does federalism secure or undermine rights', in E. Katz and G.A. Tarr, *Federalism and rights*, Lanham, Rowman & Littlefield Publishers, p. 19.

45 E.M.H. Schill, loc. cit. *supra* note 32, n. 171.

2.5. COORDINATION AND EFFICIENCY

Other drawbacks of the coexistence of multiple equality bodies in federal States have to do with possible problems of coordination and efficiency (compare also *infra* section 3). Several problems of this kind are conceivable.[46] To begin with, multiple agencies lead to higher costs, as each institution will have certain overhead costs and will need to invest in similar types of knowledge and experience, which cannot be pooled in order to benefit from economies of scale.

Moreover, there is a danger of 'reinventing the wheel' and of double work, if different equality bodies work on the same cases or problems. Related to this is a danger of creating confusion among the public if different equality bodies develop (significantly) diverging or contradictory guidelines concerning comparable or even identical cases. More generally – especially in a federal system with exclusive powers, like that in Belgium – there is likely to be some uncertainty or confusion among the public as to which body is competent for dealing with their questions or complaints; the lack of a so-called 'one stop shop'.

In most federal States, these problems are addressed by means of coordination and mutual agreements (either of a formal or informal nature). Uncertainties or difficulties citizens may experience in finding the competent institution are usually resolved by a system of referral between agencies. In Belgium such a referral system seems to be developing already. In Flanders, victims of discrimination can turn to both the federal CEOOR and to locally organised complaints offices (see *supra* section 2.1). Complainants are free to choose the body to which they submit their complaints. The local complaints offices and the CEOOR have concluded agreements for the joint treatment and mutual referral of complaints.[47] These agreements start from the principle of subsidiarity, and are aimed at having a complaint dealt with by the local complaints office in the regional area in which the (allegedly) discriminatory incident took place. Complaints that transcend local circumstances or that are unconnected to such circumstances, are transferred to the CEOOR. In the first evaluation of the local complaints offices, in 2010, this referral system was positively evaluated.[48]

---

46 See e.g. C.H. Lamb, 'Administrative coordination in civil rights enforcement: a regional approach', *Vanderbilt Law Review*, vol. 31, 1978, p. 858.

47 Gelijke Kansen in Vlaanderen [Equal Opportunities in Flanders], *Non-discriminatiebeleid in Vlaanderen, Evaluatierapport 2010* [Non-discrimination policy in Flanders, Evaluation report 2010], p. 36.

48 *Ibidem.*

2.6. CONCLUSION

Before drawing any conclusions from the foregoing for the Belgian debate, a note of caution is in order. Comparative analysis on federalism always entails a risk.[49] The federal structures and institutions of a country are highly dependent on factors such as history, culture and geography. For instance, a comparison between a large but (officially) monolingual country like the United States and a small but trilingual country like Belgium, always falls short to some extent. Nevertheless, the foregoing makes clear that the dominant Belgian discourse favouring the centralised solution is one-sided, both from a comparative point of view and on the basis of the available arguments. In practice, the coexistence of multiple equality bodies within federal States tends to be accepted as a logical consequence of the division of powers in federal States. Interestingly, the Belgian approach is at variance with this 'federal default', and while some strong and coherent arguments are brought forward for this approach, all counter-arguments have been largely ignored. Moreover, while coherent, all arguments brought to bear *against* having multiple regional and federal bodies are – in essence – arguments against the very idea of federalism.

3. A SEPARATE EQUALITY BODY VS AN INTEGRATED NATIONAL HUMAN RIGHTS INSTITUTION

Much like the dominant vision on the "interfederalisation" of the federal equality body, so too the federal government and many stakeholders advocated the simultaneous transformation of that institution into an all-encompassing national human rights institution (NHRI).

Comparatively speaking, there are an increasing number of institutions that combine the functions of an equality body with additional competences in the wider field of human rights. Examples include the United Kingdom, the Netherlands and Australia. In the UK, the Equality and Human Rights Commission (EHRC) – an agency with a broad human rights mandate – came into being in 2007, taking over the responsibilities of the three former equality commissions (the Commission for Racial Equality (CRE), the Equal Opportunities Commission (EOC – which dealt with gender equality) and the Disability Rights Commission (DRC)). In a similar vein, already in the 1980s, Australia saw the merger of its various anti-discrimination bodies into a single

[49] See V.C. Jackson, 'Comparative constitutional federalism and transnational judicial discourse', *International Journal of Constitutional Law*, 2004, p. 91.

human rights commission. More recently, in 2012, the Dutch Equal Treatment Commission was reformed to constitute a national human rights institute.[50]

However, this is by no means a general trend. In many countries equality bodies (and other institutions safeguarding specific human rights) remain separate from general human rights institutions.[51] Is this an historical coincidence or a conscious choice, based on arguments which tip the balance in favour of keeping equality bodies and general human rights institutions separate? In this section we will take a look at the advantages (3.1) and disadvantages (3.2.) of the integration of both types of bodies, in order to assess the Belgian approach.

3.1. ADVANTAGES

Some of the arguments for integration and against (retaining) a separate equality body are analogous to the arguments for a single "interfederal" equality body and against multiple regional or state bodies. To begin with, these arguments relate to a more efficient use of limited resources, both in financial terms (through a joint overhead, economies of scale, shared library, etc.),[52] and in terms of shared cognitive resources, knowledge, and experience.[53] In addition, it is argued that an integrated institution allows for 'cross-pollination': the equality agenda may gain in strength from being associated with other human rights agendas, and vice versa, and both may mutually benefit from good practices developed in other fields. In this connection, the "indivisibility" of human rights, as well as the enhanced possibility of tackling simultaneous violations of multiple rights are advanced in favour of a single human rights and equality agency.[54] Equinet, the European network of Equality bodies, more specifically lists the following advantages of an integrated institution:

---

50 For an extensive analysis, see Y. Donders and M.O. Monnikhof, 'The newly established Netherlands Institute for Human Rights: integrating human rights and equal treatment', Chapter 4 in this volume.

51 R. Carver, 'One NHRI or many? How many institutions does it take to protect human rights? Lessons from the European experience', *Journal of Human Rights Practice*, no. 1, 2011, p. 2. Although nearly all general human rights commissions in other countries do tend to be responsible for equality issues as well.

52 *Ibidem*, p. 3 and pp. 14–15; Equinet, 'Equality bodies and national human rights institutions making the link to maximise impact', Brussels, Equinet, 2011, p. 7; J. Hatchard, loc. cit. *supra* note 37, p. 34; S. Spencer and I. Bynoe, *A human rights commission: the options for Britain and Northern Ireland*, London, Institute for Public Policy Research, 1998, p. 111.

53 B.D. Jacobsen and E.O. Rosenberg Khawaja, 'Legal assistance to individuals. Powers and procedures of effective and strategic individual enforcement', in S. Obura and F. Palmer (eds.), *Report by Equinet working group 2 on strategic enforcement*, Equinet, 2006, p. 11; J. Hatchard, loc. cit. *supra* note 37, p. 35.

54 J. Hatchard, loc. cit. *supra* note 37, p. 26, p. 32 and p. 34; R. Carver, loc. cit. *supra* note 51, p. 13; C. O'Cinneide, *A single equality body: lessons from abroad*, Working paper 4, EOC, 2002, 42–43; S. Spencer and I. Bynoe, *A human rights commission: the options for Britain and Northern Ireland*, London, Institute for Public Policy Research, 1998, 111; Equinet, loc. cit. *supra* note 52, p. 8 and p. 11.

> 'Enabling the equality mandate to benefit from the protection of international standards that have been developed for national human rights instruments and institutions. Moving beyond the limitations of equality legislation with its defined grounds and its requirement for a comparator to prove discrimination [...] Enabling situations that involve an interaction of both discrimination and human rights violations to be effectively addressed.'[55]

Likewise, arguments related to visibility, familiarity and accessibility are put forward in favour of an integrated human rights institution. A single agency would benefit both victims and other stakeholders ('one stop shop') and the institution itself (greater impact and authority, greater visibility, unlikely to be marginalised as representing a 'mere' sectional interest, etc.).[56]

Closely connected to the latter is the argument that a single institution precludes the risk of multiple agencies duplicating the same work or developing contradictory practices and policies, and it avoids confusion about which agency is competent[57] (as well as preventing 'forum shopping' by complainants).[58]

Finally, integration would also make for a more powerful institution, strengthening it and thereby rendering it better able to safeguard and protect its de facto independence. As Hatchard puts it: 'An integrated body can better counter executive attempts to weaken or undermine its operation.'[59]

3.2. DISADVANTAGES

Against the arguments in favour of integrating equality bodies and general human rights institutions, there are several considerations that argue for keeping these institutions separate.

To begin with, there is the argument that the visibility of equality and non-discrimination (and of other specific human rights interests) decrease in a general human rights institution.[60] The same is argued in relation to an agency's ability to relate to target groups and specialised civil society bodies: separate equality bodies are said to offer a detailed understanding and to relate to civil society bodies in ways that will be harder to achieve for a single institution. Closely linked to this is the fact that a general human rights institution is likely to devote (relatively) less financial resources and priority to its equality and

55 *Ibidem*, p. 11.

56 *Ibidem*, p. 26 and p. 35; R. Carver, loc. cit. *supra* note 51, pp. 15–16 and pp. 18–19.

57 J. Hatchard, loc. cit. *supra* note 37, p. 26, p. 32, p. 34 and p. 35; Equinet, loc. cit. *supra* note 52, p. 8.

58 D. Juma, "Lost (or found) in transition? The anatomy of the new African court of Justice and Human Rights", in A. von Bogdandy and R. Wolfrum (eds.), *Max Planck yearbook of United Nations law*, Brill, 2009, 278; J. Hatchard, loc. cit. *supra* note 37, p. 35.

59 *Ibidem*, p. 35.

60 Equinet, loc. cit. *supra* note 52, p. 8–9; R. Carver, loc. cit. *supra* note 51, p. 3 and 9–10.

non-discrimination tasks.[61] Advocates of multiple institutions fear that the priority that they can give to the rights of their constituency cannot be reproduced by a single, non-specialised institution.

Also, a general institution entails the risk of ignoring the specific skill-sets required for distinct areas of human rights. This is particularly salient in the field of non-discrimination, which distinguishes itself from many other human rights issues by its high degree of technicality, a significant body of specialised legislation, and a complex set of evidentiary rules.[62] Within an overall, general institution, the room for achieving or maintaining the required levels of specialisation may be limited.

Closely related to this are arguments concerning the specificity of the required approach and focus. Critics of merging equality bodies and general human rights institutions point out that discrimination requires a set of very specific measures that are not always suitable for the promotion and protection of other human rights (and vice versa). Authors refer, for instance, to the greater need for 'different legal, promotional and outreach approaches in the equality field than in the broader human rights field'.[63] Furthermore, (private) employment issues are only of limited importance from the viewpoint of a general human rights agenda, while they are absolutely crucial to the equality agenda.[64] More generally, horizontal relations (amongst citizens) have traditionally been less central to human rights law, with the exception of the principle of non-discrimination. This has important consequences for the focus of equality bodies on the one hand, and general human rights institutions on the other hand:

> 'Human rights primarily govern the relationship between the state and private persons and not between individuals or between individuals and private sector institutions, although the latter are key areas for equality commissions.'[65]

In short, although there is a certain overlap between the equality agenda and the human rights agenda, there are important differences that some believe justify multiple institutions. Moreover, critics of merging specialised human rights institutions even point to tensions and outright conflicts between the two agendas, which would render a separate institutional approach desirable. Conflicts between equality and other human rights are plentiful. An obvious

---

61 J. Hatchard, loc. cit. *supra* note 37, p. 35. See also: Equinet, loc. cit. *supra* note 52, p. 2.

62 J. Hatchard, loc. cit. *supra* note 37, p. 25; Equinet, loc. cit. *supra* note 52, p. 8–9; R. Carver, loc. cit. *supra* note 51, p. 3.

63 C. O'Cinneide, 'A single equality body: lessons from abroad', Working paper 4, EOC, 2002, p. 44. See also J. Hatchard, loc. cit. *supra* note 37, p. 25.

64 *Ibidem*, p. 25.

65 *Ibidem*, p. 25. Other commentators point to the risk of a 'potential emphasis in a human rights commission on civil and political rights (in particular given the importance of the ECHR) rather than equality rights'. See: C. O'Cinneide, loc. cit. *supra* note 63, p. 44.

example is the regulation of hate speech:[66] while the right to freedom of expression is invoked to argue for restraint on the side of government intervention, advocates of government action often base themselves on the importance of equality. Numerous other examples are conceivable, such as tensions between equality and the right to freedom of religion (public officials refusing to perform same-sex marriages; wearing the face-veil; anti-gay speech by clergy, etc.) and the protection of privacy (e.g. situational testing). More generally, tensions can develop from the collectivist pursuit of (substantive) equality, and the more individual-oriented focus of many other human rights:

> 'These tensions can build on perceptions of equality as related to the group and solidarity and of human rights as related to the individual and freedom. Such tensions can also manifest themselves in the manner in which the dual mandate body seeks to present itself to the public. Communication narratives can be competing due to the different cases that can be made for equality and for human rights.'[67]

All these tensions may either paralyse a human rights institution or provide for internal schisms.[68] Even *if* a single institution succeeds in developing a clear policy line, the appearance of a hierarchy of rights can easily be created.[69]

It should also be noted that a general human rights institution may, by virtue of the sensitive issues that it inevitably has to deal with (migration, terrorism, abortion, euthanasia, privacy, prisoners, etc.), play a controversial role in public debate.[70] The work of equality bodies is generally of a less controversial nature. As a consequence, in a general human rights institution, the equality function runs the risk of being compromised or 'contaminated' by controversies in which the institution is engaged in other matters:

---

66 J. Hatchard, *The inter-relationship between Commonwealth human rights commissions and other national human rights institutions,* 2003, 25.

67 Equinet, loc. cit. *supra* note 52, p. 12. McCrudden characterises both agendas as follows: '[I]f human rights is thought to be predominantly about liberty from government, and equality is thought to be in part about redistribution by government, then the two agendas may be on a collision course, and status equality may be undermined by an overly libertarian, negative conception of human rights' (C. McCrudden, 'The contribution of the EU Fundamental Rights Agency to combating discrimination and promoting equality', in P. Alston and O. De Schutter (eds.), *Monitoring fundamental rights in Europe. The contribution of the Fundamental Rights Agency,* Oxford, Hart, 2005, p. 152).

68 Equinet, loc. cit. *supra* note 52, p. 12.

69 In part, the latter risk is compounded by international obligations that cause considerable differences and imbalances between the tasks and responsibilities vis-à-vis various human rights. For instance, an integrated human rights institution – which also includes the tasks of an equality body – will have to provide assistance to victims of discrimination, but not for victims of other human rights violations.

70 C. O'Cinneide, loc. cit. *supra* note 63, p. 44; J. Hatchard, loc. cit. *supra* note 37, p. 27.

> '[A] potential difficulty in combining human rights and equality in a single institution [is] (...) that a combined commission could by virtue of its functions be dragged into controversial terrain such as surveillance powers and bioethical issues.'[71]

A final set of arguments against integrating equality bodies and general human rights institutions is that this option, while offering economies of scale, may render the institution less manageable; the expansion may even lead to a large and unwieldy bureaucratic organisation.[72] An additional, related argument is that poor leadership of a single institution will have negative consequences for the human rights protection and enforcement system as whole.[73]

3.3. INFLUENCING FACTORS

In addition to the somewhat deceptive simplicity of the benefits and disadvantages mentioned in the two preceding sections, the literature points to several influencing factors that may increase the weight of the arguments on one side of the equation or the other.

Firstly, a successful merger of equality bodies and general human rights institutions strongly depends on the quality of the leadership of the institution (the director or the board of the institution) (cf. *supra* section 3.2). Secondly, a sufficiently long time scale is generally considered to be vital for successful integration.[74] Both these issues are evidenced by the British experience. According to critics, the transformation of the various equality bodies in the UK (the EOC, the CRE and the DRC) into one single Equality and Human Rights Commission resulted in a situation in which the previously well-functioning equality bodies currently lack vision and operational effectiveness.[75] Most critiques have focused on the chair's leadership, though underlying these criticisms is the sense that

71 C. O'Cinneide, loc. cit. *supra* note 63, p. 44. See also J. Hatchard, loc. cit. *supra* note 37, p. 27.

72 *Ibidem*, 25. Meanwhile, it should be kept in mind that there are – in countries where multiple institutions exist – relatively few problems seem to arise in ensuring minimal overlap between their respective activities and responsibilities, and a good working arrangement between them (*ibidem*, p. 35; referring to the example of the Office of the Commonwealth Ombudsman in Australia, that simply refers persons to the authorised body if it receives a complaint for which the institution itself is not competent).

73 R. Carver, loc. cit. *supra* note 51, p. 9.

74 *Ibidem*, p. 10.

75 *Ibidem*, p. 10. For additional information on the problems surrounding the British institution: A. McSmith, 'Equalities watchdog chief Trevor Phillips tried to influence inquiry', *The Independent*, 10 February 2010; L. Peacock, 'EHRC leadership rocked by three resignations', *Personnel Today*, 30 March 2009; L. Peacock, 'EHRC has faced tribunal claims for sexism, racism and religious discrimination', *Personnel Today*, 12 February 2010; T. Harper, 'Equality chief Trevor Phillips awarded friend £300,000 for £30,000 contract', *Daily Mail*, 6 September 2009; G. Peev, 'Equality chief Trevor Phillips faces inquiry for trying to influence parliamentary prob', *Daily Mail*, 10 February 2010; J. Slack, 'Equality chief Trevor Phillips clinging to job

especially equality issues have fared worse under the single body, having lost much of the momentum created by the DRC, the EOC and the CRE.

Finally, many of the risks of integrating equality bodies into a single human rights institution are strongly dependent on the object for which the merger takes place. In general, the risks are the greatest when the merger is primarily or exclusively based on considerations of cost.[76]

3.4. CONCLUSION

This section made clear that there are good arguments both in favour and against combining the functions of an equality body with that of a general human rights institution. A single institution may lead to greater efficiency and other advantages, but it may also have significant drawbacks such as internal tensions and conflicts, and other practical and institutional problems.

In Belgium, the search for the best institutional design for equality and human rights bodies is even more complicated due to the federal nature of the country. Here again the question arises as to whether the country should opt for one integrated and "interfederal" equality and human rights body, or whether the communities and the regions should establish their own integrated bodies. The first option would require the communities and the regions to transfer not only the enforcement powers concerning their anti-discrimination legislation, but also those vis-à-vis other issues of human rights to an "interfederal" institution. No doubt such a complete centralisation would have certain advantages, but it would also serve to lend added weight to some of the above-mentioned arguments *against* centralisation.

Moreover, most countries that opted to transform their equality bodies into general human rights institutions have a strongly developed tradition in both discrimination law and its enforcement through independent agencies. The obvious examples are Australia, the Netherlands and the United Kingdom. This is far less the case for Belgium. Anti-discrimination legislation in Belgium long covered only the grounds of race and ethnic origin, and was exclusively criminal in nature. More general equality laws, containing civil law provisions, were adopted only in 2003,[77] and this legislation was initially plagued by a myriad of technical and constitutional problems, which led to it being replaced in 2007. As such, the current federal equality body only recently started to enforce this new

following wave of protest resignations', *Daily Mail*, 27 July 2009; J. Pring, 'Movement slams watchdog's first year', *Disability Now*, October 2008.

76 Equinet, loc. cit. *supra* note 52, p. 8.

77 Specific sex discrimination legislation dates from 1999. However, no equality body was appointed for the enforcement of this legislation until 2002.

type of anti-discrimination legislation. Case law on the civil non-discrimination provisions remains scarce.[78]

Since the merging of equality bodies into human rights agencies seems to encounter difficulties even in those countries with a very long tradition in the field of enforcement through independent agencies, such as the UK, it is perhaps advisable for the existing Belgian equality bodies to first further develop and realise their potential as equality bodies, rather than immediately transforming them into an integrated human rights commission.

4. EPILOGUE

While the brief analysis in this chapter has its limitations, it does reveal the one-sided nature of the debate in Belgium, which was focused exclusively on centralisation, integration, and expansion. In effect, on 20 July 2012 a preliminary consensus was reached about a cooperation agreement between the federal level and the communities and regions, to first transform the federal equality body into an "interfederal" agency, and to subsequently – in the near future – further expand it into a full-fledged NHRI.[79]

It remains to be seen whether this monolithic institution will be truly beneficial for the effective enforcement of discrimination law and human rights law in general. If anything, the foregoing analysis casts doubt on that assumption.[80] On the basis of both empirical and theoretical arguments, the most appropriate solution instead would seem to be a *balance* between absolute centralisation on the one hand, and that of complete decentralisation on the other hand. However, for the time being, Belgium appears to have ignored this comparative experience.

78 For an overview, see: S. Sottiaux and J. Vrielink, '*Verschillende gelijkheden? Recente Europese en nationale rechtspraak over discriminatie*' [Different equalities? Recent European and national case law on discrimination], in A. Alen, G. Maes and S. Sottiaux (eds.), *Publiekrecht. Themis Cahier*, no. 70, 2011–12, pp. 23–67.

79 See e.g. Hrt, '*Ook Vlaanderen keurt nieuw anti-racismecentrum goed*' [Flanders also approves of new anti-racism centre], *De Standaard*, 20 July 2012.

80 These doubts are echoed in critique by human rights NGOs and minority organisations in Belgium of both the functioning of the existing federal equality bodies, and of the way in which the transformation process towards a NHRI was set up: Gom, '*Directeur nieuw mensenrechteninstituut behoort bij voorkeur zelf tot een minderheid*' [Director of the new human rights institute appertains preferably to a minority group], *De Standaard*, 26 July 2012; Amnesty International, '*Hervorming CGKR moet leiden tot onafhankelijk en omvattend mensenrechteninstituut*' [Reform CEOOR should lead towards an independent and comprehensive human rights institute], *Press release*, 20 July 2012.

PART II
EUROPEAN PERSPECTIVES

NHRI AND THEIR EUROPEAN COUNTERPARTS: SCOPE FOR STRENGTHENED COOPERATION AND PERFORMANCE TOWARDS EUROPEAN HUMAN RIGHTS INSTITUTIONS

Bruce ADAMSON[1]

1. INTRODUCTION

He aha te mea nui o te ao?
He tangata! He tangata! He tangata!

What is the most important thing in the world?
It is people! It is people! It is people!

(New Zealand Māori proverb)

Any discussion about human rights should be about people, not institutions. But in order to promote and protect human rights we need a strong human rights framework at local, national, regional and international levels. The institutions involved at all levels need to be effective and they need to work closely together.

National Human Rights Institutions (NHRIs) exist in over 100 countries across the world.[2] There is growing recognition at international and regional levels

---

[1] Legal Officer at the Scottish Human Rights Commission since its establishment in 2008. He is a lawyer qualified in three jurisdictions (Scotland, New Zealand, England & Wales). He is a member of the Edinburgh Children's Panel, a tribunal that makes decisions in relation to children who have committed offences or are in need of care and protection. He is also the chair of the Board of Trustees of the Scottish Child Law Centre. Bruce was an independent expert on Fundamental Rights for the European Commission's peer review missions to Turkey and Ukraine in 2011 and to Macedonia in 2012. At the time of writing, he was the Coordinator of the European Group of National Human Rights Institutions. Since March 2013, he is permanent representative of the International Coordinating Committee of NHRIs in Geneva.

[2] ICC, 'Chart of the status of national institutions accredited by the international coordinating committee of national institutions for the promotion and protection of human rights', Accreditation status as of May 2012, available at: http://nhri.ohchr.org/EN/Documents/Chart%20of%20the%20Status%20of%20NIs%20(30%20May%202012).pdf.

of NHRIs. In Europe they play an increasing role in providing a link between the regional human rights system and domestic systems. Yet despite Europe having perhaps the most developed regional framework for the protection and promotion of human rights, and the largest number of NHRIs, it has one of the least developed systems for the coordination of those bodies.

The regional framework for the promotion and protection of human rights in Europe is now over 60 years old and has a large and complicated structure. NHRIs in Europe are generally small and relatively new organisations.[3] They face the challenge of identifying ways in which they can interact with already established large regional institutions.

In addition, the European Group does not have the benefit of a permanent regional secretariat such as exists in Asia-Pacific and Africa. The result of the limited capacity of many NHRIs in Europe and of the network itself means that they often struggle to fully engage with the many initiatives of the regional mechanisms. This can result in regional mechanisms failing to include NHRIs in their projects due to a perceived lack of interest due to low levels of engagement, or in the regional mechanisms looking to engage with other bodies which are not NHRIs.

While the proposals to create a secretariat for NHRIs in Europe has great potential to increase engagement, it has been challenging to secure funding and it is unlikely that it will have more than minimal staffing in the near future. European NHRIs and regional institutions need to explore new ways of working with each other in a strategic way and to learn from what works in other areas of Europe and across the world.

2. THE ORIGIN, WORK AND FUNCTIONING OF THE EUROPEAN GROUP OF NHRIs

As discussed in previous chapters,[4] the origins of NHRIs can be said to date back to 1946 when United Nations Member States were encouraged by the Economic and Social Council to consider establishing 'information groups or local human rights committees' to collaborate with them in furthering the work of the Commission on human rights.[5]

The rapid creation of NHRIs in Europe in the mid 1990s was symptomatic of a global movement which allowed NHRIs to develop and organise in a more

[3] See M. Nowak, 'National Human Rights Institutions in Europe: Comparative, European and International Perspectives', Chapter 1 in this volume.

[4] See specifically M. Nowak, 'National Human Rights Institutions in Europe: Comparative, European and International Perspectives', Chapter 1 in this volume.

[5] ECOSOC Resolution 2/9 of 21 June 1946, para. 5.

formal and structured way.[6] European NHRIs were central to the development of the Paris Principles which were adopted by General Assembly resolution 48/134 of 20 December 1993. The preamble recognises the: 'significant role that institutions at the national level can play in promoting and protecting human rights and fundamental freedoms and in developing and enhancing public awareness of those rights and freedoms [...]'[7].

The global structure set up to support NHRIs, the International Coordinating Committee of National Institutions for the Promotion and Protection of Human Rights (ICC), was established in 1993. Over time it developed an increasingly sophisticated statute to manage the coordination of a growing membership.[8] The structure provides for four regional groups to ensure a fair balance of regional representation on the ICC: Africa, the Americas, Asia Pacific and Europe, each with a regional chair, coordinating committee and equal membership on the committee of management for the ICC, the ICC Bureau.[9] The members of these regional groups may establish their own procedures concerning meetings and activities.

While some European NHRIs have been established for a considerable number of years[10] most are relatively new. European NHRIs only began meeting formally in November 1994 when they met in Strasbourg along with the Council of Europe to put forward practical proposals in order to intensify cooperation among national institutions and to identify priorities and strategies for harmonising European efforts to combat racism and xenophobia.[11]

The second such meeting was held in Copenhagen in January 1997 in collaboration with the UN and other regional intergovernmental organisations. This meeting was entitled "For the Future" and recognised the need for a coordinating committee to ensure further cooperation and networking among

---

6 See United Nations Development Programme and the Office of the High Commissioner for Human Rights, 'UNDP-OHCHR Toolkit for collaboration with National Human Rights Institutions', December 2010, available at: http://www.ohchr.org/Documents/Countries/NHRI/1950-UNDP-UHCHR-Toolkit-LR.pdf.

7 UN GA, Resolution 48/134 of 20 December 1993, Annex, 'Principles relating to the Status of National Institutions' (further: Paris Principles), Preamble.

8 International Coordinating Committee of National Institutions for the Promotion and Protection of Human Rights Statute, adopted by the members of the International Coordinating Committee at its 15th session, held on 14 September 2004, Seoul, Republic of Korea, as amended, available at: www.nhri.ohchr.org. (further: ICC Statute). See also: K. Roberts, 'The Role and Functioning of the International Coordinating Committee of National Human Rights Institutions in International Human Rights Bodies', Chapter 10 in this volume.

9 Section 7 of the ICC Statute. The Asia-Pacific Forum established in 1996 in Australia is the oldest and most developed regional network. The African Coordination Committee of National Institutions was established by the Yaounde Declaration in 1996. The Americas established the Network of National Institutions in Mexico in 2000.

10 For example the Danish Institute for Human Rights. See Ch. Badse, 'The Danish Experience', Chapter 2 in this volume.

11 First European Meeting of National Human Rights Institutions, Strasbourg 7–9 November 1994, available at: http://nhri.ohchr.org/EN/Regional/Europe/Documents/1st%20European%20Meeting%20of%20National%20Human%20Rights%20Institutions.pdf.

independent statutory human rights institutions in the European region as well as cooperation with the Council of Europe, the OSCE and the United Nations, especially the United Nations High Commissioner for Human Rights.[12] The first European Coordinating Committee was duly established with the Danish Centre for Human Rights as the chair.[13]

The third meeting of European NHRIs was held in conjunction with the first round table between the Council of Europe and National Human Rights Institutions in Strasbourg, 16–17 March 2000. At this meeting there was considerable substantive discussion on protection and promotion of economic and social rights and the fight against racism and related discrimination, but there was also acknowledgment that in between the regional meetings, cooperation between the respective institutions had been rather limited.[14] This concern was addressed at the fourth meeting of the Group which took place in Belfast and Dublin, 14–16 November 2002.[15]

At the fourth meeting, European NHRIs adopted Rules of Procedure.[16] The Rules formalised the European Group and set out its membership criteria and methods of operation. The European Group operates on the basis that all NHRIs or aspiring NHRIs may participate in its work as it is considered of benefit to NHRIs that they are able to form part of the network and to share experiences and engage with colleagues. All 'A' status European Group NHRIs are members of the ICC and the other members engage with the ICC as observers.[17]

The European Group adopts a consensus-based approach wherever possible and the Guiding Principles for Activities provide that activities are to be conducted in a collegial manner as well as setting out that:

> a) In the planning and carrying out of any activity, a balance shall be sought between European sub-regions, as well as between different legal systems and the various types of National Institutions;

---

12 Second European Meeting of National Human Rights Institutions, "For the Future", Copenhagen 22 January 1997, available at: http://nhri.ohchr.org/EN/Regional/Europe/Documents/2nd%20European%20Meeting%20of%20National%20Human%20Rights%20Institutions.pdf.

13 See M. Kjærum, 'National Human Rights Institutions Implementing Human Rights', Copenhagen 2003, available at: http://www.humanrights.dk/files/Importerede%20filer/hr/pdf/n_h_r_i_h_fte_eng.pdf.

14 Third European Meeting of National Institutions, Strasbourg, 16–17 March 2000; Council of Europe NHRI(2002)012, Strasbourg, 8 November 2002, available at: http://nhri.ohchr.org/EN/Regional/Europe/Documents/NHRI(2002)012%20E%20-%20Compilation%20of%20speeches.pdf.

15 Fourth European Meeting of National Institutions, Belfast and Dublin, 14–16 November 2002, available at: http://nhri.ohchr.org/EN/Regional/Europe/Pages/4th-European-Meeting-of-National-Human-Rights-Institutions.aspx.

16 Rules of Procedure of the European Regional Group of National Institutions for the Promotion and Protection of Human Rights, adopted in Dublin on 16 November 2002, available at: http://nhri.ohchr.org/EN/Regional/Europe/Documents/European%20Regional%20group%20of%20national%20institutions%20Rules%20of%20procedure%20Rev.%203.pdf.

17 *Ibidem*, Rule 1.

b) The European Regional Group shall conduct its activities in close cooperation with the Council of Europe and other European organisations active in the field of human rights;

c) The activities of the European Regional Group shall benefit from the contributions of non-governmental organisations as well as from civil society in general.[18]

The European Group is headed by a Chair NHRI[19] which is elected by a vote of the A-status NHRIs within the Group.[20] The Chair is supported by a European Coordinating Committee of three other members of the Group,[21] all of whom represent the Group on the ICC Bureau. One member of the Group represents the Group in the Sub-Committee on Accreditation (SCA) of the ICC.[22] In order to ensure fair representation there is a general principle of rotation which applies to the nominations and positions within the European Group and its Coordinating Committee. Appointments take account, on the one hand, of the need for a balanced representation of sub-regions, and, on the other, of the need for rotation, so that all accredited National Institutions shall accede, in turn, to ICC responsibilities. In order for the principle of rotation to be fully applied, appointments are two-year terms that may only be renewed one time.[23]

The Chair is responsible, in a broadly cooperative spirit, for the respect of the principles and rules as established in the present Rules of Procedure; for strategic planning of the work of the Group including proposing initiatives; organising meetings of the Group; collecting information emanating from European organisations and disseminating such information to the European Group; representing the Group at conferences and events; as well as liaising with regional and international bodies including the OHCHR, Council of Europe, the Organisation for Security and Cooperation in Europe and its Office for Democratic Institutions and Human Rights (OSCE-ODIHR) and the EU Fundamental Rights Agency (FRA).[24]

The Chair provides technical assistance for the establishment of new NHRIs in conjunction with the OHCHR as well as in capacity building for existing

18 *Ibidem*, Rule 3.

19 The Scottish Human Rights Commission was elected as Chair in May 2011.

20 A-status NHRIs are NHRIs that are in compliance with the Paris Principles. For a further analysis, see G. de Beco, 'Assessment of the Paris Principles and the ICC Sub-Committee on Accreditation', Chapter 11 in this volume.

21 See Article 1.1 of the ICC Statute. The current members of the European Coordinating Committee are Scotland, Denmark, France and Luxembourg.

22 See Rule 2.1 of the Rules of Procedure for the ICC Sub-Committee on Accreditation, adopted by the members of the International Coordinating Committee at its 15th session, held on 14 September 2004, Seoul, Republic of Korea, as amended, available at: www.nhri.ohchr.org.

23 Rules of Procedure of the European Regional Group of National Institutions for the Promotion and Protection of Human Rights, adopted in Dublin on 16 November 2002, Rule 8.

24 See *infra* section 3 for an overview of the engagement of the European Group and European NHRIs with these bodies.

institutions in association with bodies such as the European Union,[25] OSCE[26] and UNDP.[27]

The European Group meets regularly, with an annual meeting on the fringes of the ICC meeting in Geneva and another meeting attached to a regional or international conference in the latter part of each year. It is the largest of the four regional groups of the ICC with a membership of some 40 members[28] and also contains the most diverse range of NHRI 'types' including human rights commissions, ombuds-institutions, institutes and consultative commissions.[29] In addition, the European Group operates within the most advanced regional human rights structure globally, which requires that NHRIs engage with a broad range of bodies including the OSCE, Council of Europe and EU.[30]

2.1. THE NEED FOR A SECRETARIAT FOR THE EUROPEAN GROUP

The European Group does not currently have a centralised secretariat such as has been established for two of the other regional groups of NHRIs, the Asia-Pacific Forum for NHRIs and the African Group Secretariat. Instead, support for the European Group is coordinated by a member of staff within the Chair NHRI. This is problematic as there are no centralised resources, so the Group relies on the Chair NHRI and those NHRIs who chair working groups[31] being able to divert staff time and resources to coordination and secretariat functions. NHRIs have fixed budgets and demanding domestic mandates. This means the European Group is not able to meet its full potential, and coordination often relies on the goodwill of staff taking on extra responsibilities. The lack of funding for these roles means that travel and administrative costs must be borne by the relevant NHRI from their domestic budget.

A secretariat could provide technical support, act as a focal point for regional and international bodies and civil society with NHRIs, ensure coherence in the provision of support and identify areas where capacity building or other support is needed, coordinate positions and statements of the European Group, engage with

25 See *infra* section 3.2.

26 See *infra* section 3.3.

27 See for example the UNDP-OHCHR Toolkit, loc. cit. *supra* note 6.

28 For an overview of the 36 members of the European Group, see: http://nhri.ohchr.org/EN/Documents/Chart%20of%20the%20Status%20of%20NIs%20(30%20May%202012).pdf. Moreover, Finland, Kosovo, Latvia and Lithuania are in the process of seeking accreditation (October 2012).

29 For an overview of the different types of NHRIs in Europe, see M. Nowak, 'National Human Rights Institutions in Europe: Comparative, European and International Perspectives', Chapter 1 in this volume.

30 See *infra* section 3 for an overview of the engagement of the European Group and European NHRIs with these bodies.

31 See *infra* section 2.2 for an overview of the different working groups of the European Group.

the other regional groups/secretariats and the ICC, and support the European Group Chair.

The value of a regional network has been acknowledged at both the international and regional level. The UN has repeatedly stressed the importance of international cooperation in the field of human rights, and recalled the role played by regional and international associations of national human rights institutions in promoting cooperation and sharing best practice.[32] The European Union's Fundamental Rights Agency in its May 2010 Report on NHRIs in the EU Member States gave its opinion that: 'NHRIs should be supported to contribute effectively to European and international human rights mechanisms [...] [t]his should be done through supporting the establishment of a permanent entity for the European Group of NHRIs [...] on a full time basis [...]'.[33]

Models such as the Asia Pacific Forum of National Human Rights Institutions (APF) which was established in 1996 have demonstrated the wide variety of work that such a secretariat can do:

- Advice: Specialist advice is provided to governments and civil society on the steps involved in establishing independent national human rights institutions, including compliance with the "Paris Principles", operational issues, resourcing and "best practice" models;
- Training: Tailored training programs strengthen the capacity of APF members to carry out their core functions, including investigating and resolving complaints, reviewing laws and policies and delivering human rights education. The APF's current training programs include training on the international human rights system, conducting national inquiries, torture prevention, NHRIs and human rights defenders, and media and communication skills;
- Workshops: Thematic workshops bring together APF members, governments and NGOs to discuss emerging human rights issues and develop national and regional approaches;
- Networks: Professional and issue-based networks support APF members to share information and resources, develop partnerships and establish "best practice" standards;
- Staff exchanges: Country-to-country staff exchanges help develop the individual skills of staff, strengthen links between national institutions and implement specific activities of the APF and its members;

---

32 See UN GA Resolutions 63/169 of 18 December 2008; UN GA Resolution 63/172 of 18 December 2008; UN GA Resolution 64/161 of 18 December 2009; and UN GA Resolution 65/207 of 21 December 2010.

33 FRA, 'National Human Rights Institutions in the EU Member States: Strengthening the Fundamental Rights Architecture in the EU', Vienna, Publication Office of the European Union, 2010, p. 9.

- Annual Meeting: The largest annual human rights gathering in the region, the APF Annual Meeting is the major decision-making forum and a catalyst for developing new programs and initiatives;
- International participation: The APF advocates policy as well as coordinates the participation and collaboration of member institutions in the United Nations, the International Coordinating Committee of National Institutions and other international and regional mechanisms.[34]

The European Group of NHRIs sees the APF model as the "gold standard" and is in the process of trying to replicate the model in Europe. The OHCHR has provided initial funding of approximately €77,500[35] and a number of NHRIs have committed to provide financial contributions to the secretariat. This has allowed the European Group to recruit for a Director to establish the secretariat, but there is still considerable work to do to identify sustainable funding for the Group, particularly in a time of austerity in Europe and when a number of NHRIs are facing funding cuts. This challenge has recently been recognised by the Council of Europe's current Commissioner for Human Rights who used his first comment to raise the issues of the need for human rights protections and highlighted the role of NHRIs.[36]

The APF was established in humble circumstances in 1996 with just four NHRIs and for its first six years it was hosted by the Australian Human Rights Commission. It now enjoys significant financial support. The APF receives its funding from APF's member institutions through membership fees and other financial and "in kind" donations, governments such as the Governments of Australia, New Zealand, Republic of Korea, Sweden and Thailand (often as a result of the direct advocacy of the NHRIs from those States), philanthropic organisations such as the MacArthur Foundation and the RWI, philanthropic individuals and inter-governmental organisations such as OHCHR and UNDP. Its long-term average annual funding is €1.37 million.[37] The Secretariat employs six staff members. It receives additional support through regular staff exchanges involving APF member institutions, as well as hosting student interns from academic institutions.

While the Asia Pacific Forum clearly covers a much larger geographical area and has a very different profile from Europe in terms of population size and diversity across the region, it should be noted that Europe Group has some 40 members compared to the APF's 18.

---

34 See http://www.asiapacificforum.net.

35 $100,000 US Dollars converted at mid-market rates 24 September 2012, see: Asia Pacific Forum of National Human Rights Institutions Annual Report 2010–2011, available at: http://www.asiapacificforum.net.

36 See *infra* section 3.1.3.

37 $1.8 million Australian dollars converted at mid-market rates 24 September 2012. See: Asia Pacific Forum of National Human Rights Institutions Annual Report 2010–2011, available at: http://www.asiapacificforum.net.

Another example which the European Group hopes to emulate is Equinet, the European Network of Equality Bodies, which brings together 37 organisations from 30 European countries, empowered to counteract discrimination. Equinet conducts very similar work to that of the APF. The core income comes from a grant of the European Commission which amounted to €543,286 in 2011, matched funding was met by membership fees of €54,380 and work of staff of the equality bodies valued at €128,816.[38]

Given the commitment of the international and regional organisations to the work of NHRIs and the clear need for a secretariat, it is essential that funding from regional bodies is secured, as well as from national governments committed to the work of NHRIs. Equally the European Group must seek out additional funding from external sources, while always ensuring that its independence is not compromised. One of the strengths of the Paris Principles is that they require proper funding for NHRIs,[39] which should allow them to act without independence being undermined by concern over funding.

2.2. WORKING GROUPS

At the third meeting of European NHRIs, held in 2000, the Chair of the Coordinating Group, Mr Morten Kjaerum of the Danish Centre for Human Rights made a number of proposals in relation to strengthening the Group. One was to develop working groups of professionals on the different substantial issues within the individual institutions.[40]

The European Group developed a number of working groups which consist of staff from NHRIs across the Group, chaired by an NHRI and reporting to the Chair of the European Group. As there is not yet a secretariat for the European Group, the working groups rely on a chair NHRI to coordinate their work. Usually the working groups meet once per year with continued communication through email and phone contact. The engagement of the working groups with regional bodies is discussed below in the relevant sections.

2.2.1. Asylum and Immigration Working Group

The expert Working Group on Asylum and Migration was established in Berlin in January 2008 and is led by the German Institute for Human Rights and the Belgian Centre for Equal Opportunities and Opposition to Racism. The Working

[38] Equinet Annual Report 2011, available at: http://www.equineteurope.org/Equinet-Annual-Report-2011.

[39] See further: G. de Beco, 'Assessment of the Paris Principles and the ICC Sub-Committee on Accreditation', Chapter 11 in this volume.

[40] Third European Meeting of National Institutions, Strasbourg, 16–17 March 2000; Council of Europe NHRI(2002)012, Strasbourg, 8 November 2002.

Group has contributed to a number of EU initiatives on asylum and immigration including developing a common position on non-removable persons[41] and a common position on the common European asylum system.[42]

2.2.2. Legal Working Group (LWG)

The LWG was established in March 2010 and is chaired by the Irish Human Rights Commission. The LWG has a mandate to engage with the reform of the European Court of Human Rights and *amicus curiae* interventions before the European Court. The LWG has also developed web-based accessible information for individual applicants to the European Court of Human Rights.[43]

2.2.3. CRPD Working Group

The CRPD Working Group was established in May 2010 and is chaired by the Equality and Human Rights Commission of Great Britain. The objectives of the CRPD Working Group are all related to the support and promotion of the ratification and implementation of the UN Convention on the Rights of Persons with Disabilities (CRPD). More specifically, the objectives are:

- To identify, develop, share and promote good practice guidance on the role and actions of NHRIs across Europe in promoting, protecting and monitoring implementation of the Convention in the European Group and internationally.
- To work together to influence the interpretation and implementation of the UN Convention and the development of jurisprudence in our own countries, by the Convention Expert Committee and by the European Court of Human Rights and the Court of Justice of the European Union.
- To promote and support the most effective use of the Convention's Optional Protocol (recognising that domestic legislative processes must be exhausted before the Optional Protocol can be used).
- To assist the future monitoring framework to be set up by the European Union as a party to the Convention.
- To promote the implementation of the Convention throughout Europe and by the European Union.

---

41 See: http://www.diversiteit.be/diversiteit/files/File//persberichten/EG%20NHRI%20common%20position%20non-removable%20persons.pdf.

42 See: http://www.diversiteit.be/diversiteit/files/File//Migratie/2012/120315%20EG%20-%20CEAS%20EN%20final.DOC.

43 See www.scottishhumanrights.com. For a further analysis of the interaction with the European Court of Human Rights, see *infra* section 3.1.2.

2.2.4. *Human Rights Education Working Group*

In 2011 the European Group agreed to create a human rights education working group to actively identify opportunities for engagement with regional and international organisations in the area of human rights including:

- Opportunities to make submissions to initiatives at regional and international levels;
- Opportunities for NHRI representation at meetings and events;
- Opportunities for statements at the Human Rights Council and other fora.

The Working Group will also develop a compilation of good practice in human rights education and training from the work of European Group members, which can be shared with all members of the Group and partner organisations.

2.3. PROPOSALS FOR OTHER WORKING GROUPS

During its recent meetings the European Group has identified a need for an accreditation support group. Of the 40 NHRIs in the European Group, only 22 are accredited as fully compliant with the Paris Principles. As has been discussed in earlier chapters, the Paris Principles recognise that 'it is the right of each State to choose the framework that is best suited to its particular needs at the national level', but they also provide the framework that forms the basis of an NHRI.[44] Early in its existence, the ICC set up a Sub-Committee on Accreditation (SCA) with the task of conducting assessments of NHRIs against the criteria of the Paris Principles.[45] All NHRIs believe in the importance of thorough assessment of compliance with the Paris Principles as an essential aspect of the protection of the integrity and legitimacy of all NHRIs and to maintain the status of NHRIs within the UN system. Setting up A-status institutions in all European States is an important element in creating an effective European human rights architecture.

The process of accreditation has become more robust over time, and now requires significant effort on behalf of NHRIs in terms of providing evidence of their compliance with the Paris Principles. While the OHCHR offers advice to all institutions in terms of applying for accreditation, there is a wealth of experience in building NHRIs in the European Group not properly exploited at present. The European Group coordinator is able to sit as an observer in the SCA, but as has been discussed earlier, this requires significant resource commitment from the Chair. The working group would be greatly served by some staff capacity within

---

[44] See in particular, M. Nowak, 'National Human Rights Institutions in Europe: Comparative, European and International Perspectives', Chapter 1 in this volume.

[45] See G. de Beco, 'Assessment of the Paris Principles and the ICC Sub-Committee on Accreditation', Chapter 11 in this volume.

the European secretariat dedicated to coordinating mutual help between NHRIs and countries willing to set up a NHRI and to giving advice to European NHRIs preparing their applications for (re-)accreditation. It would also be assisted by the creating of a support network made up of NHRIs with particular expertise in the accreditation system.

3. ENGAGEMENT WITH REGIONAL BODIES

A major challenge for the interaction of the European Group with the regional mechanisms is that the size of the regional human rights framework in Europe means that there are a large number of initiatives and projects being undertaken in the human rights field, and therefore there can be multiple calls on the time and resources of NHRIs. It is essential that NHRIs are seen as essential human rights actors, not simply recipients of training. Over recent years the European Group has undertaken a number of initiatives to improve cooperation and performance with regional bodies.

In September 2008 the European Group and the Council of Europe Commissioner for Human Rights organised a round table which was also attended by the members of European ombuds-institutions, the Human Rights Commissioner of the Council of Europe and members of his office, a representative of the OHCHR, the Director of the European Union's Fundamental Rights Agency, as well as individual experts. The 'Dublin Declaration' created following this event set out practical recommendations and conclusions that have given a focus to the strengthening of cooperation and performance towards regional bodies:

> 'I. Cooperation of NHRIs with other human rights actors
>
> 1. The representatives of European NHRIs acknowledged the necessity of enhanced cooperation with other human rights actors, especially at the national level, in order to jointly build an effective human rights architecture in Europe.
> 2. The representatives agreed that synergies can best be achieved by respecting the different roles and mandates of the various human rights actors. The Paris Principles constitute the normative frame of reference, as well as the benchmark for the accreditation and re-accreditation of NHRIs.
> 3. The representatives see themselves as the link between the international (i.e. global and regional) human rights protection system and the national level of implementation. They will therefore continue and enhance their cooperation with the UN treaty bodies, the UN Human Rights Council as well as with the Council of Europe mechanisms.
> 4. The representatives agreed that they should also cooperate with the recently established EU Fundamental Rights Agency. One method of institutional cooperation could be membership of NHRIs within the Management Board of the Agency.

5. The representatives acknowledged the need for international solidarity to support national human rights structures operating under dangerous circumstances. Avenues for more effective international support measures should be explored.'[46]

This was followed in December 2009 at a meeting supported by the OHCHR where the European Group Chair made a series of proposals for practical areas for greater engagement between the European Group and the regional mechanisms. These were:

- Early involvement of NHRIs on regional initiatives including the preparation of new regional Conventions, principles or policy;
- NHRIs promoting best practice initiatives between UN and regional mechanisms which may act as templates for the promotion of human rights in other regions;
- Joint work between NHRIs and regional mechanisms on awareness raising and educational activities;
- Use of NHRI expertise and experience by regional mechanisms in monitoring missions and capacity building for national human rights mechanisms;
- Involvement by regional mechanisms of NHRIs during visits to states, and follow-up activities;
- Participation or observer status given by regional mechanisms to NHRIs at meetings, conferences and events;
- And the formal recognition of the role of Paris Principle compliant NHRIs – as recognised by the UN – by regional mechanisms.[47]

3.1. ENGAGEMENT WITH THE COUNCIL OF EUROPE

3.1.1. General Observations on the Engagement with the Council of Europe

As discussed above,[48] the Council of Europe has been working with European NHRIs since before the establishment of the European Group and hosted the first regional meeting of European NHRIs in 1994. NHRIs welcomed the Council of Europe's contribution to the efforts to create and strengthen NHRIs carried out by the Steering Committee for Human Rights in October 1994 on 'aspects relating to national commissions on human rights'.[49]

46 Declaration of the European Group of National Human Rights Institutions – Conclusions on the 5th Round Table, Dublin, 16–17 September 2008.
47 Report of the Chair of the European Group of National Human Rights Institutions, ICC 23, 22–25 March 2010.
48 See *supra* section 2.
49 First European Meeting of National Human Rights Institutions, loc. cit. *supra* note 11.

The European Group has always prioritised the significance of the human rights framework of the Council of Europe. In addition to the European Convention on Human Rights and the European Court of Human Rights, this framework includes *inter alia* the European Committee on the Prevention of Torture (CPT), the European Commission against Racism and Intolerance (ECRI), the European Social Charter, the European Convention against Trafficking of Human Beings and the Framework Convention for the Protection of National Minorities.

On 5 December 2000 the Director of the Danish Centre for Human Rights requested observer status for European NHRIs at the Council of Europe's Steering Committee for Human Rights (CDDH) which was duly approved in 2001 and European NHRIs have been actively engaged ever since.[50]

Over recent years the Council of Europe has focused its engagement with NHRIs within the broader definition of 'National Human Rights Structures' (NHRSs) developed as part of the Peer-to-Peer project in association with the European Union.[51] This programme was developed in 2008 and 2009 with an aim of providing an active network of independent non-judicial National Human Rights Structures (NHRS) compliant with the Paris Principles, with special focus on non-EU Member States.

The Peer-to-Peer Project sought to enable national structures to improve their performances in terms of:

- Raising human rights awareness in their countries;
- Detecting potential or existing human rights problems;
- Proceeding to efficient investigations where this is in their mandate;
- Engaging in constructive dialogue with the authorities to avert or solve problems of human rights protection;
- Triggering rapid mobilisation of international partners if necessary.

The programme consisted of the organisation of workshops for specialised staff members of the NHRS, with accompanying training materials. In addition, missions were organised to countries where interest in setting up a NHRS is expressed, in coordination with other international organisations and with the participation of existing national structures.

In using a broader grouping to try to engage as widely as possible, the Council of Europe puts NHRIs together with a range of other national bodies who are not accredited in compliance with the Paris Principles, such as national ombudsmen,[52] thematic ombudsmen (such as Children's Ombudsmen)[53] and

---

50 Steering Committee for Human Rights, Bureau of the Steering Committee for Human Rights, (CDDH-BU), 57th Meeting, 8–9 February 2001, CDDH-BU (2001) 1, Appendix IV.

51 See: http://www.coe.int/t/commissioner/Activities/themes/nhrspeertopeer_en.asp.

52 For more information on the International Ombudsman Institute (IOI), see: www.theioi.org.

53 For more information on the European Network of Ombudspersons for Children (ENOC), see: www.crin.org/enoc/.

Equality Bodies set up under EU legislation.[54] The bringing together of all groups working to promote and protect human rights allows for a wider spread of information and coordination across a larger number of bodies. NHRIs already work cooperatively at both national and regional level with these other groups, in some cases operating as a merged body covering a number of roles.[55] However, there is a risk that the worthy aim of wider inclusion actually ends up weakening the framework of promotion and protection of human rights if institutions which are not compliant with the Paris Principles are treated the same as those that are. Since there is a UN standard that is globally recognised and supported by the infrastructure of the ICC, it needs to be used, valued and understood.

Much of the engagement has focused on training and capacity building, such as the Peer-to-Peer project which has more recently focused on workshops with the European National Preventative Mechanisms under OPCAT rather than substantive work on the policies and programmes of the Council of Europe.

The European Group regularly engages with the European Commission against Racism and Intolerance (ECRI) and the European Committee for the Prevention of Torture and Inhuman or Degrading Treatment or Punishment (CPT), by attending meetings and conferences, but lacks the capacity and opportunity to engage fully with the implementation of Council of Europe programmes.

Because of the lack of a continuous exchange between European NHRIs and the Council of Europe, it has been difficult to be admitted to some negotiations as an observer. When the European Group has participated in the negotiations on international instruments for the protection of human rights, NHRIs have been able to demonstrate valuable contributions to the process. The latest example is its work within the process for drafting the Council of Europe Convention on Violence against Women and Domestic Violence which was adopted on 12 April 2011.[56] The Group, represented by the German Institute for Human Rights, was granted observer status in the drafting committee in 2010.[57] The European Group presented a substantial statement and recommendations on the draft convention, stressing that the focus of the Convention should be on all forms of

54 For more information on EU equality bodies, see: the European Network of Equality Bodies, Equinet, www.equineteurope.org/.

55 See: Equinet, 'Equality Bodies and National Human Rights Institutions – Making the Link to Maximise Impact', November 2011, available at: http://www.equineteurope.org/136462.html.

56 Istanbul, 11.V.2011, http://conventions.coe.int/Treaty/EN/Treaties/Html/210.htm.

57 See Report of the 4th meeting Ad Hoc Committee on Preventing and Combating Violence against Women and Domestic Violence (CAHVIO), Strasbourg, CAHVIO (2010) 1 rev, 22–24 February 2010, available at: http://www.coe.int/t/dghl/standardsetting/violence/CAHVIO%20_2010_%201%20rev.pdf; Report of the 5th meeting of CAHVIO, Strasbourg, CAHVIO (2010) 11, 29 June- 2 July 2010, available at: http://www.coe.int/t/dghl/standardsetting/violence/CAHVIO_2010_11_en.pdf.

violence against women in times of peace and armed conflict.[58] Furthermore, the European Group called for a comprehensive human rights approach throughout the Convention, a strong and flexible monitoring mechanism established with due regard to the existing human rights system in the Council of Europe and the explicit inclusion of NHRIs as actors in the text of the Convention. Through the considerable efforts of the German Institute for Human Rights, the European Group has achieved several important insertions into the Convention, including an express reference to NHRIs in the text of the Convention as actors in awareness raising and monitoring (articles 13 and 68 of the Convention) and the inclusion of some Group proposals on the monitoring mechanism, in particular the need for an urgent inquiry procedure.

3.1.2. European Court of Human Rights

a) Reform of the European Court of Human Rights

One area where NHRIs have played a substantive role in the Council of Europe's work is the ongoing process of reform of the European Court of Human Rights. The reform of the Court begun as early as 2001 where it was the subject of a new protocol to the European Convention on Human Rights, Protocol No. 14.[59] This was opened for signature in 2004 and entered into force on 1 June 2010. Its purpose is to guarantee the long term efficiency of the Court by optimising the screening and processing of applications. It envisages, among other measures, the creation of new judicial formations for the simplest cases, a new admissibility criterion (the existence of "significant disadvantage") and introduces a nine-year non-renewable term of office for judges.

The European Group has contributed to the High Level Conferences in Interlaken, Izmir, and Brighton, and attends as an observer at the Council of Europe Steering Committee for Human Rights (CDDH) and its subcommittees, including the Committee of Experts on the Reform of the Court (DH-GDR), the Committee of Experts on a Simplified Amendment Procedure (DH-PS), the Committee of Experts for the Protection of Human Rights (DH-PR), and the ad-hoc working group on EU Accession (CDDH-UE).

The High Level Conference in Interlaken, Switzerland, took place in February 2010. The purpose of the conference was to reaffirm States' commitment to the protection of human rights in Europe and to draw up a roadmap for the future development of the Court. The European Group made an oral statement on the Declaration expressing the willingness of National Human Rights Institutions

---

58 The full statement of the European Group can be accessed on the website of the German Institute for Human Rights: http://www.institut-fuer-menschenrechte.de/de/themen/frauenrechte/schwerpunkte/konvention-gegen-gewalt-gegen-frauen.html.

59 Protocol No. 14 to the Convention for the Protection of Human Rights and Fundamental Freedoms, amending the control system of the Convention, Strasbourg, 13.V.2004.

throughout Europe to contribute to reform efforts while also urging that the independence of the Court be preserved:

> 'NHRIs are fundamentally different from both States and NGOs, and as such we represent a "third dimension". NHRIs work to prevent violations at the domestic level, encouraging domestic remedies and monitoring implementation of European Court judgments. Our areas of work range from legislative and policy review, follow-up of international obligations, monitoring, research, education and awareness-raising, to investigation and litigation functions. NHRIs thus play a key role in identifying and seeking to address structural and systemic deficiencies in their own countries and of the European system as a whole, thus contributing to national implementation of the Convention.
>
> It is important to acknowledge the great success enjoyed by the European Court to date. It is also key to say that any reform of the Court should be guided by the need to reduce the number of violations of the Convention by States at source, while ensuring the right of individual application remains the cornerstone of reforms.
>
> The European Group welcomes the recognition of the role of NHRIs in the Interlaken Declaration and separately the reference to consultation with civil society on effective means to implement the Action Plan. This should ensure greater transparency and participation and allow relevant stakeholders to undertake their roles in contributing to the success of our common endeavours.
>
> Mandated as we are by domestic law, NHRIs stand ready to work with Member States and the organs of the Council of Europe in all relevant stages, from the identification of the effectiveness of domestic remedies, the identification of pilot judgments, to the monitoring of execution of European Court judgments and the elaboration of domestic reform measures to address identified gaps in law or practice and thus ensure conformity with the Convention's provisions.'[60]

The Interlaken Conference was followed by a second conference in 2011 in Izmir, Turkey. The conference aimed at following up and maintaining the momentum of the process of reform of the supervisory machinery set up by the European Convention on Human Rights. The Izmir Declaration builds on Interlaken and deals with the issues of inadmissible cases and the question raised in relation to 'subsidiarity'. As with Interlaken, the European Group of National Human Rights Institutions had observer status at the High Level Ministerial Conference and made an oral statement on the Declaration expressing concern that national implementation was insufficiently addressed and that the independence of the Court should be maintained.[61]

At the latest High Level Conference in Brighton in April 2012, the European Group made a statement expressing that the right of individual petition and the

[60] See: http://www.eda.admin.ch/etc/medialib/downloads/edazen/topics/europa/euroc/inter.Par.0001.File.tmp/h-inf_2010_5.pdf.

[61] See: http://www.coe.int/t/dghl/standardsetting/conferenceizmir/Speeches/Speech%20NHRI.pdf.

independence of the Court must remain the cornerstones of the Convention system. The Group also cautioned against introducing further admissibility criteria, particularly in circumstances where the full effects of Protocol 14 have not yet been realised, and the over emphasis on the terms 'margin of appreciation' and 'subsidiarity' in the draft Declaration, stressing that States which faithfully ensure domestic compliance and remedies can have no concerns about undue Court oversight. The Group advised caution against proposals to limit the power of the Court to grant just satisfaction and welcomed the increased attention to the role of NHRIs in the implementation of the Interlaken Action Plan.[62]

In the Brighton Declaration all 47 Member States of the Council of Europe reaffirmed the need to co-operate with NHRIs[63] and to consider establishing them where this has not already been done.[64] This specific reference to NHRIs rather than NHRSs gives an indication of the developing understanding of the special role that NHRIs play and is a further recognition that NHRIs can provide a unique contribution to national efforts to protect and promote human rights.

Throughout the process European NHRIs have recognised the need to work at both the regional level, engaging the Council of Europe in the reform process, and at the local level, placing their role in implementing the Interlaken Declaration by working with states and striving to ensure that applicants are better informed of the admissibility criteria. This has been done through website guidelines,[65] engaging in deeper review of the execution of judgments process, holding roundtable information sessions on the reform of the Court, disseminating information on the Court and recent case law of prominence, in addition to the legislative, awareness and/or litigation functions of NHRIs.

Throughout the reform process NHRIs have focused on ensuring the recognition of the importance of national implementation, requiring national authorities to take responsibility through effective measures to prevent violations and ensure effective remedies. The European Group has continued to argue that national implementation, along with practical initiatives on execution and promotion in combination with the measures being implemented by the Court in addressing the backlog of applications, create the possibility of deepening Member States' commitments to prevention of abuses through strengthening domestic systems on remedies, coupled with Council of Europe oversight.

Despite the commitment by Member States to the role of the Court and to national implementation, the European Group remains concerned at some reform proposals:

---

62 See: http://www.scottishhumanrights.com/news/latestnews/article/brighton2012news.

63 High Level Conference on the Future of the European Court of Human Rights, Brighton Declaration, 20 April 2012, available at: http://hub.coe.int/en/20120419-brighton-declaration/, para. 4.

64 *Ibidem*, para. 9(c)(i).

65 See, for example, the website of the Scottish Human Rights Commission, available at: www.scottishhumanrights.com.

'There will always remain situations where the oversight of the Court is necessary to the application of Convention standards. The right of individual petition and the independence of the Court must thus remain the cornerstones of the Convention system. In light of this, the European Group cautions against introducing further admissibility criteria, particularly in circumstances where the full effects of Protocol 14 have not yet been realised.

We also caution against over emphasis on the terms "margin of appreciation" and "subsidiarity" in the draft Declaration. These are concepts underpinned by the jurisprudence of the Court in the context of individual cases. It is in the nature of the judicial function to apply principles consistently and the Court should not be instructed in regard to how to apply legal principles. States which faithfully ensure domestic compliance and remedies can have no concerns about undue Court oversight. In this regard, we caution against proposals to limit the power of the Court to grant just satisfaction.'[66]

The Council of Europe is currently in the process of drafting two additional protocols.

Protocol 15 to the European Convention on Human Rights, will include a reference to the margin of appreciation and principle of subsidiarity in the Preamble to the Convention[67] and will introduce a reduction of time limit for applying to the Court.[68] Protocol 16 will empower the Grand Chamber of the Court to give opinions at the request of domestic courts against whose decisions there is no judicial remedy under national law.[69] The European Group will continue to engage with this process through submissions to the CDDH and its subcommittees.

b) Amicus Curiae[70]

Along with the work on the reform of the Court, a number of European NHRIs make *amicus curiae* interventions in cases from their own State. The European Group also began making collective interventions in 2008 as *amicus curiae* to the case of *D.D. v Lithuania*[71] a case relating the procedures of civil commitment to psychiatric institutions and issues of capacity. The Group drew to the Court's

66 The intervention of the European Group can be found at the website of the Scottish Human Rights Commission: http://www.scottishhumanrights.com/news/latestnews/article/brighton2012news.

67 Paragraph 12(b) of the Brighton Declaration.

68 Paragraph 15 (a) of the Brighton Declaration.

69 Paragraph 12(d) of the Brighton Declaration.

70 For an extensive analysis of the potential roles of NHRIs in relation to the proceedings of the European Court of Human Rights, see: A. Buyse, 'The Court's Ears and Arms: National Human Rights Institutions and the European Court of Human Rights', Chapter 8 in this volume.

71 *D.D. v Lithuania*, Application No. 13469/06, Judgment, Strasbourg, 14 February 2012; for the submission of the European Group, see: http://www.scottishhumanrights.com/application/resources/documents/EuroGroupthirdpartyinterventionlithuania2012.doc.

attention the normative changes exemplified by the UN Convention on the Rights of Persons with Disabilities, relevant international principles and European law – a point which featured prominently in the judgment. This was the first such application before an international court made by a regional grouping of NHRIs.

The power for third parties to intervene in this way is provided for by Article 36.2 of the Convention which provides that 'the President of the Court may, in the interest of the proper administration of justice, invite any High Contracting Party which is not a party to the proceedings or any person concerned who is not the applicant to submit written comments or take part in hearings' and governed by Rule 44.3 of the Rules of the Court.

Following on from the European Group submission in *DD v Lithuania*, the Group decided, at its meeting in September 2008, to introduce a procedure for monitoring cases before the European Court of Human Rights on which the Group might make a submission. ECtHR cases involving 'priority' areas of concern are tracked and reviewed on a periodic basis in an attempt to identify strategic cases suitable for an *amicus curiae* intervention. These priority areas are: disability rights; data protection; asylum/immigration; rule of law/counter-terrorism.

It was agreed that the then Chair of the European Group, the Irish Human Rights Commission, would track newly communicated cases and compile a register with a view to considering whether NHRIs or the European Group itself should seek to intervene before the Court as an *amicus curiae*. This register is then communicated to the European Group on a monthly basis. In March 2010, when the Legal Working Group was established, this responsibility transferred to the chair of the LWG, which also happened to be the Irish Human Rights Commission.

Where a case meets the criteria for third-party intervention to the ECtHR, as agreed by the European Group (namely that it is a priority area of concern for the European Group with a systemic human rights issue arising and an *amicus curiae* intervention may be feasible and appropriate), the LWG will refer the case to the relevant NHRI for the respondent State in the case, or to the European Group with a draft proposal where no NHRI exists in the respondent State. It is of course open to the relevant NHRI to make a third-party application for intervention on its own behalf.

In 2012 the Group made a second intervention in the case of *Gauer v France*,[72] a case relating to the enforced sterilisation of intellectually disabled women. This type of cooperation with the Court allows NHRIs from across the region to assist the judiciary by drawing on comparative experience in a number of jurisdictions. However, in the *Gauer* case there were some initial procedural issues where the

[72] *Gauer and others v France* (Application No. 61521/08). Written Comments by the European Group of National Human Rights Institutions Pursuant to Article 36§2 of the European Convention on Human Rights and Rule 44§3 of the Rules of the European Court of Human Rights', 16 August 2011.The European Group submission can be found at http://www.cncdh.fr/IMG/pdf/European_Group_NHRIs_third_party_intervention_Gauer_v_France.pdf.

Court asked the NHRIs to join their submission to one being submitted by a number of civil society organisations. While NHRIs always work closely with civil society, they are not civil society actors, so it was important that the NHRIs were able to persuade the Court that the submissions should remain separate. There is a temptation to try to put NHRIs into existing classifications. To do so would not only undermine the status of NHRIs, but it would also miss an important opportunity to develop links between the international and domestic systems. Therefore the Group engaged the support of the Council of Europe Commissioner for Human Rights and appealed directly to the President of the Court to ensure there was a clear understanding of the status of NHRIs.

3.1.3. Council of Europe Commissioner of Human Rights

Successive Council of Europe Commissioners of Human Rights have made working with National Human Rights Structures a priority of their work. The current Commissioner used his first Human Rights Comment to focus on how National Human Rights Structures can help mitigate the effects of austerity measures by detecting emerging issues, prioritising vulnerable groups through outreach work and site visits, organising special telephone hotlines, providing legal assistance and representation in courts, and drawing the attention of the broader public and politicians to their plight. He highlighted the need for a proactive approach commenting that 'effective protection of human rights at national level requires good laws and efficient judiciaries – but also strong, independent national human rights structures (NHRSs). This need is especially evident in times of crisis and austerity'.[73] The Commissioner cited examples of good work from NHRIs in Portugal, Spain, Scotland and the UK. However, he also raised concerns that:

> 'Many NHRSs have seen their operational capacities curtailed through severe budget and staff cuts, the closure of regional offices, or the merger of various bodies into overarching structures that are not as focussed or accessible as the bodies they have replaced.
>
> NHRSs in Greece, Ireland, Latvia and the UK, for example, have faced cuts to their budgets or staff which may hinder their effectiveness. In some countries, such as Spain and Slovakia, regional ombudsmen or decentralised offices have been forced to close, thereby complicating individual's access to complaint mechanisms.
>
> The crisis may also represent an obstacle for countries which still have to put in place a nation-wide human rights structure compliant with the principles of

[73] Council of Europe Commissioner for Human Rights, Nils Muiznieks, 'National Human Rights Structures can help the effects of effects of austerity measures', May 2012, available at: http://www.coe.int/t/commissioner/News/2012/120531HRC_en.asp.

independence, effectiveness and competence adopted by the United Nations in 1993.

It is therefore necessary that Governments, particularly in countries undergoing serious austerity, involve NHRSs at all stages of the budget process. They can provide expert advice on the groups that need the most protection, on the impact of various policy measures and on the more general human rights consequences of the crisis, which shows no signs of abating in many European countries.'[74]

This issue of 'human rights in the time of austerity' is one of the key challenges facing Europe at present and it is essential that NHRIs and regional bodies cooperate to address it. They can do this by increasing partnership working to make best use of available resources, but also by supporting each other to oppose cuts to essential budgets, or reforms that would have a serious impact on the ability of bodies to promote and protect human rights.

3.2. ENGAGEMENT WITH THE EUROPEAN UNION AND THE EUROPEAN UNION AGENCY FOR FUNDAMENTAL RIGHTS

3.2.1. European Union[75]

There has been significant growth of human rights related legislation within the EU in recent years. The entry in force of the Lisbon Treaty means this increase is certain to continue, especially in the areas of asylum, migration, and criminal law. It also affects the EU's neighbouring states in Europe.

The Court of Justice of the European Union is likely to face a growing number of human rights issues that will benefit from third party interventions by European NHRIs (as the work of the ECtHR has benefited from them in the past). In addition, the developments in the European fundamental rights architecture, such as the accession of the European Union to the European Convention on Human Rights and the emergence of important new human rights actors, such as the EU Commissioner for Justice, Fundamental Rights, and Citizenship in 2010 and the EU Special Representative on Human Rights in 2012, demonstrate the growing importance of human rights discussions within the EU.

The European Parliament issued a resolution on 14 January 2009 on the Situation of Fundamental Rights in the European Union 2004–2008, urging

[74] *Ibidem.*

[75] For an analysis of the potential for more structured integration of NHRIs in EU human rights policy, see J. Wouters, K. Meuwissen and A. Barros, Chapter 9 in this volume.

Member States to set up NHRIs and ensure their independence, in light of the important preventative function which their work entails.[76]

The European Group Chair met with the Vice-President of the European Commission, Viviane Reding, in Brussels on 15 November 2010. The Vice-President expressed her support for the establishment of NHRIs in EU Member States that do not already have a NHRI and indicated that she would also encourage the strengthening of NHRIs where they do exist. In particular, two specific areas were proposed where there could be engagement as first steps by members of the Group:

- Regular contact with European Commission services, including the possibility of an annual meeting. This proposal was greeted positively.
- Human rights proofing of EU draft legislation. The Vice-President indicated that she felt this would be best carried out by NHRIs at the national level in terms of human rights proofing laws giving effect to EU legislation. Including the European Group formally at the consultative phase at EU level would not be possible, but there may be ways for the Group to engage in the future and in particular the possibility of NHRIs contributing to the process of the new EU Annual Report on Fundamental Rights in the future was discussed.[77]

In follow up to this meeting, the Group has worked with the Directorate General for Justice (DG Justice) to explore the following possibilities for the next stage of engagement between the European Commission and the European Group:

- Possibility for a structured process for flagging upcoming green paper public consultations to the European Group.
- Possibility of structured dialogue on the Commission's annual report with the Group and consideration to be given to convening a meeting with the Group in advance of the Commission's next annual report.
- Consideration to holding a seminar with the LWG to explore case handling practices and procedures at the national level and implications of this at community level and vice-versa.
- Consideration to be given to how the European Group might assist with the Commission's communication and awareness strategy in promoting the Charter of Fundamental Rights with the public.[78]

---

76 European Parliament Resolution of 14 January 2009 on the Situation of Fundamental Rights in the European Union 2004–2008, A6-0479/2008, para. 16.

77 Report of the Chair of the European Group of National Human Rights Institutions covering the period March 2010 to March 2011, 24th Session of The International Coordinating Committee of NHRIs, Geneva, 16–19 May 2011.

78 *Ibidem*. See also J. Wouters, K. Meuwissen, and A. Barros, Chapter 9 in this volume.

Lack of capacity has meant that the European Group's engagement with the subcommittee on Human Rights of the European Parliament (DROI) has been limited. Since it was reconstituted in 2004 the DROI has become an important European platform for the defence of human rights worldwide. The European Group's engagement has focused on specific thematic topics, although moves are underway to develop a closer relationship with the subcommittee. The DROI recently commissioned a study on the 'Role of National Human Rights Institutions in the implementation of the UN Guiding Principles on Business and Human Rights', and has organised two hearings on the issue.[79] Business and Human Rights is an important issue for NHRIs and was the topic of the 10th Biennial Conference of the ICC which resulted in the Edinburgh Declaration calling for more national and international monitoring of businesses' compliance with human rights law; that advice should be given to companies, governments, campaigners and individuals about corporate responsibility; and that institutions themselves have an important role to play in supporting companies and victims of potential human rights violations.[80]

However there is still no EU Directive specifically for NHRIs and human rights such as exists for Equality bodies. Moreover, the EU Strategic Framework and Action Plan on Human Rights and Democracy, Council of the European Union doesn't mention NHRIs.[81]

The European Commission's Technical Assistance and Information Exchange Instrument (TAIEX) supports partner countries with regard to the approximation, application and enforcement of EU legislation including the creation of NHRIs in compliance with the Paris Principles.[82] A number of experts from NHRIs have been involved in TAIEX programmes. There is significant opportunity in linking the work of the TAIEX programme to other capacity building in relation to NHRIs. Given the commitments of all of the regional bodies discussed, as well as UN bodies such as OHCHR and UNDP, to having strong NHRIs across wider Europe, there is a need for better coordination of programmes aimed at creating and building capacity of NHRIs.

3.2.2. *European Union Agency for Fundamental Rights*

Unlike the other regional bodies, the Fundamental Rights Agency (FRA) is younger than the majority of NHRIs. EU NHRIs were involved in the creation of the FRA having worked with the European Monitoring Centre on Racism and

79 See http://www.europarl.europa.eu/committees/en/droi/home.html#menuzone.

80 For more information, see the website of the Scottish Commission on Human Rights: http://www.scottishhumanrights.com/international/biennial/edinburghdec.

81 EU Strategic Framework and Action Plan on Human Rights and Democracy, Council of the European Union, Luxembourg, 25 June 2012, 11855/12 See: http://www.consilium.europa.eu/uedocs/cms_data/docs/pressdata/EN/foraff/131181.pdf.

82 See http://ec.europa.eu/enlargement/taiex/dyn/activities/justice_en.jsp.

Xenophobia which preceded it. They have actively engaged with the FRA since its establishment in 2007. This engagement is assisted in part by the recognition of NHRIs within the Regulation founding the FRA, which provides that the Agency shall cooperate with NHRIs among others.[83]

The European Group holds annual meetings with the FRA, which provide the opportunity to exchange information and discuss work being carried out both by the FRA and NHRIs and to plan and reflect on important European and international developments. The FRA has actively sought the involvement of NHRIs in its programmes providing key contacts for NHRIs across all of its work streams. The FRA has assigned staff to engage with the working groups of the European Group as well as organising regular staff level communication with the coordinator of the European Group and between the Director of the FRA and the Chair of the European Group. The FRA also communicates directly with NHRIs, through regular email updates to ensure that FRA research, tools and resources are made available to NHRIs.

EU NHRIs are invited to input into the Annual Work Programme of the Agency, and have commented on FRA's Multi-Annual Framework which will guide the FRA's work for the coming years. In relation to the latest Multi-Annual Framework the European Group made a number of comments which it hopes will be included, such as the need for robust and independent collection and analysis of information and data on the human rights impact of both police cooperation and judicial cooperation.[84]

The European Group commented on the way in which the rights of Roma were to be protected and while acknowledging the creation of the European Institute for Gender Equality (EIGE) and its mandate, expressed the importance that the category of sex/gender remain within the list of grounds of discrimination in the draft multiannual framework for FRA.[85] Not only is discrimination on the ground of sex/gender a major human rights concern, but also discrimination on other grounds cannot be adequately analysed and addressed without taking gender inequalities and intersectional discrimination into consideration. Thus, a duplication of work between EIGE and FRA should be avoided by good inter-agency coordination and cooperation rather than by restricting FRA's thematic framework.

The European Group also raised the issue that the Multiannual Framework could reflect the potential of the FRA to perform a particular role with regard to

---

83 Council Regulation (EC) No. 168/2007 of 15 February 2007 establishing a European Union Agency for Fundamental Rights, Art. 12(1)(a).

84 Statement of the European Group of National Human Rights Institutions on the proposal for a Council decision establishing a Multiannual Framework for the European Union Agency for Fundamental Rights for 2013–2017.

85 *Ibidem.*

the independent monitoring of the UN Convention on the Rights of Persons with Disabilities (CRPD) within the EU.[86]

Further the European Group referred to indivisibility and interrelatedness of human rights, enshrined in UN human rights instruments and the EU Charter on Fundamental Rights. As such, FRA's area of work should explicitly encompass economic, social and cultural rights. The relevance of these rights is emphasised by current times where the financial and economic crisis deeply affects people in their everyday lives. It is this type of cooperation and open dialogue that is the key to strengthening the relationship between NHRIs and regional bodies.

In 2010 the Agency published a report on NHRIs in EU Member States. In its report, the Agency gave its opinion that all EU Member States should have NHRIs with 'a sufficient level of independence, powers, and a mandate related to the full spectrum of rights[...]', it further recommended that NHRIs be equipped with 'strong preventative powers' and be 'sufficiently resourced'.[87] In October 2012 the Agency published a handbook on the establishment and accreditation of National Human Rights Institutions, which a number of NHRIs contributed to.[88] In December 2012, NHRIs from across Europe joined with policy makers, experts and practitioners from across the EU at the FRA's Fundamental Rights Conference on 'Ensuring Access to Justice in Times of Economic Crisis'. The conference explored how we can turn the time of fiscal consolidation into an opportunity for innovation, positive harmonisation and reform.

3.3. ORGANIZATION FOR SECURITY AND COOPERATION IN EUROPE (OSCE) OFFICE FOR DEMOCRATIC INSTITUTIONS AND HUMAN RIGHTS (ODIHR)

NHRIs are recognised by OSCE in the 1990 Copenhagen Document, which provides that participating States will 'facilitate the establishment and strengthening of independent national institutions in the area of human rights and the rule of law'.[89] A number of NHRIs have worked extensively with OSCE in Eastern Europe and Central Asia on capacity building of NHRIs and the promotion and protection of human rights. In 2007, ODIHR established a Focal Point for Human Rights Defenders and National Human Rights Institutions.

86 *Ibidem.*

87 FRA, 'National Human Rights Institutions in the EU Member States: Strengthening the Fundamental Rights Architecture in the EU', Vienna, Publication Office of the European Union, 2010, available at: http://fra.europa.eu/fraWebsite/attachments/NHRI_en.pdf.

88 Http://fra.europa.eu/en/news/2012/new-fra-handbook-accreditation-national-human-rights-institutions.

89 Document of the Copenhagen Meeting of the Conference on the Human Dimension of the Conference on Security and Co-operation in Europe, 1990, available at: http://www.osce.org/odihr/elections/14304.

In June 2009 a representative from the ODIHR Office met with the European Coordinating Committee at its meeting in Vienna. The meeting discussed the potential for ODIHR to be involved in some of the work of the European Group, particularly in relation to issues relevant to ODIHR's work in democratisation and the rule of law. It was agreed that ODIHR would forward to the European Group Chair information about its work, meetings, and upcoming events for distribution to NHRIs. In 2011 the Lithuanian Chairmanship of the OSCE set as a priority the establishment and strengthening of NHRIs and held a Supplementary Human Dimension Meeting dedicated to the topic of NHRIs. The meeting brought together 197 participants, including 115 delegates from 47 OSCE participating states.[90] This was followed by a conference in Vilnius with NHRIs in July 2011.[91] The key recommendation agreed by the meeting and the conference for OSCE participating states were to:

- Fully acknowledge that NHRIs contribute to the protection and promotion of human rights, predominantly but not exclusively at the national level;
- Establish, where they do not yet exist, NHRIs that comply with the UN Principles Relating to the Status of National Institutions (Paris Principles) as further elaborated by the Sub-Committee on Accreditation of the International Coordinating Committee of NHRIs;
- Encourage NHRIs to seek accreditation with the International Coordinating Committee of NHRIs;
- Ensure that NHRIs are provided with sufficient human capital and financial resources to allow them to exercise their mandate effectively, especially when they are given additional tasks under national or international law;
- Ensure that annual and special reports from NHRIs are discussed in parliament in a timely manner and consider the establishment of parliamentary human rights committees to engage directly with NHRIs;
- Commit to undertake all necessary steps to ensure that recommendations and initiatives of National Human Rights Institutions are given due consideration and are systematically implemented by governmental authorities;
- After consultation with and the consent of the NHRI, consider vesting the NHRI with additional functions under international agreements, such as the Optional Protocol to the United Nations Convention Against Torture or the United Nations Convention on the Rights of Persons with Disabilities, or National legislation such as anti-discrimination laws;

[90] Supplementary Human Dimension Meeting, National Human Rights Institutions (Ombuds-institutions, Commissions, Institutes And Other), 14 – 15 April 2011, Vienna, Final Report PC.SHDM.GAL/5/1120, May 2011, available at: http://www.osce.org/event/shdm2011_1.

[91] OSCE Conference For National Human Rights Institutions in the OSCE area, Vilnius, 13–14 July 2012, available at: http://www.osce.org/odihr/78607.

- When mandating NHRIs with additional functions, ensure that adequate additional resources are allocated.

Recommendations to the OSCE were:

- Continue supporting the work of National Human Rights Institutions, in cooperation with the United Nations, the Council of Europe, other relevant international organisations and the International Coordinating Committee of NHRIs;
- Ensure capacity building for and engagement with NHRIs is undertaken by field offices;
- Support the establishment of regional NHRI secretariats;
- Involve NHRIs in developing OSCE commitments;
- Consider the information provided by NHRIs when drafting reports;
- Engage NHRIs in collaborative awareness raising and educational initiatives;
- Consider NHRIs as a source of expertise and experience, and foster exchange between institutions;
- Consider NHRIs as important interlocutors on human rights issues;
- Facilitate consistent participation of NHRIs at OSCE meetings, giving recognition to their special status as independent bodies.

While the recommendations do not have official status they are useful indicators for the OSCE to reflect on how participating states are meeting their commitments to promote human rights and consider possible ways to enhance the contribution of NHRIs.

4. CONCLUSIONS

The last two decades have been a time of incredible growth in terms of the numbers of bodies created for the promotion and protection of human rights across Europe at both national and regional levels. The vast majority of states in Europe now have a NHRI in some form. As the number of NHRIs grows there is an increased need for better coordination across Europe. The growing role of the ICC and the creation of a secretariat for the European Group of NHRIs provide a framework for joint working across Europe, but this must be fully integrated into the work of regional bodies. It is essential that regional bodies understand the unique role of NHRIs and that NHRIs work with regional bodies to demonstrate their added value in core work programmes. The way in which NHRIs have contributed to the reform of the European Court and to the Fundamental Rights Agency's planning should be seen as positive examples of the role that NHRIs can play.

The growing recognition of NHRIs at the UN level provides a good model for regional bodies, but NHRIs must commit to fulfilling their obligations in support of regional bodies as well. The fact that many NHRIs are new can be both a challenge and an opportunity. It may take some time for new NHRIs to become operational, but they bring together members and staff who are experts in human rights with extensive experience in working across Europe and the world and who passionately believe in the promotion and protection of human rights. The challenge is to ensure that along with their demanding domestic mandate, they also engage through the ICC and the European Group in a structured way with regional bodies.

We must also recognise the effect of the economic situation in Europe. With the current economic austerity, the promotion and protection of human rights becomes even more important. During times of economic austerity there is a temptation for governments to reduce funding for NHRIs and other bodies that promote and protect human rights just when they are most needed. Despite the creation and strengthening of NHRIs in Europe, there have been a number of NHRIs that were established in compliance with the Paris Principles (and have been accredited) which are now under attack through debilitating budget cuts and restructuring that may bring their independence and effectiveness into question. A 2009 survey carried out by the OHCHR of 61 NHRIs across the world reported that only 21 of those surveyed considered that they had a sufficient budget to carry out their functions.[92] The survey also indicated that this may be a downward trend, with 10% reporting that their budget had significantly decreased in recent years.[93] The economic downturn affecting many European countries is further exacerbating this situation. So, just at a time when NHRIs are being recognised and engaged by regional bodies, they may lack the ability to do so. Regional bodies must play a role in supporting NHRIs when they are under threat, just as NHRIs must work to ensure that the effectiveness of the regional bodies is not threatened.

Human rights is about people, not institutions, but as institutions working to promote and protect human rights we must strive to develop new ways of working together to be more effective and we must stand together to oppose cuts that would put the human rights framework at risk.

Nā tō rourou, nā taku rourou, ka ora ai te iwi

With your food basket and my food basket, the people will thrive

(New Zealand Māori proverb)

92 OHCHR, 'Survey on National Human Rights Institutions', Geneva, July 2009, available at: http://www.nhri.net/2009/Questionnaire%20-%20Complete%20Report%20FINAL-edited.pdf, p. 17.

93 *Ibidem.*

(FUTURE) INTERACTION BETWEEN DATA PROTECTION AUTHORITIES AND NATIONAL HUMAN RIGHTS INSTITUTIONS IN THE EUROPEAN UNION

Peter J. Hustinx[1]

1. INTRODUCTION

In line with Directive 95/46/EC, all EU Member States have national authorities that monitor compliance with data protection laws. However, the way in which the Directive has been implemented in national laws varies considerably. This has resulted in discrepancies and deficiencies that have been highlighted by the EU Agency for Fundamental Rights, and also in recent case law of the European Court of Justice. In January 2012, the European Commission presented a package of proposals with the aim to update and reinforce the current legal framework for data protection. This review will also have an impact on the scope for useful interaction between data protection authorities and national human rights institutions.

The emergence of the right to the protection of personal data ("data protection") as a separate fundamental right – closely related to the right to respect for private life, but with its own special characteristics – is a typical feature of the European human rights landscape. While similar legislation developed in other regions of the world – based on theories of privacy, fair information processing, consumer protection, or just on the need to create adequate conditions for economic growth – the developments in Europe have been shaped by the early belief that the growth of the Information Society would have such an impact on the exercise of existing fundamental rights and freedoms of citizens that a more proactive and systematic approach was necessary.

1 Mr Hustinx is European Data Protection Supervisor (EDPS). Contact: edps@edps.europa.eu. Website: www.edps.europa.eu.

The first steps were taken in the context of the Council of Europe. This resulted in the adoption in 1981 of a Convention on Data Protection, also known as Convention 108, with basic principles for the processing of personal data in automated or otherwise structured data files.[2] The term 'data protection' was defined as the protection of fundamental rights and freedoms of natural persons, *in particular* their right to privacy, with respect to the processing of personal data.[3] The Convention therefore goes beyond the scope of Article 8 of the European Convention on Human Rights (ECHR),[4] and applies in principle to all personal data, regardless of whether the right to privacy is at stake. The principles of Convention 108 provide for substantive requirements for data controllers, some specific rights for data subjects, and arrangements for institutional oversight, enforcement and international cooperation. The Convention has been ratified by more than 40 member states, including all EU Member States.

When Convention 108 was implemented into national law, it quickly became clear that the general wording of its provisions allowed widely divergent national laws on data protection. At the same time, the development of an Information Society required more harmonisation and consistency among national laws than the Convention could provide. This caused the EU to become involved, eventually leading to the adoption of the Data Protection Directive 95/46/EC, which took the Convention as its starting point, but also specified it in different ways, inter alia requiring supervision and enforcement by one or more data protection authorities acting in complete independence.[5]

The next step in this development was the adoption of the EU Charter of Fundamental Rights in 2000,[6] initially as a political document. Although largely based on the ECHR, it also contained some innovations, such as the recognition of a right to the protection of personal data (Article 8), in addition to the right to respect for private and family life (Article 7). Article 8 explicitly mentions some of the main elements of the right to the protection of personal data, as further developed in Directive 95/46/EC:

---

2 Council of Europe, Convention for the Protection of Individuals with regard to Automatic Processing of Personal Data, Strasbourg, 28.I.1981 (further: Convention 108).

3 Convention 108, Art. 1.

4 Article 8 'Rights to respect for private and family life:
1. Everyone has the right to respect for his private and family life, his home and his correspondence.
2. There shall be no interference by a public authority with the exercise of this right except such as is in accordance with the law and is necessary in a democratic society in the interests of national security, public safety or the economic well-being of the country, for the prevention of disorder or crime, for the protection of health or morals, or for the protection of the rights and freedoms of others.

5 Directive 95/46/EC of the European Parliament and of the Council of 24 October 1995 on the protection of individuals with regard to the processing of personal data and on the free movement of such data, *OJL* 281/31, 23 November 1995. See especially Article 28.

6 Charter of Fundamental Rights of the European Union (2000/C 364/01), *OJL* 364/1, 18 December 2000 (the Charter).

Protection of personal data

1. Everyone has the right to the protection of personal data concerning him or her.

2. Such data must be processed fairly for specified purposes and on the basis of the consent of the person concerned or some other legitimate basis laid down by law. Everyone has the right of access to data which has been collected concerning him or her, and the right to have it rectified.

3. Compliance with these rules shall be subject to control by an independent authority.

The final step was the entry into force of the Lisbon Treaty, at the end of 2009,[7] which turned the Charter into a binding document,[8] and also inserted a horizontal legal basis for legislation on data protection, no longer dependent on the needs of the internal market, but reflecting the nature of data protection as a fundamental right, among the general principles of the Union.[9] This confirmed a legal development of several decades.

2. INDEPENDENT SUPERVISION

The existence of data protection authorities has been a standard feature of European data protection law from the beginning, but it has taken some time before the principle of *independent* supervision developed into a constitutional principle. Article 8 of the Charter provides for it now, as we have just seen, and Article 16 TFEU does the same in very similar terms. Article 28 of Directive 95/46/EC, as we will see,[10] goes into more detail on the subject.

In retrospect, it is surprising to see that, in spite of experience in Germany, Sweden and France, the concept of a 'data protection authority' played only a very limited role in the Council of Europe's Convention 108, when it was concluded in 1981. The central obligation of each Party in Article 4 of the Convention was to take 'the necessary measures in its domestic law to give effect to the basic principles for data protection' set out in the Convention. Article 10 provides that each Party must establish 'appropriate sanctions and remedies' for violations of these basic principles. The explanatory report clearly mentioned the need to guarantee *"effective protection"*, but left the way in which this should happen for each Party to decide.[11] The existence of supervisory authorities is only mentioned

7 Treaty of Lisbon amending the Treaty on European Union and the Treaty establishing the European Community (2007/C 306/01), *OJL* 306/1, 17 December 2007.

8 Consolidated Version of the Treaty on European Union, *OJL* C 115/19, 9 May 2008 (further: TEU). See Article 6.

9 Consolidated Version of the Treaty on the Functioning of the European Union, *OJL* C 115/47, 9 May 2008 (further TFEU). See Article 16.

10 See also *infra* section 4.

11 Council of Europe, Convention for the Protection of Individuals with regard to Automatic Processing of Personal Data, Explanatory Report, para. 60.

as a feature of national laws. The drafters of the Convention were obviously reluctant to impose this on all Parties as a basic legal requirement.

This situation changed with adoption of the EU Data Protection Directive 95/46. Article 28 of the Directive introduced an obligation for each Member State to have one or more supervisory authorities responsible for ensuring compliance, and 'acting with complete independence'. Recital 62 underlined that 'the establishment in Member States of supervisory authorities, exercising their functions with complete independence, is an essential component of the protection of individuals with regard to the processing of personal data'. The words '*acting* with complete independence' were a compromise formula, chosen to ensure some flexibility, but it was difficult to see how 'complete independence' could exist without sufficient institutional safeguards. This turned out highly relevant in a case before the ECJ involving Germany, to which we will return.[12]

Article 28 of the Directive also provides that supervisory authorities should have certain powers, such as consultative powers, investigative powers, effective powers of intervention, the power to engage in legal proceedings or bring violations to the attention of judicial authorities, the power to deal with complaints, etc. This seems to assure them a central position. However, they do not decide in last resort, and their decisions may be appealed to the courts.

The adoption of the Directive has led to an Additional Protocol to Convention 108, which basically takes up all elements of Article 28 of the Directive.[13] The preamble of this Additional Protocol clearly states that 'supervisory authorities, exercising their functions in complete independence, are an element of the effective protection of individuals with regard to the processing of personal data'. The explanatory report even concludes that data protection supervisory authorities 'have become an essential component of the data protection supervisory system in a democratic society'.[14] This report also puts a lot of emphasis on the notion of 'effective protection' and the role of supervisory authorities in ensuring it.[15]

This all means in the light of Article 8 of the Charter and Article 16 TFEU, that the principle of 'independent supervision' and the existence of 'independent supervisory authorities' have developed, at least at the European level, into a constitutional element of the right to data protection in a democratic society. This is based on their mission to 'ensure compliance' and closely linked to the notion of 'effective protection'.

12 See *infra*, section 4.

13 Additional Protocol to the Convention for the Protection of Individuals with regard to Automatic Processing of Personal Data, regarding supervisory authorities and trans-border data flows, ETS No.: 181, Strasbourg, 8 November 2001 (entry into force: 1 July 2004).

14 Additional Protocol to the Convention for the Protection of Individuals with regard to Automatic Processing of Personal Data, regarding supervisory authorities and trans-border data flows, ETS No.: 181, Explanatory Report, Preamble, para. 5.

15 *Ibidem*, Preamble; para. 8; para. 13; para. 16; para. 17; para. 24.

3. DIVERSITY AND DEFICIENCIES

In accordance with Directive 95/46/EC, all EU Member States have national authorities that monitor compliance with data protection laws. However, the way in which the Directive has been implemented in national laws varies considerably. This has resulted in discrepancies and deficiencies that have also been highlighted in a report published in May 2010 by the EU Agency for Fundamental Rights (FRA).[16]

As a first comment, it should be noted that some diversity is unavoidable and simply a result of different legal traditions in the Member States. The Directive leaves Member States a large margin to decide on the nature and structure of a supervisory authority in ways that fit them best. Data protection authorities (DPA) therefore exist in different forms and shapes: large or small commissions, single commissioners, elected or appointed, either or not by a national government or parliament, and so on.

However, as the FRA clearly highlighted in its report, the current diversity among Member States goes far beyond the unavoidable, and also involves rather serious deficiencies.[17] The key findings of the report have been summarised by FRA as follows:[18]

> **Rights Awareness**
> 7 in every 10 respondents to a recent Euro-barometer survey were not aware that there was a data protection authority in their country.
> **Limited powers**
> Data protection authorities are often not equipped with full powers of investigation and intervention or the capacity to give legal advice or engage in legal proceedings.
> **Lack of compliance**
> In many Member States there is a widespread disregard for the basic duty to register with the data protection authority prior to engaging in data processing operations.
> **Lack of independence**
> The lack of independence from the government of several of the data protection authorities in the EU presents a major problem for their credibility. Legislative reform modifying the nomination/appointment procedure […] could rectify the problem of lack of independence.

---

16 See: FRA, 'Data Protection in the European Union: the role of National Data Protection Authorities, Strengthening the fundamental rights architecture in the EU II', Luxembourg, Publications Office of the European Union, 2010.

17 *Ibidem*, p. 42–45.

18 See the website of FRA: http://fra.europa.eu/en/publication/2012/data-protection-european-union-role-national-data-protection-authorities.

> **Lack of financial resources and staff**
> Data protection authorities in [a number of Member States] are unable to carry out the entirety of their tasks because of the limited economic and human resources available to them.
> **Lack of sanctions and compensation**
> Legislative reform is needed to give data protection authorities an active role in procedures which lead to sanctions and compensation. Where data protection authorities have the relevant powers, they need the resources to effectively use them. [...]

The FRA report also mentions some examples of good practices,[19] but both the diversity and deficiencies exposed in the report remain rather worrying.

4. REQUIREMENT OF "COMPLETE INDEPENDENCE"

The European Court of Justice has meanwhile also expressed itself on the requirement of 'complete independence' in Article 28 of Directive 95/46.

The Court's judgment of 9 March 2010 in Case-518/07 (*Commission v Federal Republic of Germany*) dealt with the authorities in Germany that supervise the processing of personal data by *non-public bodies* at the regional level. In all states, those authorities were subject to state scrutiny. The European Commission, in Court supported by the European Data Protection Supervisor (EDPS), took the position that 'complete independence' in Article 28 of Directive 95/46 means that a supervisory authority must be free from *any* outside influence, regardless from whom.[20] The Federal Republic of Germany felt that it only required *functional* independence – i.e. from those subject to supervision – but did not exclude State scrutiny.[21]

The ECJ decided in favour of the Commission – basically saying that 'complete independence' means 'complete independence'. However, its analysis contains some interesting messages. The Court's starting point is that the meaning of the requirement must be found on the basis of the wording of Article 28 and the aims and scheme of the Directive.

As to the *wording* of Article 28, the Court mentions that in relation to a public body, 'independence' normally means 'a status which ensures that the body concerned can act completely freely, without taking any instructions or being put under any pressure'.[22] Moreover, according to the Court, the additional emphasis

19 FRA, loc. cit. *supra* note 16, pp. 47–48.
20 European Court of Justice, Judgment, Case-518/07 *Commission v Federal Republic of Germany*, 9 March 2010, para. 15.
21 *Ibidem*, para. 16.
22 *Ibidem*, para. 18.

on '*complete* independence' implies 'a decision-making power independent of any direct or indirect external influence on the supervisory authority'.[23]

As to the *objectives* of Directive 95/46, the Court considers that it aims to harmonise national law in an area where the free movement of personal data is liable to interfere with the right to privacy, and seeks to ensure a high level of protection of fundamental rights and freedoms with respect to the processing of personal data. The supervisory authorities provided for in Article 28 are the 'guardians of those fundamental rights and freedoms', and their existence is considered as 'an essential component' of the protection of individuals with regard to the processing of personal data.[24] The Court continues as follows (emphasis added):

> '24. In order to guarantee that protection, the supervisory authorities must ensure *a fair balance between, on the one hand, observance of the fundamental right to private life and, on the other hand, the interests requiring free movement of personal data.* Furthermore, under Article 28(6) of Directive 95/46, the different national authorities are called upon to cooperate with one another and even, if necessary, to exercise their powers at the request of an authority of another Member State.
>
> 25. *The guarantee of the independence of national supervisory authorities is intended to ensure the effectiveness and reliability of the supervision of compliance with the provisions on protection of individuals with regard to the processing of personal data and must be interpreted in the light of that aim.* It was established not to grant a special status to those authorities themselves as well as their agents, but in order to strengthen the protection of individuals and bodies affected by their decisions. It follows that, when carrying out their duties, the supervisory authorities must act objectively and impartially. For that purpose, they must remain free from any external influence, including the direct or indirect influence of the State or the *Länder*, and not of the influence only of the supervised bodies.'

As to the *scheme* of the Directive, the Court draws a parallel between Directive 95/46 on one hand, and Regulation 45/2001,[25] which applies to EU institutions and established the EDPS, on the other. Article 28 of the Directive should be interpreted in accordance with Article 44 of the Regulation requiring 'complete independence', but also stating that the EDPS 'may neither seek nor take instructions from anybody'.[26] The Court thus concludes that Article 28 should be interpreted:

---

23 *Ibidem*, para. 19.

24 *Ibidem*, para. 23.

25 Regulation (EC) No 45/2001 of the European Parliament and of the Council of 18 December 2000 on the protection of individuals with regard to the processing of personal data by the Community institutions and bodies and on the free movement of such data, *OJL* L 8/1, 12 January 2001.

26 *Ibidem*, Article 44 'Independence':
1. The European Data Protection Supervisor shall act in complete independence in the performance of his or her duties.

> '30. [...] as meaning that the supervisory authorities responsible for supervising the processing of personal data [...] must enjoy an *independence allowing them to perform their duties free from external influence*. That independence precludes not only any influence exercised by the supervised bodies, but also *any directions or any other external influence, whether direct or indirect, which could call into question the performance by those authorities of their task consisting of establishing a fair balance between the protection of the right to private life and the free movement of personal data*.'

The Court then considers whether state scrutiny is consistent with the requirement of independence as defined above, and arrives at the conclusion that this is *not* the case. It also points out:

> '36. [...] that the *mere risk that the scrutinising authorities could exercise a political influence over the decisions of the supervisory authorities is enough* to hinder the latter authorities' independent performance of their tasks.'

After further analysis, the Court concluded that by making the authorities responsible for monitoring the processing of personal data by non-public bodies in the different *Länder* subject to state scrutiny, the Federal Republic of Germany had failed to fulfil its obligations under Article 28 of Directive 95/46.

Thus, the Court not only decided that 'complete independence' involves the freedom from *any* external influence, but also gave some interesting messages about the role of supervisory authorities: their independence is intended to ensure the *effectiveness* of their mission, and they should act *objectively* and *impartially*, and be free to strike a *fair balance* between observance of the fundamental right to private life and other interests.

We will come back to the question what all this could mean for the interaction between data protection authorities and national human rights institutions.[27] First, it is useful to take a look at the main lines of the current review of the EU legal framework for data protection.

---

2. The European Data Protection Supervisor shall, in the performance of his or her duties, neither seek nor take instructions from anybody.
3. The European Data Protection Supervisor shall refrain from any action incompatible with his or her duties and shall not, during his or her term of office, engage in any other occupation, whether gainful or not.
4. The European Data Protection Supervisor shall, after his or her term of office, behave with integrity and discretion as regards the acceptance of appointments and benefits.

27 See *infra* section 6.

5. PROPOSALS FOR A NEW EU LEGAL FRAMEWORK FOR DATA PROTECTION

5.1. DRIVERS OF EU REVIEW

Why is this review taking place? It is possible to cite three reasons. The *first* reason is that there is a need to update the current framework, and more specifically Directive 95/46 which is still the key element of the framework. And "updating" means in this case, most of all, ensuring its continued effectiveness in practice. When the Directive was adopted, the Internet barely existed, and we now live in a world where continuous data processing is becoming increasingly relevant, so we also need stronger safeguards that deliver good results in practice. The challenges of new technologies and globalisation really require some imaginative innovation to ensure a more effective protection.

The *second* reason is that the current framework has given rise to increasing diversity and complexity, also in a much wider sense, if only for the reason that a Directive is transposed into national law – that is its nature – and we now have ended up with 27 versions of the same basic principles. That is simply too much, and translates into costs, but also a loss of effectiveness. In other words, there is a need to scale up harmonisation, and make the system not only stronger and more effective in practice, but also more consistent. This will lead to a reduction of *unhelpful* diversity and complexity.

The *third* reason has to do with the new legal framework of the EU. The Lisbon Treaty has placed a strong emphasis on fundamental rights. Among them, as we have seen, a special provision on the protection of personal data in Article 8 of the Charter of fundamental rights, and a new horizontal legal basis in Article 16 TFEU providing for comprehensive protection in all EU policy areas, regardless of whether it relates to the internal market, law enforcement, or almost any other part of the public sector.

So, the review of the framework is all about stronger, more effective, more consistent, and more comprehensive protection of personal data.

If we now look at what has been put on the table, we see a package of at least two main proposals: a Directive for – briefly put – the law enforcement area,[28] and a directly binding Regulation for what is now still Directive 95/46, applying to the commercial areas and the public sector, other than law enforcement.[29]

---

28 Proposal for a Directive of the European Parliament and of the Council on the protection of individuals with regard to the processing of personal data by competent authorities for the purposes of prevention, investigation, detection or prosecution of criminal offences or the execution of criminal penalties, and the free movement of such data, COM (2012) 10 final, Brussels, 25 January 2012.

29 Proposal for a Regulation of the European Parliament and of the Council on the protection of individuals with regard to the processing of personal data and on the free movement of such

The proposed Directive is generally considered as not satisfactory, as its level of protection is substantially lower than in the proposed Regulation. However in the present context it is also less relevant.

5.2. CONTINUITY AND CHANGE

If we now focus on the proposed Regulation,[30] there are some main messages which need to be kept in mind.

The first one is that – in spite of all innovation – there is a lot of continuity. All basic concepts and principles that we have now will continue to exist, subject to some clarification and some innovation.[31] Where the real innovation comes in, it is mainly about "making data protection more effective in practice". This implies, as we will see, a strong emphasis on implementation of principles, and on enforcement of rights and obligations, to ensure that protection is delivered in practice.

At the same time, the Regulation provides for simplification and reduction of costs. The prior notification of processing operations to the DPA has been eliminated. This is only required in situations of specific risks.[32] The Regulation also provides for a one-stop-shop for companies with establishments in different member states.[33] This involves the introduction of a "lead DPA", which is the DPA of the main establishment who will be first responsible, in close cooperation with other competent DPAs.[34]

A directly binding Regulation will of course also bring much greater harmonisation – in principle: one single applicable law in all Member States – and greater consistency. In itself, this will also bring an important simplification and reduction of costs for companies operating in different Member States.

Finally, the proposed Regulation has a general scope: it will apply both in the private and in the public sector. This is completely consistent with the situation under the present Directive 95/46. The possibility of a systematic distinction in this Directive between the public and the private sector was explicitly considered in the 1990's and rejected.

---

data (General Data Protection Regulation), COM(2012) 11 final, Brussels, 25 January 2012 (further: Proposal for a General Data Protection Regulation).

30 Further references are to this Regulation (see footnote 29).

31 An example of innovation is that there is now a stronger emphasis on data minimisation: i.e. not more data than strictly necessary (Article 5 sub c). Another example is the recognition of "Privacy by Design" as a general principle (Article 23).

32 See Article 34 on prior consultation, for instance where impact assessment indicates a high degree of specific risks.

33 See Explanatory Memorandum, p. 12, para. 3.4.6.2.

34 See Article 51.2.

This approach is reinforced by the fact that Article 8 of the EU Charter provides for an explicit recognition of the right to the protection of personal data, and that Article 16 TFEU provides an explicit horizontal legal basis for the adoption of rules on the protection of personal data, both at EU level and in the Member States, when they are acting within the scope of EU law.

5.3. SUBSTANCE OF THE PROPOSED REGULATION

If we now come to the substance of the Regulation, it strengthens the roles of the key players: the data subject, the data controller, and the data protection authorities. A brief look at the first two is important to better understand the role of the DPA.

5.3.1. Data Subject

The first perspective could also be seen as enhancing "user control": the possibility for data subjects to influence what happens to their personal data. The current rights of the data subject have been confirmed, but strengthened and extended. It will also be easier to exercise these rights in practice.[35]

The requirement of consent has been clarified: *when* you need it, it needs to be real and robust consent.[36] There is also a stronger right to object.[37] There are stronger means to ensure that the rights of the data subject are respected in practice. There is more emphasis on transparency.[38] There is a provision introducing a collective action, not a class action in US style, but still for organisations acting on behalf of their members or constituencies.[39]

There is also much talk about the "right to be forgotten", but at further analysis, it is basically an emphasis on deleting data when there is not a good enough reason to keep them.[40] The right to data portability[41] is basically also a specification of the present right to require a copy of personal data, in a particular format.

5.3.2. Data Controller

The biggest change is a much greater emphasis on real responsibility of responsible organisations. Responsibility is not a concept that only comes at the end, when

35 Articles 15–17.
36 Article 4 sub 8 and Article 7.
37 Article 19.
38 Article 5 *sub* a and Articles 11 and 14.
39 Article 73.2 and Article 76.1.
40 Article 17.
41 Article 18.

something has gone wrong. Instead, it comes as an obligation to develop good data management in practice. This appears in language such as *taking all appropriate measures to ensure compliance*, and *verifying and demonstrating that these measures continue to be effective.*[42]

This is one of the major shifts. It also implies that the burden of proof is in many cases on the responsible organisation, i.e. to demonstrate that there is an adequate legal basis, that consent is real consent, and that measures continue to be effective. This means that DPAs will be more involved *ex-post*, and will be able to require from data controllers adequate evidence of their compliance status.

The Regulation also provides for a number of specific requirements, such as the need for a privacy impact assessment,[43] the keeping of documentation,[44] and the appointment of a data protection officer.[45] These are important elements of good data management in organisations. Data protection officers can help organisations to comply and also act as contact points for DPAs.

Some of those provisions, especially on documentation, are overly detailed and would require some modification to make them more appropriate. Some exceptions in the same provisions may not be fully justified. A better balance in this part of the proposal may in fact solve both problems.

A general provision on security breach notification is also included.[46] EU law now provides for such a notification only in the case of telecommunication providers.

5.3.3. Supervision and Enforcement

A third main emphasis in the Regulation is on more effective supervision and enforcement by DPAs. The safeguards for complete independence of data protection authorities have been strengthened fully in line with the ECJ judgment in the case *Commission vs Germany.*[47]

The Regulation also provides for regulators with strong enforcement powers in all Member States, involving both investigation powers, ordering powers and imposition of administrative sanctions.[48] Presently, under Directive 95/46/EC, Member States have a very large discretion, as result of which quite a few DPAs now have weak powers and none have the full range of powers as laid down in the proposed Regulation.

Administrative fines of millions of euros – competition size fines – catch a lot of attention, but the message is: if this is important, it should be dealt with

42 Article 22.
43 Article 33.
44 Article 28.
45 Articles 35–37.
46 Articles 30–32.
47 Article 47.
48 Articles 53 and 79.

accordingly. This will drive "data protection" higher on the agenda of corporate boardrooms, which is welcome and likely to result in better data management and better delivery of data subject's rights.

International cooperation among data protection authorities is also strongly encouraged and facilitated, including mutual assistance and joint operations.[49] The introduction of a 'lead authority' for companies with multiple establishments[50] is welcome, but this lead authority will not be acting on its own, but as part of a network of close cooperation with other competent authorities. This EU wide dimension is also explicitly mentioned among the tasks of data protection authorities.[51]

Very important in this perspective is the introduction of a consistency mechanism in the context of a European Data Protection Board,[52] which is to be built on the basis of the present group of EU data protection authorities ("Article 29 Working Party").[53] This mechanism, involving all independent authorities, will ensure consistent outcomes of supervision and enforcement in all Member States. Its secretariat will be provided by the EDPS.[54]

5.3.4. Global Privacy

A final element is the wider international dimension of the Regulation, in two ways. The scope of the Regulation has been clarified and extended. These provisions now apply not only to all processing in the context of an establishment in the EU, but also when from a third country, goods or services are delivered in the European market, or when the behaviour of Europeans is being monitored online.[55]

This is a reality on the Internet nowadays. At the same time, it is a realistic approach that builds on an increasing synergy of thinking on data protection around the world. It means that European DPAs will be more and more involved in issues with international dimensions, including third countries outside the EU.[56]

International cooperation is therefore also developing among data protection authorities in a wider context – e.g. between the Federal Trade Commission in

49 Articles 55–56.
50 See *supra* section 5.2.
51 See Article 46.1.
52 Articles 57–58 and 64–72.
53 This Working Party, established by Article 29 of Directive 95/46/EC, has been active since 1996 and is now composed of representatives of all national DPAs and the EDPS. It gives advice to the European Commission, either or not at its request, and develops "soft law" guidance on different matters, but with substantial authority in practice.
54 Article 71.
55 See Article 3.
56 Recent examples are investigations against Google by the French CNIL, and against Facebook by the Irish Data Protection Commissioner, in which most other European DPAs have been involved, as well as competent authorities in Canada and the US.

the US and DPAs in the EU – in a global network (GPEN). This will make it better possible to deal with global actors on the Internet.[57]

6. INTERACTION BETWEEN DPAs AND NHRIs

So, what does all this mean for the interaction between data protection authorities and national human rights institutions?

First of all, there is an important time factor. The Commission's proposals are presently under discussion in the Council and the Parliament. This is obviously not a matter of months. Present estimates are that we will see some conclusions in the course of 2013, probably under the Irish Presidency. In any case by 2014, the proposed Regulation may well be adopted, subject to some improvements on various details. On that basis, the Regulation is likely to enter into force in 2016. In other words, the Member States and all other stakeholders will have time to prepare for transition. Until then, the current framework, and national laws implementing it, will continue to apply, only subject to partial amendments, for instance to respond to ECJ case law.

For the present, this means that some diversity will continue to exist among national data protection authorities. However, a similar diversity exists for national human rights institutions. The "Paris Principles" discussed elsewhere in this publication,[58] lay down certain standards concerning the competences, responsibilities, composition, and methods of operation of the national institutions, but no specific structure, mandate, or shape is required. This means that the way in which DPAs and NHRIs are now interacting, may be quite different in the various Member States, depending on prevailing conditions, including political culture and other traditions.

So it may well be that in some Member States, data protection authorities, just like equality bodies and national ombudsmen, are among the key stakeholders of NHRIs, and also contribute actively to their agenda, while this may not be the case in other Member States. In those cases where there is a lively interaction between data protection authorities and national institutions, it is likely that cooperation is closest in the general field of awareness raising and education, as these activities are less dependent on formal powers and procedures. In the case of complaint handling and inspection, a lively interaction would seem to be somewhat less likely. However, it may well be that national institutions have done useful work in exposing structural problems or specific issues that could be

[57] This is based on a growing convergence of data protection principles and practices around the world, involving not only formal standards, developed by OECD, Council of Europe, EU, APEC, ISO and other organisations, but also other instruments, such as codes of conduct, binding corporate rules, and so on.

[58] See in particular G. De Beco, 'Assessment of the Paris Principles and the ICC Sub-Committee on Accreditation', Chapter 11 in this volume.

the subject of a complaint or an inspection, or even that they act as the initiating party of a complaint, either or not in the general interest.

In the future, all this may continue to be the case, but the key difference will be that the current great diversity among national DPAs has disappeared or substantially been reduced. This will be the result of *directly* binding requirements in the Regulation, not only for the independent position, but also for the tasks and powers of supervisory authorities. There may well be national rules providing further details, particularly on the composition and internal structure of supervisory authorities, but the main elements will be visible in the Regulation and have direct EU wide application.

Much more than now, the situation will be that national DPAs will not only be competent to play their role within the scope of their own jurisdiction, but also be an integral part of EU wide cooperation on cross border and other common issues, and moreover be part of an EU wide consistency mechanism that is designed to ensure consistent outcomes. It is no doubt a paradox that institutional safeguards for independence will be stronger, and that at the same time arrangements are made to avoid unhelpful diversity among independent authorities. Finding the right balance in this area will of course be a key concern. Even if the appropriate legal arrangements have been made in the Regulation, once it is adopted, there will always be a need to develop effective procedures in practice. The existing Article 29 Working Party, as the current platform of DPAs in the EU, could do much in preparing the way into this direction.

For the interaction with NHRIs, this will probably not lead to major changes, but most certainly to a more consistent and predictable landscape. In any case, it would seem that the requirement of 'complete independence' and the need to avoid 'any external influence' will not prevent national DPAs from entering into appropriate relationships with NHRIs, especially in the general field of awareness raising and education, with a view to giving both more impact. Indeed, under the Paris Principles, similar standards will apply to the national institutions. It will thus be up to both parties to develop and structure mutual relationships to their best common benefit.

One additional element may still need to be considered. If the Regulation is adopted in its present form, it will also allow 'any body, organisation or association which aims to protect data subjects' rights and interests concerning the protection of their personal data' and which has been properly constituted according to national law, the 'right to lodge a complaint with a supervisory authority in any Member State on behalf of one or more data subjects', if it considers that a data subject's rights under the Regulation have been infringed as a result of the processing of personal data.[59] A similar right will apply in the context of court proceedings.[60] This will give more scope for collective actions, also in Member

[59] Proposal for a General Data Protection Regulation, *supra* note 29, Art. 73.
[60] Proposal for a General Data Protection Regulation, *supra* note 29, Art. 76.

States where this possibility does not yet exist, and thus contribute to a more active enforcement of data protection rules. It remains to be seen to which extent this would allow NHRIs or their constituencies to engage directly in data protection issues to a greater extent than they have so far.

THE COURT'S EARS AND ARMS: NATIONAL HUMAN RIGHTS INSTITUTIONS AND THE EUROPEAN COURT OF HUMAN RIGHTS

Antoine Buyse[1]

1. INTRODUCTION

Ulysses famously had his crewmen bind his arms to the mast of his ship when passing the Sirens while the crew itself was ordered to stuff their ears with wax in order to keep the ship afloat without being seduced by the songs of the mythical creatures and thereby risking shipwreck. A specific combination of ears and arms was crucial for effectiveness. The same holds for international human rights supervisory mechanisms and courts. One of their main challenges is that they are by nature functionally and institutionally detached from the national jurisdictions within which human rights problems surface. This poses problems at several levels: victims of violations may not always know how and with what kind of complaints they can turn to these courts and committees. This can either lead to an overload of unwarranted applications or, by contrast, a situation in which truly problematic human rights issues do not find their way to these mechanisms – nor are solved at the national level, one may add. The mechanisms themselves are very dependent on information provided by the two parties – mostly applicant versus state – in a particular case. This information may be incomplete or coloured by the parties' positions in the dispute. And finally, when it comes to the execution or follow-up of judgments or recommendations, international mechanisms have very limited powers to secure that states do actually offer reparations to victims and make broader legal or policy changes in order to prevent new violations.

Thus, in many ways the international level would benefit from additional "ears and arms" within national jurisdictions. In many respects non-governmental organisations may play this role in a useful way, both by providing information

[1] Dr. Antoine Buyse is associate professor and senior researcher at the Netherlands Institute of Human Rights (SIM) at Utrecht University. He also runs a weblog about the European Convention on Human Rights: echrblog.blogspot.com. Contact: A.C.Buyse@uu.nl.

and by lobbying for implementation of international judgments. But they will rarely do so on a structural basis nor even-handedly as they have their own priorities. There is, however, a category of national institutions which do fit the mould: national human rights institutions (NHRIs). As their name indicates, these are primarily geared towards the states within which they are created. This does not preclude them from connecting to human rights institutions beyond national borders. This may happen horizontally within the European group of NHRIs[2] but also globally within the International Coordinating Committee of National Institutions for the Promotion and Protection of Human Rights.[3] Functionally, NHRIs are also tasked to do more than merely function nationally by directly promoting human rights. They are also meant to fulfil a more international function: making vertical connections by supporting international human rights structures and enabling the latter to be more effective at the national level. The Paris Principles state that one of the responsibilities of an NHRI is 'to cooperate with [...] the regional institutions [...] that are competent in the areas of the promotion and protection of human rights'.[4]

The door to support for and cooperation with international institutions is thus open. This chapter will focus on how NHRIs can support the work of a specific institution: the European Court of Human Rights (ECtHR). This Court, often perceived as the most effective international human rights mechanism, still suffers from the problems described above. The work and proceedings of the Court itself can only partly remedy these problems. A key requirement is increased and more effective human rights protection within states. In the following sections the potential contributions of national human rights institutions to the European Convention on Human Rights (ECHR) machinery will be addressed in three distinct stages: *before* a complaint reaches the Court, *during* the proceedings in Strasbourg, and *after* a judgment has been delivered, when it comes to implementation.[5] As will be argued, NHRIs have an information-channelling and preventative function which may contribute to solving the challenges the European Court of Human Rights faces.

2 See: B. Adamson, 'NHRI and their European Counterparts: Scope for Strengthened Cooperation and Performance towards European Human Rights Institutions', Chapter 6 in this volume.

3 See: K. Roberts, 'The Role and Functioning of the International Coordinating Committee of National Human Rights Institutions in International Human Rights Bodies', Chapter 10 in this volume.

4 UN GA Resolution 48/134 of 20 December 1993, Annex, 'Principles relating to the Status of National Institutions', para. 3-e (Paris Principles).

5 This tripartite way of approaching the issue has also been applied in: G. de Beco, 'La contribution des institutions nationales des droits de l'homme au renforcement de l'efficacité de la Court européenne des droits de l'homme', *Revue trimestrielle des droits de l'homme*, vol. 77, 2009, pp. 165–194.

2. BEFORE: PREVENTION AND INFORMATION

The Brighton Declaration, adopted by a high level conference of all state parties to the European Convention in April 2012, reminded both states and the Council of Europe of the importance of national human rights institutions.[6] It calls upon states to 'work in a spirit of co-operation with civil society and national human rights institutions' when it talks of safeguarding the viability of the ECHR mechanism.[7] It asks the Court to consider, in consultation with the state parties, civil society and NHRIs, an extension of a pilot project of enabling electronically submitted applications. Finally, it invites those states that have not already done so to establish NHRIs. All of this means that the very existence of NHRIs and their practical helpfulness is acknowledged by European states. Simultaneously, it also implies a lot of work remains to be done. Not all countries have yet created such institutions nor do all existing ones live up to the highest standards of independence and functionality – the so-called A-status.[8] Also, this acknowledgement of the role of NHRIs is relatively recent. Neither the European Convention nor any of its additional protocols mention national human rights institutions. In addition, high level conferences preceding Brighton, in Interlaken in 2010 and in Izmir in 2011, only mentioned NHRIs in passing[9] or even not at all.[10] The Council of Europe's institutions have displayed at an earlier stage greater openness to the work of NHRIs than most European states. This may be explained by the fact that in many respects these institutions are natural allies in the promotion of human rights. The Committee of Ministers as early as 1997 expressed in a resolution that 'the importance of the role of such institutions, in particular in providing information about human rights to both the public authorities and civil society' and decided to open up channels for information exchange between the Council of Europe and NHRIs.[11] Indeed, the Council of Europe was represented at the European Group of National Human Rights Institutions' first meetings in the 1990s and the Group itself has enjoyed observer

---

6 Brighton Declaration, adopted at the High Level Conference on the Future of the European Court of Human Rights, 20 April 2012, available at: www.coe.int/en/20120419-brighton-declaration.

7 *Ibidem.*

8 A-status is the label given to NHRIs who are considered by the International Coordinating Committee of NHRIs (ICC) to be in compliance with the Paris Principles. For more information on the ICC accreditation, see: G. De Beco, 'Assessment of the Paris Principles and the ICC Sub-Committee on Accreditation', Chapter 11 in this volume.

9 Interlaken Declaration, adopted at the High Level Conference on the Future of the European Court of Human Rights, 19 February 2010. Para. 4(b) calls upon states to 'continuing to increase, where appropriate in co-operation with national human rights institutions or other relevant bodies, the awareness of national authorities of the Convention standards and to ensure their application.'.

10 Izmir Declaration, adopted at the High Level Conference on the Future of the European Court, 27 April 2011, available at: www.coe.int.

11 Committee of Ministers, Resolution (97)11, 30 September 1997.

status with the Steering Committee on Human Rights since 2001.[12] Finally, the Commissioner for Human Rights, an institution set up in 1999, is specifically mandated to facilitate the work of national ombudspersons and similar national human rights institutions.[13] Recently, the Commissioner even referred to NHRIs as 'privileged partners in his human rights dialogue with member states'.[14]

There has thus been an increasing acknowledgement of the potential usefulness of national human rights institutions from a European perspective. Let us now return to the predicament of the European Court of Human Rights, with its large load of cases and its very limited means of enforcing implementation of judgments. How could NHRIs advance the effectiveness of the Court's in the 'run up' to Strasbourg? Put differently, what role can national human rights institutions play in the phase before proceedings in Strasbourg over alleged violations start? First off, it should be noted that NHRIs cannot themselves lodge complaints at the European Court on behalf of victims. The victim requirement of Article 34 ECHR precludes this. Some have argued in favour of such an *actio popularis* mandate for NHRIs under the Convention system,[15] but the most recent high level meetings of ECHR State Parties have shown no moves in that direction. In addition, as an institution set up by the state – no matter how independent on paper and in practice – an NHRI also cannot complain about violations against itself by the state.

Nevertheless, there are many other ways in which NHRIs can contribute. First, in the broadest sense their very existence and activities are meant to promote human rights protection and thus to prevent human rights violations nationally. More specifically, they could be empowered to bring cases of human rights violations to national courts.[16] The more effective they are at this, the smaller will be the need for international supervision by the European Court.

Secondly, national human rights institutions could inform the general public about the work of the Court and about the possibilities and limits of lodging a complaint in Strasbourg. In the past few years the Court itself has done a lot to inform Europeans about its work and its procedures. It has created online manuals for lawyers about the admissibility criteria, created compilations of relevant case-law on a wide range of specific themes and there are even short and informative online documentaries about the Court. In addition the HUDOC

---

12 De Beco, loc. cit.. *supra* note 5, p. 169. See also B. Adamson, 'NHRI and their European Counterparts: Scope for Strengthened Cooperation and Performance towards European Human Rights Institutions', Chapter 6 in this volume.

13 Committee of Ministers, Resolution 99(50), 7 May 1999, art. 3(d) of the Commissioner's terms of reference.

14 Commissioner for Human Rights of the Council of Europe, Activity Report 2011, 36, http://www.coe.int/t/commissioner/default_EN.asp.

15 De Beco, loc. cit. *supra* note 5, pp. 170–171.

16 This is suggested for example in: L. R. Helfer, 'Redesigning the European Court of Human Rights: Embeddedness as a Deep Structural Principle of the European Human Rights Regime', *European Journal of International Law*, vol. 19, no. 1, 2008, pp. 125–159, at p. 156.

case-law system links whenever possible to translations of important Court judgments in more languages than just English or French.[17] NHRIs can literally bring those informational aspects of the Court closer to national audiences by translating and actively divulging these important sources of information. Maybe the most useful way of avoiding manifestly ill-founded complaints – which make up a large percentage of the European Court's caseload – would be to clearly inform potential applicants of the admissibility criteria. This requires strong, accessible and effective NHRIs which have the necessary expertise. From a European vantage point, this should most urgently be done in those State Parties from which most applications stem. In 2011, for example, only six states accounted for almost two-thirds of the Court's caseload: Russia, Turkey, Italy, Romania, Ukraine and Serbia.[18] In that sense NHRIs could be the first port of call on the way to Strasbourg. A bit provocatively perhaps, it might even be suggested to take it one step further: one could begin to require that applicants, after exhausting domestic remedies, contact the NHRI for advice and information. This it must be added is not for an assessment of the merits of the claim, but rather to help and check whether the main admissibility criteria appear to be complied with. On receiving such advice, it would be the free choice of applicants whether to go to Strasbourg or not. To avoid that states would indirectly abuse such a structure to preclude that victims of human rights violations could turn to the Court, such a scheme would only be allowed in countries where NHRIs have A-status under the Paris Principles and are thus fully and effectively independent. In that sense, NHRIs could become gatekeepers: not by shutting the gates to Strasbourg, but rather by informing anyone who wants to pass through the gates about what lies behind them.

3. DURING: INTERVENTIONS

Once proceedings have started at the European Court of Human Rights, national human rights institutions can again contribute in an important way to the work of the Court. The Court values information from independent sources to supplement the views of the applicant and the state. It could be said that NHRIs can contextualise a case for the Court in a broader way than an individual applicant *could* ever do and in a more independent way than the defendant state *would* ever do. NHRIs can help to answer the following questions for the Court: is the legal issue at stake in the country involved broader or more general than the applicant's individual situation? And which structural issues – either laws or policies – form part of the problem? By providing information NHRIs can in this respect function as true *amici curiae*.

17 All of this is available at: www.echr.coe.int/echr.

18 European Court of Human Rights, Annual Report 2011, p. 13.

The European Convention on Human Rights allows for third party interventions in several ways. Article 36 reads as follows:

> 1. In all cases before a Chamber or the Grand Chamber, a High Contracting Party one of whose nationals is an applicant shall have the right to submit written comments and to take part in hearings.
> 2. The President of the Court may, in the interest of the proper administration of justice, invite any High Contracting Party which is not a party to the proceedings or any person concerned who is not the applicant to submit written comments or take part in hearings.
> 3. In all cases before a Chamber or the Grand Chamber, the Council of Europe Commissioner for Human Rights may submit written comments and take part in hearings.

This enables an intervention of NHRIs in two different ways. Either directly, when given leave by the president of the Court, or indirectly, by supplying the Commissioner for Human Rights with the necessary information.[19] The latter option has the advantage that the Commissioner has a formal right to intervene. In fact, the Commissioner would benefit from NHRI input in any submission made about national situations. It could be a good channel to group and coordinate the input of a group of NHRIs, even though they could also do that by themselves.[20] The Commissioner stands in close contact with NHRIs and in 2003 even established a liaison office with the particular goal of strengthening ties and coordinating information exchange.[21]

The option in which an NHRI or a group of NHRIs asks for leave to intervene in theory carries the risk that the Court could refuse an intervention. After all, the Court receives more requests for interventions than it can accommodate and selects on the basis of whether the intervention will really assist the Court's decision-making. Nevertheless, in practice NHRIs stand very good chances of having their submissions accepted. First, because the Court is generally open to interventions, even if it may at times request interveners to group their submissions.[22] Secondly and more importantly, because NHRIs, with both their unique rootedness in national societies and their independence, are in an excellent position to play an assisting role for the Court. One could even argue that their

---

19 See in this sense also: De Beco loc. cit. *supra* note 5, pp. 174–188.

20 For more information on the European Group of NHRIs and its activities in the context of third party interventions to the ECtHR cases, see: B. Adamson, chapter 6 in this volume, section 3.1.2., b).

21 *Ibidem*, pp. 177–178. For more information on the interaction of European NHRIs with the European Commissioner on Human Rights, see also: B. Adamson, 'NHRI and their European Counterparts: Scope for Strengthened Cooperation and Performance towards European Human Rights Institutions', Chapter 6 in this volume, at 3.1.3.

22 D. Harris, M. O'Boyle, E. Bates and C. Buckley, *Harris, O'Boyle & Warbrick: Law of the European Convention on Human Rights*, Oxford University Press, 2009, 2nd ed., pp. 855–856.

legitimacy can be higher than that of NGOs, since these might be driven by very specific interests.

In any event, whichever of these two paths is chosen, a third party intervention of this kind offers NHRIs the possibility to contextualise a pending case. An intervention can inform the Court of the wider context in which a specific law or policy was adopted, changed or abolished. This permits the Court to look beyond the particularities of an individual case and become more conscious of possible systemic or structural problems. One could call this "factual contextualisation". But NHRIs can also undertake "legal contextualisation", in a similar vein to NGOs which submit interventions to the Court. Whenever an important legal point of interpretation of the Convention presents itself, a comparative exercise can be very useful. Especially if one considers that the Court itself has only limited research resources for that purpose. Such a comparison could serve either to indicate the situation under other international human rights treaties or adjudicating bodies or to indicate whether a common ground or European consensus exists on a specific legal issue by comparing a large number of European states.[23] It goes without saying that the latter could best be undertaken by a group of NHRIs. Taking it even one step further, one may also argue that national human rights institutions may offer suggestions as to the direction in which more general action needs to be undertaken by the government.

The possibility for intervention by NHRIs thus exists. But is this possibility actually used? Although the first instances of third party interventions date from the late 1970s, it was mostly (human rights) NGOs which seized the opportunity. In fewer cases, states or persons directly affected were given leave to intervene.[24] Cases in which national human rights institutions participated as third parties are still relatively rare and recent. This can partly be explained by the fact that NHRIs themselves are in most states a very new phenomenon. Nevertheless, it seems that the call for greater NHRI involvement by the Council of Europe has not yet been taken up fully in this respect. In what follows I will go into a few examples of third party interventions by national human rights institutions in order to illustrate the possibilities and limitations.

The earliest examples of NHRI intervention come from the context of Northern Ireland. In the case of *Brannigan and McBride,*[25] decided by the Court in 1993, the Northern Ireland Standing Advisory Commission on Human Rights – predecessor to the Northern Ireland Human Rights Commission – was given leave to intervene. As De Beco notes, it is not surprising that this Northern Irish institution was the first NHRI to intervene as a third party. It had already, in the national context, been frequently intervening in court cases and was thus

23 Ph. Leach, *Taking a Case to the European Court of Human Rights*, Oxford University Press, 2011, 3rd ed., p. 50.

24 For examples, see: *ibidem*, pp. 50–55.

25 ECtHR, *Brannigan and McBride v. the United Kingdom*, 25 May 1993 (Applications No. 14553/89 and 14554/89).

experienced in that respect.[26] The case focused on the question whether the United Kingdom's derogation of the ECHR in the context of its fight against terrorism was justified. The Standing Advisory Commission argued it was and in turn the Court came to the same conclusion, although it is difficult to establish whether the third party intervention was in any way decisive. Intervening human rights NGOs had argued for very strict scrutiny by the Court.[27] The Court did indicate that it made its assessment 'in the light of all the material before it as to the extent and impact of terrorist violence in Northern Ireland and elsewhere in the United Kingdom'.[28] Undoubtedly, such information also included the contents of the Standing Advisory Commission's intervention. This example also shows that NHRIs will not always 'side' with the applicants – a concern some states may have.

Four more cases from the same context, decided almost a decade later – in Spring 2001 and thus months before the September 11 attacks on New York's World Trade Center – also led to intervention by the Northern Irish Human Rights Commission. This series of cases, *Hugh Jordan*, *Kelly and others*, *McKerr*, and *Shanagan*,[29] related to killings of persons allegedly involved in terrorism. In these cases, the Human Rights Commission pointed at the deficiencies in the investigation of these killings, referred to the Scottish system which allowed for more access to the investigation by immediate family members and asked the Court to give guidance on how such investigations should be conducted.[30] The Court concluded that the shortcomings in the investigations had violated article 2 ECHR, the right to life, and did so on several of the points brought forward by the Human Rights Commission. It is therefore probable that the Commission's submission informed the Court's decision-making.[31] References to earlier case-law pointed out how national authorities should carry out investigations in line with the requirements of the European Convention.

More recently, in the very different context of migration and social policy, the (English) Equality and Human Rights Commission was given leave to intervene in *Bah v. the United Kingdom*.[32] The case concerned a woman from Sierra Leone who came to the United Kingdom (UK) as an asylum seeker and was eventually given a permanent residence permit. When she had her son (a 13 year old) come

26 De Beco loc. cit. *supra* note 5, p. 184.
27 *Brannigan and McBride*, para. 42.
28 *Ibidem*, para. 47.
29 All judgments were delivered by the European Court of Human Rights on 4 May 2001. The respective application numbers are: 24746/94 (*Hugh Jordan*), 30054/96 (*Kelly and others*), 28883/95 (*McKerr*), and 37715/97 (*Shanagan*).
30 See for example, *Hugh Jordan*, para. 101.
31 This was pointed out by several authors: B. Dickson, 'The Contribution of Human Rights Commissions to the Protection of Human Rights', *Public Law*, 2003, pp. 272–285, at p. 282; L.-A. Sicilianos, 'La tierce intervention devant la Cour européenne des Droits de l'Homme', in H. Ruiz Fabri and J.-M. Sorel, *Le tiers a l'instance devant les jurisdictions internationales*, Pedone, 2007, p. 137, both mentioned in: De Beco loc. cit. *supra* note 5, p. 184, footnote 64.
32 ECtHR, *Bah v. the United Kingdom*, 27 September 2011 (Application No. 56328/07).

over from Sierra Leone as well, he, by contrast, was given a *conditional* permit to stay. The condition was that he would not have recourse to any public funds. When the son arrived in the UK, the private landlord where Ms Bah was renting ended the contract since he did not want more than one person living in the room. Ms Bah applied for social housing with priority need, since there was a threat that she and her son would become homeless. Normally families with minor children would be given precedence, but Ms Bah child did not count as the law provided for an exception: children with a conditional permit did not count. She complained in Strasbourg that the UK violated her right to respect for the home in conjunction with Article 14 ECHR: the non-discrimination clause. An English Court of Appeal had held in another case that the legal provision at stake (about children on conditional permits not counting) was contrary to the ECHR. By contrast, the UK government argued that this provision was meant to prevent welfare tourism.

In its intervention,[33] the Equality and Human Rights Commission contextualised the issue. It labelled the case as involving ongoing structural discrimination in English housing legislation. In addition, the Commission informed the European Court that the authorities had been particularly slow and grudging to change the law after the Court of Appeals had criticised it. Eventually, the law was changed but according to the Equality and Human Rights Commission, it simply replaced one form of discrimination (conditional status) with another (nationality). This intervention is an example of a case in which an NHRI offered information which the government would obviously not be keen to inform the Court about and which is too specialised for an individual applicant to be aware of.

Unfortunately, in these proceedings the NHRIs information did not strike at the core of the Court's *ratio decidendi* which focused on a broad margin of appreciation in socio-economic matters and held that the distinction was justified and not disproportionate in the context of a scarce stock of social housing. Thus, in the *Bah* case the NHRI's intervention did not make a decisive difference in the outcome of the case. This may seem surprising as the Equality and Human Rights Commission has acquired some experience over the past few years in intervening in national court cases. The *Bah* judgment shows that involvement of a national human rights institution is no legal panacea and that it may not be predictable to an intervening NHRI what the Court would consider to be the heart of the matter. Nevertheless, the Court's questions to the state could offer some pointers in this regard.

A final example is a common intervention by an alliance of more than thirty NHRIs, the European Group of National Human Rights Institutions.[34] As a

33 Summarised in paragraphs 33–34 of the judgment.

34 For more information on the European Group of NHRIs, see: B. Adamson, 'NHRI and their European Counterparts: Scope for Strengthened Cooperation and Performance towards European Human Rights Institutions', Chapter 6 in this volume.

pan-European group it is in an excellent position to provide the Commissioner for Human Rights and the European Court with representative overviews of national laws and policies. The case of *D.D. v. Lithuania*[35] is the first in which it intervened, but more may follow. D.D. suffered from schizophrenia and was legally incapacitated. At the request of her legal guardian, her adoptive father, she was placed in a care home against her will. The legal capacity rights of people with (mental) disabilities were at the core of the case and *D.D.* was widely seen as an opportunity for the Court to provide more clarity in the issue: apart from the European Group of NHRIs, the Harvard Project on Disability also was given leave to intervene. In addition, the Court itself referred in the case to other non-ECHR sources, such as the Convention on the Rights of Persons with Disabilities, a Committee of Ministers recommendation on the issue, and a report on Lithuania by the European Committee for the Prevention of Torture and Inhuman or Degrading Treatment or Punishment.[36] Thus, there certainly was no lack of information for the Court in this case.

The comments of the European Group of NHRIs summarise the key international documents on the issue, but most added value can be found in their comparative European overview on national laws concerning legal capacity. In those, the Group discerns a shift in national legislation in a large number of countries towards a concept of disability which puts more emphasis on self-determination and autonomy.[37] In the Group's submission it is striking that Lithuania as such is barely mentioned: the comments focus on European and global legal trends and argue for a different approach. Clearly, the Group saw the specific case as a broader opportunity for a clearer stance in the European Court's case-law. In its judgment, the Court did no go into the shifts in national legislation in the continent but it did seem to follow the underlying concept. First, it highlighted the European Group of NHRI's assertion that the Convention guaranteed rights for everyone regardless of their individual level of capacity. Secondly, the Court also reiterated the Group's mentioning of its reference to the landmark *Winterwerp*[38] case with its emphasis on mental illness being able to legitimise limitations on access to courts, but not warranting total absence of a right to access. Thirdly, in its own argumentation on whether the proceedings in Lithuania in D.D.'s case violated the right to access to court, the European Court held crucially:

> 'The Court accepts that there may be situations where a person deprived of legal capacity is entirely unable to express a coherent view or give proper instructions to a lawyer. It considers, however, that in many cases the fact that an individual has to

35 ECtHR, *D.D. v. Lithuania*, 14 February 2012 (Application No. 13469/06).

36 See paras. 84–91 of the judgment for these documents.

37 Written Comments by the European Group of National Human Rights Institutions in the case of *D.D. v. Lithuania*, 22 April 2008, pp. 6–10.

38 ECtHR, *Winterwerp v. the Netherlands*, 24 October 1979 (Application No. 6301/73).

> be placed under guardianship because he lacks the ability to administer his affairs does not mean that he is incapable of expressing a view on his situation and thus of coming into conflict with the guardian. In such cases, when the conflict potential has a major impact on the person's legal situation, such as when there is a proposed change of guardian, it is essential that the person concerned should have access to court and the opportunity to be heard either in person or, where necessary, through some form of representation. Mental illness may entail restricting or modifying the manner of exercise of such a right, but it cannot justify impairing the very essence of the right, except in very exceptional circumstances such as those mentioned above. Indeed, special procedural safeguards may prove called for in order to protect the interests of persons who, on account of their mental health issues, are not fully capable of acting for themselves (see, *mutatis mutandis*, *Winterwerp*, cited above, § 60).'[39]

The Court went on to find a violation of Article 6 ECHR, which includes the right to access to court. In many ways the concepts of self-determination and autonomy thus seem to be present implicitly, although it may have come as a disappointment to many civil society organisations that the Court did not go into the recent shifts in national legislation in a large number of countries and the more thorough emphasis on autonomy these reflect than the old 1979 *Winterwerp* case. The *D.D.* judgment thus offers a mixed bag as far as the usefulness and direct effect of NHRI interventions are concerned. The intervention may have highlighted certain key issues but that does not mean the Court very *explicitly* shows it took these issues into account, even if the general gist of the judgment seems to point in that direction.

Is there room for more of these interventions? As this short overview has shown, the cases in which NHRIs have intervened are still very few and far between. Nevertheless, they offer a promising venue to increase the quality of the adjudicatory process. Obviously, national human rights institutions cannot intervene in each case, but there is a strong argument in favour of intervention in two kinds of cases.

First, as was alluded to above, instances in which the human rights problem at stake is broader than the individual case which the Court adjudicates. This would apply to large-scale structural or systemic problems in a country. In the system of adjudication under the European Convention a specific tool has been developed by the Court to deal with such situations: the pilot judgment procedure. This procedure allows the Court to single out a case among many comparable ones, decide on the merits, and subsequently indicate general measures to be taken by the defendant state.[40] This can both prevent new human rights violations as well as allow the Court to deal more expediently with its large caseload. The Court can

39 *D.D.v Lithuania*, para. 118.

40 For a more elaborate overview, see my own 'The Pilot Judgment Procedure at the European Court of Human Rights: Possibilities and Challenges', *Nomiko Vima (the Greek Law Journal)*, vol. 57, 2009, pp. 1890–1902, available at: ssrn.com, no. 1514441.

itself become aware of a structural issue and choose to tackle it by way of a pilot judgment procedure by the mere fact that large amounts of claims on the same issue reach its doorsteps. But NHRIs could also actively highlight cases to the Court which are representative of wider problems which merit the more efficient pilot judgment approach. NHRIs could help to identify problematic national laws or policies warranting change and also, through the information provided in the intervention, prevent that the Court would indicate general measures for the state to take which would fall foul of their goal rather than striking at the core of the matter.

Secondly, NHRI interventions can be useful in cases in which the practice in the country at stake is clearly out of line with most other European countries. This entails that the level of European consensus and the scope of the margin of appreciation become relevant. The NHRI can here clarify the national context. This does not necessarily mean that a national human rights institution would argue in favour of less or more margin: both are possible. An NHRI could argue that a state is lagging behind compared to a common European standard or it could clarify why a different national position can be justified as it protects human rights equally but in a different way than other state parties to the Convention do – this latter situation admittedly being much more rare. Especially when a Strasbourg verdict could have consequences which the judges at the European Court cannot entirely foresee, the input of an NHRI can be crucial. In summary, NHRIs can contribute to *informed, legitimate* and *feasible* European Court judgments.

4. AFTER: IMPLEMENTATION AND PREVENTION OF RENEWED VIOLATIONS

Once a judgment is delivered by the Court, it is up to the state to implement the judgment. Of course, formally the Committee of Ministers supervises the execution of judgments of the European Court of Human Rights, as provided by Article 46 ECHR. But that can only be part of the solution. In fact, supervision has not been free of problems.[41] Political representatives, with a limited staff, having to supervise each other through peer pressure: it works to get the compensation paid to the victim in most cases, but broader reforms following from a judgment can never be sufficiently pushed and supervised from the international level. The work of the Committee of Ministers barely features in most national discussions.

41 See more elaborately: L. Zwaak, 'The Role of the Council of Europe and its Committee of Ministers. Analysing the Efficiency of Measures Taken Under Article 46(2) of the ECHR', in: I. Boerefijn and J. Goldschmidt, *Changing Perceptions of Sovereignty and Human Rights*, Intersentia, 2008, pp. 355–380.

At the national level, parliaments have a role to play, as the Parliamentary Assembly of the Council of Europe has pointed out,[42] as well as civil society. But again, NHRIs could be a focal point: as an independent watchdog which structurally supervises from within the country itself whether national authorities truly and faithfully implement Strasbourg judgments. The more effective they are in doing so, the better they can help to prevent new claims about similar problems going to Strasbourg. This entails that also in this third stage, the emphasis should be on cases reflecting large-scale or structural problems. That is where human rights are most at stake and that is also where the largest gains can be made. In that sense, Strasbourg judgments could be pointers for NHRIs on the fields in which advocacy for change is necessary.

National human rights institutions could also complement the information provided by states to the Committee of Ministers on how and to what extent they are implementing the Court's judgments. Protocol 14 which led to a reform of the supervisory system of the ECHR even provides that the Committee of Ministers, by a majority of two-thirds of the votes, can refer a situation back to the Court.[43] Both to inform such a referral and also the eventual decision by the Court on compliance, NHRIs could offer substantive input in order to come to more informed decision-making. Additionally, NHRIs can offer advice on the best ways – most fitting in a particular national jurisdiction – in which a judgment should be implemented: whether and in which precise form the setting up of a new administrative or judicial remedy is most effective, for example.

In taking upon themselves the aforementioned roles, national human rights institutions also have a preventative function. The more effectively they advise and induce national authorities to pay due regard to Strasbourg's judgments – even when addressed to other State Parties – the more new human rights complaints could be prevented from arising and going to the European Court. This is beneficial not only to the Court, but also to national authorities and, most importantly, to the protection of human rights in general.

5. CONCLUSION

National human rights institutions may be a relative newcomer on the stage of human rights. Nevertheless, as I have tried to demonstrate above, they can be conveyors of information and tools of leverage in three different phases: before a human rights complaint goes to the European Court, during the proceedings in Strasbourg, and in the implementation phase. In doing so, they can help smoothening the sometimes fraught dialogue or tango between national

42 See e.g. the report of Parliamentary Assembly member Marie-Louise Bemelmans-Videc, 'Guaranteeing the authority and effectiveness of the European Court of Human Rights', Doc. 12811, 3 January 2012, available at: assembly.coe.int.

43 Article 46(4) ECHR.

authorities and international human rights institutions such as the European Court of Human Rights.

A note of caution is in place here however, with the danger of stating the obvious. NHRIs can neither replace the decision-making of the European Court of Human Rights itself nor take upon them the responsibility for securing human rights which State Parties to the European Convention carry as a difficult but crucial burden. They can advise, lobby, supplement and inform, but ultimately state authorities remain responsible under international law.

Concluding, NHRIs may be a new partner for regional human rights courts such as the European Court of Human Rights, but I would argue that they can be an extremely useful one. In line with the Paris Principles, their cooperation with regional institutions can help to increase human rights protection. NHRI's can channel national expertise and information to the European level and vice versa. By supporting the work of the Court from within national jurisdictions, they can help to make European human rights more effective and the Court's judgments more legitimate – and in passing help to reduce the Strasbourg case-load. From the Court's perspective NHRIs can truly be the much needed ears and arms. And for State Parties to the European Convention, the activities of NHRIs can be a strong inducement to take the Strasbourg machinery and more fundamentally the protection of human rights more seriously. After all, one may be tempted to pay more attention when one's own watchdog barks than when the neighbour's dog does.

THE EUROPEAN UNION AND NATIONAL HUMAN RIGHTS INSTITUTIONS

Jan Wouters,[1] Katrien Meuwissen[2] and Ana Sofia Barros[3]

1. INTRODUCTION: THE EU MULTI-LAYERED HUMAN RIGHTS ARCHITECTURE[4]

As reflected in the post-Lisbon Treaty on European Union (TEU), 'respect for human rights' is one of the foundational values of the European Union[5] (EU or Union) and the 'protection of human rights' is one of the central objectives in the Union's relations with the wider world.[6] Moreover, with the entry into force of the Lisbon Treaty on 1 December 2009, the EU Charter of Fundamental Rights has been given the status of primary Union law,[7] and the EU is set to accede to the European Convention of Human Rights.[8] In terms of actors, there have also been novelties: among the members of the European Commission, there is a Commissioner who is specifically competent for fundamental rights,[9] and in July 2012 an EU Special Representative for Human Rights was appointed.[10] A Joint Communication of the European Commission and the High Representative of

1 Jan Wouters is Full Professor of International Law and International Organisations and Director, Leuven Centre for Global Governance Studies – Institute for International Law, KU Leuven.

2 Katrien Meuwissen is researcher at the Leuven Centre for Global Governance Studies and teaching assistant at the KU Leuven Institute for International Law.

3 Ana Sofia Barros is researcher at the Leuven Centre for Global Governance Studies and at the Institute for International Law, KU Leuven.

4 In accordance with EU terminology we use the terms 'fundamental rights' and 'human rights' throughout the text. While the EU refers to 'fundamental rights' in its internal policy (in light of the Charter of Fundamental Rights of the European Union), 'human rights' is used for its external policies (in light of the international conventions on human rights).

5 See Article 2, Consolidated Version of The Treaty on European Union (TEU), *OJ* C 83/13, 30 March 2010.

6 Article 3(5) TEU.

7 Article 6(1) TEU.

8 Article 6(2) TEU.

9 Viviane Reding, Commissioner for Justice, Fundamental Rights and Citizenship. See: http://ec.europa.eu/commission_2010-2014/reding/index_en.htm.

10 Stavros Lambrinidis; see Council of the European Union, 'Council decision 2012/440/CFSP of 25 July 2012 appointing the European Union Special Representative for Human Rights', *OJ* L200/21, 27 July 2012.

the European Union for Foreign Affairs and Security Policy of December 2011 considers that 'the promotion and protection of human rights is a silver thread running through all EU action both at home and abroad'.[11] The multi-faceted internal and external EU human rights policies interrelate with national, regional and international mechanisms in the area of human rights.

From all of this, a complex web emerges of a multi-layered EU human rights architecture. While the EU is uniquely placed to protect and promote human rights, the density of actors, instruments and policy areas poses itself a challenge to a coherent human rights policy. As fundamental rights become binding on the EU itself, its institutions are increasingly in need of expert advice in this area. Moreover, the many mechanisms in place also enhance the need for information of EU citizens, especially on the question of where they can turn to in case of a violation of their human rights. Finally, as recently indicated by the Commissioner for Justice, Fundamental Rights and Citizenship, while many human rights standards are in place, a better connection needs to be made between 'abstract legal texts and the reality'.[12] The present chapter aims to demonstrate that National Human Rights Institutions (NHRIs) can be important partners for the EU in rendering its human rights policy more effective. Whether they deliver expert advice on human rights from within the EU or across the globe, spread valuable information that can be used by the EU in its multi-faceted human rights promotion and protection, monitor the implementation of European and international human rights instruments, or even monitor EU development policy in third countries, NHRIs can constitute important bridges across the multiple layers of the EU internal and external human rights architecture.

This chapter is built up in two parts. The first part explores the potential for EU-NHRI cooperation *within* the EU with a view to fostering a fundamental rights culture across Europe. Attention is paid to (i) the potential role of NHRIs in the process of EU policy and law-making, particularly in view of the need for the consideration of fundamental rights in impact assessments, (ii) the relevance of NHRIs to ensure respect for the Charter on Fundamental Rights when Member States act within the scope of EU law, and (iii) the potential that NHRIs offer to connect EU citizens with their fundamental rights, through providing information on the appropriate means of redress when their fundamental rights are violated. The second part explores the potential synergies of EU-NHRI cooperation in EU *external* relations, in particular (i) in the field of development cooperation, (ii) before the UN Human Rights Council, and (iii) cooperation on common human rights priorities across human rights fora.

---

11 European Commission and High Representative of the European Union for Foreign Affairs and Security Policy, Joint Communication to the European Parliament and the Council, 'Human Rights and Democracy at the Heart of the EU External Action- Towards a More Effective Approach', COM(2011) 886 final, 12 December 2011, p. 4.

12 Viviane Reding, 'The binding EU Charter of Fundamental Rights: Key trends two years later', Speech/12/266, Brussels, 16 April 2012, p. 3.

A note of caution is due, however: this chapter does not intend to provide an all-encompassing overview of the potential for EU cooperation with NHRIs in internal and external human rights domains. Rather, it deals with a number of relevant issue areas in both domains in order to highlight opportunities for a more structured cooperation between the EU and NHRIs.

2. EU-NHRI COOPERATION: CONTRIBUTION TO A FUNDAMENTAL RIGHTS CULTURE WITHIN THE EU

Over the past 15 years, a fundamental rights culture has evolved within the EU. A decisive step in this regard was the proclamation of the Charter of Fundamental Rights of the European Union on 7 December 2000 (Charter).[13] Although initially not legally binding, the Charter soon gained the status of an authoritative catalogue of fundamental rights and had a transformative impact on the working culture and practices of EU institutions.[14] With the entry into force of the Lisbon Treaty, the Charter was accorded the same legal status as the European Treaties, giving a new boost to the EU's work concerning the protection of fundamental rights.[15] The Charter applies primarily to the institutions and bodies of the EU, and concerns in particular the legislative and decision-making work of the Commission, Parliament and the Council, which must be in conformity with it (Article 51(1) Charter). Moreover, it applies to EU Member States when they are acting within the scope of EU law (*ibid.*). Aimed at enabling individuals to enjoy their fundamental rights in situations governed by EU law, the Charter, and its implications, must be duly disseminated. By ensuring an effective implementation of the Charter across the Union, and the outreach of the rights set therein, the EU contributes to enhancing the confidence of EU citizens in its policies and actions, while rendering the Charter a practical tool for the protection of fundamental rights.

NHRIs can support the EU to further strengthen a fundamental rights culture throughout the Union. Notably, their expertise can be linked to the means currently used to ensure that the Charter rights are complied with. This applies in the first place to the process of EU policy and law-making (2.1). Furthermore, NHRIs can play a relevant role in helping to ensure Member States' compliance with the Charter when acting within the scope of EU law (2.2). Finally, NHRIs can have an important role in connecting citizens with the procedures that are in place to protect their fundamental rights on the ground (2.3).

13 *OJ* C 364, 18 December 2000.

14 This was reflected, for instance, in the frequent allusions by the Union Courts to the provisions of the Charter. See K. Lenaerts and P. Van Nuffel, *European Union Law*, Sweet and Maxwell, 2011, p. 832.

15 As referred to by the European Commission in its Communication 'Strategy for the Effective Implementation of the Charter of Fundamental Rights by the European Union', COM (2010) 573/4, 19 October 2010, p. 2 (European Commission Implementation Strategy 2010).

2.1. NHRIS' RELEVANCE FOR EU POLICY AND LAW-MAKING IN ACCORDANCE WITH FUNDAMENTAL RIGHTS

EU institutions, bodies, offices and agencies are the first addressees of the Charter and therefore have to 'respect the rights, observe the principles and promote the application thereof in accordance with their respective powers' (art. 51(1) Charter). Accordingly, as acknowledged by some of its institutions,[16] the EU needs to adopt a proactive, rather than a reactive approach to fundamental rights. NHRIs can be important partners for the EU, as they can provide the latter's institutions with information and expertise on fundamental rights promotion and protection. Specifically, European NHRIs and their coordinating network (the European Group of National Human Rights Institutions) should be consulted by the EU whenever it develops fundamental rights-related policy initiatives and/or adopts legislative measures, in order to translate NHRI expert knowledge from the ground into consistent and efficient EU policy and action.

A concrete example in this regard is provided by the Commission's consultation practices preceding the adoption of Green and White Papers. In order for the Commission to fuel discussions at European level on topical themes possibly leading to legislative initiatives, there is a solid institutionalised practice of launching Green Papers in which a wide range of stakeholders is invited to participate. Transparency and inclusiveness are, in fact, seen as crucial for EU policy formulation.[17] The results of Green Papers are typically reflected in Commission White Papers, which, in turn, contain recommendations for EU action in a specific area. Green Paper consultation processes purport to provide the Commission with factual information, concrete insight and consistent data, which can naturally be imparted by NHRIs where the issues at stake concern fundamental rights. For instance, a Green Paper adopted by the Commission on

---

16 See for example Conclusions of the Presidency, European Council 4–5 November 2004, Annex I, 'The Hague Programme: Strengthening freedom, security and justice in the European Union', 14292/1/04 Rev 1, p. 14: '2. Protection of fundamental rights. Incorporating the Charter into the Constitutional Treaty and accession to the European Convention for the protection of human rights and fundamental freedoms will place the Union, including its institutions, under a legal obligation to ensure that in all its areas of activity, fundamental rights are not only respected but also actively promoted.'. See also: Council of the European Union, 'EU Strategic Framework and Action Plan on Human Rights and Democracy', Press Release 11855/12, Luxembourg, 25 June 2012: 'Pursuing Coherent Objectives [...] Within their own frontiers, the EU and its Member States are committed to be exemplary in ensuring respect for human rights. Outside their frontiers, promoting and speaking out on human rights and democracy is a joint responsibility of the EU and its Member States.'

17 Under Article 11 TEU, '1. The institutions shall, by appropriate means, give citizens and representative associations the opportunity to make known and publicly exchange their views in all areas of Union action; 2. The institutions shall maintain an open, transparent and regular dialogue with representative associations and civil society; 3. The European Commission shall carry out broad consultations with parties concerned in order to ensure that the Union's actions are coherent and transparent.'.

14 June 2011 on the application of EU criminal justice legislation in the field of detention[18] benefited from substantial comments provided by the European Group of National Human Rights Institutions[19] as well as the Spanish Ombudsman.[20]

Such positive examples illustrate that EU-NHRI cooperation in the field of fundamental rights is taking off. The European Group of NHRIs has met with the Commissioner for Justice, Fundamental Rights and Citizenship (November 2010) and with the head of DG Justice (February 2011) in order to delineate the scope for cooperation, especially with regard to (i) consultation of the European Group in the context of green papers, (ii) a structured dialogue with NHRIs on the Commission's Annual Report on the Application of the EU Charter of Fundamental Rights, (iii) information-sharing on case-handling practices and procedures, and (iv) assistance with the awareness-raising and promotion of the Charter among EU citizens.[21] The European Parliament has been a vocal promoter of the establishment of Paris Principles compliant NHRIs by EU Member States.[22] Especially the Parliament's LIBE[23] and DROI[24] Subcommittees would benefit from a more structured EU cooperation with NHRIs. While some interaction between the European Parliament and European NHRIs is taking place, this is limited due to resource constraints and priority-setting of the European NHRIs.[25]

The EU Agency for Fundamental Rights (FRA) was established in 2007 to provide EU institutions and Member States (when implementing EU law) with assistance and expertise when they take measures or formulate courses of action to fully respect fundamental rights.[26] FRA appears to function as the EU's own "NHRI". Indeed, when establishing the FRA, the European Commission referred to '*national institutions for the protection and promotion of human rights set up by some Member States on the basis of UN principles*' as a source of inspiration.[27] The FRA's main functions consist in data collection, the production of expert opinions,

18 Green Paper, 'Strengthening mutual trust in the European judicial area – A Green Paper on the application of EU criminal justice legislation in the field of detention', COM(2011) 327 final, 14 June 2011.

19 The document is available at: http://ec.europa.eu/justice/newsroom/criminal/opinion/files/110510/irish_human_rights_commission_ihrc_response_en.pdf.

20 The document is available at: http://ec.europa.eu/justice/newsroom/criminal/opinion/files/110510/reply_from_es_ombudsman_en.pdf.

21 Report of the Chair of the European Group of National Human Rights Institutions covering the period March 2010 to March 2011, 24th Session of The International Coordinating Committee of NHRIs, Geneva, 16–19 May 2011. See also *infra* 2.3 and B. Adamson, Chapter 6 in this volume.

22 European Parliament Resolution of 14 January 2009 on the Situation of Fundamental Rights in the European Union 2004–2008, A6-0479/2008, para. 16.

23 Subcommittee on Civil Liberties, Justice and Home Affairs: cooperation with NHRIs would be mainly relevant to the fundamental rights issues relating to the internal EU policy.

24 Subcommittee on Human Rights: cooperation with NHRIs would be mainly relevant to the fundamental rights issues relating to the external EU policy.

25 As observed by B. Adamson in Chapter 6.

26 Article 2 of Council Regulation (EC) No 168/2007, 15 February 2007.

27 Communication from the Commission, 'The Fundamental Rights Agency Public Consultation Document', COM(2004) 693 final, 25 October 2004, p.4.

and the establishment of a communication strategy in order to raise public awareness of fundamental rights.[28] These competences mirror functions that are also attributed to NHRIs on the basis of the Paris Principles.[29] A further element indicating the FRA's position as "the EU's NHRI" is the reference made to the Paris Principles in the FRA's founding regulation. According to the latter: 'having regard to [...] the Paris Principles, the composition of [FRA's Management] Board should ensure the Agency's independence from both Community institutions and Member State governments and assemble the broadest possible expertise in the field of fundamental rights'.[30]

Whereas the mandate and composition of the FRA seem to point to a position as the "EU's NHRI", it is clear that the FRA's founding regulation does not attribute to the Agency a sufficiently comprehensive mandate nor a truly pluralistic and independent composition[31] which would allow it to function as a "Paris Principle compliant" fundamental rights institution. To some extent, this is due to the specificity of the EU. As the European Commission noted, the FRA could not have, for example, quasi-judicial powers (dealing with complaints and petitions) as some NHRIs do,[32] since 'the Commission's role of supervising the proper application of Community law must be respected'.[33] More importantly, however, the FRA does not have the competence to adequately monitor human rights compliance of the EU's internal and external policy and legislative initiatives. For example, its conclusions, opinions and reports which 'concern' legislative proposals from the Commission or positions taken by the EU institutions in the course of the legislative procedure can be formulated only if the respective institution has requested it to do so.[34] This restriction clearly falls short of the Paris Principles, which require that NHRIs may freely consider any questions falling within their competence, irrespective of whether they are submitted by the

28 See Article 4 of Council Regulation (EC) No 168/2007 for the enumeration of the eight specific tasks attributed to FRA. See also G. L. Toggenburg, 'The role of the new EU Fundamental Rights Agency: Debating the "sex of angels" or improving Europe's human rights performance?', *European Law Review*, 2008, vol. 33, no. 3, pp. 385–398, at p.387.

29 'Principles relating to the status of national institutions', as adopted by UN General Assembly, resolution A/RES/48/134 of 20 December 1993 (further: Paris Principles), 'Competence and responsibilities', para. 3, especially (a) and (g).

30 Considerans (20), Preamble of Council Regulation (EC) No 168/2007.

31 It can be noted, for example, that even if FRA cooperates with civil society, civil society representatives are not members of any of FRA's Boards. In contrary, the FRA's Management Board includes two representatives of the Commission (Article 12(1)(c) Council Regulation), one of which is also member of the Executive Board (Article 13(1) Council Regulation). The Paris Principles, however, do require an 'independent and pluralistic' composition of NHRIs, encompassing 'the social forces (of civilian society) involved in the promotion and protection of human rights'. See: Paris Principles, 'composition and guarantees of independence and pluralism', para. 1.

32 Paris Principles, 'additional principles concerning the status of commissions with quasi-jurisdictional competence'.

33 Commission Communication, *supra* note 27, p. 4.

34 Article 4(2) of Council Regulation (EC) No 168/2007.

government and especially 'without referral to a higher authority'.[35] These kinds of restrictions in the FRA's mandate undermine the EU's purported aim to adopt a more proactive approach towards fundamental rights promotion and protection. Accordingly, a better alignment of the FRA's mandate with the standards put forward in the Paris Principles would enhance its potential contribution to EU compliance with fundamental rights.[36]

In view of its embedment in the EU's institutional framework on the one hand, and its explicit mandate to cooperate with NHRIs on the other hand,[37] the FRA seems to be the most prominent EU interlocutor for NHRIs. The FRA interacts with NHRIs on a regular basis, with regard to the annual planning of its activities as well as its involvement in specific fundamental rights programmes.[38] It has the mandate to cooperate with 'public bodies competent in the field of fundamental rights in the Member States, *including* national human rights institutions'.[39] As the FRA is mandated to cooperate with the full spectrum of domestic human rights bodies simultaneously, it has been issuing extensive reports providing an overview of the different national bodies in EU Member States 'with a mandate to monitor fundamental rights'.[40] The FRA can thus offer a unique platform to engender better cooperation and synergies between the various EU domestic institutions with a human rights mandate, thereby contributing to a stronger "European fundamental rights architecture".[41]

---

35 Paris Principles, 'competence and responsibilities', para. 3(a): '[...] either at the request of the authorities concerned or through the exercise of its power to hear a matter without higher referral, opinions, recommendations, proposals and reports on any matters concerning the promotion and protection of human rights [...].'; G. L. Toggenburg, 'The role of the new EU Fundamental Rights Agency: Debating the "sex of angels" or improving Europe's human rights performance?', European Law Review, 2008, vol. 33, no. 3, pp. 385–398, at p. 394.

36 See also: Cost Action IS0702 'The Role of the EU in UN Human Rights Reform, recommendations on National Human Rights Institutions (NHRIs)', included as an annex to this book, namely recommendation 12.

37 Article 8(2)(a) of Council Regulation (EC) No 168/2007.

38 For a detailed overview of the interaction of FRA with European NHRIs, see B. Adamson, Chapter 6 in this volume.

39 Article 8(2)(a) of Council Regulation (EC) No 168/2007, emphasis added. Europe is the continent with the strongest diversity in domestic institutions with a human rights mandate, ranging from data protection agencies to equality bodies, children commissions or Paris Principle compliant NHRIs. For an overview of the NHRI landscape in Europe, see M. Nowak, Chapter 1 in this volume.

40 FRA, 'Fundamental rights protection bodies need more support', press release 7 May 2010: 'Four new reports issued today by the European Union Agency for Fundamental Rights (FRA) give evidence that data protection authorities, equality bodies and national human rights institutions across the European Union are in need of additional support'. More information and the reports are available at: http://fra.europa.eu/en/press-release/2011/fundamental-rights-protection-bodies-need-more-support.

41 See especially the foreword of M. Kjaerum (Director of FRA) in: FRA, *National Human Rights Institutions in EU Member States, Strengthening the fundamental rights architecture in the EU*, Luxembourg, Publication Office of the European Union, 2010.

Currently, one of the main means for the EU to ensure compatibility of legislative proposals with the Charter is through taking account of fundamental rights in Impact Assessments (IAs).

Respect for fundamental rights is a condition for the lawfulness of EU acts and is subject to scrutiny of the European Court of Justice (ECJ), which can declare EU legislation invalid if it does not comply with the Charter.[42] The ECJ requires EU institutions to demonstrate that they have carefully considered different policy options and have chosen the most proportionate response to a given problem in light of the fundamental rights protected by the Charter.[43] The Charter thus supports the interpretation of the Treaties and the measures adopted in conformity with them, and sets the standards against which the validity of such measures must be judged.

As stated above, with the entry into force of the Lisbon Treaty, the Charter became legally binding as part of EU primary law. Hence, it is fundamental to ensure that at all stages of EU law-making processes, legislative proposals are scrutinised to ensure compatibility with it.

Impact Assessments (IAs) are valuable tools to achieve this end, as they enable informed judgments to be made in the evaluation of different policy options and may lead to discarding one of those options when it does not (fully) conform to fundamental rights.[44] The Commission launched IAs in 2002[45] and this tool is currently being used prior to all its major initiatives. Initially, fundamental rights were not prioritized in IAs: according to a Commission Communication from 2002, IAs should focus on economic, social and environmental impacts, and fundamental rights were only fleetingly mentioned as an example of a social impact that could arise.[46] To reflect the new legal status of the Charter, the Commission is reinforcing the structural assessment of the impact on fundamental rights across all sectors.[47] It issued Operational Guidance on taking account of fundamental

42 The compatibility of EU acts with Charter requirements has been scrutinised by the ECJ in various recent cases, inter alia: judgment of 26 February 2013 in Case C-399/11 *Stefano Melloni v Ministerio Fiscal*, not yet published in the ECR, and judgment of 22 January 2013 in Case C-283/11 *Sky Österreich GmbH v Österreichischer Rundfunk*, not yet published in the ECR. In Joined Cases C-92/09 and C-93/09 *Schecke and Eifert v Land Hessen* [2010] ECR I-11063 and Case C-236/09, *Association Belge des Consommateurs Test-Achats ASBL and Others v Conseil des ministres* [2011] ECR I-773, the Court found a conflict between EU legislative acts and the Charter, leading to the invalidation of some of the former's provisions.

43 *Schecke and Eifert*, paras. 81–83.

44 Checks on the legality of the final text are carried out at a later stage through processes internal to the Commission.

45 Communication from the Commission, 'Impact Assessment', COM(2002) 276 final, 5 June 2002.

46 *Ibid.*, p. 15.

47 Contrary to economic, social or environmental impacts, that are addressed in separate categories, fundamental rights impact assessments need to be done across all sectors. See: European Commission, 'Commission Staff Working Paper, Operational Guidance on taking account of Fundamental Rights in Commission Impact Assessments', SEC(2011)567 final, Brussels, 6 May 2011, p. 17 (Operational Guidance 2011). See also: Council of the European Union, 'EU Strategic Framework and Action Plan on Human Rights and Democracy', Press

rights in Commission Impact Assessments.[48] Importantly – and as recently remarked by the European Parliament when considering the new EU's human rights strategy[49] –, human rights IAs should also be undertaken by the EU before negotiating any bilateral or multilateral agreement with third countries. In this regard, the European Parliament called upon the Commission and the European External Action Service (EEAS) to 'develop a robust methodology which enshrines the principles of equality and non-discrimination so as to avoid any negative impact on certain populations and which provides for mutually agreed preventive or remedial measures in the event of any negative impact, before negotiations are finalised'.[50]

IAs should be based on high-quality and reliable data: apart from the information gathered within the Commission services, it is often necessary to rely on sources concerning specific national contexts.[51] In addition, as the 2011 Operational Guidance indicates, when interpreting the Charter, the IAs should also take account of the European Convention on Human Rights and United Nations (UN) human rights conventions.[52] Member State and stakeholder support can therefore be required to identify and use such information. As far as fundamental rights issues are concerned, NHRIs appear to be obvious and well-equipped entities for the Commission to consult and seek input from, as they are explicitly mandated to monitor and report on national human rights situations and to cooperate in this regard with regional or international institutions.[53] The expertise of NHRIs as actors monitoring the national implementation of international and regional human rights standards enables them to provide information to the Commission, taking into account the multi-layered European human rights protection system. Regrettably, while NHRIs fall within the ambit of the Commission's definition of 'relevant parties for consultation' in the preparation of an IA,[54] the Commission seems to focus on the consultation of

Release 11855/12, Luxembourg, 25 June 2012, Outcome, I. 1. 'Incorporate human rights in all Impact Assessment: Insert human rights in Impact Assessment, as and when it is carried out for legislative and non-legislative proposals, implementing measures and trade agreements that have significant economic, social and environmental impacts, or define future policies.'.

48 Operational Guidance 2011, *ibid.*

49 European Parliament, Committee on Foreign Affairs, 'Report on the review of the EU's human rights strategy (2012/2062(INI)), A7-0378/2012, 19 November 2012, paras. 50–55.

50 *Ibid.*, para. 54.

51 Impact Assessment Guidelines, SEC(2009) 92, 15 January 2009, p. 17. It is often the case that the required information is highly contextualised, as a complete IA may require *inter alia* a comprehensive collection of the existing legal framework, an understanding of the legal traditions of the Member States and an analysis of the extent to which the transposition of a new directive affects existing legislation, in terms of demanding the abrogation and/or amendment of different legislative instruments, both in their substantive and procedural dimensions.

52 Operational Guidance 2011, p. 8–9.

53 Paris Principles, Competence and Responsibilities, 3(d)-(e).

54 See Communication from the Commission, 'Towards a reinforced culture of consultation and dialogue – General principles and minimum standards for consultation of interested parties by the Commission, COM(2002) 704 final, 11 December 2002, p. 19.

NGOs and does not mention NHRIs in its Communications or Guidance relating to IAs.[55]

Screening of draft legislation should be done both by the European Parliament and the Council prior to the adoption of any substantive amendments to Commission proposals.[56] However, this has not been done as often as desirable.[57] In the area of fundamental rights, some efforts can nevertheless be noted: the European Parliament recommended in a Resolution of 2009[58] that every new policy, legislative proposal and programme should be accompanied by an IA concerning respect for fundamental rights. The Council, recognising its key role in ensuring the effective implementation of the Charter,[59] established "Guidelines on methodological steps to be taken to check fundamental rights compatibility at the Council's preparatory bodies".[60] While in none of these documents NHRIs are explicitly mentioned as partners for consultation, the Council and Parliament may consider cooperation with NHRIs in light of their broad human rights expertise, as indicated in relation to the Commission's IAs.

Member States have also been recommended by different EU institutions to conduct IAs whenever involved in EU law-making processes.[61] Accordingly, when Member States use their right of initiative in specific cases provided for by the Treaties, such as in the field of judicial cooperation in criminal matters

---

55 See, for example, Commission Operational Guidance 2011, p. 13: 'There are a number of stakeholders working in the field of fundamental rights that can provide valuable input during the consultation phase, such as non-governmental organisations specialising in human rights, health, development, environmental and social issues more generally.'. In addition, it can be noted that when the European Group of NHRIs met with the Vice-President of the Commission in November 2011, the latter 'indicated that she felt that [human rights proofing of EU draft legislation] would be best carried out by NHRIs at the national level in terms of human rights proofing laws giving effect to EU legislation. Including the European Group formally at the consultative phase at EU level would not be possible [...].' See: Report of the Chair of the European Group of National Human Rights Institutions covering the period March 2010 to March 2011, 24th Session of The International Coordinating Committee of NHRIs, Geneva, 16–19 May 2011. See further: B. Adamson, Chapter 11 in this volume.

56 Such commitment was made in the Inter-Institutional Agreement on Better Law-making of 2003 (Doc. 2003/C *OJ* C 321/1, 31 December 2003, para. 30) and was later complemented by the 'Common approach to impact assessment', agreed by the three EU institutions in November 2005', available at: http://ec.europa.eu/governance/impact/key_docs/docs/ii_common_approach_to_ia_en.pdf.

57 Communication from the Commission, 'Smart Regulation in the European Union', COM(2010) 543 final, 8 November 2010, p. 8.

58 European Parliament resolution on the situation of fundamental rights in the European Union (2009) – effective implementation after the entry into force of the Treaty of Lisbon (2009/2161(INI)), 15 December 2010.

59 Council conclusions on the role of the Council of the European Union in ensuring the effective implementation of the Charter of Fundamental Rights of the European Union, 3071st Justice and Home Affairs Council Meeting, Brussels, 24 and 25 February 2011, especially para. 4.

60 Doc 10140/11, 18 May 2011. In this document, the use of the expertise of national experts is suggested in cases of doubt regarding a fundamental rights issue, a role that might be progressively taken up by NHRIs.

61 See Council Conclusions loc. cit. *supra* note 59, paras. 9 and 10, and Commission Communications loc. cit. *supra* notes 45, p. 4 and 57, p. 9.

and police cooperation,[62] or when in general, they submit proposals for legislative amendments to the Council, they are expected to examine beforehand the conformity of these initiatives with the Charter and their impact on the rights set therein. In these instances too, it is submitted that the involvement of NHRIs is desirable.[63]

While direct NHRI-EU cooperation needs to be further elaborated, indirect participation of NHRIs in the EU law-making process is also feasible through cooperation of NHRIs with the FRA. The FRA is explicitly mentioned as a stakeholder that can be consulted for IAs.[64] Accordingly, through their cooperation with the FRA, NHRIs' expertise can indirectly trickle down into EU law-making. However, as the FRA can only deliver 'conclusions, opinions and reports' with regard to EU law-making to the extent that the European instances ask it to do so,[65] the scope for integration of NHRI expertise in EU-law making through the FRA is limited.[66]

NHRIs are well equipped for the EU to enhance the human rights knowledge base and to get input from for policy and law-making processes in accordance with fundamental rights. As the FRA notes, since the entry into force of the Lisbon Treaty, NHRIs have an ever more important role to play in the EU's fundamental rights architecture.[67] While NHRIs can be included as stakeholders to be consulted by the EU – especially when national contextual information is needed – it is striking that NHRIs are generally not mentioned in the EU's policy documents. This omission may be partly due to a lack of knowledge of EU institutions with regard to the functioning of NHRIs in Europe. Also, the diversity of national institutions competent in the area of human rights across Europe is a factor that can cause difficulties for EU institutions to structurally cooperate with NHRIs. NHRIs are not present in all EU Member States, and the scope and strength of NHRIs varies where such institutions are established.[68] The European Group of NHRIs, the network coordinating the NHRIs in Europe, could therefore serve as a focal point for EU-NHRI interaction.[69] The active cooperation of the European Group with organisations beyond the EU, such as the Council of Europe and the OSCE, and with UN human rights institutions, is an asset in view of the need of EU institutions for "multi-layered" information

62 See Articles 76(b) and 294(15) of the Treaty on the Functioning of the European Union (TFEU).

63 As indicated *infra*, 2.2 the consultation of NHRIs by EU Member States should be further strengthened.

64 See: Operational Guidance 2011, p. 13.

65 As mentioned above, note 35.

66 Article 4(2) of Council Regulation (EC) No 168/2007.

67 European Union Agency for Fundamental Rights, *National Human Rights Institutions in the EU Member States, Strengthening the Fundamental Rights Architecture in the EU*, Luxembourg, Publication Office of the European Union, 2010, p. 6.

68 Currently, 23 NHRIs exist in 16 of the 27 EU Member States. Out of these, 11 fully comply with the international standards relating to NHRIs. For more information, see M. Nowak, Chapter 1 in this volume.

69 See B. Adamson, Chapter 6 in this volume.

for proactive fundamental rights compliance of the Union. However, it must be noted that the European Group of NHRIs has a weak institutional structure and very limited resources. The strengthening of its institutional structure through the establishment of a Permanent Secretariat seems to be an important step in enhancing the capacity of the European Group to effectively advocate for a better integration of NHRIs in EU policy- and law-making processes.[70]

2.2. NHRIS' RELEVANCE FOR ENSURING MEMBER STATES' COMPLIANCE WITH THE CHARTER

According to Article 51(1) of the Charter, the provisions of the Charter are addressed 'to the Member States only when they are implementing Union law'. The 2010 Strategy on the Implementation of the Charter clarifies that 'the upholding of fundamental rights by EU Member States when they implement Union law is in the common interest of all Member States, because it is essential to the mutual confidence necessary for the operation of the Union.'[71] Indeed, particularly in view of the expansion of the EU *acquis* into fields where fundamental rights are especially relevant – such as the area of freedom, security and justice -, respect for fundamental rights across the 27 EU Member States has gained importance.

Whenever Member States act within the scope of Union law, e.g., when they apply Treaty provisions or transpose EU directives into national law,[72] they are bound to observe Union requirements regarding the protection of fundamental rights. To ensure the quality of transposition, ministries are required to conduct IAs domestically.[73] According to the Paris Principles,[74] NHRIs have the responsibility to examine legislative proposals and make recommendations to ensure that they are in conformity with the fundamental principles of human rights.[75] In view of the institutional linkage of NHRIs with their states and their broad human rights expertise, they are highly relevant partners to be consulted by national (and depending on the division of competences within Member States:

[70] *Ibid.*

[71] Communication from the Commission, 'Strategy for the effective implementation of the Charter of Fundamental Rights by the European Union', COM/2010/573 final, 19 October 2010.

[72] For an understanding of what it means to "act within the scope of Union law", see K. Lenaerts and P. Van Nuffel, *European Union Law*, Sweet and Maxwell, 2011, pp. 834–835.

[73] In the Commission Communication on Impact Assessment from 2002, mentioned above in note 45, Member States were already encouraged to establish standards for consultation and IAs when transposing directives leaving them broad margins for implementation. See also: Council Conclusions loc. cit. *supra* note 59, para. 9, and Commission Communication loc. cit. *supra* note 57, p. 9.

[74] United Nations Principles Relating to the Status of National Institutions, Annex to United Nations General Assembly resolution 48/134, 20 December 1993. See G. de Beco, Chapter 11 in this volume.

[75] Paris Principles, competences and responsibilities, Article 3(a)(i).

regional and/or local) authorities on how to ensure that their fundamental rights obligations are accounted for.

A 2006 study of Olivier De Schutter, however, indicates that in the majority of EU Member States, fundamental rights screening of national legislation is primarily done within governments or parliaments, with scarce external input from NHRIs.[76] While in that period human rights IAs did not play a significant role in the Member States, the binding force of the Charter today should be an incentive to enhance the importance attached to the respect for fundamental rights in IAs on the national level, and to strengthen the role of NHRIs in this context.

Beyond the need for respect of fundamental rights in the implementation of EU legal acts at the national level, there is also a need to enhance knowledge across the EU on the actual implementation of EU fundamental rights obligations in Member States. The recent *N.S.* case before the ECJ illustrates this.[77] The Court stressed that Member States are under the obligation to respect the Charter when they establish the responsibility for examining an asylum application under the Dublin II Regulation.[78] Even though the Common European Asylum System is based on mutual confidence and a presumption of compliance of the Member States, the Court found that Member States must not transfer an asylum seeker to another Member State if they cannot be aware of systemic deficiencies in the asylum procedure and reception conditions amounting to substantial grounds for believing that the person would face a real risk of being subjected to inhuman or degrading treatment.[79] The Court noted that Member States should be aware of these risks, and could do so through taking into account relevant reports provided by stakeholders such as international NGOs or the UN High Commissioner for Refugees.[80] In noting this, the ECJ referred to the similar *M.S.S.* judgment of the

76 O. De Schutter, 'When can National Human Rights Institutions successfully intervene in the process of adopting legislation?', Fourth Round Table of European National Institutions for the Promotion and Protection of Human Rights and the Council of Europe Commissioner for Human Rights, Athens, 27–28 September 2006, available at: http://www.coe.int/t/commissioner/Source/CommDH-NHRI(2006)2_E.doc.

77 ECJ, Joined Cases C-411/10 and C-493/10 *N.S. v Secretary of State for the Home Department and M.E. e.a. v Refugee Applications Commissioner* [2011] ECR I-0000. See in the same sense: European Court of Human Rights, *M.S.S. v. Belgium and Greece*, Application no. 30696/09, 21 January 2011, paras. 358, 360 and 367, referred to by the ECJ in its *N.S.* judgment, para. 88.

78 Under the Dublin II Regulation, EU Member States are required to determine, based on certain criteria, which Member State is responsible for examining an asylum application lodged in one of the Member States by a third-country national. Article 3(2) of the Regulation prescribes that each Member State may examine an application for asylum lodged with it by a third-country national, even if such examination is not its responsibility under the criteria laid down in the Regulation. The question before the Court was essentially whether, and if so under which circumstances, a Member State is required under EU law to assume responsibility for examining asylum applications itself, even though another Member State is primarily responsible for the examinations under the Dublin II Regulation.

79 See in particular *N.S.* judgment, paras. 94 and 123.

80 *N.S.* judgment, paras. 90–91. The ECJ refers in this regard to the ECtHR *M.S.S.* case at paras. 347–350.

European Court of Human Rights (ECtHR) and the human rights reports that were relied upon by the ECtHR in that case.[81] Remarkably, an explicit reference was made to NHRI reports, as at para. 348 of its judgment the ECtHR referred to the reports issued by the Greek National Commission for Human Rights.[82] The *N.S.* case shows that a lack of consideration for the actual implementation of fundamental rights among EU Member States can give rise to a finding of violation of EU law by the ECJ. The *N.S.* and *M.S.S.* cases indicate that both the ECJ and the ECtHR take reports of NHRIs into consideration.[83] The effective sharing of information on the implementation of fundamental rights across EU Member States, and the adequate consideration of this information, could prevent similar judgments in the future and are necessary in order not to undermine the mutual confidence between EU Member States.

While individual NHRIs can offer valuable information on specific national human rights situations, thematic reports of the FRA can offer insights on fundamental rights problems across EU Member States. As indicated above (*supra*, 2.1), NHRIs are valuable partners for the FRA as they offer information upon which such reports can be based.[84] Moreover, according to the 2010 Implementation Strategy of the Charter, the Commission started to present Annual Reports on the implementation of the Charter.[85] These reports are also helpful to enhance insight across the EU on the implementation of the Charter. When preparing the drafting of the Report, the Commission takes on board information provided by all stakeholders and explicitly refers in this regard to independent national human rights bodies.[86]

Next to advising States on the fundamental rights compliance of legislative proposals and reporting on the national implementation of fundamental rights obligations, NHRIs can also serve as implementation mechanisms of fundamental rights. NHRIs sometimes function as non-judicial complaint handling mechanisms.[87] In these instances, they need to apply the Charter themselves: whenever they receive a complaint whereby it is necessary to apply or consider the validity of a national measure implementing EU law, their interpretation

81 *N.S.* judgment, paras. 88–91.

82 For more information on NHRIs and the European Court of Human Rights, see A. Buyse, Chapter 8 in this volume. See also B. Adamson, Chapter 6 in this volume.

83 The ECJ in the *N.S.* case took into account a report submitted by the NHRI of the United Kingdom (the Equality and Human Rights Commission) as a third party: *N.S.* judgment, para. 56.

84 It can be noted, for example, that the Danish Institute for Human Rights and the German Human Rights Institute even take up the role as National Focal Point for the FRA research network 'FRANET'. See: http://fra.europa.eu/fraWebsite/research/franet/franet_en.htm.

85 EC Implementation Strategy 2010, p. 12–13.

86 EC Implementation Strategy 2010, p. 13.

87 See: Paris Principles, additional principles concerning the status of commissions with quasi jurisdictional competence, (a)-(d).

will have to be done in light of the provisions contained in the Charter.[88] This is specifically relevant for NHRIs that follow the "ombudsman"-model and are mainly entrusted with handling individual complaints.[89]

Lastly, it can be observed that NHRIs are sometimes mandated to implement Member State obligations flowing from EU directives concerning specific fundamental rights. The directives on racial discrimination and on gender discrimination both require that national bodies are set up by the Member States to independently promote and monitor the rights protected by them.[90] Member States have a margin of appreciation in implementing this obligation and in establishing or appointing such a national body. Sometimes, Member States' NHRIs do get the role to act as an independent mechanism under these directives. The Danish Institute for Human Rights and the Polish Ombudsman, for example, have the mandate to serve as equality body under both the directive on racial discrimination and the directive on gender equality.[91]

While NHRIs vary widely across the EU, it is clear that Member States should take better account of the roles that can be played by these actors as fundamental rights advisors, reporters and implementers. As the FRA indicated in its 2010 report on NHRIs in Europe, 'there is a clear need to adopt a more comprehensive approach to human rights at the national level, with efforts and resources focused on key institutions – such as a visible and effective overarching NHRI.'.[92]

2.3. THE RELEVANCE OF NHRIs IN CONNECTING CITIZENS WITH THEIR FUNDAMENTAL RIGHTS

In the 2010 Strategy on the Implementation of the Charter, the Commission underlines that the Charter is not a text setting out abstract values, but rather an instrument to enable people to enjoy the rights enshrined in it when they are in a situation governed by Union law.[93] The Commission points to multiple problems in

---

88 For an overview of the agenda and speakers, see: http://www.europarl.europa.eu/document/activities/cont/201109/20110930ATT27926/20110930ATT27926EN.pdf.

89 For more information on the different typologies of NHRI, see M. Nowak, Chapter 1 in this volume. For an example of the ombudsman-model, see A. Gliszczyńska-Grabias and K. Sękowska-Kozłowska, Chapter 3 in this volume.

90 Article 13 of Council Directive 2000/43/EC of 29 June 2000 implementing the principle of equal treatment between persons irrespective of racial or ethnic origin, *OJL* 180/22, 19 July 2000; Article 20 of Directive 2006/54 EC of the European Parliament and of the Council of 5 July 2006 on the implementation of the principle of equal opportunities and equal treatment of men and women in matters of employment and occupation (recast), *OJL* 204/23, 26 July 2006.

91 For more information on the Danish Institute for Human Rights, see C. Badse, Chapter 2 in this volume; for more information on the Polish Ombudsman, see A. Gliszczyńska-Grabias and K. Sękowska-Kozłowska, Chapter 3 in this volume.

92 FRA, *National Human Rights Institutions in the EU Member States, Strengthening the Fundamental Rights Architecture in the EU*, 2010, p. 9.

93 EC Implementation Strategy 2010, p. 3.

this respect, such as the lack of awareness of people (in particular children) on how to defend their rights, the difficulties of knowing the appropriate legal remedies and the lack of suitable information for the public on how to take action.[94] In its 2010 and 2011 Reports on the Implementation of the Charter, the Commission concluded that the greatest confusion of the public concerns the application of the Charter: while it applies to Member States when implementing EU law, it does not apply to them when they are exercising a national competence.[95]

The fulfilment of the information needs of EU citizens regarding their Charter rights and the means of redress in cases of violation is understood as a shared responsibility between EU institutions and Member States' national, regional and local authorities.[96] For their part, the Commission has manifested its willingness to strengthen information activities by providing training for legal professionals and judicial authorities and making information available on legal remedies existing in Member States through the European E-Justice Portal.[97] However, this task cannot be performed in isolation, and thus the Commission has been pursuing a closer dialogue with different institutions in Member States, seeking enhanced multilevel cooperation among all actors involved in the application of the Charter. On 6 October 2011 it organised a seminar jointly with the European Parliament Committee on Petitions, bringing together European NHRIs, equality bodies, ombudsman institutions and children's ombudsman institutions.[98] With these multilevel dialogues, the Commission and Parliament intend to share knowledge on good practices and to discuss common challenges as well as identify opportunities for action at European and national levels to connect EU citizens better with their fundamental rights.

Since NHRIs themselves are active at the different levels relevant for the protection of fundamental rights of citizens (the local, national and European level), they are in a good position to advise the Commission on how to enhance the outreach of fundamental rights to EU citizens. While some NHRIs get in touch with citizens through handling individual complaints, all of them have the specific responsibility to increase public awareness in the area of human rights protection.[99] Importantly, NHRIs can inform citizens on the different actors that can be addressed when they seek protection of their fundamental rights, thereby avoiding confusion about the appropriate legal remedies and the functions

94 EC Implementation Strategy 2010, p. 11.

95 European Commission 2011 Report on the Application of the EU Charter of Fundamental Rights, p. 10.

96 *Ibid.*

97 The European e-Justice Portal (https://e-justice.europa.eu/) provides information about Charter rights and legal remedies existing in the Member States to deal with allegations of breaches of fundamental rights. As of March 2013, it is possible to find information on national courts and bodies handling complaints on fundamental rights, such as NHRIs and Equality bodies, existing in twelve Member States.

98 For an overview of the agenda and participants, see: http://www.europarl.europa.eu/document/activities/cont/201109/20110930ATT27926/20110930ATT27926EN.pdf.

99 See: Paris Principles, Competence and responsibilities, 3, (g).

performed by each actor. Accordingly, NHRIs can play an important role in empowering citizens to claim the rights they are entitled to under the Charter more effectively. As in most EU Member States a variety of national authorities competent in a specific area of fundamental rights exist (such as the children ombudsman, the racial equality bodies, the data protection agencies, etc.), the broad mandate of NHRIs makes them arguably the most effective actors to serve as central focal points or "one stop shops" to inform citizens of their fundamental rights in a comprehensive manner.

3. EU-NHRI COOPERATION IN EU EXTERNAL RELATIONS

In accordance with its Treaty commitments in this respect, the EU has invested much in elaborating instruments and policies to enhance the promotion and protection of human rights across the globe. The EU's external human rights policy has nevertheless been facing extensive criticism, such as the lack of differentiation of policies according to local human rights situations, the application of double standards regarding 'pro-Western' countries compared to others, and/or a lack of implementation of its promoted policies.[100] This reveals the need for more contextualised and effective outreach and third country implementation of the EU's human rights policy and tools.[101] In this respect, the globally embedded networks of NHRIs that gather human rights expertise from countries of all regions of the world can be of great interest to the EU. NHRIs are increasingly active on the international scene, an active role which is supported by the UN.[102] The success of NHRIs as international actors is reflected in the continuous strengthening of their status and participation rights in international organisations, with the support of countries from all over the world.[103] As NHRIs are established with the explicit mandate to promote and protect human rights in a national setting, and as they are increasingly involved in regional and international human rights promotion and protection across the globe, they seem to be natural partners for the EU in its external human rights policy.

With the entry into force of the Lisbon Treaty, various initiatives have been taken by the EU to enhance the effectiveness of its external human rights

---

[100] See for example: G. de Búrca, 'The Road Not Taken: The EU as a Global Human Rights Actor', *American Journal of International Law*, vol. 105, no. 4, 2011, pp. 649–694.

[101] As reflected in the Joint Communication of the European Commission and High Representative of the European Union for Foreign Affairs and Security Policy, p. 15, *supra* note 11.

[102] United Nations Office of the High Commissioner for Human Rights, *National Human Rights Institutions: History, Principles, Roles and Responsibilities*, Professional Training Series No. 4 (Rev. 1), 2010, p. 13. See also Part three 'International Perspectives' of this volume.

[103] See further Part Three 'International Perspectives' in this volume, particularly K. Roberts, Chapter 10.

policy.[104] They reveal an enhanced attention for local actors and civil society.[105] While NHRIs are not explicitly mentioned in the latest human rights policy documents,[106] the revised policies do constitute new opportunities for an effective engagement of the EU with NHRIs.

Since 2011, the EU has been preparing specific human rights strategies for over 150 countries (and ultimately all third countries) that should enable a tailored approach and a stronger positive impact of its human rights policies on the ground.[107] Obviously, where NHRIs are established in third countries, the EU (especially the EEAS and the Union Delegations around the world[108]) engages with these actors, both in the definition and development of the country strategies as well as in the implementation thereof.[109] Provided their independence is ensured, the EU considers NHRIs a cost-effective means of strengthening its human rights policies, and therefore obvious stakeholders in consultation processes. At the occasion of the human rights dialogues, which the EU holds with more than 30 third countries,[110] the institutionalisation of NHRIs is often discussed. Where

104 See in particular: Joint Communication of the European Commission and the High Representative of the European Union for Foreign Affairs and Security Policy, *supra* note 11. See also: Council of the European Union, EU Strategic Framework on Human Rights and Democracy, *supra* note 47.

105 See for example, p. 9 'Working in partnership with civil society' of the Joint Communication of the European Commission and the High Representative of the European Union for Foreign Affairs and Security Policy, *supra* note 11.

106 A notable exception is the reference to NHRIs contained in the EU Guidelines on Human Rights Defenders, Doc. 16332/2/08, REV 2, Council of the European Union, Brussels, 10 June 2009 (12.06), namely pp. 9 and 10.

107 See p. 8 of the Joint Communication of the European Commission and the High Representative of the European Union for Foreign Affairs and Security Policy, *supra* note 11. See also: European Parliament, Committee on Foreign Affairs, 'Report on the review of the EU's human rights strategy (2012/2062(INI))', A7-0378/2012, 19 November 2012, paras 32–38; European Parliament resolution of 13 December 2012 on the annual report on Human Rights and Democracy in the World 2011 and the European Union's policy on the matter (2012/2145(INI)), 13 December 2012, paras 11; 61–62; 91.

108 Of the 141 Union Delegations, 133 bilateral delegations – including regional delegations – are accredited to nearly 160 countries. There are currently 8 Union delegations in multilateral fora; to the United Nations (UN) in New York, to the UN and other international organisations in Geneva, to the World Trade Organization in Geneva, to the UN, the OSCE and other international organisations in Vienna, to the UN in Rome, to the Council of Europe in Strasbourg, to the OECD and UNESCO in Paris, and, to the African Union in Addis Ababa. For a detailed assessment, see: J. Wouters and S. Duquet, 'The EU and International Diplomatic Law: New Horizons?', *The Hague Journal of Diplomacy*, vol. 7, No.1, (2012) pp. 31–49.

109 While EU human rights country strategies are not public documents, this was confirmed in an interview with EEAS Human Rights Division officials (March 2013). The European Parliament requested the publicising of the key priorities of the human rights country strategies, without putting at risk the safety of human rights defenders and civil society in the countries concerned. The Parliament stressed that such publicised priorities 'would demonstrate the EU's commitment to human rights in third countries and provide support to those struggling to exercise and protect their human rights'. See: European Parliament, Committee on Foreign Affairs, Report *supra* note 107, para. 35. In the same sense, European Parliament, resolution *supra* note 107, para. 62.

110 The impetus for a more systematic inclusion of human rights issues into the political dialogues held by the EU with third countries was given in 2001, which is reflected in the Communication

these institutions are weak, the EU is persistent in pleading for their further strengthening in line with the Paris Principles, and where they have not yet been set up, the EU is vocal in encouraging this.[111] The EU human rights dialogue with Morocco held on 10 December 2012 was a case in point: apart from ensuring the participation of the Moroccan NHRI (*Conseil national des droits de l'homme*), the EU adopted a EUR 2.8 million programme aimed at strengthening the work of the institution.[112]

In addition, the Special Representative for Human Rights, who has the mandate to 'strengthen dialogue with civil society organisations and other relevant actors to ensure the effectiveness and visibility of the Union's human rights policy'[113] should also consistently integrate NHRIs in his work, especially since these institutions offer avenues to link up European human rights policy to local situations. In the same light, EU institutions should consult NHRIs and their regional and international coordinating networks when determining their human rights priorities and action plans, and before drafting the annual EU report on human rights and democracy around the world.[114]

Hereafter three specific issue areas are considered which are relevant for the EU's external human rights policy and where an enhanced cooperation with NHRIs carries potential: EU development cooperation, external outreach at the UN Human Rights Council and cooperation on common thematic human rights priorities across human rights fora. These three issue areas are also part of the 'EU Strategic Framework and Action Plan on Human Rights and Democracy'.[115]

---

from the Commission 'The European Union's Role in Promoting Human Rights and Democratisation in Third Countries', COM(2001) 252 final, 8 May 2001, particularly pp. 9 and 10. The approach was endorsed by the Council of the European Union, leading to the adoption, in the same year, of the EU Guidelines on Human Rights Dialogues, Doc. 14469/01, Council of the European Union, 3 December 2001.

111 This information was mentioned in an interview with EEAS Human Rights Division officials (March 2013).

112 See the European Commission press release, entitled 'European Union supports human rights promotion in Morocco', available at: http://europa.eu/rapid/press-release_IP-12-1346_en.htm.

113 Article 3(c) of Council Decision 2012/440/CFSP of 25 July 2012 appointing the European Union Special Representative for Human Rights, *OJL* I. 200/21, 27 June 2012.

114 See also: Cost Action IS0702 'The Role of the EU in UN Human Rights Reform, recommendations on National Human Rights Institutions (NHRIs)', reproduced as annex to this book, recommendation 14.

115 Council of the European Union, EU Strategic Framework on Human Rights and Democracy, *supra* note 47, p. 2: 'The EU will promote human rights in all areas of its external action without exception. In particular, it will integrate the promotion of human rights into [...] development [...]'; p. 3–4: '[...] The EU underlines the leading role of the UN Human Rights Council in addressing urgent cases of human rights violations and will contribute vigorously to the effective functioning of the Council [...]'; p. 2: 'Pursuing coherent objectives [...] Within their own frontiers, the EU and its Member States are committed to be exemplary in ensuring respect for human rights. Outside their frontiers, promoting and speaking out on human rights and democracy is a joint responsibility of the EU and its Member States [...]'.

3.1. NHRIs AND EU DEVELOPMENT COOPERATION

Respect for human rights and fundamental freedoms has become an integral part of the development cooperation discourse, as multilateral and bilateral donor agencies have integrated human rights in various ways. The advancement of human rights is upheld by the EU as an objective in all its external policies and as a necessary component of its cooperation strategies with third countries.[116] Since 2001, the Commission has set out a policy for integrating human rights as a cross-cutting theme in the EU's development assistance programmes through 'mainstreaming'. In 2011, the Commission Communication *'Increasing the impact of EU Development: Agenda for Change'* underlined the need to attach enhanced importance to human rights, democracy and good governance in determining the mix of EU instruments and aid modalities at country level.[117] The EU's 2012 Strategic Action Plan on Human Rights and Democracy reaffirms that human rights should be mainstreamed in all sectors, and in particular in development cooperation, and that steps should be taken to apply a 'human rights-based approach'.[118] The integration of human rights in EU development policy implies including human rights considerations in the planning, design, implementation and monitoring of policies and programmes.[119] Moreover, it implies ensuring, throughout the development process, the participation of those actors best suited to provide input on human rights-related issues. In line with the Declaration on Aid Effectiveness and the subsequent Accra Agenda for Action, EU policy statements underline that "ownership" of country strategies by the partner

116 As stipulated in the Treaties (Article 208(1) TFEU and Article 21 TEU) EU policy in the field of development cooperation is to be conducted within the framework of the principles and objectives of the EU's external action, which include the advancement of human rights and fundamental freedoms, as well as the promotion of democracy and the rule of law.

117 Communication from the Commission, 'Increasing the impact of EU Development: an Agenda for Change', COM(2011) 673 final, 13 October 2011, pp. 4–6.

118 Council of the European Union, EU Strategic Framework on Human Rights and Democracy, supra *note* 47. The 'human rights-based approach to development' is a policy concept whereby the human rights framework serves as the basis and objective of all development cooperation activities. It has been elaborated most comprehensively within the context of UN development agencies such as the UNDP and UNICEF. In addition, several bilateral donor agencies and non-governmental development organisations have developed their own human rights-based approaches. The OECD Development Assistance Committee has not specifically endorsed a human rights–based approach, but has instead set out guiding principles for promoting human rights in development serving as basic orientations in areas where harmonised donor action is of particular importance. See: UN Development Group, 'The Human Rights Based Approach to Development Cooperation, Towards a Common Understanding Among UN Agencies', 2003; UN Development Programme, 'Mainstreaming Human Rights in Development Policies and Programming: UNDP Experiences', New York, 2012; OECD-DAC 'Action-Oriented Policy Paper on Human Rights and Development', 2007; UNESCO, 'Empowering the Poor Through Human Rights Litigation', Paris, 2011; UNIFEM, 'CEDAW and the Human Rights Based Approach to Programming', New York, 2007.

119 Communication from the Commission, 'The European Union's role in promoting human rights and democratisation in third countries', COM(2001) 252 final, 8 May 2001.

countries is of paramount importance to the success of development policies.[120] The most wide-ranging participation of all segments of society has thus been encouraged[121] through the gradual involvement of civil society organisations (CSO) since the mid-1970s[122] and other non-state actors, national assemblies, parliaments and local authorities.[123]

The Union's structured relationship with the African, Caribbean and Pacific (ACP) countries, as shaped in the revised Cotonou Agreement,[124] reflects the developments described above. The Cotonou Agreement provides, at least in theory,[125] the most progressive and comprehensive framework for the involvement of CSOs in the development process.[126] Among these non-state agents and other state entities, NHRIs are not specifically mentioned as local partners, although practice has revealed the involvement of these institutions in the design and implementation of development strategies.[127] As will be explained below, the role foreseen for CSOs within the realm of human rights can in fact be played as well, *mutatis mutandis*, by NHRIs, not so much as implementing entities but rather as governance actors, i.e., dialogue partners and monitoring agencies.[128] As NHRIs are statutorily established and funded by the government, while functioning

120 The Paris Declaration on Aid Effectiveness was endorsed in 2005 by a large number of international development actors and identified five key principles for more effective development assistance: ownership, alignment, harmonisation, managing for results and mutual accountability. See: OECD, 'The Paris Declaration on Aid Effectiveness (2005) and Accra Agenda for Action (2006), available at http://www.oecd.org/development/effectiveness/34428351.pdf.

121 Communication from the Commission, 'Participation of non-state actors in EC Development Policy', COM (2002) 598 final, 7 November 2002; Communication from the Commission, 'The roots of democracy and sustainable development: Europe's engagement with Civil Society in external relations', COM(2012) 492 final, 12 September 2013.

122 M. Carbone, 'Mainstreaming Non-State Actors: Assessing Participation in EU-Pacific Relations', in P. Hoebink (ed.), *European Development Cooperation: In Between the Local and the Global*, Amsterdam University Press, 2010, pp. 73–92, at p. 77.

123 Participation is not only deemed a means to improve aid effectiveness but also a tool to contribute to accountable States and effective democracies. See for example: COM(2012) 492 final, 12 September 2012, para. 4.1., pp. 6–7.

124 Agreement amending for the second time the Partnership Agreement between the members of the African, Caribbean and Pacific Group of States, of the one part, and the European Community and its Member States, of the other part, signed in Cotonou on 23 June 2000, as first amended in Luxembourg on 25 June 2005, *OJ* L. 287/3 of 4 November 2010.

125 See M. Carbone, 'Theory and Practice of Participation: Civil Society and EU Development Policy', *Perspectives on European Politics and Society*, vol. 9, no. 2, June 2008, pp. 250–251, for an overview of the criticism that has been raised with regard to the practice of participation within the EU-ACP context.

126 Illustrative of this are Articles 4, 9(2), 33(5), 57(3) of the Cotonou Agreement.

127 This information was obtained in telephone interviews with two EU officers working in DG EuropeAid with ACP countries, in June 2012 and further discussed in an interview with EEAS Human Rights Division officials, held in March 2013.

128 In some cases, NHRIs have been the implementing actors of human rights-related development activities, mostly as part of programmes managed by their respective national (bilateral) development agency. For example, the Danish International Development Agency cooperates with the Danish Institute for Human Rights in organising capacity building projects in developing countries. See Danish Institute for Human Rights, 'Annual Report 2010', 2010.

independently from the latter,[129] they might suffer less from the drawbacks often associated with CSOs in ACP countries, such as competition, fragmentation, governance issues or lack of a solid representative structure.[130]

The EU's development cooperation with ACP countries is based on Country Strategy Papers (CSPs),[131] the function of which is to guide, manage and review EU assistance programmes in light of the priorities of the EU, its partner countries and other donors. These instruments are always accompanied by National Indicative Programmes, whereby focal and non-focal sectors are identified for funding through the European Development Fund (EDF), which is the main instrument providing EU aid for development cooperation in the ACP countries. While the involvement of CSOs is foreseen in all phases of the programming process, it is submitted that the same requirement should apply to NHRIs when human rights issues are at stake. For instance, the formulation of CSPs entails a "country diagnosis", where the country's political, institutional and security situation, including observance of human rights, is analysed in a broad context.[132] In this context, NHRIs can be consulted and take part in policy debates on CSP preparation and the definition of sector strategies, once the priority focal sectors have been determined.[133] Moreover, CSOs, as well as NHRIs, are to be involved in the later stages of project implementation and in the CSP review. Throughout the latter phase of the programming exercise, there is space for criticism and for a constructive dialogue to take place towards the improvement of development cooperation performance. Here, again, NHRIs can be provided the space in which to offer their views on the country's development strategy and its impact on the enjoyment of human rights. Even if EU officials indicate that NHRIs are involved in CSP programming and implementation,[134] reference to the potential role of NHRIs is largely absent in EU policy or guidance documents for development programming.

---

129 See: Paris Principles, 'composition and guarantees of independence and pluralism'.

130 J. Bossuyt, 'Mainstreaming Civil Society in ACP-EU Development Cooperation', in M. Lister and M. Carbone (eds.), *New Pathways in International Development, Gender and Civil Society in EU Policy*, Ashgate, 2006, pp. 123–138, at p. 128.

131 It should be noted that CSPs are instruments generally used in EU development assistance programming, including within the European Neighbourhood Policy framework, referred to below.

132 According to the Communication from the Commission, 'Increasing the Impact of EU Aid: A Common Framework for Drafting Country Strategy Papers and Joint Multiannual Programming', COM(2006) 88 final, 2 March 2006, Annex, pp. 12–13, the political situation section of the country diagnosis should examine, among others, 'the main obstacles at national level to progress towards a situation in which human rights are respected, protected and promoted', 'the content and any shortcomings of the partner country's plans/policies concerning social cohesion, employment and gender equality' and the government's position with regard to the key international human rights conventions.

133 European Commission Guidelines on Principles and Good Practices for the Participation of Non-State Actors in the development dialogues and consultations, November 2004, p. 5.

134 This information was obtained in telephone interviews with two EU officers working in DG EuropeAid with ACP countries, in June 2012 and in a subsequent interview with EEAS Human Rights Division officials, held in March 2013.

The EU-ACP Partnership Agreement includes a political dimension whereby developments concerning respect for human rights, democratic principles, the rule of law and good governance must be taken into account through joint assessments.[135] NHRIs can certainly be associated to such political dialogues and to the evaluation of the country's policy performance. Needless to say, the extent to which NHRIs participate depends on them being sufficiently independent from the government, as such independence sets the difference between effectively participating in a constructive dialogue or merely being consulted. The international accreditation of NHRI according to the International Coordinating Committee of NHRI (ICC) can be applied as a standard to assess whether NHRIs can be considered independent or not.[136] As noted by the UN, it is rare that a NHRI can be more effective or stronger than the governance structure or environment in which it operates.[137] This can be particularly problematic in ACP countries, which often lack well-embedded governance structures and suffer from corruption. In line with its aim to strengthen the attention for governance and respect for human rights in its development policy, the EU can, in parallel to such efforts, engage in the strengthening of NHRIs and their independent and effective functioning in these countries.[138] Where political dialogue between the EU and the ACP partner fails and the commitments imposed by Article 9(2)[139] are disregarded by one of the parties, NHRIs arise as watchdogs of national human rights compliance which could alert to such defaults and support, through the provision of relevant information and guidance, the triggering of the consultation procedures contained in Article 96.[140]

135 Article 8(4) of the Cotonou Agreement, *supra* note 125.

136 UNDP also focuses its NHRI cooperation on NHRIs that comply with the Paris Principles and engages in the strengthening of national governance structures and NHRIs specifically in order to render them more effective. For more information on the accreditation procedure, see G. de Beco, Chapter 11 in this volume.

137 UNDP-OHCHR Toolkit for Collaboration with National Human Rights Institutions, December 2010, available at http://www.ohchr.org/Documents/Countries/NHRI/1950-UNDP-UHCHR-Toolkit-LR.pdf, Introduction, p. x.

138 As UNDP interestingly indicates in this regard, 'UNCTs [United Nations Country Teams], whose primary working partner is the State itself, need to understand [national human rights] institutions and should support their work when needed. UNCTs are frequently called on to support and strengthen NHRIs, on the one hand, while carrying out broader governance and justice programmes in partnership with national authorities, on the other'. See: UNDP-OHCHR Toolkit for Collaboration with National Human Rights Institutions, December 2010, available at: http://www.ohchr.org/Documents/Countries/NHRI/1950-UNDP-UHCHR-Toolkit-LR.pdf, Introduction, p. vi.

139 The commitments foreseen in Article 9(2) include the respect for human rights and human dignity, democratic principles and the rule of law and the promotion of equality of men and women.

140 Article 96 provides for a set of measures to ensure compliance with human rights, democratic principles and the rule of law, starting with consultation procedures. As a measure of last resort, the agreement can be suspended.

Financing the work of NHRIs is also a way of contributing to the EU's goal of advancing human rights through development cooperation. With regard to the EDF, NHRIs can be financially supported for instance in light of Article 33 of the Cotonou Agreement,[141] and within the programming framework mentioned above, as institutions that help to promote the respect and protection of human rights, to strengthen the rule of law and ensure transparency and accountability in governance and administration. In the field of human rights, this geographical programme is complemented by the European Instrument for Democracy and Human Rights (EIDHR), which focuses primarily on public institution-building.[142] NHRIs fit the eligibility criteria set out in Article 10 of the Regulation establishing the EIDHR, and can therefore be financed by such instrument.[143] Accordingly, the current Multiannual Financial Framework for the EIDHR (2007–2013) reflects the EU's commitment to promote democracy and human rights, by supporting human rights institutions worldwide, in addition to CSOs.[144] For example, the Commission has funded or co-funded the Human Rights Commission in Rwanda (2002 and 2004), in Mexico (2003), in Kenya (2005), in the Philippines (2006), and the National Council for Human Rights and Women in Egypt (2006).[145]

With regard to its "neighbouring countries", the EU operates through the European Neighbourhood Policy (ENP). The ENP has been recently revised in light of both the opportunities afforded by the Lisbon Treaty for a more integrated and effective EU foreign policy and recent developments relevant for the partnerships, especially the upheavals in the Southern Mediterranean.[146]

---

141 According to Article 33(1), 'Cooperation shall pay systematic attention to institutional aspects and in this context, shall support the efforts of the ACP States to develop and strengthen structures, institutions and procedures that help to: a) promote and sustain democracy, human dignity, social justice and pluralism, with full respect for diversity within and among societies; b) promote and sustain universal and full respect for and observance and protection of all human rights and fundamental freedoms; c) develop and strengthen the rule of law; and improve access to justice, while guaranteeing the professionalism and independence of the judicial systems; and d) ensure transparent and accountable governance and administration in all public institutions.'

142 See the objectives of the instrument in Art. 1 of Regulation (EC) N° 1889/2006 of the European Parliament and of the Council, of 20 December 2006, on establishing a financing instrument for the promotion of democracy and human rights worldwide, *OJ* L. 386/1, of 29 December 2006.

143 According to Article 10(1)(b) of Regulation (EC) N° 1889/2006, public sector non-profit agencies, institutions and organisations and networks at local, national, regional, and international level, operating on an independent and accountable basis, are eligible for funding.

144 See p. 9 of the Joint Communication of the European Commission and the High Representative of the European Union for Foreign Affairs and Security Policy, *supra* note 11.

145 Consortium PARTICIP–ADE–DIE–DRN-ECDPM-ODI, 'Thematic evaluation of the European Commission support to respect of Human Rights and Fundamental Freedoms (including solidarity with victims of repression) – Volume 3: Inventory of Human Rights Interventions', Brussels/Freiburg, 2011.

146 Joint Communication by the High Representative of the Union For Foreign Affairs and Security Policy and the European Commission, 'A New Response to a Changing Neighbourhood, a

The revised ENP indicates that EU support will be tailored to the needs of each country and to the regional context,[147] and places particular emphasis on "partnerships with societies" (especially CSOs and parliaments) to support and strengthen democracy, respect for human rights and the rule of law.[148] On the basis of country reports covering the political, economic, social and institutional situation in each country, action plans are negotiated between each of the ENP partner countries and the EU. The action plans spell out the planned economic and political reforms with short and medium term priorities. Each country's action plan differs according to the priorities the country has agreed upon with the EU but will in any case consider actions with regard to democracy, the rule of law and human rights.

Observations on EU-NHRI cooperation in the ACP framework can be similarly applied to the context of the ENP: when elaborating and implementing ENP country reports and action plans, the EU actors should consult NHRIs when they exist, taking into account the reliability of the NHRI at hand, especially on the basis of the Paris Principle compliance of the NHRI. Even if NHRIs are not mentioned in the ENP policy documents, practice does reveal the integration of NHRIs as local partners for the EU in its efforts to strengthen good governance and human rights in its neighbouring countries.[149] It can be noted that some of the ENP action plans do explicitly refer to NHRIs.[150] The EU/ Egypt action plan, for example, purports to: '[s]upport Egyptian government efforts to protect human rights and fundamental freedoms in line with international conventions to which Egypt is party, and to elaborate a human rights strategy in partnership with the NCHR [*National Council for Human Rights*] and with appropriate consultation of other relevant organisations. [...]'.[151] Beyond the cooperation with existing NHRIs in ENP countries, the EU also supports the establishment and strengthening of

review of European Neighbourhood Policy', COM(2011) 303, 25 May 2011 [hereinafter 'A New Response to a Changing Neighbourhood']. See also: Joint Communication by the High Representative of the Union For Foreign Affairs and Security Policy and the European Commission, 'Delivering on a new European Neighbourhood Policy', JOIN(2012) 14 final, 15 May 2012 [hereinafter 'Delivering on a new European Neighbourhood Policy'].

147 'A New Response to a Changing Neighbourhood', p. 3.

148 *Ibid.*, especially at 1.2 'A partnership with societies'.

149 This information was obtained in an interview with EEAS Human Rights Division officials, held in March 2013.

150 See for example: EU/ Jordan Action Plan at 2.1. Human rights and fundamental freedoms, Medium Term: '[...] Strengthen the capacity and effectiveness of the National Commission for Human Rights [...]'; EU/ Egypt Action Plan at 2.1.1. b). All ENP action plans can be consulted at: http://ec.europa.eu/world/enp/documents_en.htm#2.

151 EU/ Egypt Action Plan at 2.1.1. b) Human rights and fundamental freedoms.

these NHRIs in accordance with the Paris Principles, both through political (e.g. in the context of human rights dialogues)[152] and financial means.[153, 154]

As noted, the EU is currently elaborating human rights country strategies, establishing country-specific priorities and objectives. On the one hand, the human rights analysis contained in these documents can aptly feed into the country diagnosis included in CSPs and ENP action plans; on the other hand, the priorities and objectives outlined in the human rights strategy papers should be integrated in all relevant EU external policies, including development.[155] Obviously, if NHRIs would be consistently involved in both the elaboration of the human rights country strategies and the CSPs and ENP action plans, these institutions could monitor and assist with the appropriate inclusion of national human rights priorities in the EU's development policy.

Supporting the creation of NHRIs or their work is significant in that it places the question of human rights compliance on the political agenda, and it ensures that monitoring functions are not solely left in the hands of CSOs. It can be noted that, contrary to the EU, the United Nations Development Programme (UNDP) does explicitly consider the support for, and cooperation with NHRIs as a strategic priority in order to enable a sustainable, human rights based approach to development.[156] While it is true that involving various actors, including NHRIs, may raise some problems of competition for funding and confusion about which actors should do what, it is essential to ensure that EU development policy manages this type of multi-actor partnerships as, in fact, the different roles played complement each other and contribute to more collaborative, contextualised and

---

152 Note that in the context of 'A New Response to a Changing Neighbourhood', *supra* note 147, the strengthening of human rights dialogues was singled out as a specific focus, at p. 4. See also *supra* note 112 for a reference to the NHRI of Morocco in the context of the EU-Morocco human rights dialogue.

153 The European Neighbourhood and Partnership Instrument (ENPI) is the main funding mechanism for the ENP. NHRIs can receive ENPI funding as they fall under the scope of 'Community assistance' as defined by ENPI. See: Regulation (EC) No 1638/2006 of the European Parliament and of the Council of 24 October 2006 laying down general provisions establishing a European Neighbourhood and Partnership Instrument, *OJ* L310/1, 9 November 2006, Article 2, para. 2: 'Community assistance shall be used to support measures within the following areas of cooperation [...](c) strengthening of national institutions and bodies responsible for the elaboration and the effective implementation of policies in areas covered in association agreements, partnership and cooperation agreements, and other multilateral agreements to which the Community and/or its Member States and partner countries are parties, whose purpose is the achievement of objectives as defined in this Article. ENPI will be replaced by the European Neighbourhood Instrument (ENI) from 2014 on.

154 This information was obtained in an interview with EEAS Human Rights Division officials, held in March 2013.

155 See p. 8 of the Joint Communication of the European Commission and the High Representative of the European Union for Foreign Affairs and Security Policy, *supra* note 11. In the same sense, European Parliament report *supra* note 107, para. 5; European Parliament, resolution *supra* note 107, para. 11.

156 For an extensive overview, see: 'UNDP-OHCHR Toolkit for Collaboration with National Human Rights Institutions', December 2010, available at: http://www.ohchr.org/Documents/Countries/NHRI/1950-UNDP-UHCHR-Toolkit-LR.pdf.

effective development strategies. The EU should explicitly include NHRIs in its policy frameworks on development cooperation, as this would back up its current cooperation with NHRIs in the field.

3.2. NHRIs AS CROSS-REGIONAL PARTNERS IN THE UN HUMAN RIGHTS COUNCIL

As indicated by the EU's annual reports on human rights and democracy around the world, the EU has invested strongly in the functioning of the UN Human Rights Council (HRC or Council).[157] The HRC is an intergovernmental UN body made up of 47 States responsible for the promotion and protection of all human rights around the globe. The membership of the HRC is based on "equitable geographical distribution": the 47 seats of the Council are distributed between countries from five different regional groupings.[158] The inter-governmental character of the HRC entails that the EU is an observer at the Council, while EU Member States can be, and are, elected to Council membership. During HRC sessions, the Union Delegation in Geneva leads daily coordination meetings with the EU Member State delegations in order to foster a common European voice at the Council. In light of the division of seats in the HRC, the EU and its Member States (together with other Western countries) are in a minority position. Pursuing cross-regional cooperation and support for the EU's human rights priorities at the Council is therefore one of the EU's main challenges in the HRC.[159]

NHRIs seem to enjoy wide support from all actors in the Council, and just recently saw their status upgraded in the context of the HRC review process.[160] The active participation of NHRIs in the Council is limited to A-status NHRIs, i.e. NHRIs that comply with the Paris Principles.[161] Therefore, NHRIs active in the Council can be regarded as functioning independently from their government,

157 European External Action Service, 'EU Annual Report on Human Rights and Democracy in the World in 2010', 2011, pp. 72–75.

158 HRC, Resolution 60/251 of 3 April 2006, para. 7: '[...] seats shall be distributed as follows among regional groups: Group of African States, thirteen; Group of Asian States, thirteen; Group of Eastern European States, six; Group of Latin American and Caribbean States, eight; and Group of Western European and other States, seven.'

159 Recently, the EU has invested much in more effective cross-regional cooperation at the UN HRC. As indicated by the European Council on Foreign Relations (ECFR): 'Several EU successes in 2011, including on Libya and Syria, overturned the assumption that the UN Human Rights Council is irredeemably anti-Western.' Accordingly, the EU's performance at the UN HRC is graded with a B+ in the 2013 ECFR Report, while in the ECFR's 2010/2011 reports it was still graded with C+. See: ECFR, 'Scorecard 2012', available at: http://www.ecfr.eu/scorecard/2012/issues/71.

160 UN HRC, Resolution 16/21, 'Review of the work and functioning of the Human Rights Council', 25 March 2011, paras. 9, 13, 22(a), 28 and 59.

161 HRC, Resolution 5/1 of 18 June 2007, VII, Rule 7, 'Participation of and consultation with observers of the Council'.

and can constitute fairly reliable partners for the EU in the Council.[162] NHRIs are observers in the Council: they do not have a voting right, but are able to attend HRC proceedings, submit written statements to the HRC, make oral interventions, participate in debates and organise "parallel events" on issues relevant to the work of the HRC.[163] While NHRIs have a strong observer status at the Council and can participate in all of its procedures, their actual participation is rather low. Due to resource constraints and priority setting, not all NHRIs actively participate in the Council's work.[164] A 2010 report indicates, however, that the participation of NHRIs (from all regions of the world) in the HRC is on the rise.[165] Moreover, continuous representation of NHRIs in the HRC is guaranteed by the presence of a permanent representative of the International Coordinating Committee of National Human Rights Institutions (ICC) in Geneva.[166] The ICC has the explicit mandate to coordinate the activities of NHRIs in the framework of the HRC, and also supports NHRIs to participate in the procedures of the Council. In addition, the regional coordinating networks of NHRIs can represent NHRI opinions in the Council, and engage in HRC debates.[167]

EU cooperation with NHRIs in the HRC has an important potential both regarding thematic issues and country-specific engagement. Even if the resources of NHRIs to engage at the international level are limited, the cross-regional character and independent position of NHRIs in the Council makes them interesting partners for the EU. On common thematic human rights priorities (such as business and human rights or the protection of children),[168] the EU can engage with NHRIs and their regional networks that are present in the HRC, while the ICC can serve as a permanent focal point for cooperation in the UN body. Cooperation with NHRIs –and particularly the regional and international networks – on common human rights priorities can strengthen the EU's knowledge base on the issues concerned from a "non-European perspective", and can feed into the EU's outreach activities towards third countries and other regions in the Council. Moreover, through the delivery of statements in the HRC, NHRIs and their networks can support EU initiatives on common issues of concern. At its turn, the EU can raise awareness and support for NHRIs in the Council, and can co-organise or provide financial support for NHRIs' side-events on thematic initiatives in the Council that are in line with EU priorities.

---

162 According to the Paris Principles, NHRIs have to function in an independent manner. See G. de Beco, Chapter 11 in this volume for more information on the NHRI accreditation relating to the Paris Principles.

163 UN HRC, A/HRC/RES/5/1, para. 11(a) and (b) *juncto* A/HRC/RES/2005/74, para. 11(a).

164 UN Office of the High Commissioner for Human Rights, *Survey on National Human Rights Institutions*, July 2009, Geneva, p. 45.

165 ICC, Report on the 23th session of the ICC, Geneva, 22–25 March 2010, p. 2, para. 7.

166 ICC Statute, Article 7. For more information, see K. Roberts, Chapter 10 in this volume.

167 These regional coordinating committees are: the Network of African NHRIs; the Network of Americas; the Asia Pacific Forum; and the European Group of NHRIs.

168 See *infra*, 3.3 for an analysis of the potential EU-NHRI cooperation on common thematic priorities across human rights fora.

While generally participation of individual NHRIs in the HRC is rather low, the participation of NHRIs during the Universal Periodic Review (UPR)[169] sessions of the Council is high. A 2009 OHCHR survey indicates that each of the respondents (originating from the four different regions in the Council) did participate in the UPR process of its own state.[170] Accordingly, EU-NHRI cooperation on country-specific situations in the framework of the UPR seems to carry a particularly promising potential. Through cooperation with the NHRI of the state under review, the EU can obtain local information on the human rights situation in that state. This information can be taken up in the EU's position and statements during the UPR process, but can also feed into the EU's action when addressing country-specific situations beyond the UPR. Information obtained in the context of the UPR can for example be used in the outreach activities of Union Delegations around the world, especially regarding the elaboration and implementation of human rights country strategies. As indicated before (*supra* 3.1), NHRIs can constitute important local partners for the implementation of the EU's human rights (and development) policy in third countries. Bridging the local EU-NHRI cooperation with the EU's international engagement can entail interesting synergies for a more coherent EU external human rights policy. Furthermore, by supporting the international engagement of NHRIs, their independent functioning from their government can be further strengthened.

3.3. COHERENT THEMATIC ENGAGEMENT ACROSS HUMAN RIGHTS FORA

Through annual and biannual ICC meetings, NHRIs from all over the globe identify common priorities and best practices that feed into the national, regional and international activities of NHRIs and their coordinating bodies. Interestingly, the thematic priorities identified by NHRIs align to a large extent with the thematic priorities of the EU in its internal and external human rights policy. Common priorities appear to be the furtherance of the rights of the child, women's rights, the prevention of torture, business and human rights and the rights of persons with disabilities.[171] The national, regional and global networks of NHRIs can interrelate with the national, internal and external European human rights policy, aptly feeding into Europe's multi-layered human rights objectives. A case in point which serves to illustrate the potential for NHRI-EU cooperation

---

169 In the framework of the UPR, the human rights situation of all UN Member States are reviewed in a cycle of four years. For more information: http://www.ohchr.org/EN/HRBodies/UPR/Pages/UPRMain.aspx.

170 Survey of the UN Office of the High Commissioner for Human Rights, *supra* note 166, pp. 43–44.

171 For an overview of the ICC thematic priorities, see the ICC website: http://nhri.ohchr.org/EN/Themes/Pages/default.aspx.

on common thematic priorities across human rights fora is the protection of rights of persons with disabilities.

As recent international human rights treaties tend to focus more on the implementation of rights, NHRIs are increasingly involved in international standard-setting and national implementation of international human rights conventions.[172] NHRIs were involved in the negotiations leading to the drafting of the UN Convention on the Rights of Persons with Disabilities (CPRD)[173] and can function as national implementation and monitoring mechanisms based on that convention.[174] In a recent survey, 44% of the NHRI respondents reported that they play a role as an independent mechanism under Article 33(2) CRPD.[175] A study on the European implementation of Article 33(2) of the CRPD indicates that various European NHRIs fulfil the function of independent mechanism under Article 33(2) CRPD.[176]

While the expertise of NHRIs on human rights priorities is grounded in national know-how, this expertise is extrapolated in their actions and undertakings on the regional and international level. During the nineteenth session of the HRC, for example, the ICC made a statement in the Panel Discussion on Persons with Disabilities.[177] At the same time, European NHRIs have been actively involved in the research project of the FRA on "fundamental rights of persons with intellectual disabilities and persons with mental health problems", taking part in the stakeholder consultation meetings, which the FRA organised.[178] While NHRIs singled out the CRPD as a priority issue for their work across different policy levels, the EU also attaches particular importance to the

172 See K. Roberts, Chapter 10 in this volume.

173 For an extensive analysis, see: G. De Beco, 'Article 33(2) of the UN Convention on the Rights of Persons with Disabilities: Another Role for National Human Rights Institutions?', *Netherlands Quarterly of Human Rights*, vol. 29, no. 1, 2011, pp. 84–106.

174 Article 33(2) of the CRPD maintains that States Parties shall have at their disposal an independent mechanism to promote, protect and monitor the implementation of the Convention, taking into account the principles relating to the status and functioning of national institutions for protection and promotion of human rights.

175 ICC and Canadian Human Rights Commission, *Survey of National Human Rights Institutions on Article 33(2) of the Convention on the Rights of Persons with Disabilities*, August 2011, p. 7.

176 In three EU Member States, the A-status NHRI fulfills the function of independent mechanism under the CRPD: Denmark, Germany and the UK. Moreover, NHRI without A-status fulfill this function, such as the Centre for Equal Opportunities in Belgium. Probably, the newly constituted *Netherlands Institute for Human Rights* and the French *Commission nationale consultative des droits de l'homme* will also fulfill this function. See: UN OHCHR Europe Regional Office (G. De Beco), *Study on the Implementation of Article 33 of the UN Convention on the Rights of Persons with Disabilities in Europe*, available at: http://europe.ohchr.org/Documents/Publications/Art_33_CRPD_study.pdf.

177 ICC Statement, 'Human Rights Annual Panel Discussion on Persons with Disabilities, Participation on Political and Public Life by Persons with Disabilities', 1 March 2012, available at: www.nhri.ohchr.org.

178 For more information, consult the FRA website: http://fra.europa.eu/fraWebsite/research/projects/proj_disability_en.htm.

effective implementation of the rights of persons with disabilities, and became a party to the CRPD in December 2010.[179]

As the European Disability Strategy indicates, the CRPD will apply throughout the EU since all Member States and the EU itself are ratifying the Convention.[180] This EU-wide ratification of a UN human rights convention sets a strong example of how the EU can engender a coherent approach to international human rights standards. The Disability Strategy explicitly mentions important areas of action for the EU's internal policy and adds that the EU and its Member States should promote the rights of people with disabilities in their external action, connecting the internal and external EU disability policy.[181] The EU Disability Strategy points out four instruments that have to underpin EU action: awareness raising; financial support; statistics and data collection and monitoring; and the mechanisms required by the Convention.[182] NHRIs can be effective partners for three out of four instruments: awareness raising, data collection and monitoring, and functioning as mechanisms under the CRPD.

Moreover, NHRIs (and especially the ICC and its regional coordinating networks) can provide the EU with relevant expertise and information on the rights of persons with disabilities beyond the EU, an important asset in light of the linking up of the EU's internal and external human rights policy as envisaged by the European Disability Strategy. However, while the European Strategy refers to the need for cooperation with and support of stakeholders,[183] and explicitly refers to NGOs as important partners,[184] it does not explicitly mention NHRIs.

As indicated by the involvement of NHRIs in the FRA's research project on disability rights, the EU does interact with NHRIs to some extent. However, a structural engagement on common thematic human rights priorities is currently lacking. Since EU-NHRI cooperation has the potential to engender synergies across the multiple human rights fora, an explicit integration of EU-NHRI cooperation in documents spelling out the implementation of EU thematic human rights priorities (such as the EU Disability Strategy) is desirable.

---

179 Council Decision of 26 November 2009 concerning the conclusion, by the European Community, of the United Nations Convention on the Rights of Persons with Disabilities (2010/48/EC), *OJ* L23/35, 27 January 2010. See also: Communication from Commission, 'European Disability Strategy 2010–2020: A renewed Commitment to a Barrier-Free Europe', COM(2010) 636 final, 15 November 2010 (European Disability Strategy).

180 European Disability Strategy, p. 3. In March 2013, 26 out of 27 EU Member States did ratify the Convention. The Netherlands signed the treaty (30 March 2007), but did not ratify it yet. For an updated overview of the ratifications of the UNCRPD, see the United Nations Treaty Collection: http://treaties.un.org/.

181 European Disability Strategy, p. 9.

182 European Disability Strategy, pp. 9–10.

183 European Disability Strategy, pp. 4 and 34.

184 European Disability Strategy, p. 6.

4. CONCLUDING THOUGHTS: TOWARDS A MORE STRUCTURED INTEGRATION OF NHRIs IN THE EU HUMAN RIGHTS ARCHITECTURE?

NHRIs are recognised and supported by the UN as 'cornerstones of the protection of human rights' in view of their specific human rights expertise and their potential to constitute a bridge between international human rights standards and national human rights performance.[185] Even if the various EU institutions and bodies working in the field of human rights expressed support for NHRIs and do cooperate to some extent with these institutions, NHRIs are not structurally integrated into the European human rights working culture yet.[186] Especially the non-inclusion of NHRIs in relevant policy documents indicates the lack of their effective integration in the EU's human rights policy.

The entry into force of the Lisbon Treaty created a momentum for the further strengthening of the promotion and protection of human rights in the EU's internal and external policies. At the same time, the increasing establishment and activity of NHRIs all over the globe *and* in the EU[187] enhances the potential gains of cooperation with NHRIs for the EU.

This chapter has demonstrated that there is scope for NHRIs to become more important partners of the EU in the implementation of different issue areas relevant to the EU's human rights architecture. NHRIs can help to foster a fundamental rights culture across the EU, through the delivering of human rights expertise in the context of EU policy and law-making initiatives and advising States on the fundamental rights compliance of legislative proposals. Stronger participation policies bring with them greater quality, transparency and legitimacy of policy and law-making processes both within the EU and its Member States when acting within the scope of EU law. NHRIs can report on the national implementation of fundamental rights, or serve as central focal points to inform citizens about their fundamental rights. These examples also point to the significance of NHRIs in ensuring that the fundamental rights contained in the EU Charter become a practical tool for the protection of individuals.

In a second part, this Chapter outlined several options for the EU to integrate NHRIs in its external human rights policy. The active involvement of NHRIs in

---

[185] United Nations Office of the High Commissioner for Human Rights, *National Human Rights Institutions: History, Principles, Roles and Responsibilities*, Professional Training Series No. 4 (Rev. 1), 2010, p. 13.

[186] Interestingly, various Commission 'Progress Reports' adopted within the framework of the EU enlargement policy include considerations regarding the performance of Ombudsmen in EU accession countries. In general, the point is made that these institutions' capacity should be strengthened in order to enhance human rights protection. See, for example, Commission Staff Working Paper, Albania 2011 Progress Report, SEC(2011) 1205 final, 12 October 2011, p. 10; Commission Staff Working Paper, Croatia 2011 Progress Report, SEC(2011) 1200 final, 12 October 2011, p. 6; and Commission Staff Working Paper, Kosovo 2011 Progress Report, SEC(2011) 1207 final, 12 October 2011, p. 14.

[187] See part One 'Comparative Perspectives' of this volume.

the different stages of UN development work clearly indicates that the former can be structurally involved in EU development programmes as well. Furthermore, the cross-regional character and independence of NHRIs in the HRC makes NHRIs and their coordinating networks interesting partners for the EU in this UN body: NHRIs can deliver cross-regional human rights expertise on common issues of concern, while they can also provide information on local human rights situations in the context of the UPR. The prioritisation by both NHRIs and the EU of the enhancement of the rights of persons with disabilities illustrates that there is room for a structural engagement of the EU with NHRIs on common issues of concern across multiple human rights fora. NHRIs can help the EU to more effectively bridge its human rights policy with actual implementation on the ground, and can offer human rights know-how based on national experience, embedded in regional and global networks, linking up the international, regional and national facets of human rights promotion and protection.

While there is considerable potential for more cooperation of the EU with NHRIs, we also indicated several obstacles that have to be taken into account. NHRIs lack resources and do not always have the capacity to effectively carry out their diverse functions.[188] Many NHRIs prioritise their national functions over the interaction with international institutions. Also, the diversity of national actors competent in the field of human rights (such as equality bodies, or data protection agencies), and the variety of structures and mandates among NHRIs themselves jeopardise a coherent EU approach towards NHRIs.

While the EU human rights policy is undergoing adaptations in order to implement the Lisbon Treaty, NHRI interaction with the new EU human rights structures is taking off.[189] However, despite the novelties introduced by the Lisbon Treaty,[190] the EU human rights architecture continues to lack coherence and consistency between internal and external policies.[191] The EU's engagement with NHRIs indeed reflects an important disjuncture between the approach towards NHRIs internally and externally. *Externally,* the EU consistently encourages the establishment and strengthening of NHRIs in accordance with the Paris

188 See also B. Adamson, Chapter 6 in this volume; K. Roberts, Chapter 10 in this volume.

189 On 15 November 2010, the European Group of NHRI met with Viviane Reding, Vice-President of the European Commission and Commissioner responsible for justice, fundamental rights and citizenship. The Chair of the European Group highlighted that the meeting was a first step in a structured engagement with the Commission. See: Irish Human Rights Commission, Report of the Chair of the European Group of National Human Rights Institutions Covering the Period March 2010 to March 2011, 24th Session of the ICC, Geneva, 16–19 May 2011.

190 Article 21(3) second para. TEU affirms: 'The Union shall ensure consistency between the different areas of its external action and between these and its other policies. The Council and the Commission, assisted by the High Representative of the Union for Foreign Affairs and Security Policy, shall ensure that consistency and shall cooperate to that effect'.

191 See in this regard for example: G. de Búrca, 'The Road Not Taken: The European Union as a Global Human Rights Actor', *The American Journal of International Law*, vol. 105, no. 4, 2011, pp. 649–693.

Principles.[192] *Internally*, though, emphasis is put mostly on national institutions with a specific human rights mandate,[193] and only 10 out of 27 EU Member States have an NHRI that fully complies with the Paris Principles. In order to strengthen its fundamental rights architecture internally, and to enhance the credibility of its external human rights policy and action, the EU should encourage and support EU Member States to establish effectively functioning NHRIs, which are in compliance with the Paris Principles.[194] This way, the EU's engagement towards third states will be backed up by its internal initiatives.

EU institutions, Member States and NHRIs need to enhance their awareness and insights regarding the potential of EU-NHRI cooperation, identifying common priorities and recognising each other's strengths and weaknesses. A structured dialogue between the EU and NHRIs and their networks could offer opportunities to delineate a common agenda. Guidelines or a communication on National Human Rights Institutions (and other national institutions competent in the area of human rights) could offer guidance for the relevant EU actors cooperating with NHRIs and their networks.

Enhanced attention by the EU on NHRIs should also encompass more support for these actors given their need for increased resources to fulfil their functions. Coherent support from the EU would consolidate the attention that is paid to these actors in the context of the EU's human rights policy. Arguably, EU support could also increase the independent functioning and the reliability of NHRIs, especially of NHRIs in third countries.

NHRIs do not replace other stakeholders in the field of human rights and will not always be the most appropriate partner for the EU. However, consistent consideration for NHRIs in the different areas of its human rights policy can help the EU to more effectively deal with various challenges it faces today, ranging from an enhanced outreach at the UN Human Rights Council to the fulfilment of EU citizens' information needs with regard to their fundamental rights and legal remedies.

---

192 See for example the EU/ Jordan Action Plan and the EU/ Egypt Action Plan, referred to *supra* note 151. This was also confirmed in an interview with EEAS Human Rights Division officials, held in March 2013.

193 As noted (see *supra* note 90), the EU directives on racial discrimination and on gender discrimination both require that national bodies are set up by the Member States to independently promote and monitor the rights protected by the respective Directives. These institutions with a 'specific mandate' do not fully comply with the Paris Principles and are accorded B-status by the ICC.

194 See also: Cost Action IS0702 'The Role of the EU in UN Human Rights Reform, recommendations on National Human Rights Institutions (NHRIs)', included as an annex to this book, namely recommendation 1.

PART III
INTERNATIONAL PERSPECTIVES

THE ROLE AND FUNCTIONING OF THE INTERNATIONAL COORDINATING COMMITTEE OF NATIONAL HUMAN RIGHTS INSTITUTIONS IN INTERNATIONAL HUMAN RIGHTS BODIES[1]

Kirsten Roberts[2]

1. INTRODUCTION

About half of the countries in the world currently have some form of national human rights institution (NHRI), and approximately one-third of all countries have an institution that has been recognised as independent and meeting the requirements of the Paris Principles, that is, an A-status NHRI.[3] While there is already a large number of NHRIs around the world, there is also increasing pressure at the international level on states to establish NHRIs and ensure their compliance with the Paris Principles, particularly since 2008 with the

1 This chapter draws on two previously published works by the author, K. Roberts, 'National Human Rights Institutions as Diplomacy Actors' in M. O'Flaherty, U. George, K. Zdzislaw and M. Amrei (eds.), *Human Rights Diplomacy: Contemporary Perspectives*, Martinus Nijhoff, 2011, pp. 221–247; K. Roberts, 'National Human Rights Institutions in Europe', in W. Benedek, F. Benoît-Rohmer, W. Karl, M. Nowak (eds.), *European Yearbook on Human* Rights, 2011, pp.257–539, as well as a paper presented by the author at the University of Melbourne Law School Workshop: 'Creating Change? NHRIs (in) Action in the Asia-Pacific Region', June 2009. This chapter represents the views of the author and does not necessarily reflect the views or position of the Irish Human Rights Commission or the International Coordinating Committee of NHRIs.

2 Kirsten Roberts BCL, M.Litt. is Acting Deputy Chief Executive and Director of Research, Policy and Promotion in the Irish Human Rights Commission (IHRC), Ireland's A-status National Human Rights Institution (NHRI). From 2008 – 2011 she was also coordinator of the European Group of NHRIs. From 2012–2013 Ms Roberts was a Visiting Researcher at Harvard Law School.

3 A-status is the term given to NHRIs who are considered by the International Coordinating Committee of NHRIs (ICC) to be in compliance with the Paris Principles (see *infra* note 5). See *infra*, section 3.2 for more information on the ICC accreditation of NHRIs. See also, G. De Beco, 'Assessment of the Paris Principles and the ICC Sub-Committee on Accreditation', Chapter 11 in this volume.

operationalisation of the universal periodic review process (UPR) at the Human Rights Council. Combined with this international push towards establishing NHRIs is an increased targeting by international and regional organisations of NHRIs as monitors and implementers of international human rights standards, policies and initiatives.

While there is a push at the international level to promote NHRIs, their establishment and functioning has not been without its criticism. Yet to date there has not been a significant amount of attention focussed on their actual work and there are still considerable efforts to be made to ensure that the role of NHRIs at the national and international level is both understood and their work and impact assessed. It can be noted at the outset that there is a disjoint between the aspirations for NHRI engagement internationally and the reality. A 2009 survey undertaken by the Office of the High Commissioner for Human Rights (OHCHR) of 61 NHRIs indicated that NHRI engagement with the Human Rights Council, for example through submitting documents, contributing to reports or making oral statements, averaged around 20%.[4]

This chapter demonstrates some of the ways in which NHRIs have the expertise and the unique positioning to provide significant added-value at the international level within the UN system, and outlines some examples of NHRI engagement with international human rights bodies.

2. RATIONALE FOR NHRI ENGAGEMENT AT THE INTERNATIONAL LEVEL

The United Nations *Principles relating to the status of national institutions* or 'Paris Principles' aimed at the creation of institutions based in the constitution or national legislation of states that would act independently of government both at the domestic and international levels for the promotion and protection of human rights.[5] The Principles provide a relatively general outline of what a NHRI should be, leaving the issue of the form of NHRI to be established to be determined by the particular state. Globally, this has resulted in a well-documented diversity of NHRI models, including human rights commissions, ombuds-institutions and multi-member institutions (for example, consultative commissions).[6] While the Principles set out some functions for NHRIs, such as providing advice to government and issuing reports on human rights issues, each NHRI is different

4 OHCHR, 'Survey on National Human Rights Institutions, Report on the findings and recommendations of a questionnaire addressed to NHRIs worldwide', Geneva, Switzerland, July 2009, p. 45.

5 UN GA, Resolution 48/134 of 20 December 1993, Annex, 'Principles relating to the Status of National Institutions' (further: Paris Principles).

6 For an extensive analysis of the different types of NHRIs in Europe, see M. Nowak, 'National Human Rights Institutions in Europe: Comparative, European and International Perspectives', Chapter 1 in this volume.

in form and function and operates within a distinct social, political and economic context. Thus, despite the overarching terminology used to describe "NHRIs", they are heterogeneous. Not only does the form and function of NHRIs differ from state to state, but their activities and areas in which they work are also tailored to national needs and situations within the broad heading of "promoting and protecting human rights". In addition, the effectiveness of each NHRI is dependent on a range of factors – and can fluctuate over time – including how the form and function of the NHRI meets the needs of the relevant country, the NHRI's own leadership, the reality of their independence and how they choose to exercise it, the existence of other independent national actors (such as thematic ombudsmen or bodies), the resources allocated to the institution and the issues they choose to prioritize, as well as the national context in which they operate.

The diversification in both form and function means that viewing NHRIs as a block can be problematic. However, there are common features of NHRIs that mean they have the ability and potential to influence the promotion and protection of human rights at the international level. These features include their independence, unique positioning, focus on human rights, cross-regional nature and role in connecting the international with the national.

2.1. ROLE OF NHRIs: DOMESTIC V. INTERNATIONAL

As national level institutions for the promotion and protection of human rights, it may seem somewhat strange that NHRIs are active at the international level. Indeed, from the domestic viewpoint and in the day to day functioning of NHRIs, this role may be difficult to reconcile. This is in part due to what might be considered as an inherent contradiction in discussing the regional and international role of entities defined as 'national' institutions and the duality of functions that NHRIs have in engaging with national as well as international issues. Indeed, it is a particular challenge for many NHRIs to engage at the international levels. Many NHRIs lack either a specific mandate to engage internationally or the human and financial resources to enable them to participate actively in international meetings and events. Anecdotally, some NHRIs have acknowledged criticism from national parliaments or in the media for their international engagement.[7] In part, this may arise from a lack of understanding of the role and functions of NHRIs, as well as a desire by national actors for NHRIs to fulfil the roles wished of them by states, non-governmental organisations (NGOs) or other national actors.

7 Sidoti states that 'governments and civil society will criticize institutions that seem to be giving too much priority to international engagement rather than domestic human rights issues [...]'. C. Sidoti, 'National Human Rights Institutions and the International Human Rights System' in R. Goodman and T. Pegram (eds.), *Human Rights, State Compliance, and Social Change*, Cambridge University Press, 2012, pp. 93–124.

From the international perspective, particularly that of the United Nations, involving NHRIs in international meetings and more specifically, engaging with them as key actors who directly interact with international bodies, has become standard practice. The UN General Assembly in a resolution on NHRIs adopted at its 66th Session in December 2011, once again welcomed 'the increasingly important role of [NHRIs] in supporting cooperation between their Governments and the United Nations in the promotion and protection of human rights'.[8] In addition to this encouragement from the international level, and while there is a duality in the role and functions of NHRIs between the domestic and international, there is also a clear mandate to engage internationally. The Paris Principles specifically reference the engagement of NHRIs at the international level, including encouraging ratification and implementation of international human rights treaties, contributing to the reporting procedure under international instruments, and cooperating with the UN human rights mechanisms and regional human rights bodies.[9] This mandate, combined with support from international human rights mechanisms, particularly the Office of the High Commissioner for Human Rights (OHCHR), has meant that NHRIs are directly engaged in the international human rights framework in a manner and to an extent which may not have been envisaged at their inception.[10] The mandate to engage internationally and support from the international level, combined with the factors considered below, places NHRIs in a unique position to contribute to the promotion and protection of human rights at the international level.

2.2. INDEPENDENCE

At the heart of the added value that NHRIs can bring to engagement at the international level (as well as at the national level), is the independence of NHRIs. Independence is a core feature of the Paris Principles, and the element on which the most emphasis has been placed by the international community as well as by NHRIs themselves, particularly through the accreditation process, discussed

8 UNGA Resolution A/RES/66/169 of 16 December 2011. This statement is also reflected in Human Rights Council Resolution A/HRC/17/L.18 adopted on 16 June 2011. The Resolution calls on the Secretary General to report on the implementation of the Resolution at the 20th Session of the Human Rights Council, which will be held in June 2012.

9 For general information on NHRIs see: United Nations Development Programme and the Office of the High Commissioner for Human Rights, 'UNDP-OHCHR Toolkit for collaboration with National Human Rights Institutions', December 2010, available at: http://www.ohchr.org/Documents/Countries/NHRI/1950-UNDP-UHCHR-Toolkit-LR.pdf.

10 UN Secretary-General Ban Ki-Moon's 2010 Report on NHRIs states that NHRIs 'play a crucial role in promoting and monitoring the effective implementation of international human rights standards at the national level, a role which is increasingly recognised by the international community'. See: UNGA, 'Report of the Secretary-General on National Institutions for the Promotion and Protection of Human Rights', *UN Doc.* A/HRC/13/44, 15 January 2010, p. 3.

further below.[11] It is the independence of NHRIs that goes to the core of their legitimacy in undertaking their activities. A consideration of the Paris Principles and the General Observations of the sub-Committee on Accreditation of the International Coordinating Committee of NHRIs indicates that independence requires that the NHRI is unrestrained by the state in its operations and in carrying out its mandate and free to work and comment – including publicly – on any human rights issue as it sees fit. Independence also requires that a NHRI has the human and financial resources to fully carry out its mandate. The mandate and functioning of the NHRI is key to ensuring its independence, this includes a president (head) and board chosen and appointed through an open and transparent process; a stable and sufficient budget; selection and appointment of its own staff; no government representation on the board or on the staff; and the ability in practice to freely, transparently and publicly work to promote and protect all human rights in the country.

2.3. POSITIONING OF NHRIs: THE "FOURTH SPACE"

Despite the heterogeneous nature of NHRIs from country to country, all Paris Principle compliant NHRIs are established as independent state institutions. As neither state representatives, nor NGOs, nor international organisations, they occupy a "4th space".[12] This space is one which has been enhanced through the activities of NHRIs in a broad range of contexts, and which primarily exists due to the engagement of NHRIs in what were previously the exclusive roles of the three existing key actors within the international human rights framework: international human rights mechanisms, NGOs and states themselves.[13] Within the international human rights system NHRIs are thus *sui generis* and this positioning means that in addition to the existing actors they can provide added value to the international system.

To elaborate, the role that NHRIs can and do play in monitoring the application and implementation of international human rights agreements, and NHRIs' advisory function in relation to the implementation of international standards at national level, was traditionally the almost sole remit of international human rights

11 See *infra* section 3.2. For an analysis of the accreditation process, see G. De Beco, 'Assessment of the Paris Principles and the ICC Sub-Committee on Accreditation', Chapter 11 in this volume.

12 A number of commentators have referred to NGOs/civil society as the "3rd space", for example: R. P. Fairbanks II, 'The Political Economic Gradient' in R. A. Cnaan and C. M. Milofsky (eds.), *Handbook of Community Movements and Local Organisations*, Berlin, Springer, 2007; T. Kaplan, 'Women's Rights as Human Rights: Women as Agents of Social Change' in M. Agosín (ed.), *Women, Gender & Human Rights: A Global Perspective*, New Brunswick, Rutgers University Press, 2001. Gérard Fellous referred to NHRIs as institutions of the "third type" , G. Fellous, *Les Institutions Nationales des Droits de l'Homme: Acteurs de Troisième Type*, Commission Nationale Consultative Des Droits de l'Homme, 2006.

13 K. Roberts, 'National Human Rights Institutions as Diplomacy Actors', loc. cit. *supra* note 1.

mechanisms. The Paris Principles clearly identified an international function for NHRIs in linking the international human rights system to the national level.[14] This specific role for NHRIs can be seen as an enhancement of the work of international human rights mechanisms through the creation of national-level monitors and advocates for standards elaborated at the international level, as well as acting as promoters of the work of international organisations themselves at the national level. For example, where NHRIs are active in the UPR, considered further below,[15] this can enhance the quality and awareness of this process both within the Human Rights Council and at the domestic level. The engagement of NHRIs with Special Procedure mandate holders, also considered further below,[16] has the potential to raise awareness of mandate holders' activities, enhance their ability to focus on the most relevant national issues and arguably increase pressure on governments to provide full and frank information as NHRIs themselves can independently provide such detail should the state fail to do so.

Secondly, some of the space that NHRIs occupy was traditionally the almost sole remit of human rights NGOs. NGOs are often regarded as the primary custodians of the concerns of civil society and individuals in relation to human rights at the national level. Because of their active engagement with national civil society and awareness of a broad range of domestic human rights concerns, national institutions also assume an active role in this area as custodians of a wide range of national human rights concerns arising out of the activism or experiences of groups and individuals at the domestic level. For example, NHRIs can establish and maintain strong relationships with civil society organisations at the national level and many NHRIs directly receive complaints or information from individuals in their country.[17] In the absence of a NHRI acting as a national conduit for human rights issues and concerns, such complaints and information relating to human rights would frequently rest solely with NGOs. While civil society activism is a vital component in any democratic country, it is advantageous both to the NGO and to the individual to have multiple avenues open to them for any human rights complaint or concern. Additionally, the position of the NHRI within the national framework means they can also utilise individual issues to work on broader systemic policy concerns. Indeed, NHRIs, as state-based institutions are arguably ideally placed to promote access to justice and policy change at the national level. Although this will of course depend on a range of

---

14 For example, the Paris Principles provide that '3. A national institution shall, inter alia, have the following responsibilities: [...] (e) To cooperate with the United Nations and any other organization in the United Nations system, the regional institutions and the national institutions of other countries that are competent in the areas of the protection and promotion of human rights;'. See *supra* note 5.

15 *Infra,* section 4.3.

16 *Infra*, section 4.6.

17 *See for example* OHCHR Survey on National Human Rights Institutions, *loc. cit.* supra note 4.

factors noted above,[18] including the political climate in which the NHRI operates, its independence and effectiveness.

Third, NHRIs may be said to provide an alternative to the traditional role of the state where they provide an authoritative, national-level voice on domestic human rights issues at the international level. Where a country has an A-status institution,[19] the state will be aware that their report on the human rights situation in their country may not be the only state voice on the issue. The NHRI report may indeed provide a contradictory assessment of a human rights situation, which in the case of A-status institutions is given considerable weight at the international level, particularly by the UN treaty bodies.[20] NHRI engagement in discussions on the development of new treaties or conventions, for example, in the case of the Convention on the Rights of Persons with Disabilities (CRPD),[21] provides a further counterpoint to the role of states.

That NHRIs occupy these spaces does not however mean that the roles of other actors are or should be diminished. It is important for NHRIs to work with other actors, particularly civil society organisations, and to ensure that its own work does not reduce or restrict civil society action on the ground. Renshaw and Fitzpatrick highlight the 'desirability of cooperation between NGOs and NHRIs' and note the formalised engagement between NGOs and NHRIs in the Asia-Pacific region as one example of NHRI-NGO collaboration.[22]

While the position of NHRIs incorporates some of the traditional roles of states, NGOs and international mechanisms, it also has its own specific elements arising from the remit and focus of NHRIs' work. Thus the "4th space" that NHRIs occupy is not just attributable to the combining of the three areas discussed above. The "4th space", covering some of the traditional roles of the three key actors at the international level, with the addition of unique elements rising from the attributes of NHRIs, provides an important position from which NHRIs can distinctively contribute to the international human rights system.[23] This role for NHRIs as a new actor within the international framework is also promoted and championed by international organisations, notably the OHCHR.

In addition, this space which NHRIs occupy is strengthened by the internationalised nature of their work and collective engagement. NHRIs individually and collectively draw on international human rights standards in

18 *Supra*, section 2.

19 As mentioned *supra* note 3, A-status NHRIs are considered by the ICC to be in compliance with the Paris Principles, and thus should be able to function independently from government (see *supra* 2.2).

20 *Infra*, section 4.5.

21 *Infra*, section 4.5.

22 C. Renshaw and K. Fitzpatrick, 'National Human Rights Institutions in the Asia Pacific Region: Change Agents under Conditions of Uncertainty' in R. Goodman and T. Pegram (eds.), *Human Rights, State Compliance, and Social Change*, Cambridge University Press, 2012, p. 159.

23 See further K. Roberts, 'National Human Rights Institutions as Diplomacy Actors in Human Rights Diplomacy: Contemporary Perspectives', loc. cit. *supra* note 1.

their substantive engagement. The cross-regional nature of NHRIs' collective engagement, discussed further below,[24] means that their statements at the international level cannot be dismissed as merely reflecting the interests or views of one region, political persuasion or faith. Statements by the International Coordinating Committee of NHRIs represent national institutions from every region of the world. This adds to the value of NHRI collective engagement at the international level and enhances their legitimacy as human rights actors.

Finally, because of their unique positioning, NHRIs are increasingly targeted to enhance a 'two-way system' between what happens within the UN and what is happening on the ground in terms of human rights. NHRIs bring international initiatives both from and to the international level. At the same time, international initiatives and procedures are to be reinforced by NHRIs on the ground. Thus, an idea which begins at the international level can be discussed directly at the national level between the NHRI and their respective state structures, including national parliaments; simultaneously, it can also be discussed and reinforced by NHRIs individually and collectively at the international level.

2.4. HUMAN RIGHTS FOCUS AND EXPERTISE

A further factor strengthening the value of NHRI engagement at the international level is their human rights focus. Paris Principles compliant NHRIs should maintain independence and impartiality from particular agendas or political positions; their sole purpose is the promotion and protection of human rights. Where they function in this manner, they can be said to be almost exclusively "loyal" to human rights principles and are free to engage with all actors on the human rights stage. *Sidoti* for example, argues that NHRIs 'have the information and the experience to bring a measure of honesty to international forums where it is lacking'[25]. The general human rights expertise of NHRIs and in relation to the specific human rights situation at the national level can add value to the forums in which they engage. States come to human rights discussions with a range of interests and concerns apart from the sole improvement of human rights. Even where NGOs come to the table with only improvement of human rights as their aim, their views can sometimes too easily be dismissed by states' collective willingness to support each other and focus on political interests. NHRIs, which are given legitimacy by the member state itself, and have a sole remit to promote and protect human rights, are harder to dismiss as coming from a "vested interest" and their views are therefore more difficult to ignore.

The combination of factors: engagement with civil society and the public, providing an alternative "state" voice and undertaking international

24 *Infra*, section 3.1.

25 C. Sidoti, loc. cit. *supra* note 7, p.100.

organisation-type monitoring functions combined with a focus and expertise on human rights, a cross-regional approach and a clear mandate to engage at the international level, means that NHRIs are in a position to make real progress in promoting and protecting human rights at the international level. While NHRIs may not have fully exploited to date the added value they bring to the international stage, they are increasingly active in this area and there is considerable potential for NHRIs to utilise their unique positioning into the future.

3. THE INTERNATIONAL COORDINATING COMMITTEE OF NHRIs

It is a particularly interesting aspect of the collective engagement of NHRIs, that they take an active part in developing their own role as well as in promoting the establishment of independent NHRIs around the world and assessing existing NHRIs for their independence. Indeed, the Paris Principles were elaborated with the input of NHRIs and subsequently adopted by the United Nations.[26] This unique type of engagement within the international human rights system has primarily been driven through an international network – the International Coordinating Committee of NHRIs (or 'ICC'). The ICC was first established in 1993 and became a legal entity under Swiss law in 2008.[27] It acts as a forum through which NHRIs can coordinate their international engagement,[28] and is headed by a Chair from one of its A-status NHRI members, who, among other tasks, acts as a high-level representative of the ICC in international meetings and events. Currently there are 69 full members (A-status) of the ICC and 32 observers (non A-status).[29] The ICC has also developed a Statute[30] and has a permanent representative in Geneva who supports NHRIs' engagement in the international human rights system as well as supporting the Chair of the ICC. While the ICC is primarily funded through a membership fee from its A-status members, to date it has also received a limited annual amount from the OHCHR. The ICC Secretariat – comprising

[26] See for example, C. Sidoti, 'National Human Rights Institutions and the International Human Rights System', loc. cit. *supra* note 7, pp. 93–123.

[27] See OHCHR website at: http://www.ohchr.org/en/countries/NHRI/pages/NHRImain.aspx. UNGA Resolution 50/176 of 27 February 1996 on National Institutions for the Promotion and Protection of Human Rights, notes the establishment of the ICC in 1993, at para 7.

[28] The ICC Statute provides that the functions of the ICC include 'to coordinate at an international level the activities of NHRIs established in conformity with the Paris Principles, including such activities as: Interaction and cooperation with the United Nations, including the OHCHR, the Human Rights Council, its mechanisms, United Nations human rights treaty bodies, as well as with other international organisations; To promote the establishment and strengthening of NHRIs in conformity with the Paris Principles.'. See: Statute of the International Coordinating Committee of National Human Rights Institutions as amended 24 March 2009 (Statute of the ICC), Art. 7, available at: nhri.ohchr.org.

[29] ICC, Chart of the Status of National Institutions, Accreditation Status as of May 2012, available at: http://nhri.ohchr.org.

[30] *Supra* note 28.

the Chair, Secretary (vice-chair) and members of the governing Bureau – is also supported by the OHCHR by way of practical assistance.

The ICC meets on an annual basis in Geneva – 2012 saw the 25th annual ICC meeting – and also meets biennially to discuss specific thematic issues in-depth. In November 2012, the ICC biennial in Amman, Jordan discussed gender equality, including the rights of women and girls. The annual meetings of the ICC provide an opportunity to discuss both structural issues (such as the workplan for the ICC and financial matters), as well as thematic issues. The 2012 annual meeting for example discussed NHRIs and the environment, monitoring, the Optional Protocol to the Convention Against Torture (OPCAT), indigenous people's rights, transitional justice, the right to development and the UPR. There were also side-events held on the accreditation process and lesbian, gay, bisexual and transgender (LGBTI) rights. Although these discussions are NHRI-centric, focussing on how NHRIs can work on these areas, they provide important opportunities to identify and discuss how NHRIs can develop their work at the national level, and learn from best practice of their peers.

3.1. REGIONAL GROUPS

A particular strength of the ICC network is its regional focus. The regional groups are in ways stronger than the overarching ICC structure in that they actively and regularly engage their members and undertake a considerable number of substantive initiatives at the regional level. The regional groups provide regular updates to their members, and focus on NHRIs' work and development within a specific region. They also take the lead on engagement with regional human rights mechanisms. There are four regional networks of national institutions, each with a coordinating structure, covering Africa, the Americas, Asia-Pacific and Europe. The four regional networks, each led by a Chair elected from among the A-status NHRIs of the respective region and supported by a coordinating committee of three other A-status members, act autonomously at the regional level but form part of the ICC structure. Indeed the chair and the coordinating committee of each region combine to form the 16-member Bureau of the ICC. Two interesting examples of regional networks are the European Group and Asia Pacific Forum of NHRIs.

The European Group of NHRIs, representing 34 NHRIs from the European Region, 22 of which are A-status, actively engages with the three main human rights mechanisms in Europe: the Council of Europe, the Organisation for Security and Cooperation in Europe (OSCE), and the EU Fundamental Rights Agency.[31] The European Group has taken some groundbreaking collective initiatives such

[31] For an extensive overview, see: B. Adamson, 'NHRI and their European Counterparts: Scope for Strengthened Cooperation and Performance towards European Human Rights Institutions', Chapter 6 in this volume.

as submitting third party (*amicus curiae*) interventions to the European Court of Human Rights.[32] The European Group has also made a number of detailed submissions to the process for reform of the European Court of Human Rights and has presented statements at high-level ministerial conferences on the issue.[33] Although the European Group forms part of the ICC, these initiatives are undertaken independently of the ICC and are coordinated by the Chair of the European Group (from 2006–2011 the Irish Human Rights Commission and since May 2011, the Scottish Human Rights Commission) and the regional coordinator, who to date has been a member of staff of the Chair NHRI. Since 2009, the European Group has been working to establish a regional secretariat to support and enhance the work of the Group. By the end of 2012, a Director has been recruited to further establish the Secretariat.[34]

The Asia Pacific region has one of the strongest regional coordinating mechanisms within the ICC. The Asia Pacific Forum of National Human Rights Institutions (APF) was established in 1996, with the aim of providing support to governments in the region to establish and develop national human rights institutions, and expanding mutual support, cooperation and joint activity among member institutions.[35] The APF has grown considerably since that time, and now provides a range of services including advice, training, capacity building, supporting NHRI accreditation, professional networks and staff exchanges.[36] The APF is also a leader in initiatives at the international level, and was particularly active in the Convention on the Rights of Persons with Disabilities' recognition of the role of independent national bodies, as well as in securing participation rights for NHRIs in the Human Rights Council, and in advocating for the role of NHRIs in the Commission on the Status of Women.

These international and regional structures have a coordinating and networking function. While they cannot be said to 'set policy' for the global community of NHRIs, they do act as an important forum for NHRIs to have a collective voice at the regional and international level and are a key source of initiatives and substantive engagement by NHRIs at the regional and international level.

---

32 In the cases of *DD v. Lithuania*, Application No. 13469/06, and *Gauer v. France*, Application No. 61521/08. See also: A. Buyse, 'The Court's Ears and Arms: National Human Rights Institutions and the European Court of Human Rights', Chapter 8 in this volume.

33 See for example: Oral Statement of the European Group of National Human Rights Institutions at the Brighton High-Level Ministerial Conference on the Future of the European Court of Human Rights, 19–20 April 2012, available at: www.ihrc.ie.

34 See also: B. Adamson, 'NHRI and their European Counterparts: Scope for Strengthened Cooperation and Performance towards European Human Rights Institutions', Chapter 6 in this volume.

35 Larrakia Declaration, Asia Pacific Forum of National Human Rights Institutions, First Regional Workshop, Darwin, Australia, 8–10 July 1996, available at: http://www.asiapacificforum.net/about/history/annual-meetings/1st-australia-1996/downloads/larakia.pdf.

36 See the APF website: www.asiapacificforum.net. See also: B. Adamson, 'NHRI and their European Counterparts: Scope for Strengthened Cooperation and Performance towards European Human Rights Institutions', Chapter 6 in this volume.

Finally, it should also be noted that although there are international and regional coordinating structures, NHRIs also actively engage individually with regional and international mechanisms for the promotion and protection of human rights. Because of the regional structure and the coordinating role of the ICC, such engagement is fed back into the collective discussions and information sharing of the whole ICC. Accordingly, information, initiatives and issues circulate globally among NHRIs.

3.2. THE ACCREDITATION PROCESS[37]

A particularly important role of the ICC is its peer-review system for assessing the independence of NHRIs. As noted above, independence is the crucial hallmark of NHRIs and vital for their added value to and legitimacy within the international system. Despite the diversity of models of NHRIs internationally, the Paris Principles remain the benchmark for the mandate and structure of national institutions. Early on in its establishment, the ICC set up a committee to review the compliance of national institutions with the Paris Principles.[38] NHRIs that are fully compliant with the Principles are given an A-status accreditation by the ICC. This brings with it the recognition of the respective NHRI within the UN system, and includes the right to make statements before the Human Rights Council.[39] As of 2012, there were sixty nine NHRIs accredited as fully compliant with the Paris Principles and some thirty others that were accredited as partly compliant or non-compliant.[40] This peer-review mechanism is in the unique position of being recognised within the UN system and has approval as the process by which the independence of NHRIs can be assessed. A side event on the margins of the 25th meeting of the ICC in Geneva in March 2012, considered the accreditation process and the increasing levels of scrutiny and difficulties in obtaining and retaining 'A'-status accreditation were noted, particularly as the

37 For more information on the accreditation procedure, see G. De Beco, 'Assessment of the Paris Principles and the ICC Sub-Committee on Accreditation', Chapter 11 in this volume.

38 The first accreditations took place in 1999, see ICC Chart loc. cit. *supra* note 29.

39 UN GA Resolution 60/251 of 3 April 2006 establishing the Human Rights Council provides that the Council is to 'work in close cooperation in the field of human rights with Governments, regional organisations, national human rights institutions and civil society'. UN HRC Resolution 5/1 of 18 June 2007, Rule 7 provides for the participation of NHRIs.

40 See ICC Chart, loc. cit. *supra* note 29. The SCA assesses the compliance of NHRIs with the Paris Principles in law and practice. It has developed a series of guidelines known as General Observations and Templates, which serve as interpretative tools of the Paris Principles. The General Observations and Templates are available at: http://nhri.ohchr.org/. See also UN GA, Report of the Secretary-General on Process Currently Utilized by the International Coordinating Committee of National Institutions for the Promotion and Protection of Human Rights to Accredit National Institutions in Compliance with the Paris Principles, *UN Doc.* A/HRC/13/45, 18 January 2010.

ICC has finished the first accreditation cycle and begins its review of all NHRIs in addition to new accreditations.

The role of the SCA is particularly important when examined in the light of the above-mentioned unique attributes of NHRIs within the international system. Maintaining the process of assessment of independence, which could otherwise become easily politicised, separate from member states goes to the heart of the ability of NHRIs to promote and protect human rights both nationally and internationally.

In some ways, the SCA process mirrors NHRIs role in parallel reporting to treaty bodies[41] in that NHRIs undertake their own, independent assessment and propose recommendations. It is an unusual process when the fact that the NHRI has not been responsible for its own establishment is taken into account, nor is the NHRI responsible for many of the issues that the SCA repeatedly highlights such as its basis in national legislation, the procedure for the appointment of members and staff, and designation and level of budgets. The recommendations of the SCA, although addressed to NHRIs, are in reality issues which the state must often rectify. The SCA's recommendations can hold particular importance for NHRIs in their efforts to advocate for their improved compliance with the Paris Principles. In this way, the ICC itself is working to strengthen NHRIs globally, and to rectify situations where states may have created weak institutions. In relation to the Asia Pacific Region, Renshaw and Fitzpatrick, citing Cardenas, note that the establishment of NHRIs has often been undertaken as a result of international obligations, resulting in institutions that were weak and reflected the state's reluctance to concede any elements of sovereignty.[42] A review of the reports of the SCA demonstrates that its recommendations have real impact in improving the compliance of NHRIs. For example, in the case of the NHRI in Nigeria, which had been downgraded from A-status to B-status,[43] the SCA noted in 2010 the work of the NHRI in pursuing amendments to its own legislation, and that an amending bill had gone before the Parliament.[44] With the enactment of the legislation, the National Human Rights Commission of Nigeria was re-accredited with A-status in 2011.[45] Similarly, in 2009 in relation to Qatar, the SCA expressed 'appreciation for the legislative changes that have increased the number of civil society representatives on the NHRC, their majority status on the NHRC and the

41 See *infra* section 4.5 for more information on NHRI interaction with the UN treaty bodies.

42 C. Renshaw and K. Fitzpatrick, loc. cit. *supra* note 22 at p.154, citing S. Cardenas 'National Human Rights Commissions in Asia', *Human Rights Review* vol. 30, 2002, p. 48.

43 B-status NHRIs are not in full compliance with the Paris Principles. See further: G. De Beco, 'Assessment of the Paris Principles and the ICC Sub-Committee on Accreditation', Chapter 11 in this volume.

44 ICC, Report and Recommendations of the Session of the Sub-Committee on Accreditation (SCA), Geneva, October 2010, p. 6.

45 ICC, Report and Recommendations of the Session of the Sub-Committee on Accreditation (SCA), Geneva, May 2011, p. 18.

removal of voting rights for Government representatives'.[46] In relation to Algeria, the SCA took note of 'a letter dated 25 March 2009 from the [NHRI] President to the ICC Chair informing that the Prime Minister has instructed the Minister of Justice to elaborate a legislative text on the status of the [NHRI]'.[47]

4. THE ICC AND INTERNATIONAL HUMAN RIGHTS MECHANISMS

4.1. PROMOTING INTERNATIONAL ENGAGEMENT

In addition to providing both a forum for NHRIs and a means of assessing NHRI compliance with the Paris Principles, the ICC actively engages and promotes engagement with international human rights mechanisms. The ICC thus lobbies to promote the role of NHRIs, works to promote the use of international standards by NHRIs, and to promote the strengthening of international mechanisms. As noted above, there may be a conflict between the domestic and international engagement of NHRIs and both separate to and sometimes because of this conflict, NHRIs may be reluctant or restricted in engaging internationally. The ICC has an important role in encouraging NHRI engagement at the international level, and in highlighting the value of such engagement to NHRIs and international human rights actors. While to some extent this push for international engagement has come via the strong links between NHRIs and OHCHR, which has its own institutional reasons for encouraging NHRI engagement, the main impetus has come from the collective leadership of the ICC over a number of years. The ICC, including through its Geneva-based representative, identifies and lobbies for space for NHRIs in international forums, and encourages active participation by its members. The ICC also provides support to NHRIs to assist them in their participation, for example by assisting with accreditation for access to the UN in Geneva or through the delivery of information on how to access a treaty body. Regular updates are sent both from the ICC Chair and the respective Regional Chairs to ICC members to alert NHRIs to opportunities for engagement and encourage active participation.

4.2. THE HUMAN RIGHTS COUNCIL

The Human Rights Council provides an important opportunity for NHRIs to highlight domestic and international human rights issues. A-status NHRIs

[46] Report and Recommendations of the Session of the Sub-Committee on Accreditation (SCA), Geneva, March 2009.

[47] *Ibidem.*

are explicitly referenced as independent interlocutors with the Human Rights Council. In its Resolution 60/251 establishing the Human Rights Council, the UN General Assembly specifically urged the Council to work in close cooperation with NHRIs.[48] NHRIs have been increasingly active within the Human Rights Council in recent years, both individually and collectively. A-status NHRIs are entitled to submit documents and make oral and written statements to the Council, and also have a role in the Council's universal periodic review process.[49] NHRIs even have their own designated seating, separate from NGOs and government.

The ICC and individual NHRIs have utilised this position through submissions and statements on a wide range of issues. In the most recent sessions of the Council, the ICC has participated in High Level Panels, and made statements on a range of reports and thematic areas.[50] NHRIs' individual and collective statements have covered a wide range of topics including thematic issues such as human rights education,[51] transitional justice,[52] the Convention on the Rights of Persons with Disabilities,[53] human rights and countering terrorism,[54] the Optional Protocol to the Convention on the Rights of the Child,[55] issues relating to the relationship

---

48 UN HRC, Resolution 60/251 of 3 April 2006. See also: K. Meuwissen, 'NHRI Participation in United Nations Human Rights Procedures: International Promotion versus Institutional Consolidation', Chapter 12 in this volume.

49 See *infra*, section 4.3.

50 For example, at the 17th session of the Human Rights Council in Geneva the ICC made statements on transnational corporations best practices in combating racism and the consideration of an optional protocol to the Convention on the Rights of the Child to provide a communications procedure.

51 See, for example: ICC Additional Statement on the Submission of the Draft Statement on Human Rights Education and Training to the Human Rights Council, 16 March 2009; Advisory Committee of the HRC, 'Draft "United Nations Declaration on Human Rights Education and Training", Concerted Contribution National Human Rights Institutions Presented at the session of the Advisory Committee of the Human Rights Council, to be held in Geneva from 3 to 7 August 2009', *UN Doc.* A/HRC/AC/3/NI/1, 4 August 2009, annex.

52 See, for example: Statement by the Network of African National Human Rights Institutions on behalf of A-status national human rights institutions in Africa on the report by the Office of the High Commissioner for Human Rights on transitional justice, 12th Session of the Human Rights Council, 14 September to 2 October 2009, *UN Doc.* A/HRC/12/NI/1, 4 September 2009, annex.

53 See, for example: ICC Chairperson statement on Article 33 and the Role of National Human Rights Institutions during a Panel Discussion on the Rights of Persons with Disabilities, 13th Session of the Human Rights Council, 5 March 2010, available at: http://www.ohchr.org/EN/Issues/Disability/Pages/SecondDebate.aspx; European Group of National Human Rights Institutions Statement on the Effective Implementation of National Frameworks on the Implementation and Monitoring of the Convention on the Rights of Persons with Disabilities, 5 March 2010, available at: http://www.equalityhumanrights.com/uploaded_files/humanrights/hrc13_crpd_panelstatement.pdf.

54 For example: Joint NHRI Statement of Denmark, Greece, France, Afghanistan, Germany, Great Britain, Norway, Ireland, Luxembourg and South Africa, under Agenda item 3: Report of the Special Rapporteur on the Promotion and Protection of Human Rights while Countering Terrorism, 8 March 2010.

55 For example: Joint NHRI Statement of Korea, Ireland, Morocco, Germany, Namibia, Togo, Indonesia, Great Britain, the Philippines, and Ukraine on the Rights of the Child, delivered at the 13th Regular Session under Agenda item 3: Report of the Working Group on the Optional

between NHRIs and the UN human rights mechanisms – including the role and functions of NHRIs –,[56] and the need to strengthen international mechanisms such as the treaty bodies and the special procedures of the Human Rights Council.[57]

NHRIs have also sought to both support and develop international human rights standards. For example, the ICC has been particularly active in engaging on the issue of Business and Human Rights. The ICC Working Group on Business and Human Rights[58] has made a number of submissions to the development of the Ruggie Framework[59] as well as advocating for the role of NHRIs within the framework, and is now actively promoting the role of NHRIs in the implementation of the framework at the national and international level. In June 2011, the Human Rights Council specifically recognised the role of NHRIs in this area.[60]

Collectively, NHRIs have also been active in promoting their own role within the Council. During the Human Rights Council review process, the ICC made a number of submissions aimed at enhancing the process and strengthening the role of NHRIs within the Council.[61] The efforts of NHRIs, supported by Member States and the OHCHR, resulted in the inclusion in the second round of the UPR of a separate section in the UPR OHCHR stakeholder review document for the submissions of A-status NHRIs. NHRIs are also now entitled to speak directly after the state under review, during the adoption of the outcome report by the

---

Protocol to the Convention on the Rights of the Child, 13th Session of the Human Rights Council (Geneva, 1–26 March 2010).

56 For example: ICC Statement 3 March 2010 during the General Segment of the 13th Session of the Human Rights Council, reiterating the importance of independent national institutions, the need for adequate funding, and urging Member States to establish Paris Principles Compliant NHRIs, and to strengthen those already in existence. ICC Statement on Secretary General's Reports on NHRIs and the Accreditation Process, 4–5 March 2010.

57 For example: ICC Statement under Agenda Item 2: Annual Report of the High Commissioner for Human Rights, 4–5 March 2010, noting the linking role of NHRIs, and encouraging the OHCHR to continue to facilitate and support NHRI engagement with the international mechanisms including special procedures and treaty bodies.

58 The Working Group was established in 2009 and comprises 2 members from each of the ICC Regions. In October 2010, the ICC Biennial focussed on the theme of Business and Human Rights. For more information, see the ICC website: http://nhri.ohchr.org/EN/Themes/BusinessHR/Pages/Home.aspx.

59 For further information on the Ruggie Framework see http://198.170.85.29/Ruggie-protect-respect-remedy-framework.pdf.

60 UN HRC Resolution 17/4 of 16 June 2011, para. 11: '11. *Also welcomes* the important role of national human rights institutions established in accordance with the Paris Principles in relation to business and human rights, and encourages national human rights institutions to further develop their capacity to fulfil that role effectively, including with the support of the Office of the High Commissioner and in addressing all relevant actors;'.

61 See: ICC, 2011 Human Rights Council Review ICC Position Paper, available at: http://www.nanhri.org/index2.php?option=com_docman&task=doc_view&gid=61&Itemid=28; ICC, Human Rights Council Review ICC Proposals for the Outcome Document, February 2011, available at: http://nhri.ohchr.org/EN/IHRS/HumanRightsCouncil/Review/ICC%20Proposal%20for%20the%20outcome%20document%20Feb.%202011.pdf.

Council.[62] A procedure for facilitating NHRIs to make statements to the Council by video-link or video statement has also been introduced, with the first NHRI video statement being delivered in March 2012.[63]

4.3. UPR

Within the UPR process, NHRIs have a particularly active role in advocating for the adoption of strong and pertinent recommendations for the report on their state and there is increasing engagement in the UPR process by NHRIs, supported by the ICC.[64] To give just one example, the (A-status) Irish Human Rights Commission submitted a report for the stakeholder compilation, held briefing sessions on UPR in different parts of Ireland, published suggested voluntary commitments, developed a section on its website to provide information on the UPR and a simple template for submissions and provided advice and support to civil society organisations on how they could submit information for the process. At the adoption of Ireland's UPR Report, the Irish Commission also made an oral statement and circulated a longer written statement of its concerns.[65]

In addition to engagement by individual NHRIs in the process at the national level, the UPR itself has a strong focus on NHRIs with recommendations on the establishment or strengthening of NHRIs featuring in almost every UPR report.

NHRIs are also a focus in UPR follow-up, which arguably represents the greatest challenge in terms of the utility and success of the UPR process in terms of ensuring substantive human rights improvements in states. This issue has been discussed within the ICC itself, and good practice examples of follow-up procedures, such as that undertaken by the Danish Institute for Human Rights

62 See UN HRC, Resolution 16/21 of 25 March 2011.

63 On 5 March 2012, the *Provedoria* for Human Rights and Justice of Timor Leste spoke via video statement under Item 3, during the Interactive Dialogue with the Working Group on Enforced Disappearances.

64 UN HRC Resolution 5/1 of 18 June 2007 (Institution-building package of the United Nations Human Rights Council), Annex, part VII (Rules of Procedure), rule 7(b). The participation and speaking rights of NHRIs were strengthened as a result of the Human Rights Council Review Process 2011: see UN HRC Resolution 16/21 of 25 March 2011, para. 28 and para. 22, a). NHRIs provide stakeholder reports to the stakeholder summary, encourage and assist NGOs and civil society organisations to provide information, raise awareness of the UPR at the national level and comment on the state report. Prior to the hearings, NHRIs may engage directly with the diplomats of other member states during side events, and can directly lobby on issues of concern for their county's UPR report. After the adoption of the report, NHRIs can make statements at the Human Rights Council concerning the implementation of the recommendations made to their state. See for example, Irish Human Rights Commission http://www.ihrc.ie/international/upr.html See also universal periodic review information presented by the Asia Pacific Forum of National Human Rights Institutions, *UN Doc.* A/HRC/14/NI/10, 31 May 2010.

65 See the website of the IHRC: www.ihrc.ie.

have been shared with the other members of the ICC.[66] The ability of NHRIs to be proactive in the follow-up process will be a test for the strength of their engagement in the UPR process, and this will only begin to come to light as the second cycle of UPR begins in 2012. However, already the Human Rights Council has recognised the added value of NHRIs to the process by giving them a separate section in the stakeholder compilation for the second cycle.

4.4. GENERAL ASSEMBLY AND OTHER UN BODIES

NHRI engagement with the General Assembly has been somewhat more limited than their engagement with the Human Rights Council. However, it has been an arena that has seen lobbying by NHRIs in support of their role and the strengthening of NHRIs globally. The General Assembly has adopted biennial resolutions on NHRIs in recent years, reaffirming its support for NHRIs.[67] In 2011, the General Assembly adopted Resolution 66/169 on NHRIs, co-sponsored by more than eighty countries reaffirming the importance of developing such institutions and the contribution they make to promoting and protecting human rights. The ICC undertook advocacy to support both the content and adoption of the Resolution. In particular, the ICC was invited to submit its preliminary comments and objectives to the main sponsor of the Resolution.[68] NHRIs at the national level also supported the adoption of the resolution through engagement with their own ministries of foreign affairs by calling on them to support the Resolution. The work of the ICC in both advocating for and supporting such resolutions demonstrates the active nature of NHRIs in promoting the establishment and strengthening of NHRIs globally.

In other United Nations forums there has been a mixed but increasing level of engagement. The ICC has participated in the Commission on the Status of Women (CSW), the Conference of State Parties to the Convention on the Rights of Persons with Disabilities, the Permanent Forum on Indigenous Issues, the Anniversary of the Durban Declaration and Programme of Action and the Open Ended Working Group on Ageing. In relation to CSW, the ICC has been advocating for recognition of the role of NHRIs in the Commission for a number of years, including lobbying

---

66 See for example Universal Periodic Review – First Cycle Reporting Methodologies from the Position of the State, Civil Society and National Human Rights Institutions, 2011, Danish Institute for Human Rights, Copenhagen, Distributed by The International Coordinating Committee of National Institutions for the Promotion and Protection of Human Rights. For more information on the Danish Institute for Human Rights, see: Ch. Badse, 'The Danish Experience: the Danish Institute for Human Rights', Chapter 2 in this volume.

67 See for example: General Assembly Resolutions 63/172 and 64/161 of 18 December 2009.

68 See Recommended Objectives by the ICC, 66th Session of the General Assembly Resolution on National Human Rights Institutions. See: http://nhri.ohchr.org/EN/ICC/BureauMeeting/Documents/Bureau%20meeting%20October%202011/GA%20resolution%20on%20NHRIs%20-%20recommended%20objectives.doc.

directly with member states. The Asia-Pacific Forum, with the support of the ICC, lobbied the CSW to give a formal position to NHRIs. To date, these efforts have resulted in formal government statements promoting the role of NHRIs in the CSW, a statement by the Chair of the Committee on the Elimination of All Forms of Discrimination Against Women (CEDAW Committee) strongly encouraging CSW to consider how NHRIs could be fully integrated into its work, and the first specific reference to NHRIs in the 'Agreed Conclusions' of the CSW, but these efforts have not yet seen the formalisation of the role of NHRIs in CSW.[69]

4.5. TREATY BODIES

The ICC and individual NHRIs have been particularly active in their engagement with the United Nations treaty bodies both through substantive contributions to the treaty monitoring process and in the process for reform of the treaty body system. Engagement with the treaty bodies, combined with interaction with the Human Rights Council, probably represents the most active areas of formal engagement for the ICC and individual NHRIs at the international level. A number of treaty body general comments and recommendations specifically refer to NHRIs, and some treaty bodies have developed formal guidelines on their working relationship with NHRIs.[70] The Committee on the Elimination of Racial Discrimination (CERD) for example has formalised the role of NHRIs in the hearing process, allowing NHRIs to speak during the state hearing.[71] The CEDAW Committee has issued a statement on its relationship with NHRIs and the roles of NHRIs in monitoring and protecting the rights of women.[72] The Committee on the Rights of the Child has elaborated working methods specifically encouraging NHRIs to provide reports and the Committee can meet

[69] See Report on ICC Advocacy at the 54th Session of UN Commission on the Status of Women, New York, 1–12 March 2010. For further information see also: http://www.asiapacificforum.net/working-with-others/un/commission-on-the-status-of-women.

[70] For example: General Comments 10, 16 and 19 of the Committee on Economic, Social and Cultural Rights; General Comments 1, 2, 5, 8, 9 and 11 of the Committee on the Rights of the Child; General Comment 31 of the Human Rights Committee; General Recommendations 27 and 33 of the Committee on the Elimination of Racial Discrimination; General Recommendation 28 of the Committee on the Elimination of All Forms of Discrimination against Women. For more information, see: ICC, Position Paper, 'The Treaty Body Strengthening Process: Effective Participation of National Human Rights Institutions', April 2012. See also: K. Meuwissen, 'NHRI Participation in United Nations Human Rights Procedures: International Promotion versus Institutional Consolidation', Chapter 12 in this volume.

[71] See CERD, Rules of Procedure *UN Doc.* CERD/C/35/Rev.3, 1 January 1989, Rule 40.

[72] CEDAW, 'Statement by the Committee on the Elimination of Discrimination against Women on its relationship with national human rights institutions', *UN Doc.* E/CN.6/2008/CRP.1, Annex II.

with NHRIs at their request in private.[73] The Human Rights Committee has also invited NHRIs to submit reports and NHRIs may make oral statements to the Committee during the first morning meeting of every plenary session.[74] Since 2006, the ICC has participated in the annual inter-committee meeting of the treaty bodies and special procedure mandate holders. In working to strengthen the treaty body process itself, including through participation in the Treaty Body Strengthening Process (Dublin Process) the ICC has sought to make a substantive contribution to the promotion and protection of human rights at the international level. The ICC developed a position paper on the Treaty Body Strengthening Process in April 2012.[75] The paper outlines a number of ways in which NHRIs can contribute to strengthening the treaty body process, including proposing that NHRIs should be able to contribute to all stages of the General Assembly's Treaty Body Strengthening Processes: by attending meetings and consultations and presenting oral and written interventions, and highlighting the need to limit NHRI participation to A-status institutions.[76]

The ICC has also engaged in the inter-state process regarding international treaties. At the fourth meeting of the Conference of States Parties (COSP) to the Convention on the Rights of Persons with Disabilities held in New York in September 2011, NHRIs were given *de facto* recognition by the Chair of the Bureau of the COSP.[77] This included a designated NHRI seat, the right to make a statement and the right to participate in discussions. ICC representatives at the Conference worked to strengthen the role and visibility of the ICC and NHRIs through meeting with key stakeholders and sponsoring a side-event on Article 33.2 of the CRPD, which deals with domestic monitoring of implementation.[78]

Individually, NHRIs regularly provide 'shadow' or alternative reports to Treaty Bodies, support the involvement of NGOs and civil society organisations in the national level treaty body monitoring process, raise awareness of specific treaties and the examination process at the national level, and meet directly with the treaty body to pass on concerns and recommendations.[79] Thus both

---

[73] Committee on the Rights of the Child, Working Methods, VIII. Participation of non-governmental organizations and national human rights institutions in the activities of the Committees.

[74] Human Rights Committee, Working Methods, VIII. Participation of non-governmental organizations and national human rights institutions in the activities of the Committees.

[75] ICC, Position Paper, 'The Treaty Body Strengthening Process: Effective Participation of National Human Rights Institutions', April 2012.

[76] *Ibidem.*

[77] See Progress Report on ICC Operational Plan for ICC Bureau meeting and ICC, 25 March 2012, p. 6.

[78] *Ibidem.*

[79] See for example: Conclusions of the International Roundtable on the Role of National Human Rights Institutions and Treaty Bodies, Berlin, 23 and 24 November 2006, presented at Nineteenth meeting of chairpersons of the human rights treaty bodies Geneva, 21–22 June 2007, available at: http://www.nhri.net/pdf2006/Conclusions_Int_RT_rev8dec.pdf; A. Müller and F. Seidensticker, *The Role of National Human Rights Institutions in the UN Human Rights Treaty Body Process*, Berlin, German Institute for Human Rights, 2007. See also OHCHR

at the international level and through their work on the ground, NHRIs make a substantive contribution to the monitoring of international human rights standards contained in the core UN treaties. NHRI engagement with the treaty bodies both nationally and internationally provides a good indication of how their unique positioning allows them to bring added value to the promotion and protection of human rights. For example, because NHRIs are active participants in the national monitoring of the treaties, they are well positioned to contribute to the international reform process. Because they are independent voices for human rights concerns at the national level their views are given a certain weight by the treaty bodies. And because they work collectively at the international level they can as a collective engage with authority in promoting an improved process in the ongoing discussion on treaty body reform.

4.6. SPECIAL PROCEDURES

While there has been somewhat of a lower level of engagement from NHRIs with special procedure's mandate holders to date compared to the treaty bodies, this engagement is also on the increase. The Human Rights Council review for example has resulted in NHRIs in compliance with the Paris Principles (A-status) being allowed to nominate candidates as special procedures mandate holders and being entitled to intervene immediately after the state under consideration.[80] NHRIs have also been given the right to make contributions to the Human Rights Council by video-conferencing and video-statements.[81] Individually, NHRIs meet with special procedures when they undertake country visits, and regularly provide information to surveys or questionnaires on human rights issues relevant to the special procedure's mandate. Similarly to their engagement with the treaty bodies, NHRIs unique positioning and collective action through the ICC allows them to make a substantive contribution to the work of the special procedures.

Information Note on National Human Rights Institutions (NHRIs) interaction with the UN Treaty Body System http://nhri.ohchr.org/EN/ICC/AnnualMeeting/24/4NHRI%20Treaty%20Bodies%20Engagement/NHRIs%20and%20the%20Treaty%20Bodies.Infonote.11.4.2011.doc. To give one example, the Irish Human Rights Commission engages actively with treaty bodies and in the last four years has submitted shadow reports under ICCPR, CERD and CAT, as well as appearing before each Committee, and publicising each process at the national level. The results of this engagement have clearly been seen by the Irish Commission in the concluding observations of the Committees.

80 HRC Resolution 16/21 of 25 March 2011, para. 28. According to this paragraph, the A-status NHRI of the country concerned shall be entitled to intervene immediately after the state during the interactive dialogue, following the presentation of a country mission report by a special procedure mandate holder. Resolution 16/21 also grants A-status NHRIs the right to nominate candidates as special procedures mandate holders (para. 22 a).

81 HRC Resolution 16/21 of 25 March 2011, para. 59.

5. CHALLENGES AND OPPORTUNITIES

NHRIs are not a "cure-all" that can improve global human rights standards overnight. They are, however, an important addition to the existing international human rights framework. Their unique positioning, independence, "loyalty" to human rights and on the ground expertise can strengthen the current structures – supporting civil society's work, highlighting government shortcomings and enhancing the universality of human rights. But expectations on their ability to improve human rights standards must be tempered by a range of factors, including an understanding of their actual role and functions and the national contexts in which they operate, and the importance of independence and resourcing.

The potential added value of NHRIs has been recognised by international human rights mechanisms, and this has resulted in a high demand for NHRI engagement. Yet the increasing level of attention and focus on NHRIs is not without its risks. The tasks demanded of NHRIs both nationally and internationally are frequently not matched by the necessary resources either to individual NHRIs or their networks. NHRIs are asked to monitor and scrutinise human rights at the national level, implement international initiatives, engage with civil society, the state, regional and international organisations and to play an active role collectively at the international level. When NHRIs are unable to undertake the multitude of tasks assigned to them, there can be disappointment and criticism that NHRIs are not doing enough or that they are simply taking space or resources away from other actors who are in a better position to contribute. For NHRIs, international engagement, while recognised as valuable and important, often constitutes an additional workload on top of an already demanding domestic focus. Thus, while NHRIs are increasingly targeted as the implementers of the initiatives of regional and international human rights mechanisms, they may not always be in a position to actually undertake these tasks. More work may need to be undertaken by the ICC and NHRIs regionally and nationally to promote understanding of both the abilities and constraints of NHRIs to ensure that expectations are in keeping with the realities of NHRIs' individual and collective engagement. In addition, the Sub-Committee on Accreditation may need to increase scrutiny in its assessment of NHRIs on the need for resources and the potential down-grading (or non up-grading) of institutions lacking necessary resources. Finally, the targeting of NHRIs as implementers of international initiatives needs to be combined with the provision of resources. It is also worth recalling that both individually and within the international human rights framework, NHRIs are still a relatively new actor. Although the concept of establishing NHRIs has been in place since 1993, many institutions have only been created in the last ten years, and many are still being established or developed into A-status institutions. The ICC accreditation procedure has only formally been in place for five years. It is easy to criticise, but it must be remembered that it is not a single body that has been set up, but over a hundred national institutions, in a multiplicity of regions and national contexts. That there is such coherence in the network of NHRIs and that NHRIs have developed their own internal accreditation system should be reason for praise. Furthermore, this unique system of accreditation is not required for other bodies in the international human rights system, and while it can and is being strengthened, it is important that it is supported by the international community as a peer-review process and without undue interference or politicisation. With most states accepting the UPR recommendations to establish and strengthen NHRIs, it can be conjectured that the profile of NHRIs will increase in coming years as their numbers mount. With an increasing number of NHRIs and an increasing focus on their work, there is a risk that the accreditation process may become politicised. Removal of the accreditation process from its current locus within the community of NHRIs could pose a serious threat to the role and functioning of NHRIs globally – and particularly to their independence, which would seriously damage their legitimacy to promote and protect human rights. While it is acknowledged that the current accreditation process can be strengthened, the value of a peer-review system cannot be underestimated in the context of maintaining independent institutions.

Increasing the effectiveness of NHRIs both nationally and internationally may also result in increased risk to NHRIs independence. Already it has been seen that some NHRIs that were A-status have been downgraded, and other A-status institutions have had their budgets and resources reduced to the point where their effectiveness is threatened through lack of ability to undertake their functions. Where NHRIs actively criticise their government, even the most benign of states may take measures to reduce their effectiveness and independence. An important counter to such action is the role of the ICC and Sub-Committee on Accreditation in monitoring the compliance of NHRIs with the Paris Principles and reducing their status when appropriate. International pressure on states to ensure their NHRI has A-status combined with the critical assessment of the Sub-Committee may help to prevent or mitigate such attacks on NHRIs independence.

NHRIs themselves also need to be supported to recognise the value of international engagement, and how it connects with their work on the national level. The ICC has and will continue to play a key role in this area. However, the ICC itself lacks resources. There may be steps taken in coming years to further strengthen the role of the ICC. For example, a consideration to be made is whether a permanent secretariat for the ICC can be established in order to further enhance the services to members of the ICC and the engagement of the ICC on a regular basis in Geneva and in other UN fora. Permanent regional secretariats exist in Asia-Pacific and Africa, and one is in the process of being established for Europe. Strengthening of NHRIs regionally will also support the ICC at the international level. Additional funding, for example from philanthropic or donor organisations, could also assist the ICC in undertaking and increasing work.

NHRIs are important additions to the framework for the promotion and protection of human rights both nationally and internationally. Through the support and strategic engagement of the ICC, their ability to influence and shape human rights protection globally has the potential to significantly increase in the coming years. With the 20th Anniversary of the Paris Principles in 2013, it may be an opportune time to take stock and see how and where the role of these unique institutions can be enhanced on the international stage. In particular, increased academic and policy-level assessment of the role and functioning of NHRIs through for example an empirical study of their effectiveness may help to understand how NHRIs can positively develop and increase their contribution to the promotion and protection of human rights in the coming twenty years.

COMPLIANCE WITH THE PARIS PRINCIPLES AND THE ICC SUB-COMMITTEE ON ACCREDITATION

Gauthier DE BECO[1]

1. INTRODUCTION

The accreditation of national human rights institutions (NHRIs) is an important topic. To qualify as such, NHRIs should meet certain criteria without which their legitimacy might be questioned. NHRIs are governed by the 'Principles relating to the status and functioning of national institutions for the protection and promotion of human rights', commonly called the Paris Principles. Compliance with these Principles is considered essential to enable NHRIs to fulfill their mandates. The issue, however, has been little discussed and the accreditation procedure is not well known, which is problematic considering its important consequences at both national and international levels. Understanding how a body gets a label is crucial before it gets any attention.

This chapter will study how NHRIs are accredited. It will look at the body competent for examining their compliance with the Paris Principles and analyse the accreditation procedure step-by-step. The chapter is divided into four parts. The first part introduces the Paris Principles and examines their adoption, recognition and content, including the fundamental principles of independence and pluralism. The second part discusses the role and composition of the ICC Sub-Committee on Accreditation as well as the characteristics of the accreditation procedure and the consequences of the accreditation of NHRIs. The third part examines the different parts of the accreditation procedure as well as efforts done to strengthen it and provides a few examples of its practical application. The fourth and last part gives an evaluation of the accreditation procedure.

---

1 Post-doctoral researcher at KU Leuven, Leuven Institute for Human Rights and Critical Studies (LIHRCS). Ph.D. in Law, University of Louvain; LL.M., University of Nottingham. Developments are updated until March 2013.

2. PARIS PRINCIPLES

2.1. INTERNATIONAL RECOGNITION OF THE PARIS PRINCIPLES

The Paris Principles outline the responsibilities, composition and working methods of NHRIs.[2] They were drafted by NHRIs at their first International Workshop held in Paris in 1991 and subsequently endorsed by the UN Commission on Human Rights (now UN Human Rights Council) and the UN General Assembly.[3] The Paris Principles still constitute the basic standards for NHRIs worldwide. Although they were drafted by NHRIs, they have gradually been recognised at the international level. The World Conference on Human Rights held in Vienna in 1993 acknowledged the importance of creating NHRIs that comply with the Paris Principles.[4] Treaty bodies encouraged states worldwide to establish or strengthen NHRIs in line with the Paris Principles.[5] The UN also encouraged their creation and supports their networking activities through its various bodies. The Office of the UN High Commissioner for Human Rights (OHCHR) has been particularly active in this regard and created a National Institutions Unit.[6]

2.2. NATIONAL HUMAN RIGHTS INSTITUTIONS (NHRIs)

2.2.1. Responsibilities

According to the Paris Principles, NHRIs have mainly three functions: the monitoring and advising of state authorities, the promotion and providing of human rights education and the handling of complaints on alleged human rights

---

2 The Paris Principles are divided into the following headings: Competence and responsibilities; Composition and guarantees of independence and pluralism; Methods of operation; and Additional principles concerning the status of commissions with quasi-jurisdictional competence. See Annex 2 to this book for the integral text of the Paris Principles.

3 UN CHR Resolution 1992/54 of 3 March 1992, *UN Doc.* E/CN.4/RES/1992/54; UN GA Resolution 48/134 of 20 December 1993, *UN Doc.* A/RES/48/134.

4 Vienna Declaration and Programme of Action, 25 June 1993, *UN Doc.* A/Conf.157/23, Part I., para 36.

5 See Committee on the Rights of the Child, General Comment No. 2, 'The role of independent national human rights institutions in the promotion and protection of the rights of the child', 15 November 2002, *UN Doc.* CRC/GC/2002/2; Committee on Economic, Social and Cultural Rights, General Comment No. 10, 'The role of national human rights institutions in the protection of economic, social and cultural rights', 10 December 1998, *UN Doc.* HRI/GEN/Rev.7; Committee on the Elimination of Racial Discrimination, General Recommendation No. 17, 'Establishment of national institutions to facilitate implementation of the Convention', March 1993, *UN Doc.* A/48/18, 25.

6 The OHCHR also published a handbook to assist governments in the establishment and strengthening of NHRIs which was recently updated: OHCHR Professional Training Series No. 4 (Rev.1), 'National Human Rights Institutions. History, Principles, Roles and Responsibilities', 2010.

violations (the last function being optional according to the Paris Principles). Regarding the first function, NHRIs examine the compliance of both legislation and practice with human rights. They evaluate not only their conformity with human rights treaties but also the broader implications of policies for human rights enjoyment. NHRIs may also conduct general inquiries and submit reports on human rights issues that seem important or urgent to state authorities. Regarding the second function, NHRIs aim to increase awareness of human rights by disseminating information on human rights. This includes not only education within or outside the school system but also training for all those responsible for their implementation. Some NHRIs also focus on research in order to promote a better understanding of human rights.

NHRIs aim to ensure that national human rights policies are consistent. Thanks to their broad mandate, they can help states to adopt coherent human rights policies. They can elaborate a general approach to human rights issues, including those issues straddling the competence of different public organs or different levels of powers in federal or decentralised states and, by so doing, ensure the mainstreaming of human rights. Moreover, NHRIs can foster a national dialogue on specific human rights issues. A NHRI can also prove to be valuable to the general public by setting up information points and special desks in order to direct individuals to other competent institutions.

2.2.2. Fundamental Principles

Besides setting out the functions of NHRIs, the Paris Principles lay emphasis on two fundamental principles: independence and pluralism.

Independence requires that NHRIs be free from governmental interference. This has a triple meaning under the Paris Principles. First, NHRIs should be functionally independent. To guarantee this, they should be established 'by a constitutional or legislative text'.[7] Secondly, NHRIs should be personally independent. This means that their members should be able to act in a pressure-free environment and be appointed (and, if necessary, dismissed) according to a fair and clear procedure. They must also be able to choose their own staff and to determine their priorities. Thirdly, NHRIs should be financially independent. They must have sufficient resources at their disposal, which should be determined preferably by parliament.[8]

Pluralism links NHRIs with civil society. The Paris Principles provide that the composition of NHRIs should ensure 'the pluralist representation of the social forces (of civilian society) involved in the promotion and protection of

7 Paris Principles, Principle 2, A. Competence and responsibilities.

8 Paris Principles, Principle 2, B. Composition and guarantees of independence and pluralism.

human rights'.[9] They also mention a series of actors who should be involved in the work of NHRIs:

- Non-governmental organisations responsible for human rights and efforts to combat racial discrimination, trade unions, concerned social and professional organisations, for example, associations of lawyers, doctors, journalists and eminent scientists;
- Trends in philosophical or religious thought;
- Universities and qualified experts;
- Parliament;
- Government departments (if these are included, their representatives should participate in the deliberations only in an advisory capacity).[10]

NGOs are the actors that have the strongest links with NHRIs. NHRIs and NGOs can mutually benefit from cooperation. On the one hand, through NHRIs NGOs can channel their demands to state authorities and thereby increase their impact. NHRIs also give NGOs the opportunity to coordinate their action, by allowing them to collectively deal with human rights issues that are in the ambit of different organisations. On the other hand, NGOs can help NHRIs to get in touch with local communities and to be appraised of the day-to-day problems affecting vulnerable groups. They can also make available their sound knowledge and the deeply rooted expertise they possess in the field of human rights to these institutions.

NGOs, however, tend to be over-represented in NHRIs at the expense of other actors, such as trade unions, concerned social and professional organisations as well as universities and qualified experts, which are mentioned in the Paris Principles.[11] NGO dominance may lead to forgetting that these actors are also concerned with human rights, even if this might be incidental, and they should therefore be associated in their implementation. Furthermore, a better balance in NHRI membership would lead to a better understanding between both NGO and non-NGO forces.

Pluralism can be achieved in two ways: representation or cooperation. The Paris Principles state that NHRIs should ensure 'the pluralist representation of the social forces (of civilian society) involved in the promotion and protection of human rights' either 'by powers which will enable effective cooperation to be established with, or through the presence of, representatives of' the abovementioned actors.[12] This means that these representatives should either be members of the NHRIs or be able to effectively cooperate with these institutions.

9 Paris Principles, Principle 1, B. Composition and guarantees of independence and pluralism.
10 *Ibidem.*
11 *Ibidem.*
12 *Ibidem.*

3. ICC SUB-COMMITTEE ON ACCREDITATION

3.1. THE ICC AND THE ICC SUB-COMMITTEE ON ACCREDITATION

At the international level, NHRIs created the International Coordinating Committee of National Institutions for the Promotion and Protection of Human Rights (ICC).[13] The ICC is a representative body composed of four regional groups, namely Africa, Europe, the Americas and Asia-Pacific, all of which have their own regional coordinating committees. It is an association recognised under Swiss law with its own statutes.[14] The ICC is headed by a Chairperson and run by a Bureau comprising 16 NHRIs.[15] Its members form together the General Meeting which meets at least once a year.[16] The ICC promotes the establishment and strengthening of NHRIs in compliance with the Paris Principles and facilitates their cooperation worldwide and their interaction with UN human rights mechanisms. It gradually acquired an international position by increasing its engagement in policy making with regard to NHRIs.[17] Since its inception, the ICC has considered that the Paris Principles are the criteria defining which bodies are to be included or excluded and undertook to verify that its members continue to comply with these Principles.[18] The ICC also organises biannually international conferences, which include thematic sessions. The OHCHR is closely linked to the ICC and its National Institutions Unit serves as ICC Secretariat.

To determine if NHRIs are in compliance with the Paris Principles, the ICC established a Sub-Committee on Accreditation. The accreditation procedure is outlined in the ICC Statute and further developed in the Rules of Procedure of the ICC Sub-Committee on Accreditation which are annexed to the ICC Statute.[19] With the support of the National Institution Unit, the ICC Sub-Committee on Accreditation is compiling a list of those institutions that comply, do not fully comply, or fail to comply with the Paris Principles. Those that comply are granted

---

13 See also K. Roberts, 'The Role and Functioning of the International Coordinating Committee of National Human Rights Institutions in International Human Rights Bodies', Chapter 10 in this volume.

14 Statute of the International Coordinating Committee of National Institutions for the Promotion and Protection of Human Rights, 30 July 2008, amended 21 October 2008, amended 24 March 2009 (further: ICC Statute).

15 ICC Statute, Article 43.

16 ICC Statute, Article 36.

17 See A.-M. Garrido and B. Kofod Olson, 'Coordination of the Work of NHRIs – From Liaison to Joint Achievements', in R.F. Jorgensen and K. Slavensky (eds.), *Implementing Human Rights. Essays in Honour of Morten Kjaerum*, Danish Institute for Human Rights, 2007, pp. 190–203.

18 M. Brodie, 'Progressing Norm Socialisation: Why Membership Matters. The Impact of the Accreditation Process of the International Coordinating Committee of National Institutions for the Promotion and Protection of Human Rights', *Nordic Journal of International Law*, vol. 80, 2011, pp. 153–154.

19 Rules of Procedure for the ICC Sub-Committee on Accreditation, 14 September 2004, amended 15 April 2008 (Rules of Procedure).

A-Status, those that do not fully comply are granted B-Status, and those that fail to comply receive C-Status.[20] This is one of the key tasks of the ICC. As a result, it is now possible to know how many NHRIs are recognised as such both globally and regionally.[21] Only NHRIs with A-Status can become voting members of the ICC and its regional groups and be elected to sit in the ICC Bureau.[22] Importantly, they can also participate in the sessions of the Human Rights Council where they have their own tribune and may circulate documents under their own symbol number.[23] NHRIs with B-Status are granted observer status in the ICC and in its regional groups as well as in the sessions of the Human Rights Council. Those with C-Status have no rights, although they may be invited to participate as observers in meetings and workshops. There may be more than one NHRI with A-Status per state,[24] but only one can have voting rights in the ICC.

---

20 (R)-Status, i.e. accreditation with reserve, was previously granted if documentation was lacking to be granted A-Status. This category is no longer used now.

21 A regularly updated list of accredited NHRIs is available at: http://www.ohchr.nhri.net. As of February 2013, 69 NHRIs had A-Status. See ICC, 'Chart of the Status of National Institutions Accredited by the International Coordinating Committee of National Institutions for the Promotion and Protection of Human Rights', February 2013. In the Council of Europe, these are (in alphabetical order): the Republic of Albania's People's Advocate, the Human Rights Defender of Armenia, the Human Rights Commissioner in Azerbaijan, the Human Rights Ombudsman of Bosnia and Herzegovina, the Ombudsman of the Republic of Croatia, the Danish Institute for Human Rights, the French *Commission Nationale Consultative des Droits de l'Homme*, the Public Defender's Office in Georgia, the German Institute for Human Rights, the Equality and Human Rights Commission in the United Kingdom, the Greek National Commission for Human Rights, the Irish Human Rights Commission, the Luxembourg *Commission Consultative des Droits de l'Homme*, the Northern Ireland Human Rights Commission, the Norwegian Centre for Human Rights, the Polish Commissioner for Civil Rights Protection, the *Provedor de Justiça* in Portugal, the Commissioner for Human Rights in the Russian Federation, the Scottish Human Rights Commission, the Protector of Citizens of the Republic of Serbia, the *Defensor del Pueblo* in Spain and the Ukrainian Parliament Commissioners for Human Rights. See also M. Nowak, 'National Human Rights Institutions in Europe: Comparative, European and International Perspectives', Chapter 1 in this volume. For more information on the European Group of NHRIs, see B. Adamson, 'NHRI and their European Counterparts: Scope for Strengthened Cooperation and Performance towards European Human Rights Institutions', Chapter 6 in this volume.

22 ICC Statute, Article 24 (1).

23 Resolution 60/251 of the General Assembly provides that NHRIs can participate in the sessions of the Human Rights Council in the same way as they could in those of the Commission on Human Rights (where those with A-Status had already the right to speak). See UN GA Resolution 60/251 of 3 April 2006, *UN Doc.* A/RES/60/251, para. 11. While NHRIs could initially only speak under the item relating to NHRIs themselves, those that were accredited were subsequently authorised to discuss all issues relating to their mandates. See UN Commission on Human Rights Resoultion 2005/74 of 20 April 2005, *UN Doc.* E/CN.4/RES/2005/74, para. 11 (a). The participation of NHRIs is also explicitly provided for in the Rules of Procedure of the Human Rights Council which refers to Resolution 2005/74 of the Commission on Human Rights. See UN Human Rights Council, Resolution 5/1 'Institution-building of the United Nations Human Rights Council, VII. Rules of Procedure' of 18 June 2007, *UN Doc.* A/HRC/RES/5/1, para. 7 (b).

24 This is only the case with the United Kingdom which has three NHRIs: the Equality and Human Rights Commission, the Scottish Human Rights Commission and the Northern Ireland Human Rights Commission. The Equality and Human Rights Commission is the NHRI for England, Wales and Scotland with the exception of matters falling under the remit

The ICC Sub-Committee on Accreditation was created in 2002.[25] It is composed of one NHRI of each regional group, which consist of four NHRIs in total.[26] It meets each time after the General Meeting of the ICC but additional meetings may be convened by the Chair.[27] Members are elected by regional groups for a period of three years renewable.[28] Currently, these are the Canadian Human Rights Commission, the National Human Rights Commission of Korea, the National Commission for Human Rights of Togo and the French *Commission nationale consultative des droits de l'homme.* In its capacity of ICC Secretariat, the OHCHR has permanent observer status in the ICC Sub-Committee on Accreditation.[29]

The ICC Sub-Committee on Accreditation developed General Observations which serve to '[g]uide [it] in its determination of new accreditation applications, reaccreditation applications or special reviews'.[30] The General Observations aim to provide a clarification of the Paris Principles and also to help both NHRIs and governments to increase the NHRIs' compliance with these Principles. Further guidance on the Paris Principles however would be required, considering the succinct nature of these Observations.[31]

3.2. ADVANTAGES AND DISADVANTAGES OF A "PEER REVIEW" ACCREDITATION

The accreditation of NHRIs is a peer review. This peer review has both advantages and disadvantages.

On the positive side, NHRIs which drafted the Paris Principles have an interest in accreditation being done seriously, because the presence of unqualified members might affect their own reputation. High consideration for the benchmark against which they are measured is necessary to uphold their legitimacy. Trying to influence their peers would therefore work against them. The absence of pressure between the members ensures that evaluation takes place equitably.[32] Since the

of the Scottish Human Rights Commission. The Scottish Human Rights Commission is the NHRI for Scotland and the Northern Ireland Human Rights Commission is the NHRI for Northern Ireland.

25 The ICC had already started to accredit NHRIs a few years before the creation of the ICC Sub-Committee on Accreditation.

26 Rules of Procedure, Article 2.1.

27 Rules of Procedure, Articles 4.1 and 3. In practice, the ICC Sub-Committee on Accreditation meets twice a year.

28 Rules of Procedure, Article 2.2.

29 Rules of Procedure, Article 2.4.

30 Rules of Procedure, Article 6.3 (c).

31 The General Observations are currently being reviewed by the ICC Sub-Committee on Accreditation.

32 G. de Beco, 'Networks of European National Human Rights Institutions', *European Law Journal*, vol. 14, 2008, p. 865.

members of a network are easily aware of the difficulties faced by their colleagues, peer review also provides for reliable examination. On the other hand, should actors other than NHRIs participate in the accreditation procedure they might try to lower the requirements set forth in the Paris Principles. This is obviously the case with governments on whom compliance with the Paris Principles mainly depends. The fact that the accreditation procedure is completely separated from state politics and carried by NHRIs themselves guarantees its credibility.[33] In this regard, the question is whether or not it is the governments that are being held accountable by the peer review. Peer review is actually a means for NHRIs to inform their peers about how governments treat them, which eventually determines membership of the ICC.[34]

On the negative side, NHRIs have a double role of regulator and promoter of NHRIs. While the ICC is accrediting NHRIs according their compliance with the Paris Principles, it encourages their establishment and strengthening in compliance with the Paris Principles. This double role can be problematic and questions whether peer review is good for their accreditation.[35] Given its aim to have as much as possible NHRIs with A-status internationally, the ICC might evaluate NHRIs too lightly in order to expand its membership. While the ICC Sub-Committee on Accreditation may guarantee that minimal requirements are met, it will not consider their concrete role in the implementation of human rights, including their potential engagement in critical issues and their impact on the work of other actors.[36] The accreditation procedure is moreover secretive with limited input of other actors, except the OHCHR.[37] The ICC Sub-Committee on Accreditation may receive information from NGOs[38] and invite experts as observers in its meetings,[39] but there is no requirement to do so. This prevents it from examining closely how NHRIs work. The consequence is that the evaluation of NHRIs might be inconsistent having mainly the sole interests of the ICC in mind.

---

33 C. Sidoti, 'National Human Rights Institutions and the International Human Rights System', in R. Goodman and T. Pegram, (eds), *Human Rights, State Compliance, and Social Change. Assessing National Human Rights Institutions*, Cambridge University Press, 2012, p. 98.

34 G. de Beco, loc. cit. *supra* note 32, p. 865.

35 R. Murray, *The Role of National Human Rights Institutions at the International and Regional Levels: The Experience of Africa*, Hart Publishing, 2007, pp. 87–88.

36 P. Rosenblum, 'Tainted Origins and Uncertain Outcomes: Evaluating NHRIs', in Goodman and Pegram, loc. cit. *supra* note 33, p.301.

37 *Ibidem*, p. 317.

38 Rules of Procedure, Article 3.6.

39 Rules of Procedure, Article 4.2.

3.3. CONSEQUENCES OF THE ACCREDITATION OF NHRIs BEYOND MEMBERSHIP OF THE ICC

The consequences of the accreditation of NHRIs go further than membership of the ICC. As already mentioned, NHRIs with A-status can participate in the sessions of the Human Rights Council. Their participation in these sessions raises further questions about their accreditation, because the A-status enhances their position internationally, which shows indeed that the Paris Principles are now fully recognised at the international level. Participation in international *fora*, in turn, increases the legitimacy of NHRIs nationally.[40] Furthermore, A-status gives NHRIs legitimacy at home not only with state authorities but also towards civil society and the general public. Although it is not the only criterion affecting their legitimacy, this can be used to prove their independence and pluralism or counter criticism from other actors. A last factor that further adds to the consequences of being accredited is the reference to the Paris Principles in two recent human rights treaties, namely the Optional Protocol to the Convention against Torture and other Cruel, Inhuman or Degrading Treatment or Punishment (OPCAT) and the Convention on the Rights of Persons with Disabilities (CRPD), which require that states establish or designate national preventive mechanisms to visit places of detention and independent mechanisms to promote, protect and monitor the implementation of the CRPD, respectively, in compliance with the Paris Principles. Given the explicit mentioning of these Principles in these treaties,[41] NHRIs will usually be designated, alone or together with other actors. Their accreditation will be used to demonstrate their compliance with these Principles and their suitability to be designated national preventive mechanism under OPCAT and independent mechanism under the CRPD. This however does not necessarily mean that they are best suited to play this role.[42] The impact of the accreditation procedure shows therefore the importance to have a clear, fair and objective process granting A-status to NHRIs.

4. ACCREDITATION PROCEDURE

4.1. PERIODIC REVIEW AND SPECIAL REVIEW

NHRIs that wish to apply for membership of the ICC should follow the accreditation procedure outlined below. Originally, they had to do so only once. As requested by the UN Secretary General, the accreditation procedure was

40 R. Murray, loc. cit. *supra* note 35, pp. 71 and 85.
41 OPCAT, Article 18 (4); CRPD, Article 33 (2).
42 G. de Beco, 'Article 33(2) of the UN Convention on the Rights of Persons with Disabilities: Another Role for National Human Rights Institutions?', *Netherlands Quarterly of Human Rights*, vol. 29, 2011, p. 95.

subsequently strengthened, especially in view of the participation of NHRIs with A-status in the sessions of the Human Rights Council.[43] Since 2006, NHRIs are reviewed every five years starting immediately for those that were accredited more than five years before. Members who fail to send the supporting documentation in due time are suspended until this documentation is submitted to the ICC Sub-Committee on Accreditation.[44] An NHRI, however, may ask that its re-accreditation be deferred provided it gives written justifications that are compelling and exceptional,[45] such as prospective changes in its enabling statutes. This can be done for a period of one year after which it loses its membership. The ICC also took a series of measures in order to improve the accreditation procedure by making it more rigorous, efficient and transparent and by including recommendations to improve the NHRIs' compliance with the Paris Principles.[46]

Besides the initial application and every five years review, NHRIs can be specially reviewed if circumstances so require. The ICC Chairperson or any member of the ICC Sub-Committee on Accreditation may initiate the special review of an NHRI with A-status, if it appears that new circumstances have affected its compliance with the Paris Principles.[47] This could be, for instance, a prospective change in its enabling statutes.[48] NHRIs also have an obligation to notify these changes to the ICC Chairperson who will inform the ICC Sub-Committee on Accreditation.[49] The special review must be done within 18 months after which the NHRI loses its membership if it fails to show that it still complies with the Paris Principles.[50] It can then re-apply for A-status. Another possibility is to immediately suspend an NHRI with A-status in exceptional circumstances in which case a special review will be started with the same conditions. The Chairperson will notify this to the ICC Bureau and the NHRI in question,[51] which may challenge it within thirty days.[52] Although an immediate suspension never took place so far, members of the regional group of the Americas

---

43 UN Commission on Human Rights, 'Effective Functioning of Human Rights Mechanisms: National Institutions and Regional Arrangements. Enhancing the Participation of National Human Rights Institutions in the Work of the Commission on Human Rights and its Subsidiary Bodies. Report of the Secretary General', *UN Doc.* E/CN.4/2005/107, 19 January 2005, para. 16.

44 Rules of Procedure, Article 3.4.

45 Rules of Procedure, Article 3.5.

46 OHCHR, 'Process currently utilized by the International Coordinating Committee of National Institutions for the Promotion and Protection of Human Rights to accredit national institutions in compliance with the Paris Principles. Report of the Secretary General', *UN Doc.* A/HRC/16/77, 3 February 2011, p.4.

47 Article 16.2, ICC Statute.

48 OHCHR Professional Training Series No. 4 (Rev. 1), loc. cit. *supra* note 6, p. 48.

49 ICC Statute, Article 16.1.

50 ICC Statute Article 17.

51 ICC Statute Article 18.1.

52 ICC Statute Article 18.2.

have proposed to define the term 'exceptional circumstances' in order to limit its scope at the last meeting of the ICC.[53]

As will be seen in the next section, the current accreditation procedure has four steps.[54] First, the NHRI has to send the supporting documentation for its accreditation to the ICC Secretariat. Secondly, the OHCHR reviews the application and provides a summary to the ICC Sub-Committee on Accreditation. Thirdly, the ICC Sub-Committee on Accreditation makes a recommendation on accreditation to the ICC Bureau. Fourthly, the ICC Bureau decides on the accreditation of the NHRI.

4.2. ACCREDITATION PROCEDURE

4.2.1. Application

An NHRI seeking accreditation has to submit its application to the Chairperson of the ICC through the ICC Secretariat. It should send the following supporting documentation:

- a copy of the legislation or other instrument by which it is established and empowered in its official or published format;
- an outline of its organisational structure including staff complement and annual budget;
- a copy of its most recent annual report or equivalent document in its official or published format;
- a detailed statement showing how it complies with the Paris Principles as well as any respects in which it does not so comply and any proposals to ensure compliance. The ICC Bureau may determine the form in which this statement is to be provided.[55]

This documentation, including the statement of compliance which requires specific information on the NHRI's compliance with the Paris Principles,[56] should be submitted to the ICC Secretariat at least four months before the next meeting of the ICC Sub-Committee on Accreditation.[57] Civil society organisations may also provide information relating to the accreditation within the same time

[53] Proposed amendments to the ICC Statute, 12 January 2012, available at http://nhri.ohchr.org/EN/ICC/AnnualMeeting/25/Meeting%20Documents/FINAL%20ICC%2025%20-%20ICC%20Statute%20Amendments%20Paper%20-EN.pdf.

[54] OHCHR Professional Training Series No. 4 (Rev. 1), loc. cit. *supra* note 6, p. 45.

[55] ICC Statute, Article 10.

[56] See ICC, 'Compilation of the Rules and Working Methods of the SCA, 6. Template of the Statement of Compliance', http://nhri.ohchr.org/EN/AboutUs/ICCAccreditation/Pages/NextSession.aspx.

[57] Rules of Procedure Article 3.4.

period of time.[58] This information is shared with the NHRI. Although the ICC Sub-Committee is not required to do so, it sometimes consults civil society organisations on its own initiative.

4.2.2. *Summary*

In its capacity of ICC Secretariat, the OHCHR reviews the application and makes a summary which examines the NHRI's compliance with the Paris Principles for the attention of the ICC Sub-Committee on Accreditation.[59] The ICC Secretariat may ask additional information to the NHRI and will share the summary with the NHRI whose comments are forwarded together with this summary to the ICC Sub-Committee on Accreditation.

4.2.3. *Recommendation*

The ICC Sub-Committee on Accreditation considers the application of the NHRI on the basis of the summary and its statement of compliance with the Paris Principles, in cooperation with the OHCHR. Using its General Observations, it prepares a report which includes any recommendations to improve the NHRI's compliance with the Paris Principles. It can consult the NHRI and should do so if a negative response to the application is to be recommended.[60] It also has a contact person who can be reached by phone during the review in case additional information is necessary to make the evaluation. Regional coordinating committees may participate as observers. OHCHR desk officers and, if necessary, OHCHR regional offices are also invited to share their views. The ICC Sub-Committee on Accreditation will then recommend A-, B- or C-status for the NHRI to the ICC Bureau. Its recommendation on accreditation will first be sent to this NHRI which can challenge it within 28 days of receipt.[61]

4.2.4. *Decision*

The ICC Bureau receives the recommendation of the ICC Sub-Committee on Accreditation and any challenges by the NHRI after the twenty-eight day period.[62] Any member who disagrees with the recommendation can notify it within twenty days and, if at least four members coming from at least two different regional groups also object within twenty days, the recommendation will be deferred to the next meeting of the ICC Bureau;[63] if at least four members coming from at least

[58] Rules of Procedure Article 3.6.
[59] OHCHR Professional Training Series No. 4 (Rev. 1), loc. cit. *supra* note 7, p. 47.
[60] Rules of Procedure, Article 4.5.
[61] ICC Statute, Article 12; Rules of Procedure Article 6.1 (i) and (ii).
[62] ICC Statute, Article 12; Rules of Procedure Article 6.1 (iii).
[63] ICC Statute, Article 12; Rules of Procedure Article 6.1 (iv).

two different regional groups do not object within twenty days, it is approved.[64] The ICC Bureau decides then on the accreditation of the NHRI. Its decision is final.[65]

4.3. ILLUSTRATIONS OF THE ACCREDITATION PROCEDURE

A few examples can illustrate the practical application of the accreditation procedure. The accreditation of three NHRIs will be examined: the French *Commission nationale consultative des droits de l'homme*, the Swedish Equality Ombudsman and the Norwegian Centre for Human Rights.[66]

First, the French *Commission Nationale Consultative des Droits de l'Homme* was the first NHRI ever to be created and served as example for many NHRIs.[67] As any NHRI, it had to be reviewed in 2006 following the strengthening of the accreditation procedure. Astonishing as it may sound, it was so far established by ministerial decree (against the Paris Principles which provide that an NHRI should be established 'by a constitutional or legislative text'[68]) and was not sufficiently independent from government. Its re-accreditation was deferred until a bill relating to its composition and functioning was adopted in 2007 in order to remedy this.[69] It received again A-Status from the ICC in 2009 but its re-accreditation was again deferred for a period of one year in 2012.

Secondly, the Swedish Equality Ombudsman failed to send the supporting documentation in 2006 and its accreditation was deferred twice, until 2007 and until 2008, awaiting the future merger of the four Swedish Ombudsmen for which it was leading the application for membership of the ICC. So far, it was the Ombudsman against Ethnic Discrimination who had A-status on behalf of the four Swedish Ombudsmen.[70] Its accreditation therefore lapsed in 2008. In 2011, the (new) Swedish Equality Ombudsman applied for (re-) accreditation but received only B-status because of its lack of independence from the government

64 ICC Statute, Article 12; Rules of Procedure Article 6.1 (v).

65 ICC Statute, Article 12; Rules of Procedure Article 6.1 (vi).

66 Since this volume has a focus on NHRIs in Europe and their cooperation with European organisations, examples have been chosen only from European states.

67 The French *Commission Nationale Consultative des Droits de l'Homme* was established in 1947.

68 Paris Principles Principle 2, A. Competence and responsibilities.

69 While recommending A-status for the French *Commission Nationale Consultative des Droits de l'Homme*, the ICC Sub-Committee on Accreditation still noted the continuous involvement of the Prime Minister's office in issues related the Commission. See ICC, Report and Recommendations of the Sub-Committee on Accreditation, October 2007, p. 4, available at http://nhri.ohchr.org/EN/AboutUs/ICCAccreditation/Documents/2007_October%20SCA%20Report.pdf.

70 M. Brodie, loc. cit. *supra* note 18, p. 169. The four Swedish Ombudsmen are, besides the Ombudsman against Ethnic Discrimination, the Equal Opportunities Ombudsman, the Disability Ombudsman and the Ombudsman against Discrimination because of Sexual Orientation.

(which can give instructions to the Ombudsman and appoint and dismiss its head with full discretion, as it did with the then mandate holder[71]) and because its mandate is restricted to matters of equality.[72]

Thirdly, the Norwegian Centre for Human Rights was granted A-status following its re-accreditation in 2006. Its next re-accreditation was however differed for six months in 2011. The Norwegian Centre for Human Rights is both Norway's NHRI and part of the University of Oslo which expressed its intention to put an end to this dual role. In collaboration with the government, it is examining how to establish an NHRI in compliance with Paris Principles that is separated from the University of Oslo. In the meanwhile, the Norwegian Centre for Human Rights was recommended B-Status and received recommendations regarding the ongoing process for the establishment of the NHRI.[73] As provided for by the ICC Statute, it lost its A-status one year later, since continued compliance with the Paris Principles was not by then demonstrated.[74]

5. EVALUATION OF THE ACCREDITATION PROCEDURE

The ICC has shown great willingness to strengthen the accreditation procedure. This is positive, given the important consequences of the accreditation of NHRIs. Compliance with the Paris Principles should be strictly evaluated, considering that these Principles are referred to in two recent human rights treaties and since A-status gives access to the Human Rights Council. The strengthening of the accreditation procedure has obliged NHRIs as well as governments to take the accreditation of NHRIs more seriously. This has raised attention to the Paris Principles which still need further guidelines to improve compliance with them.

As demonstrated with the aforementioned examples, the ICC is not taking its task lightly. All NHRIs, including older ones with strong reputation, such as the French *Commission Nationale Consultative des Droits de l'Homme*, had to be evaluated again after a long period of time and had sometimes their enabling statutes to be amended in order to secure their re-accreditation. The ICC Sub-Committee on Accreditation will not hesitate to downgrade an NHRI

71 Although she had four years left before the end of her mandate, Katri Linna was sacked by the government without justification.

72 See ICC, 'Report and Recommendations of the Session of the Sub-Committee on Accreditation (SCA)', May 2011, pp. 9–10, available at http://nhri.ohchr.org/EN/AboutUs/ICCAccreditation/Documents/SCA%20REPORT%20MAY%202011%20-%20FINAL%20%28with%20annexes%29.pdf.

73 See ICC, 'Report and Recommendations of the Session of the Sub-Committee on Accreditation (SCA)', October 2011, pp. 15–16, available at http://nhri.ohchr.org/EN/AboutUs/ICCAccreditation/Documents/SCA%20REPORT%20OCTOBER%202011%20-%20FINAL%20%28with%20annexes%29.pdf.

74 ICC Statute, Article 18.1. Since this was decided in October 2011, the Norwegian Centre for Human Rights definitively received B-status in November 2012.

if necessary, as happened with both the Swedish Equality Ombudsman and the Norwegian Centre for Human Rights. It has become more severe with the latter, although no changes took place which would justify its downgrading, but the mere perspective of improving the NHRI's compliance with the Paris Principles seems to have led to a stricter evaluation. In Sweden, there was no NHRI with A-status for three years after a failure to send the supporting documentation.[75]

The accreditation procedure could however still be improved. The accreditation of NHRIs is more theoretical than practical. Too little attention is given to effectiveness. Independence, for instance, could be guaranteed on paper but should also be in practice. Questions, such as whether NHRI members act independently and provide sufficient leadership, whether NHRIs use their resources efficiently and are held accountable and whether civil society is properly involved and given support where necessary, often remain unanswered. The evaluation of NHRIs focusses mostly on the state *vis-à-vis* the NHRI and not the functioning of the NHRI as such. The accreditation of NHRIs should also require more input of other actors. Civil society organisations should be allowed to participate fully in the accreditation procedure, which could also involve experts familiar with NHRIs. The accreditation procedure also lacks visibility. Besides the reports of the ICC Sub-Committee on Accreditation which state the outcome, the supporting documentation for the accreditation and information from civil society organisations as well as comments from the NHRIs are not publicly available.[76] Greater transparence could encourage other actors to share their views and the general public to pay more attention to the accreditation of NHRIs.

More broadly, the question is also whether an A-status is the end of the story, which leads to that of the utility of the Paris Principles. While the Paris Principles provide a clear set of criteria for the establishment and strengthening of NHRIs, they somewhat fail to do so for their subsequent operation. The reason is that when they were drafted, the focus was principally on the necessity to create NHRIs, whereas now it is more on their functioning. The Paris Principles provide minimal standards relating to their structure, mandate and powers but do not help to examine their performance.[77] Whether the Paris Principles should continue to be the only benchmark against which NHRIs are measured could therefore be discussed. In the meanwhile, the ICC Sub-Committee should be able to examine

75 Actually, the Ombudsman for Ethnic Discrimination submitted the supporting documentation for the re-accreditation to the ICC Sub-Committee on Accreditation in 2008. There is no reference to this in the report of the ICC Sub-Committee on Accreditation which simply recommended that the accreditation of the Swedish Equality Ombudsman should lapse. See M. Brodie, loc. cit. *supra* note 18, pp. 169–170.

76 According to the OHCHR, information from civil society organisations and comments from the NHRIs are posted on the ICC website but they cannot be retrieved. See OHCHR, loc. cit. *supra* note 6, p. 5. Note however that the ICC website has recently migrated which might explain why some information is no longer available.

77 C. Sidoti, loc. cit. *supra* note 33, p. 97.

the effectiveness of NHRIs, which would require that the accreditation procedure focuses more on their working, while ensuring the full participation of their most concerned actors.

NHRI PARTICIPATION TO UNITED NATIONS HUMAN RIGHTS PROCEDURES: INTERNATIONAL PROMOTION VERSUS INSTITUTIONAL CONSOLIDATION?

Katrien MEUWISSEN[1]

1. INTRODUCTION

> 'National human rights institutions – at least those that are in compliance with the Paris Principles – are the cornerstone of national human rights protection systems and, increasingly, serve as relay mechanisms between international human rights norms and the State.'
>
> (UN Office for the High Commissioner on Human Rights)[2]

This statement of OHCHR clearly reflects the international promotion of Paris Principles compliant NHRIs[3] to connect United Nations human rights procedures with domestic realities. While the international human rights system suffers from a lack of state compliance,[4] independent national institutions with an explicit state mandate to promote and protect human rights are natural partners for the

---

1 PhD and teaching assistant KU Leuven Institute for International Law, researcher Leuven Centre for Global Governance Studies. Contact: katrien.meuwissen@law.kuleuven.be. The author especially wishes to thank the OHCHR Secretariats of the Human Rights Committee and the ESCR Committee, as well as Professor Cees Flinterman, member of the Human Rights Committee, for providing very insightful information that assisted in elaborating this chapter.

2 United Nations Office of the High Commissioner for Human Rights, 'National Human Rights Institutions: History, Principles, Roles and Responsibilities', Professional Training Series No. 4 (Rev. 1), 2010, p. 13.

3 'Principles relating to the Status of National Institutions', adopted by UN GA, Resolution 48/134 of 20 December 1993, Annex. For more information on the Paris Principles and NHRI accreditation on the basis of these Principles, see G. De Beco, 'Assessment of the Paris Principles and the ICC Sub-Committee on Accreditation', Chapter 11 in this volume.

4 A recent report of the High Commissioner on Human Rights (HCHR) indicates, for example, that while the number of ratifications of UN human rights treaties has doubled since 2000, the number of reports submitted by state parties to the conventions has relatively decreased over the same period. See: OHCHR, 'Strengthening the United Nations human rights treaty body system', *UN Doc.* A/66/860, June 2012, p. 17.

United Nations to get a firmer foothold in countries around the world. The strong connection between UN promotion and the international engagement of NHRIs is adequately illustrated by the work of the OHCHR in this field.

OHCHR set up a National Institutions and Regional Mechanisms Section (NIRMS) which leads the global UN assistance for the establishment and capacity-building of NHRIs in accordance with the Paris Principles. OHCHR therefore cooperates with states worldwide, but also directly engages with NHRIs, the regional networks of NHRIs, as well as the international coordinating committee of NHRIs (the ICC)[5]. At the same time, OHCHR also functions as Secretariat to the UN human rights mechanisms; the treaty bodies and the UN Human Rights Council (HRC). Accordingly, OHCHR plays an important role in better connecting NHRIs with the UN human rights mechanisms. OHCHR NIRMS and the Permanent Representative of the ICC in Geneva brief each other on a daily basis. In addition, the OHCHR Secretariats function as the contact points for NHRIs that want to engage with the UN mechanisms, and provide these NHRIs with practical information on the international procedures.[6] Conversely, the OHCHR Secretariats also inform the UN mechanisms on the functioning of NHRIs, especially in the context of country specific procedures such as the state reporting procedures of the UN treaty bodies.

As indicated in a 2009 survey conducted by OHCHR, NHRI participation in international procedures is still generally rather low.[7] However, the UN support for the international engagement of NHRIs seems to bear fruit, and Paris Principles compliant NHRIs 'increasingly serve as relay mechanisms between international norms and the state'.[8]

In light of the increasing relevance of NHRIs for the international human rights system, this chapter aims to elucidate the interaction of NHRIs with the main UN

---

5 OHCHR functions as secretariat to the coordinating NHRI networks. For more information on the ICC, see K. Roberts, 'The Role and Functioning of the International Coordinating Committee of National Human Rights Institutions in International Human Rights Bodies', Chapter 10 in this volume.

6 For example, in 2011, the OHCHR Human Rights Treaty Division elaborated an information note for NHRIs compiling relevant information relating to the opportunities for NHRI engagement with each of the nine UN treaty bodies, available at: http://www.ohchr.org/EN/HRBodies/HRC/Pages/NHRIParticipation.aspx.

7 See: OHCHR, 'Survey on National Human Rights Institutions, Report of the findings and recommendations of a questionnaire addressed to NHRIs worldwide', Geneva, July 2009, at p. 4: 'Despite some variation amongst the four regions, the level of NHRI engagement with international and regional human rights mechanisms – particularly in following up on recommendations – remains significantly underdeveloped overall and reflects a limited familiarity with these systems.'

8 As the 2012 report of the UN Secretary General on NHRI for example indicates: 'In 2011, an average of 21 NHRIs participated in each of the Human Rights Council sessions. They were active before and during the sessions, presenting statements, submitting written documentation, participating in general debates, organising parallel events and interacting with special procedures.'. See: UN GA, 'National institutions for the promotion and protection of human rights, Report of the Secretary-General', *UN Doc.* A/HRC/20/9, 1 May 2012, para. 69.

human rights mechanisms: the UN Human Rights Council and the UN treaty bodies.[9] The chapter will especially focus on the extent to which the promotion of NHRIs as "bridge builders" between the national and international level of human rights protection is translated in the institutional frameworks of these UN human rights mechanisms. Consequentially, the bulk of the chapter (section 2) is dedicated to a detailed analysis of how NHRI participation in UN human rights procedures has been consolidated in the rules and practices of the UN human rights mechanisms. Each of the UN mechanisms functions according to their own institutional framework, and the approaches towards NHRIs vary concurrently. First, the institutionalisation of NHRIs in the intergovernmental UN Human Rights Council will be examined. Then, the integration of NHRIs as participants in the procedures of the UN expert treaty committees will be assessed. A final part of this chapter will evaluate which kind of NHRIs can participate in the UN human rights procedures.

2. NHRI CONSOLIDATION IN INSTITUTIONAL FRAMEWORKS OF UN HUMAN RIGHTS MECHANISMS

2.1. UN HUMAN RIGHTS COUNCIL

2.1.1. From Human Rights Commission to Human Rights Council

In 2006, the Human Rights Council (HRC) was established to replace the former Commission on Human Rights (CHR), as the Commission suffered from polarisation and a lack of credibility.[10] Through resolution 60/251, the UN

9 Each of the nine core international human rights treaties have established a treaty body monitoring the implementation of the treaty obligations: the Human Rights Committee for the International Covenant on Civil and Political Rights (ICCPR), the ICERD Committee for the International Convention on the Elimination of All Forms of Racial Discrimination (ICERD), the ICESCR Committee for the International Covenant on Economic, Social and Cultural Rights (ICESCR), the CEDAW Committee for the Convention on the Elimination of All Forms of Discrimination against Women (CEDAW), the CAT Committee for the Convention against Torture and Other Cruel, Inhuman or Degrading Treatment or Punishment (CAT) – and the Sub-Committee on the Prevention of Torture under the Optional Protocol to CAT –, the CRC Committee for the Convention on the Rights of the Child (CRC), the CMW Committee for the International Convention on the Protection of the Rights of All Migrant Workers and Members of their Families (ICMW), the CRPD Committee for the Convention on the Rights of Persons with Disabilities (CRPD), and the CPPED Committee for the International Convention for the Protection of All Persons from Enforced Disappearance (ICPPED).

10 As UN Secretary-General Kofi Annan observed, 'States ha[d] sought membership of the Commission not to strengthen human rights but to protect themselves against criticism or to criticise others'. See: UN Secretary General, 'In larger freedom: towards development, security and human rights for all', *UN Doc.* A/59/2005, para. 182.

General Assembly established the UN Human Rights Council, and regarding national institutions specified that:

> 'the Council shall apply the rules of procedure established by the Committees of the General Assembly, as applicable, unless subsequently otherwise decided by the Assembly or the Council, and also decides that the participation and consultation with observers, including [...] national human rights institutions, as well as nongovernmental organizations, shall be based on arrangements, including ECOSOC resolution 1996/31 of 25 July 1996, and practices observed by the Commission on Human Rights, while ensuring the most effective contribution of these entities'[11].

This provision both entailed uncertainty and reassurance for NHRIs.[12] The rules of procedure of the Committees of the General Assembly did not provide for rules of participation for NGOs or NHRIs. Accordingly, while resolution 60/251 reassured that the arrangements and practices of the former Commission would continue to apply, it also specified that subsequent rules could change the previous arrangements. ECOSOC resolution 1996/31 established very specific rules of procedure for the consultative relationship of NGOs with the United Nations, but the participatory arrangements of NHRIs in the Commission on Human Rights were less clear and thus constituted an uncertain basis for participation of NHRIs in the UN Human Rights Council. In order to fully grasp the institutionalisation of NHRIs in the rules of procedure of the HRC, the next section will first address the integration of NHRIs in the practices and rules of the HRC predecessor, the Commission on Human Rights.

2.1.2. NHRI Institutionalisation in the Procedures of the Commission on Human Rights

The very inception of the notion that 'national committees' could play a role in connecting UN mechanisms with UN member states emerged very early. In 1946, the UN Economic and Social Council (ECOSOC) adopted a resolution inviting UN member states to '[...] consider the desirability of establishing information groups or local human committees within their respective countries to collaborate with them in furthering the work of the Commission on Human Rights'[13]. While the idea to establish national human rights committees was not widely accepted

---

11 UN GA, Resolution 60/251 of 15 March 2006, *UN Doc.* A/RES/60/251, §11.

12 As remarked by Ch. Sidoti, 'NHRIs and the International Human Rights System', in R. Goodman and Th. Pegram (eds.), *Human Rights, State Compliance and Social Change*, Cambridge University Press, 2012, pp. 104–105.

13 ECOSOC, resolution 2/9 of 21 June 1946, section 5, as referred to in: UN ECOSOC, 'Enhancing the participation of national human rights institutions in the work of the Commission on Human Rights and its subsidiary bodies, Report of the Secretary-General', *UN Doc.* E/CN.4/2005/107, 19 January 2005, para. 4.

at first, discussions in the context of the UN gradually lead to the international acceptance of the conception of 'national human rights institutions' as reflected in the Paris Principles: independent institutions established by the state with a broad mandate to promote and protect human rights.[14]

In 1992 the Commission on Human Rights was the first UN body to adopt the Paris Principles.[15] The Paris Principles stipulate that cooperation of NHRIs with United Nations human rights bodies is one of the core responsibilities of NHRIs,[16] and specify provisions regarding the guarantees of independence and pluralism of NHRIs.[17] Nevertheless, in the early 90s, NHRIs were not considered to be independent participants at the Commission. National institutions were rather considered to be part of government delegations: if their government allowed NHRIs to take up part of their speaking time, NHRIs could address the Commission from the seats of their governments.[18] During the 90s, the conception of NHRIs by governments evolved, and the CHR regularly requested the UN Secretary-General to draw up reports to recommend possible forms of participation by national institutions. In the early reports, the opinions of states on NHRI participation in the CHR procedures diverged widely. Some states agreed with the 'Paris Principles compliant' conception of NHRIs as independent participants in the Commission's procedures,[19] while other states

14 For an elaborate overview of the development of the notion of 'NHRIs' in the UN context, see: A. Pohjolainen, 'The Evolution of National Human Rights Institutions – The Role of the United Nations', Danish Institute for Human Rights, 2006, available at http://www.nhri.net/pdf/Evolution_of_NHRIs.pdf.

15 Commission on Human Rights, Resolution 1992/54, not available online. For references: see UN Economic and Social Council, 'Enhancing the participation of national human rights institutions in the work of the Commission on Human Rights and its subsidiary bodies, Report of the Secretary-General', *UN Doc.* E/CN.4/2005/107, 19 January 2005, para. 5.

16 Paris Principles, 'Competence and responsibilities', 3(e).

17 Paris Principles, 'Composition and guarantees of independence and pluralism'.

18 See for example: UN Commission on Human Rights, resolution 1997/40, 11 April 1997, *UN Doc.* E/1997/23, p. 135–136: 'Noting the importance of finding an appropriate form of participation by national institutions in relevant United Nations meetings dealing with human rights, and noting that a number of national institutions have for some time taken a constructive part in such meetings as part of the delegations of Member States, [...]'. During the World Conference on Human Rights of 1993 NHRIs could for the first time participate in an international conference in their own right. This was approved by the Commission on Human Rights in its resolution 1993/55, §11. See: UN General Assembly, Report of the World Conference on Human Rights, *UN Doc.* A/CONF.157/24 (Part I), 13 October 1993, para. 17.

19 For example: Canada (See: 'National institutions for the promotion and protection of human rights, Report by the Secretary-General submitted in accordance with Commission on Human Rights resolution 1996/50', *UN Doc.* E/CN.4/1997/41, 5 February 1997, para. 9); India (*Ibidem*, §12); Nigeria (See: 'National institutions for the promotion and protection of human rights, Report by the Secretary-General submitted in accordance with Commission on Human Rights resolution 1995/50', *UN Doc.* E/CN.4/1996/48, 26 January 1996, para. 51); Iraq (See: National institutions for the promotion and protection of human rights, Report by the Secretary-General submitted in accordance with Commission on Human Rights resolution 1994/54', *UN Doc.* E/CN.4/1995/48, 24 January 1995, paras. 11–12).

continued to consider NHRIs as being part of the government delegations.[20] The Secretary-General himself, however, strongly favoured the Paris Principle compliant conception of NHRIs, and supported the independent participation of NHRIs in the procedures of the Commission.[21] Throughout the late 90s, states increasingly agreed on a distinct role for Paris Principles compliant NHRIs, independent from government delegations. Accordingly, the Chairman of the CHR granted these NHRIs (and their regional and international coordinating committees) yearly arrangements that enabled them to address the Commission in their own right, first from behind the desks of national delegations,[22] but later also from separate seating.[23] The participation of NHRIs in the Commission remained however issue-specific, as it was limited to agenda item 18, b) 'effective functioning of human rights mechanisms: national institutions and regional arrangements'.

In his 2005 report, the Secretary-General proposed to abolish the specific agenda item on national institutions, and to grant participation rights to Paris Principles compliant NHRIs under each agenda item of the Human Rights Commission.[24] These modalities would grant Paris Principles compliant NHRIs participation rights as fully-fledged independent observers in the Commission; a position similar to that of accredited NGOs.[25] The CHR accepted the Secretary-General's proposal, and requested the Chairman to elaborate the NHRI participation modalities.[26] Before the Commission formally accepted the new modalities, however, the CHR was abolished and replaced by the Human Rights Council. This entailed a continued uncertain position for NHRIs at the inception of the HRC, as has been indicated in section 2.1.1 above.

---

20 For example: Germany (See: *UN Doc.* E/CN.4/1997/41, 5 February 1997, §10); Belise (*UN Doc.* E/CN.4/1996/48); Uganda (*UN Doc.* E/CN.4/1995/48, para. 16).

21 *UN Doc.* E/CN.4/1997/41, loc. cit. *supra* note 19, para. 41.

22 This arrangement is made from 1996 on. See: Economic and Social Council, 'National institutions for the promotion and protection of human rights, Report by the Secretary-General submitted in accordance with Commission on Human Rights resolution 1999/95', *UN Doc.* E/CN.4/1999/95, 3 February 1999, para. 58.

23 This is agreed from 1998 on. The practice is welcomed by the Commission on Human Rights in its Resolution 1999/72, para. 15.

24 This is partly in answer to the objections that were raised against the participation of NHRIs under all the agenda items of the Commission on the basis of the time constraints of the Commission. See SG report 2005, paras. 22 and 27.

25 *UN Doc.* E/CN.4/2005/107, loc. cit. *supra* note 13, para. 24.

26 Commission on Human Rights, 'national institutions for the promotion and protection of human rights', Human Rights Resolution 2005/74, *UN Doc.* E/CN.4/2005/L.10, Chap. XVIII, 20 April 2005, para. 11.

2.1.3. *NHRI Participation Rights in the UN Human Rights Council*

The establishment of the HRC rules of procedure was a difficult exercise, influenced by the politicised context of the former Commission.[27] However, national institutions succeeded in ensuring that the rules of procedure of the newly established Human Rights Council did incorporate resolution 2005/74 of the Commission on Human Rights, enabling Paris Principles compliant NHRIs as well as their international and regional coordinating committees to speak from their own seats under each of the agenda items of the Council.[28] NHRIs intensively lobbied and put pressure on the negotiations in Geneva, both through engaging at the national level with their governments, and by installing permanent representatives in Geneva to follow up the negotiations.[29] NHRIs succeeded in finding sufficient support from states across the traditionally divided regional groupings in the Council, as well as from NGOs. The incorporation of a distinctive role for Paris Principles compliant national institutions in the rules of procedure of the Council ensured certainty for NHRI participation in all procedures of the Council over the longer term. Since the establishment of the HRC, Paris Principles compliant NHRIs are taken up in the rules of procedure of the Human Rights Council as observers that need to be consulted.[30] Similar to accredited NGOs, Paris Principles compliant NHRIs are allowed to submit documents, make written statements and oral interventions on each agenda item of the Council, and organise parallel events on any issue of interest to NHRIs.

As resolution 60/251 (which established the HRC in 2006) indicated, the HRC would review its work and functioning five years after its installation.[31] As independent observers of the HRC, NHRIs were allowed speaking time during the review process at the end of each agenda item under negotiation. Again, NHRIs actively lobbied for an enhanced position in the Council, and individual NHRIs as well as the international and regional coordinating committees of NHRIs participated in the review negotiations.[32] NHRIs cooperated with NGOs on common issues of concern,[33] while a variety of states expressed their support

27 See for example the UK statement after the adoption of the Rules of Procedure: 'We must ensure that in the Programme of Work we get away from the selectivity we have experienced over the past year and in the Commission', 19 June 2007, available on the OHCHR extranet.

28 Human Rights Council, 'Institution-building of the United Nations Human Rights Council, *UN Doc.* A/HRC/RES/5/1, 18 June 2007, Rule 7, (b).

29 Ch. Sidoti, loc. cit. *supra* note 12, pp. 107–109.

30 *UN Doc.* A/HRC/RES/5/1, VII, Rule 7, 'Participation of and consultation with observers of the Council'.

31 *UN Doc.* A/RES/60/251, para. 16.

32 See for example: Human Rights Council, Open-Ended Intergovernmental Working Group on the Review of the Work and Functioning of the Human Rights Council First session, *UN Doc.* A/HRC/WG.8/1/CRP.2/Rev.1, 22 November 2010: interventions were made by the ICC, the Asia Pacific Forum of NHRIs, the German Institute for Human Rights, as well as the French National Consultative Commission for Human Rights.

33 See for example: ICC, '2011 Human Rights Council Review, ICC Position Paper', available online: http://www.nanhri.org/index2.php?option=com_docman&task=doc_view&gid=61&

for the enhancement of the position of NHRIs in the Council.[34] Contentious relations among states of the different regions in the Council prevented a thorough review of the Council, but one of the few points of consensus among the HRC member states concerned the enhancement of the participation rights of NHRIs. Accordingly, in the outcome document of the review of the work and functioning of the Human Rights Council most of the NHRIs' priorities were adopted, and their position in the HRC strengthened.[35]

Since the HRC review, Paris Principles compliant NHRIs obtained some participation rights in the Council that reach beyond the opportunities offered to accredited NGOs. Before the adoption of the outcome of the universal periodic review, the NHRI of the state under review is now allowed to make an intervention immediately after the state has been given the floor.[36] In the same sense, during the interactive dialogue of the Council in the context of a country specific mandate, the NHRI of the state under review is entitled to intervene immediately after the presentation of the country report by the special procedure mandate holder.[37] These additional participation rights for NHRIs in the context of country-specific procedures reflect the acceptance of a special role for Paris Principles compliant NHRIs in linking the international procedures of the HRC with domestic human rights situations.

2.1.4. HRC as Promoter of UN-NHRI Cooperation Beyond the HRC

Even before the elaboration of the Paris Principles, the Commission on Human Rights has been supporting the establishment of national human rights institutions.[38] Initially, opinions about the character and role of the national institutions diverged widely in the Council. Over the past fifteen years, however, the Paris Principles have become the clear standard for NHRIs in the HRC, and Paris Principles compliant NHRIs have been accepted as independent actors, with a role and position separate from the state, and with participation rights that go beyond those of accredited NGOs. Since the HRC review, the attention for NHRIs

Itemid=28, stating that: 'A status accredited NHRIs, as well as NGOs in consultative status with the UN Economic and Social Council, should be able to submit video statements as oral interventions at Council sessions'.

34 Inter alia: Australia; Canada; Chile; Morocco; UK; Peru; Qatar; Spain. See: UN HRC, 'Open-Ended Intergovernmental Working Group on the Review of the Work and Functioning of the Human Rights Council First session', *UN Doc.* A/HRC/WG.8/1/CRP.1/Rev.1, 15 November 2010.

35 For an overview of the NHRI priorities, see: ICC, '2011 Human Rights Council Review, ICC Position Paper', available online: http://www.nanhri.org/index2.php?option=com_docman&task=doc_view&gid=61&Itemid=28.

36 *Ibidem*, para. 13.

37 *Ibidem*, para. 28.

38 The CHR called for the organisation of the first international workshop on national institutions for the promotion and protection of human rights. See: UN Commission on Human Rights, Resolution 1990/73 of 7 March 1990.

has been reinvigorated in the Council, and two resolutions on NHRIs have been adopted with broad cross-regional support.[39] Notably, the HRC promotes its own cooperation with NHRIs as a model to be adopted by other UN organs and organisations. In its 2012 resolution on NHRIs, the HRC expressly recommended the UN General Assembly to explore the feasibility of enabling Paris Principles compliant NHRIs to participate in its meetings on the same basis as they do in the Human Rights Council.[40] Accordingly, it appears that in the intergovernmental UN procedures Paris Principles compliant NHRIs are increasingly integrated as actors in their own right, with a distinct role in bridging the international procedures with domestic realities.

2.2. UN TREATY PROCEDURES

As indicated in an information note of the OHCHR,[41] NHRIs can play a supportive role in relation to many of the activities of the treaty bodies: the reporting process, the individual complaints procedure, the inquiry procedure, and also the development of general comments. NHRIs have the potential to contribute to the UN treaty body procedures at different stages of the procedures: through promoting the national ratification of treaties and optional protocols, through lobbying and advising governments to comply with treaty obligations, through providing treaty bodies with information on the human rights situation within a state, and through following-up the domestic implementation of treaty body recommendations or decisions.[42] While NHRIs thus can play an important role for treaty compliance both at the national and international level, the following sections focus on one specific aspect: the consolidation of NHRI functioning in the UN treaty body institutional frameworks.

2.2.1. UN Human Rights Treaties

The most obvious treaty basis for NHRI interaction with treaty bodies can be found in recently negotiated treaty texts: the Optional Protocol to the Convention against Torture (OPCAT),[43] and the Convention on the Rights of

39 UN HRC, *UN Doc.* A/HRC/RES/17/9 of 16 June 2011; UN HRC, *UN Doc.* A/HRC/RES/20/14 of 5 July 2012.

40 UN HRC, *UN Doc.* A/HRC/RES/20/14 of 5 July 2012, para. 16.

41 OHCHR, 'Information Note National Human Rights Institutions Interaction with the UN Treaty Body System', 5 April 2011, loc. cit. *supra* note 6.

42 For an extensive overview of the potential roles of NHRIs in UN treaty procedures, see: *ibidem*. For a detailed illustration of how NHRI-UN treaty body cooperation can be effectuated, see: Christoffer Badse, 'The Danish Experience: The Danish Institute for Human Rights', Chapter two in this volume, especially section 6.3.

43 Optional Protocol to the Convention against Torture and Other Cruel, Inhuman or Degrading Treatment or Punishment, New York, 18 December 2002. Entry into force: 22 June 2006.

Persons with Disabilities (CRPD)[44]. OPCAT requires state parties to establish an independent national preventive mechanism for the prevention of torture at the domestic level, and thereby demands State parties to give due consideration to the Paris Principles.[45] Similarly, the CRPD requires state parties to establish an independent mechanism to promote, protect and monitor the implementation of the Convention, and also requires states to take into account the Paris Principles when designating or establishing this domestic mechanism.[46] To the extent that NHRIs are mandated by their state to function as national mechanisms under CRPD or OPCAT, the participation of NHRIs in the international procedures is a direct result of the treaty texts.[47] Moreover, in many cases, the possibility for interaction of the treaty bodies with NHRIs can be implicitly derived from certain provisions in the treaties. The Convention on the Rights of Children (CRC), as well as the International Convention on the Rights of Migrant Workers (ICMW), for example, stipulate that their respective treaty committees may invite 'competent bodies' to provide expert advice and to submit reports on matters that fall within the ambit of the Convention.[48] Even in the oldest of the human rights treaties, the International Convention on the Elimination of All Forms of Racial Discrimination (ICERD), an indirect reference can be found to NHRIs, since article 14(2) of ICERD provides for the possibility for state parties to establish a national body to consider individual complaints under the convention.[49] The conclusion is that even if NHRIs are not specifically mentioned in any of the UN human rights treaties, the interaction of UN treaty bodies with NHRIs fits within the functions that are accorded to the UN treaty bodies on the basis of the treaty texts.

---

44 Convention on the Rights of Persons with Disabilities, New York, 13 December 2006. Entry into force: 3 May 2008.

45 OP CAT, art. 17 *juncto* art. 18, para. 4.

46 CRPD, art. 33, para. 2.

47 This is, however, not required by any of the treaties, nor is it always the best option to designate the specific treaty obligations to a NHRI. See, for more information: APF, APT, and OHCHR, 'Preventing Torture: An Operational Guide for National Human Rights Institutions', May 2010; G. De Beco, 'Study on the Implementation of Article 33 of the UN Convention on the Rights of Persons with Disabilities in Europe, United Nations Human Rights Office of the High Commissioner, Europe regional Office, available at: http://europe.ohchr.org/Documents/Publications/Art_33_CRPD_study.pdf.

48 CRC, art. 45(a); ICMW, art. 74, para. 4. Note that the CRC Committee considers in its General Comment on the role of national independent institutions in the promotion and protection of the rights of the child that: 'the establishment of such bodies [...] falls within the commitment made by States parties upon ratification to ensure the implementation of the Convention [...]'. See: *UN Doc.* CRC/GC/2002/2, 15 November 2002, para. 1.

49 ICERD, art. 14, para. 2.

2.2.2. *Treaty Bodies and NHRIs: Rules of Procedure; Working Methods and General Comments or Statements*

Each of the treaty bodies has expressly incorporated modalities for NHRI interaction in their institutional frameworks; be it in rules of procedure, working methods or general comments and statements. Since the rules and arrangements for NHRI participation in the work of the committees are scattered over different documents, it is not easy to get a complete overview of the opportunities for NHRI interaction. Some committees provide an up to date overview of their arrangements for NHRI participation on their website.[50] This appears to be a best practice that should be encouraged in order to enhance the transparency and clarity of treaty body interaction with NHRIs.

The UN human rights treaties regulate the respective treaty procedures in general terms, but allow the treaty bodies to elaborate their own rules of procedure. Rules of procedure are adopted through formal decisions of the Committees; amendments to the rules require a new formal decision of the Committees.[51] Only five out of the nine treaty bodies have incorporated the interaction with NHRIs in their rules of procedure: the ICERD, CAT, ICMW, CRPD and ICED committees. All of the treaty committees, however, address NHRI participation in their working methods. Contrary to the rules of procedure, working methods do not require decisions of the committees, but reflect established practice of the committees that can be adapted through subsequent practice. Accordingly, there is a lower threshold to adopt NHRI participation modalities in treaty body working methods than to do this in rules of procedure. Working methods can be easily adapted which allows treaty bodies some room of manoeuvre when interacting with NHRIs. From a legal perspective, however, working methods constitute a less stable and weaker basis for participation of NHRIs to treaty body procedures than rules of procedure. The mere adoption of NHRI participation modalities in working methods does not ensure predictability or certainty for NHRIs that wish to participate in the procedures of the UN committees.

The rules of procedure and working methods of the treaty bodies rather briefly express the participation opportunities of NHRIs to the treaty procedures. Generally, the rules and methods of the treaty bodies outline the possibilities for NHRI participation in the framework of the different stages of the committees' reporting procedures. Most often, the role of NHRIs in the context of other treaty body procedures (such as communication procedures, inquiry procedures or general comments) is not specified, and the treaty bodies' rules and methods do not address the role of NHRIs regarding the follow-up of the UN procedures on the domestic level.

---

[50] See for example the website of CAT: http://www2.ohchr.org/english/bodies/cat/follow_up_ngo.htm.

[51] See for example: Rule 82, CRC Rules of procedure: 'These rules of procedure may be amended by a decision of the Committee, without prejudice to the relevant provisions of the Convention'.

In line with the arrangements on the reporting procedure as determined in the rules and methods, NHRIs can submit written information to the committees and can also orally interact with the committees in Geneva before the consideration of a state report. NHRIs can furthermore attend the interactive dialogues between the committees and the states under consideration as observers, without the opportunity to participate in these dialogues. Only the ICERD and ICMW Committees grant NHRIs of the state concerned the opportunity to orally intervene during the interactive dialogue between the state and the committee, if the state party's delegation does not object to this.[52] To the extent that treaty bodies established follow-up procedures in relation to state reporting procedures, NHRIs can also submit information in relation to these follow-up procedures.[53] Accordingly, the participation opportunities for NHRIs largely concur with the possibilities for participation for NGOs in treaty body reporting procedures.[54]

In addition to working methods and rules of procedure, treaty body general comments or recommendations are of particular relevance to reveal the opportunities for NHRI participation in the treaty procedures. Treaty bodies deliver general comments or recommendations with the aim to promote the further implementation of their convention and to assist and stimulate state parties to fulfil their obligations under the conventions.[55] Three treaty bodies (the ESCR Committee,[56] the ICERD Committee,[57] and the CRC Committee[58]) have issued specific general comments on NHRIs, while some treaty bodies mention NHRIs in wider general comments.[59] The CEDAW Committee and the Human Rights Committee issued statements on their relationship with NHRIs.[60] From

52 CERD, Rules of Procedure, rule 40; CMW, *UN Doc.* A/61/48, §20.

53 This is the case in relation to the CAT. The CAT Committee provides an extensive overview of the participation opportunities for NHRIs in its procedures on its website. See: http://www2.ohchr.org/english/bodies/cat/follow_up_ngo.htm.

54 See for example: Human Rights Committee, working methods, VIII, 'participation of NGOs and NHRIs in the activities of the Committee'.

55 M. Nowak, *U.N. Covenant on Civil and Political Rights CCPR Commentary*, N.P. Engel Publisher, Kehl-Strasbourg-Arlington, p. 576, note 144; W. Vandenhole, *The Procedures Before the UN Human Rights Treaty Bodies*, Intersentia, Antwerp-Oxford, 2004, p. 177.

56 Committee on Economic, Social and Cultural Rights, Draft General Comment No. 10: 'the role of national human rights institutions in the protection of economic, social and cultural rights', *UN Doc.* E/C.12/1998/25, 10 December 1998.

57 Committee on the Elimination of Racial Discrimination, General recommendation XVII 'Establishment of national institutions to facilitate the implementation of the convention', 25 March 1993.

58 Committee on the Rights of the Child, General Comment No. 2 'The role of independent national human rights institutions in the promotion and protection of the rights of the child', *UN Doc.* CRC/GC/2002/2, 15 November 2002.

59 See for example: Human Rights Committee, General Comment No. 31, 'The Nature of the General Legal Obligation Imposed on State Parties to the Covenant', *UN Doc.* CCPR/C/21/Rev.1/Add.13, 26 May 2004, §15.

60 Statement by the Committee on the Elimination of Discrimination against Women on its relationship with national human rights institutions, *UN Doc.* E/CN.6/2008/CRP.1, 2008; Human Rights Committee, 'The relationship of the Human Rights Committee with National Human Rights Institutions, Human Rights Committee 106th session, Geneva,

the general comments and statements on NHRIs, it can be deduced that treaty bodies accept NHRIs as actors with a specific role in their procedures. While the ICERD Committee's General Comment of 1993 recommended that NHRIs should be included in government delegations, the subsequent comments and notes reflect the treaty bodies' acknowledgement that NHRIs have a function which is distinct from that of governments and NGOs.[61] The general comments and statements specifically dedicated to NHRIs reflect the particular importance attached by treaty bodies to NHRIs, and clarify the approach of treaty bodies towards NHRIs in a more comprehensive manner than the rules of procedure and working methods. Contrary to working methods and rules of procedure which regulate the internal treaty body procedures, general comments and statements address states and NHRIs themselves and encourage these actors to facilitate the effective contribution of NHRIs in the treaty body procedures. Importantly, general comments and statements explicitly link the roles of NHRIs at the domestic level (e.g. to encourage governments to ratify treaties and optional protocols or to follow-up treaty body recommendations and decisions within a country) with the participation of NHRIs in the procedures before the UN committees (e.g. to submit domestic information to the treaty bodies in relation to their procedures).

NHRIs are not yet institutionalised in each of the treaty body procedures to the same extent, as indicated by the fact that only five out of nine treaty bodies issued a general comment or statement on NHRIs. Moreover, the practical arrangements for treaty body interaction with NHRIs diverge quite widely. For example, the deadlines for submission of written documents by NHRIs vary between the treaty bodies.[62] Also, the opportunities to engage orally with the committees differ from committee to committee, as some of the committees interact with NHRIs during public meetings and other committees prefer to organise private meetings to encourage the sharing of information by national

---

15 October-2 November 2012, advance unedited version, available at the Committee's website: http://www2.ohchr.org/english/bodies/hrc/.

61 See, for example: CERD General Recommendation 33 on the Follow-up to the Durban Review Conference, adopted at the Seventy-fifth session, August 2009, at I, g): 'Recommends that the States parties to the International Convention on the Elimination of Racial Discrimination [...]Engage with national human rights institutions and civil society, in a spirit of cooperation and respect, while preparing their periodic reports and with regard to follow-up; [...]'.

62 Compare, for example: CRPD, Note on National Human Rights Institutions Participation for the 8th session of the Committee: 'The Committee welcomes National Human Rights Institutions to provide country-specific information on issues relevant to the implementation of the Convention in the months prior to the adoption of the LOIs or the examination of the State party's report'. While, CAT, 'Reporting to the Committee, Information for NGOs and NHRIs', available at: http://www2.ohchr.org/english/bodies/cat/follow_up_ngo.htm: 'The written information that NGOs and NHRIs wish to submit to the Committee for the LOIs must be received by the Secretariat (see contacts below) no later than 10 weeks before the opening of the session. [...]For the November 2012 session (29 October to 23 November), the deadline is 17 August 2012. For the May 2013 session (6 to 31 May), the deadline is 22 February 2013.'

institutions.[63] The wide variety and diversity of existing practices among treaty bodies in their interaction with NHRIs is burdensome for the NHRIs that wish to participate in the UN procedures.[64] Since each treaty body has different engagement rules, national actors are not gaining from their experience, and rather have to acquire knowledge on how to cooperate with individual treaty bodies.[65] Accordingly, the OHCHR secretariats of the treaty bodies play a vital role in connecting NHRIs with UN procedures by intimating the NHRIs of crucial deadlines and time scheduled of the treaty bodies and by briefing NHRIs on the opportunities to participate in the different procedures.[66] The ICC also functions as an information platform for NHRIs, and cooperates intensively with OHCHR to transmit accurate and timely information to NHRIs that wish to participate in the treaty body procedures.[67]

From the consideration of the patchwork of rules, methods, comments and statements of UN treaty bodies on NHRIs, it can be concluded that also in the context of the UN human rights treaty procedures NHRIs are increasingly integrated as actors with a distinct role to play. Nevertheless, the opportunities for participation diverge among the treaty bodies, and only half of the committees adopted a comprehensive comment or statement that is especially dedicated to the role of NHRIs in their procedures. Contrary to the increasingly prominent opportunities for oral interventions of NHRIs in the HRC, the role of NHRIs in the context of the treaty body procedures lies in the first place in providing information that will be assessed by treaty body experts before it is taken up in the discussions with or recommendations towards state party delegations. The essential role for NHRIs lies then in the follow-up of the treaty body recommendations on the domestic level, in order to encourage states to better comply with their treaty obligations.[68]

---

63 Compare: CMW and CRPD interact with NHRIs in public meetings; HRC, CAT and CRC interact with NHRIs in closed meetings; while CERD, CESCR and CEDAW interact with NHRIs both in public and private meetings. For an overview, see: Inter-Committee Meeting of the human rights treaty bodies, twelfth meeting Geneva, 27–29 June 2011, *UN Doc.* HRI/ICM/2011/2, paras. 43–44.F.

64 As noted by the ICC in its Marrakesh Statement on Strengthening the relationship between NHRIs and the human rights treaty body system, 10 June 2010, para. 6.

65 As noted by OHCHR in the 2012 report on strengthening the UN treaty body system, loc. cit. *supra* note 4, p. 66.

66 This is for example made explicit in the statement of the UN Human Rights Committee on NHRIs, loc. cit. *supra* note 59, para. 13; para. 18; para. 22.

67 For more information on the ICC functioning, see K. Roberts, 'The Role and Functioning of the International Coordinating Committee of National Human Rights Institutions in International Human Rights Bodies', Chapter 10 in this volume.

68 Note that according to the OHCHR report of June 2012, only 16% of the state parties submit their reports to treaty bodies on time. See: OHCHR, 'Strengthening the United Nations human rights treaty body system', *supra* note 4, p. 9.

2.2.3. *Towards Harmonised Treaty Body Interaction with NHRIs*

The elaboration of the nine core human rights treaties has been a gradual undertaking that took place over the past 65 years. While all the treaties have some elements in common, each of the treaties has been the product of separate negotiations among interested stakeholders, and contains differing procedures and provisions. The divergent interaction of treaty bodies with NHRIs is as a consequence directly related to the ramification of the UN human rights treaties and the procedures established on the basis of these treaties. Moreover, the discrepancy between the treaty procedures is further amplified by the fact that each of the treaty bodies can independently elaborate the treaty procedures through specific rules and practices. The diverging treaty body rules and practices obviously lead to a sub-optimal functioning of the treaty procedures, and entail difficulties for stakeholders to efficiently engage with the treaty procedures, as indicated specifically for NHRIs in section 2.2.2 above.

In order to enhance the effective functioning of the treaty bodies as a whole, the chairpersons of the treaty bodies meet annually to discuss matters of common concern. Since 2002, Inter-Committee Meetings (ICMs) are also organised, specifically to discuss the harmonisation of working methods of the committees.[69] In this context, an International Roundtable on the Role of National Human Rights Institutions and Treaty Bodies has been organised in 2006, with the participation of NHRIs, civil society and treaty body representatives. At the end of the conference the participants to the Roundtable adopted a 'draft harmonised approach for treaty-body engagement with NHRIs' (the Berlin Statement), which would be submitted for consideration of the treaty bodies during their next ICM.[70] The Berlin Statement outlines in general terms how treaty bodies could integrate NHRIs in each of their procedures: the reporting procedure, petition and enquiry procedures, follow-up procedures, and thematic engagement of the Committees. The Berlin Statement was, however, never formally adopted by the treaty bodies.

Since the elaboration of the Berlin Statement, the development of a harmonised approach towards NHRIs is regularly discussed within the ICM. Treaty body experts are informed on practices regarding treaty body-NHRI cooperation by the OHCHR secretariats that prepare the ICMs, and by the ICC, which is regularly invited to the Inter-Committee meetings. It can be noted that treaty bodies do take the recommendations made in the context of the ICMs into account. The CAT Committee, for example, explicitly refers to the recommendations of the Chairperson meetings and ICMs when outlining the participation opportunities

69 ICMs bring together the Chairpersons and two additional members of each of the Committees.

70 Conclusions of the International Roundtable on the Role of National Human Rights Institutions and Treaty Bodies, Berlin, 23 and 24 November 2006, Annex to *UN Doc.* HRI/MC/2007/3, 7 February 2007.

for NHRIs in its procedures.[71] Moreover, the recently adopted general comments and statements on NHRIs reflect a more comprehensive approach towards NHRI interaction which runs in line with the proposals adopted in the Berlin Statement. Nevertheless, the impact of the discussions in the context of the ICMs remains limited until now, since the rules and practices of the treaty bodies continue to diverge considerably. Whereas the ICMs offer a platform for treaty body representatives to be informed on the diverse rules and practices of the different committees and to share best practices regarding NHRI-treaty body interaction, the recommendations formulated in the context of the ICMs are not binding upon the committees, which remain fully independent in deciding upon their rules and methods.

In addition to the Chairperson Meetings and ICMs, various reform initiatives have been undertaken in order to render the functioning of the treaty bodies more effective.[72] The current High Commissioner, Ms. Navi Pillay, started her 'treaty body strengthening process' in 2009.[73] Resisting from amending the texts of the treaties, the strengthening process aims for gradual improvements and harmonisation of the working methods of the treaty bodies on the basis of open consultations with all stakeholders involved (including states, treaty bodies, civil society and NHRIs). In the context of the High Commissioner's initiative, NHRIs have been actively consulted,[74] and the participation of NHRIs to treaty body procedures has been widely discussed. On the basis of the consultations, the High Commissioner issued a report in June 2012. This report includes various proposals that can be relevant for a more efficient participation of NHRIs to UN treaty procedures (such as for example the proposal to introduce a comprehensive reporting calendar)[75], and also specifically puts forward a detailed model to harmonise the interaction between the treaty bodies and NHRIs in the context of the reporting procedures.[76]

It remains an open question what the impact will be of the treaty body strengthening process on the further institutionalisation of NHRI participation

71 See CAT Committee website: http://www2.ohchr.org/english/bodies/cat/follow_up_ngo.htm: 'NHRIs are bridges between the national and international protection mechanisms and treaty bodies should have procedures that allowed them to hear their views during the reporting process, as recommended by the Chairpersons and Inter-Committee Meetings'.

72 OHCHR, 'Strengthening the United Nations human rights treaty body system', loc. cit. *supra* note 4.

73 For an overview of the HCHR treaty body strengthening process, see the OHCHR website: http://www2.ohchr.org/english/bodies/HRTD/.

74 In June 2010, the "Marrakesh" consultation meeting was organised specifically for NHRIs to reflect on the future of the human rights treaty bodies. See: Marrakesh Statement on strengthening the relationship between NHRIs and the human rights treaty bodies system, 10 June 2010, available at: http://www2.ohchr.org/english/bodies/HRTD/hrtd_process.htm.

75 OHCHR, 'Strengthening the United Nations human rights treaty body system', loc. cit. *supra* note 4, p. 37

76 *Ibidem*, pp. 65–66.

in UN treaty procedures, especially since an inter-governmental treaty body strengthening process is initiated at the UN General Assembly.[77] It is clear, however, that the treaty body strengthening initiatives open up new windows of opportunity for the further integration, and a more harmonised consolidation of NHRI participation in the treaty bodies' institutional frameworks. Notably, shortly after the issuing of the High Commissioner's report, the Chairpersons put forward 'the participation of NHRIs in the work of the treaty bodies' as a specific focus of their next meeting.[78]

3. NHRI CONCEPTUALISATION: PARTICIPATION OF "NATIONAL INSTITUTIONS"

3.1. ICC ACCREDITED NHRIs IN THE UN HUMAN RIGHTS COUNCIL

Even before the elaboration of the Paris Principles, the Commission on Human Rights has been involved in the elaboration of international standards relating to national human rights institutions.[79] Ever since the adoption of the Paris Principles, the Commission on Human Rights, and its successor the Human Rights Council, have encouraged states to establish and strengthen NHRIs in accordance with these standards. The Paris Principles do not contain a definition of an NHRI, and merely prescribe that 'a national institution shall be vested with the competence to promote and protect human rights'[80]. The Paris Principles give leeway to states to establish an NHRI in a manner best suited to the national context, but especially lay emphasis on the requirement that NHRIs should be capable to carry out their mandate independently of government interference.[81] The Human Rights Council confirms that 'it is the right of each state to choose the framework for national institutions that is best suited to its particular needs at the national level in order to promote human rights in accordance with international

77 The ICC and NHRIs are also allowed to participate in this process and a first ICC statement has been delivered to the UN GA by the ICC. See: ICC, 'response of NHRIs to the UN HCHR Report on the Strengthening of the Human Rights Treaty Body System (the Belfast Statement)', July 2012, Available at the website of the ICC: http://nhri.ohchr.org/EN/IHRS/TreatyBodies/Pages/default.aspx.

78 UN GA, 'Implementation of human rights instruments, Note by the Secretary-General', *UN Doc.* A/67/222, 2 August 2012, para. 39.

79 In 1978 already, the UN Commission on Human Rights organised a seminar on National and Local Institutions for the Promotion and Protection of Human Rights in order to draft guidelines for the structure and functioning of these institutions. For an overview of the early conceptualisation of NHRIs, see: Centre for Human Rights, 'National Human Rights Institutions, a Handbook on the Establishment and Strengthening of National Institutions for the Promotion and Protection of Human Rights', Professional Training Series No. 4, 1995, especially para. 22.

80 Paris Principles, 'Competence and responsibilities', art. 1.

81 Paris Principles, 'Composition and guarantees of independence and pluralism'.

human rights standards'[82]. At the same time, in line with the requirements of the Paris Principles, the Council encourages governments to provide national institutions with more autonomy and independence.[83]

The rules of procedure of the HRC grant participation rights to 'national institutions that are accredited by the Accreditation Subcommittee of the International Coordinating Committee of National Institutions under the auspices of the Office of the High Commissioner'[84]. Consequentially, the interpretation of the Paris Principles according to the ICC Sub-Committee on Accreditation (SCA) determines which NHRIs can participate in the procedures of the Council.[85] Notably, the ICC SCA developed General Observations which supplement the Paris Principles and serve to guide the ICC SCA in its accreditation procedure.[86] Various types of NHRIs have been accredited by the ICC SCA as being Paris Principles compliant. As indicated in chapter 1 of this volume, human rights commissions, as well as ombuds-institutions, or advisory committees have received A-status accreditation.[87] In light of the requirement of the Paris Principles to establish NHRIs with 'a broad mandate as possible'[88], the ICC considers NHRIs with a thematic mandate (such as children commissions or anti-racism institutions) or with a sub-national mandate, as being 'not fully in compliance with the Paris Principles'.[89] Consequentially, these thematic and sub-national institutions do not get the opportunity to participate in the proceedings of the HRC as 'NHRIs', even though they often dispose of information that would be of interest for the HRC's procedures.

The acceptance of ICC accreditation as a benchmark for NHRI participation to the Human Rights Council is remarkable. The accreditation of participants in international forums is generally decided by the Member States of the international institutions. The participation of NGOs in the UN system, for example, is depending on the accreditation of NGOs by the UN Committee

82 See, for example the 2011 resolution of the Human Rights Council on NHRIs: *UN Doc.* A/HRC/RES/17/9 of 16 June 2011, para. 5.

83 *Ibidem*, para. 5 and para. 15.

84 UN Human Rights Council, *UN Doc.* A/HRC/RES/5/1, 18 June 2007, Rule 7, 'Participation of and consultation with observers of the Council' *juncto* UN Human Rights Commission, Resolution 2005/74, para. 11, a).

85 For more information on the ICC accreditation procedure, see G. De Beco, 'Assessment of the Paris Principles and the ICC Sub-Committee on Accreditation', chapter 11 in this volume.

86 See: Rules of Procedure for the ICC Sub-Committee on Accreditation, 14 September 2004, amended 15 April 2008, Article 6.3 (c).

87 M. Nowak, 'National Human Rights Institutions in Europe: Comparative, European and International Perspectives', Chapter 1 in this volume.

88 Paris Principles, 'Competence and responsibilities', art. 2.

89 The thematic and sub-national NHRIs are thus accorded with a B-status. See: ICC, Chart of the Status of National Institutions, Accreditation Status as of May 2012, available at: http://nhri.ohchr.org/. For more information, see, for example: L. Reif, 'The Shifting Boundaries of NHRI Definition in the International System', in R. Goodman and Th. Pegram (eds.), *Human Rights, State Compliance and Social Change, Assessing National Human Rights Institutions*, Cambridge University Press, 2012, chapter 2, pp. 52–73.

of NGOs, which ECOSOC can approve or overturn. The decisions of the UN Committee of NGOs are widely criticised for being politicised, and it is argued that the UN Committee is largely in hands of states that do not support a 'vibrant' civil society.[90] The accreditation of NHRIs in the intergovernmental HRC on the basis of the ICC accreditation process, which does not include states at any point, is exceptional, and adds to the independent status of NHRIs in the HRC. The strong support of the UN Secretary-General and the OHCHR for NHRIs, and the involvement of OHCHR in the ICC accreditation procedure, definitely has facilitated the acceptance of the ICC accreditation as benchmark for NHRI participation in the HRC.[91] At the same time, however, it should be noted that the ICC accreditation procedure is also subject to criticism. The ICC SCA's procedure is for example being criticised for lacking transparency and accountability.[92] As Gauthier De Beco indicates elsewhere in this book,[93] the ICC is both regulator and promoter of NHRIs, and the evaluation of NHRIs in the context of the accreditation procedure 'might be inconsistent having mainly the sole interests of the ICC in mind'. Since the accreditation procedure of the ICC determines which NHRIs can participate in the procedures of the Council, the further strengthening of this procedure is a matter that deserves particular attention of the international community. The participation of NHRIs in international procedures does strengthen the credibility of NHRIs as independent actors that foster the promotion and protection of human rights. As the time allocated to NHRIs in the context of the inter-governmental HRC procedures entails that less time can be given to other stakeholders, it should be ensured that participating NHRIs are credible and independent information providers, and do not act as mouthpieces for their governments.

3.2. UN TREATY BODIES: THEMATIC FOCUS REGARDING NHRI PARTICIPATION

In 1993, in the aftermath of the Vienna World Conference on Human Rights, the ICERD Committee was the first UN treaty body to encourage state parties to establish national human rights institutions in accordance with the Paris

---

90 See: International Service on Human Rights, 'UN Committee on NGOs accredits 129 NGOs, defers 130', 8 June 2012, available at: http://www.ishr.ch/other-new-york-news/1319-un-committee-on-ngos-accredits-129-ngos-defers-130#_ftnref2.

91 See also *supra* section 2.1, especially at 2.1.2.

92 See for example: M. Brodie, 'Progressing Norm Socialisation: Why Membership Matters. The Impact of the Accreditation Process of the International Coordinating Committee of national Institutions for the Promotion and Protection of Human Rights', *Nordic Journal of International Law*, vol. 80, 2011, pp. 143–192.

93 G. De Beco, 'Assessment of the Paris Principles and the ICC Sub-Committee on Accreditation', chapter 11 in this volume.

Principles.[94] Since the nineties, more UN treaty bodies have gradually started to promote the establishment and strengthening of Paris Principles compliant NHRIs. Today, the general comments and the concluding observations of all the UN treaty committees encourage state parties to establish and strengthen Paris Principles compliant NHRIs.[95] In two recent treaties, the Paris Principles have even been integrated in binding treaty law, as the CRPD and OPCAT oblige state parties to establish a national body to monitor the implementation of treaty obligations, and thereby require state parties to take the Paris Principles into account.[96]

Contrary to the emphasis on the establishment of Paris Principles compliant NHRIs by the UN treaties and the UN treaty bodies, the rules of procedure or working methods of the UN committees generally do not refer to the Paris Principles as the benchmark for NHRI participation in their own procedures. Only the ICERD Committee's rules of procedure state that the opportunity to make an oral intervention during the interactive dialogue (in an independent capacity and from separate seating) is limited to NHRIs that are accredited to take part in the UN Human Rights Council.[97]

As pointed out above, the participation of NHRIs in the context of the Human Rights Council is limited to ICC accredited NHRIs. The Paris Principles require NHRIs to have a broad mandate as possible,[98] which leads to the exclusion of thematic and sub-national NHRIs to the work of the HRC. The UN treaty bodies, however, rather seem to attach particular importance to "thematic" competences of NHRIs to promote and protect the specific rights related to the treaty the UN committee in question is monitoring. The ESCR Committee, for example, calls upon states to ensure that the mandates accorded to NHRIs include appropriate attention to economic, social and cultural rights.[99] The CRC Committee, at its turn, welcomes the establishment of ombudspersons and commissioners with a specific focus on children's rights, and even seems to perceive the establishment of an NHRI with a broad mandate including children's rights, only as a second best option.[100] With one specific exception, the rules of procedure and working

---

94 CERD, General Comment No. 17 'Establishment of national institutions to facilitate implementation of the Convention', 25 March 1993.

95 OHCHR regularly updates a compilation of all treaty bodies' concluding observations and recommendations referring to NHRIs (available at: http://nhri.ohchr.org) and sends the concluding observations to the NHRIs concerned. See: Report of the Secretary-General, 'National Institutions for the promotion and protection of human rights', *UN Doc.* A/HRC/20/9, 1 May 2012, para. 78.

96 As mentioned above, section 2.2.1.

97 CERD, rules of procedure, rule 40.

98 See *supra* note 80.

99 ESCR Committee, General Comment No. 10 'The role of national human rights institutions in the protection of economic, social and cultural rights', E/C.12/1998/25, 10 December 1998, para. 4.

100 See: CRC Committee, General Comment No. 2 (2002) 'The role of independent national human rights institutions in the promotion and protection if the rights of the child', CRC/GC/2002/2, 15 November 2002, especially para. 6: 'Specialist independent human rights institutions for

methods of the UN treaty bodies do not require NHRIs to be in compliance with the Paris Principles in order to be able to participate in their procedures. Particularly in view of their mandate to monitor specific human rights treaties, it is important for UN committees to also gather information from specialised thematic NHRIs, even if these institutions do not comply with the Paris Principles.

The independence of NHRIs is one of the central standards put forward in the Paris Principles.[101] The lack of a threshold for NHRI participation in the UN treaty procedures may raise concerns regarding the legitimacy of "national human rights institutions" as independent participants to these procedures. National institutions with a human rights mandate exist in a wide variety, and certainly not all of these institutions function in an independent manner and constitute reliable partners for UN treaty bodies. As a matter of practice, however, it appears that the treaty bodies are informed by the OHCHR secretariat about the status and reliability of the NHRIs with which they cooperate. As indicated by an OHCHR secretariat, 'the weight that is given to NHRI contributions may depend on the status that it has been given by the ICC'.[102] The information provided by OHCHR thus constitutes the basis for the treaty body experts to assess the reliability of NHRI information that is provided in the context of their procedures.

Contrary to the intergovernmental processes at the UN HRC, the UN treaty procedures are in hands of independent experts. Accordingly, less focus is put on the Paris Principles compliance of NHRIs, since the information gathered in the context of the treaty body procedures is filtered and interpreted by independent experts before they are taken up in the recommendations and decisions concerning state parties. Nevertheless, in order to enhance the legitimacy of NHRIs as independent participants to the UN treaty body procedures, it would also seem to be appropriate for treaty bodies to make their approach towards the assessment of NHRIs more explicit in their institutional frameworks. In view of the limited time and resources available to UN treaty committees, it is important to be aware of the reliability of the information providers. The "special position" accorded to NHRIs in the treaty system does not seem to be legitimate whenever these institutions do not function in a reliable and independent manner.

---

children, ombudspersons or commissioners for children's rights have been established in a growing number of States parties. Where resources are limited, consideration must be given to ensuring that the available resources are used most effectively for the promotion and protection of everyone's human rights, including children, and in this context development of a broad-based NHRI that includes a specific focus on children is likely to constitute the best approach [...]'.

101 See G. De Beco, 'Assessment of the Paris Principles and the ICC Sub-Committee on Accreditation', Chapter 11 in this volume.

102 E-mail of the ICCPR secretariat, August 2012. On file with author.

4. CONCLUSION

This chapter has analysed to what extent the function of NHRIs as "bridge builders" between the national and international layers of human rights promotion and protection is integrated in the institutional frameworks of the UN human rights mechanisms. In each of the UN procedures, NHRIs get opportunities to participate as actors in their own right, next to states and civil society. However, there is great divergence between the approaches of the different UN mechanisms towards NHRI cooperation: both with regard to the consolidation of NHRI participation in the institutional frameworks of the UN mechanisms (first part of the chapter), as with regard to the interpretation of the kind of NHRIs that can participate in the UN procedures (second part of the chapter).

While in the early nineties NHRIs were still considered as appertaining to government delegations in the Commission on Human Rights, Paris Principles compliant NHRIs (and their regional and international coordinating committees) are now clearly recognised as independent observers in the Council. Accordingly, these NHRIs can submit documents, make written statements and oral interventions on each agenda item of the Council, and can organise parallel events on any issue of interest to NHRIs. Since the HRC review, Paris Principles compliant NHRIs obtained some participation rights in the Council that go beyond the opportunities offered to accredited NGOs. Especially in the context of country-specific procedures (UPR and special procedures), it seems to be important that the voices of NHRIs can be heard. The additional participation rights for NHRIs in the context of country-specific procedures reflect the acceptance of a special role for Paris Principles compliant NHRIs in linking up the international procedures of the HRC with domestic human rights situations.

Also in the context of UN treaty body procedures, NHRIs are currently recognised as actors in their own right, next to government delegations and NGOs. Contrary to the clear arrangements for NHRI participation in the Human Rights Council's institutional framework, the participation opportunities for NHRIs in UN treaty body procedures are not as comprehensively integrated in the institutional frameworks of the treaty bodies. Whereas the UN treaty bodies all acknowledge the role NHRIs can play as information providers in their reporting procedures, many of the treaty bodies did not yet stipulate a comprehensive set of rules that aptly reflects the multiple roles NHRIs can play in the context of the treaty procedures. Especially in view of the lack of state compliance with human rights treaty obligations, more attention for the role of NHRIs in following-up the treaty procedures, both on the domestic level (monitor national compliance with treaty body recommendations and decisions) and the international level (report to the treaty bodies on national follow-up of treaty body recommendations and decisions), would be desirable. Moreover, the variety of existing rules and methods of treaty bodies on their interaction with NHRIs is burdensome for NHRIs that wish to participate in the treaty procedures. In the context of ICMs and the treaty body strengthening process, momentum is created to better harmonise and further consolidate NHRI participation in UN treaty body procedures. In light of the divergent approaches as well as the lack of clear, transparent and harmonised rules, the information provided to NHRIs by OHCHR and the ICC currently remains crucial to enable effective NHRI engagement with the UN treaty committees.

In a second section, this chapter indicated which type of NHRIs can participate in the procedures of the UN mechanisms. Both the UN HRC and the UN treaty bodies promote the establishment and strengthening of NHRIs in accordance with the Paris Principles. In the UN HRC, NHRI participation is limited to NHRIs that are accredited by the ICC Sub-Committee on Accreditation as being in compliance with the Paris Principles. The accreditation of NHRIs in the HRC on the basis of the ICC process – which does not include states at any point – is exceptional for an intergovernmental organisation such as the Human Rights Council, and adds to the independent status of NHRIs in the procedures of the Council. However, as the interpretation of the Paris Principles according to the ICC determines which NHRIs can participate in the procedures of the Council, the further strengthening of the ICC accreditation procedure is a matter that deserves particular attention of the international community.

While the UN treaty bodies also encourage states to establish Paris Principles compliant NHRIs, the participation of NHRIs in the UN treaty procedures is not confined to Paris Principle compliant NHRIs. The UN treaty committees generally do not specify a threshold for NHRI participation in their procedures, and all kinds of NHRIs can thus participate in the procedures of the UN committees. However, as a matter of practice, the OHCHR secretariats inform the treaty bodies of the status and reliability of NHRIs that engage with them. Accordingly, the UN committees do take the compliance of NHRIs with the Paris Principles into account when interacting with these bodies, and when assessing the information provided by NHRIs on an informal basis. The lack of explicit reference to the Paris Principles as benchmark for NHRI participation in the treaty procedures can be traced back to the fact that – in view of their mandate to monitor specific human rights treaties – UN treaty bodies attach great importance to the expert-information that can be provided by thematic NHRIs on the implementation of UN treaties in their countries. Even if these thematic institutions do not comply with the standards put forward in the Paris Principles (they generally are accorded B-status), they do constitute important partners for UN treaty bodies, which essentially have a thematic mandate themselves. Yet, in order to enhance the transparency and accountability of their processes, it also seems to be appropriate for the UN treaty bodies to make their approach towards the assessment of information delivered by different types of NHRIs more explicit in their institutional frameworks.

NHRIs are rather new actors on the international scene; only twenty years ago these bodies were still considered to be part of government delegations in UN human rights procedures. The current integration of NHRIs as independent actors in the institutional frameworks of the UN human rights mechanisms indicates that NHRIs have conquered their own spot in the international human rights arena. This privileged position of NHRIs on the international scene definitely has been made possible because of the UN promotion and support for these actors. It is remarkable that even if the participation of NHRIs in international procedures is rather low, and while the impact of NHRIs on human rights compliance is not clear, these national institutions have acquired a privileged position in UN human rights procedures already.[103] The swift integration of NHRIs in UN human rights procedures seems to be grounded in the need of the UN mechanisms to become better connected with domestic systems in order to more easily gather comprehensive information on local human rights situations, and to facilitate more effective follow-up of UN recommendations on the national level.

This chapter has shown that the approach of UN human rights mechanisms towards NHRIs is still evolving, both with regard to their position and role in the UN procedures as well as in relation to defining which NHRIs can participate in their procedures. While the current integration of NHRIs in UN human rights procedures indicates that these new actors will not disappear from the international scene anymore, the institutional consolidation of these actors in UN human rights procedures is a work in progress which needs to be further refined and harmonised.

103 While being beyond the scope of this chapter, further research should analyse the capacity and effectiveness of NHRIs to constitute "bridges" between the different layers of the human rights system. An interesting contribution that focuses on how NHRIs carry out the function of 'agents of international law within the domestic system' is: R. Carver, 'A New Answer to an Old Question: National Human Rights Institutions and the Domestication of International Law', *Human Rights Law Review*, vol. 10, March 2010 pp. 1–32.

PERSPECTIVES ON THE NEED FOR NATIONAL HUMAN RIGHTS INSTITUTIONS IN EUROPE AND THE WORLD

Jan JAŘAB[1]

1. ROLE OF NHRIs AS LAID DOWN IN THE PARIS PRINCIPLES

From OHCHR's perspective, NHRIs are firmly rooted in the system of international human rights law. The Principles Relating to the Status of National Institutions (the Paris Principles which were adopted by General Assembly Resolution 48/130 of 20 December 1993) clearly lay down, among the responsibilities of NHRIs, that they shall:[2]

- Promote and ensure the harmonisation of national legislation, regulations and practices with the international human rights instruments to which the state is a party, and their effective implementation;
- Encourage ratification of the above mentioned instruments or accession to those instruments;
- Contribute to reports which states are required to submit to United Nations bodies and committees, and to regional institutions, pursuant to their treaty obligations, and where necessary, to express an opinion on the subject, with due respect for their independence;
- Cooperate with the United Nations and any other organisation in the UN system, regional organisations and national organisations of other countries that are competent in the area of protection and promotion of human rights.

The international human rights mechanisms – treaty monitoring bodies, special procedure mandate holders and the universal periodic review (UPR) – pay

[1] Regional Representative for Europe of the UN High Commissioner for Human Rights.
[2] Principles Relating to the Status of National Institutions for the Protection and Promotion of Human Rights (The Paris Principles), endorsed by General Assembly Resolution 48/134 of 20 December 1993, Annex.

considerable attention to the existence or lack of a NHRI and to their quality, as expressed by their status. In the first cycle of the UPR for example, approximately ninety states which do not yet have a NHRI received recommendations to establish such an institution; and nearly forty states which have one of B, C or non-accredited status received recommendations to proceed to accreditation or upgrade their institution to A-status, which usually involves overcoming a lack of necessary independence.

In the European Union, there are at present twelve A-status NHRIs in ten member states,[3] fully compliant with Paris Principles, plus several countries which are in the process of upgrading their B-status NHRI, or of creating an entirely new one.[4] Most of these NHRIs are fairly young, having come into existence after 2000. OHCHR hopes that in ten to fifteen years, it will be an exception not to have an A-status NHRI in Europe, and indeed that the majority of states worldwide will have at least some kind of NHRI, if not always one of A-status.

2. REASONS FOR CREATING NHRIs BASED ON INTERNATIONAL LAW

The very idea for NHRIs was generated by the international human rights system when, in 1946, ECOSOC proposed the establishment in Member States of 'local human rights committees within their respective countries to collaborate with them in furthering the work of the Commission on Human Rights'.[5]

Thereafter, a number of UN treaties have called for the establishment of NHRIs or similar bodies namely the International Convention on the Elimination of Racial Discrimination (ICERD),[6] the Optional Protocol to the Convention against Torture (OP CAT)[7] and the Convention on the Rights of Persons with Disabilities (CRPD).[8] Both the OP CAT and CRPD also explicitly request that the member states take the Paris Principles into consideration when creating or designating the appropriate national entity. In addition to references in the treaties, the UN treaty bodies have also issued a number of recommendations

3 Denmark, France, Germany, Greece, Ireland, Luxembourg, Poland, Portugal, Spain, United Kingdom (with an NHRI in its constituent countries: Great Britain, Northern Ireland and Scotland). See for more information: M. Nowak, 'National Human Rights Institutions in Europe: Comparative, European and International Perspectives', Chapter 1 in this book.

4 For example: Italy or Finland.

5 ECOSOC Resolution 2/9 of 21 June 1946, para. 5.

6 ICERD, Art. 14(2).

7 OP CAT, Art. 3.

8 CRPD, Art. 33(2).

dealing either specifically,[9] or in part,[10] with NHRIs and the treaty bodies and special procedure mandate holders have also reinforced the need for NHRIs in their concluding observations.

The Council of Europe and other regional bodies have also adopted similar measures.[11] At the EU level, a number of Directives call for the establishment of entities that have similar, although not identical features, to NHRIs or may alternatively be included within NHRIs. These include the Racial Equality Directive[12] and the Gender Equality Directive on Goods and Services.[13] In some Member States, bodies do exist (or are currently being created) which fulfil both the functions of an NHRI and an equality body. This can prove problematic, however, if the resulting structure takes on more of the characteristics of an equality body whose independence is often less strictly defined than under the Paris Principles. An improvement is contained in the draft Equal Treatment Directive ("Horizontal Directive") which specifically refers to the designated institution's independence and its compliance with the Paris Principles.[14]

International human rights law also affords a special position to NHRIs within its system. They have the right of audience before the UN Human Rights Council (HRC) and their views are taken on board in the creation of international treaties.[15]

---

9 CERD Committee, General Recommendation XVII 'Establishment of national institutions to facilitate the implementation of the convention', 25 March 1993; Committee on Economic, Social and Cultural Rights, Draft General Comment No. 10: 'The role of national human rights institutions in the protection of economic, social and cultural rights', *UN Doc.* E/C.12/1998/25, 10 December 1998.

10 Committee on the Rights of the Child, General Comment No. 2 'The role of independent national human rights institutions in the promotion and protection of the rights of the child', *UN Doc.* CRC/GC/2002/2, 15 November 2002, para. 1; CERD Committee, General Recommendation No. 33 'Follow-up to the Durban Conference', 29 September 2009, para. 1(g).

11 Council of Europe, Recommendation No. R (97) 14 of the Committee of Ministers to Member States on the Establishment of Independent National Human Rights Institutions for the Promotion and Protection of Human Rights, 30 September 1997.

12 Council Directive 2000/43/EC of 29 June 2000 implementing the principle of equal treatment between persons irrespective of racial or ethnic origin, *OJ L* 180, Art. 13.

13 Council Directive 2004/113/EC of 13 December 2004 implementing the principle of equal treatment between men and women in the access to and supply of goods and services, *OJ L* 373/37, Art. 12.

14 Commission of the European Communities, Proposal for a Council Directive on implementing the principle of equal treatment between persons irrespective of religion or belief, disability, age or sexual orientation, 2008/0140(CNS), para. (28), and Art. 12.

15 See also K. Roberts, 'The Role and Functioning of the International Coordinating Committee of National Human Rights Institutions in International Human Rights Bodies', Chapter 10 in this volume; K. Meuwissen, 'NHRI Participation in United Nations Human Rights Procedures: International Promotion versus Institutional Consolidation', Chapter 12 in this volume.

3. REASONS FOR CREATING NHRIs IN ALL EUROPEAN DEMOCRACIES

At present, just above one third of EU Member States have an A-status NHRI, and in some of the other member states it seems difficult to persuade the authorities to move ahead in this direction. Unfortunately, the lack of fully Paris Principles-compliant NHRIs in European states makes it harder for the EU and its Member States to argue for the establishment of NHRIs in Africa or Asia; it undermines the credibility of EU Member States and of the EU as a whole when they invest major – and generally laudable – efforts in improving the situation of human rights in other parts of the world.

One of the most frequent arguments articulated by EU Member States as a reason for reluctance to create an NHRI is the lack of need for such a body. They claim that NHRIs may be useful for states in transition, but are not necessary for mature democracies based on the rule of law. However, there is clear evidence to show that even well-established democracies benefit, and indeed need, NHRIs.

The philosopher and sociologist Professor Zygmunt Bauman, when speaking at a Council of Europe, European Commission against Racism and Intolerance (ECRI) conference in 2004,[16] was asked what he would consider to be the best possible society. He answered that for him, this would be a society which would always remain aware of its imperfections while continuing to strive to overcome them.[17] This applies also to the development of human rights in free and open societies: recognising the imperfections in the area of human rights is a necessary precondition for improving them. It is also broadly in line with Karl Popper's definition of open societies[18] which emphasises that democratic elections do not provide states with perfect governments, nor do they provide those elected with a "mandate" overriding all others who have been less popular. The main advantage of an open society is that it allows imperfect governments to be replaced by other imperfect ones, errors to be corrected (often by errors of a different type), and actors who do not take part in the electoral process to nonetheless have a voice in society.

Echoing both Bauman and Popper, it can be argued therefore, that one essential role for NHRIs is to remind societies of their imperfections (in terms of human rights, as laid down in international human rights law) and to look for constructive ways of overcoming these, while acknowledging that this will be an open-ended task. To do so effectively, NHRIs must be equipped with several key attributes of independence, as laid down in the Paris Principles.

---

16 ECRI Conference 'All Different, All Equal: ECRI 10 years of combating racism' Strasbourg, 18 March 2004.

17 Professor Zygmunt Bauman, Philosopher and Sociologist, Emeritus Professor at the University of Leeds, 'Insecurity and Fear of the Stranger in liquid-modern times' speaking at ECRI Conference 'All Different, All Equal: ECRI 10 years of combating racism', 18 March 2004.

18 K. Popper, *The Open Society and Its Enemies, Volume One*, Routledge, 1945, chapter 10, part I.

Even without these attributes, NHRIs can sometimes play the aforementioned role if the persons in charge are sufficiently independent-minded. For instance, in the case of the Government Commissioner for Human Rights in the Czech Republic, the office tried to act in an independent-minded way, doing everything it could to alert the government, and broader society, to a number of imperfections in the area of human rights; to issues which had been overlooked or willfully ignored in the first decade after the democratic revolution. But this is always easier in the early days of a new government, when deficiencies can still be blamed on the previous governments, than in later years when authorities grow increasingly impatient with continued criticism of what they, by then, perceive to be their own record. In the long run, there is no effective alternative to real independence, to compatibility with the Paris Principles –in terms of selection of commissioners, office holders and staff; of the modus operandi; of financing etc.

Open societies should not be tempted by triumphalism about their achievements in human rights (or for that matter, in any other area). In OHCHR, when we see a country being aggressively defensive about its human rights record, blaming all problems on past regimes or even attributing all criticism to enemies from the outside, we know it is in much deeper trouble than those which admit to having problems.

3.1. CENTRAL AND EASTERN EUROPE: RISKS OF IMMATURE DEMOCRACIES

In the EU itself, it is telling that the lack of interest in a NHRI or a dismissive attitude towards its establishment on the basis that "democracies do not need this" is much more prevalent among the "new" Central and Eastern European Member States, which have emerged from a totalitarian system just two decades ago, than among "old" Member States. Out of the twelve A-status NHRIs in the EU, only one – Poland – is in a new Member State. After the fall of Communism, there was a degree of naïve optimism in most Central and Eastern European countries that political freedom and democracy were bound to deliver the full enjoyment of human rights for all almost automatically – and challenges to that view were usually greeted with distrust, as an accusation that the state in question had not yet fully achieved its transition from totalitarianism to democracy.

In fact, inappropriate triumphalism on the part of new and immature democracies often obscures the existence of many human rights problems (or labels them as minor "residues of the past" which will resolve themselves in due time without policy attention). Many human rights problems in Central and Eastern Europe are indeed at least partly due to the heritage of the Communist past, with its authoritarian, top-down decision-making and contemptuous attitude to those who do not have power; but they are likely to remain submerged if not addressed by policies. NHRIs have a potentially major role in this context. OHCHR, of course encourages all EU Member States to establish Paris-Principles-compliant NHRIs, but we believe that they could be of particular value for the states of Central and Eastern Europe.

In some of these new democracies we have witnessed a populist "winner takes all" mentality prevail – whoever wins the elections has a mandate to impose "the democratic will of the people", even against human rights. And even where there is no clear majority and the political sphere is divided between many parties, the public discourse tends to favour the view that one's voice in a democratic society ought to be proportionate to the number of votes received – more for the big parties, less for the smaller ones, and hardly anything for the unelected. We see leading politicians claiming that "human right-ism" or "NGO-ism" is subversive to democracy; that evoking international human rights law is at best a form of irrelevant elitism detached from the real needs of the people, and at worst a part of conspiracy of the nation's enemies.

3.2. IMPERFECTIONS OF MATURE DEMOCRACIES

Even in well-established democracies, human rights often become targets of cheap populist attacks, particularly in the media. And indeed, the very fact that NHRIs themselves are sometimes targeted by such populist attacks shows how useful and necessary they are – precisely because they are independent and not fishing for votes. That is why populists seek to delegitimize them. In March 2012, a British tabloid attacked the UK's Equality and Human Rights Commission (EHRC), calling it a "left-wing quango" arguing that 'prisoners, terrorists and gipsies should be handed MORE rights'.[19]

The description of the EHRC as a "left-wing quango" shows, of course, also another difficulty with which NHRIs need to struggle: real misunderstanding or a deliberately manipulative misreading of their innovative character. NHRIs are public bodies but they are independent of the ruling power which enjoys a democratic mandate. Yet in many democratic societies, the dominant discourse tends to operate in simple dichotomies of government vs. opposition, and state vs. non-state (civil society).

4. SUBSTANTIVE REASONS FOR ESTABLISHING NHRIs IN THE 21st CENTURY

Even if our reluctant governments acknowledge that having an independent NHRI is in principle healthy in terms of feedback, they might argue – sometimes

[19] I. Drury, 'Prisoners, terrorists and gipsies should be handed MORE human rights, declares equality quango', *Daily Mail*, 5 March 2012.

with conviction – that there is simply not enough to do for a NHRI. This, too, is in our view an error. Even in democratic systems with a long tradition, human rights violations may occur – and indeed, they may arise without that being the explicit or deliberate policy of the state. For instance, human rights of various groups at risk may suffer as an (unintended) consequence of other mainstream policies of a socio-economic nature when these policies are not consciously rights-based. Furthermore, states can violate human rights not only through action ("by commission") but also by failing to act ("by omission").

In this context, it is important to emphasise that beyond the obligation to *respect* human rights (which means refraining from violating them), states also have the obligation to *protect* them from being violated by third parties and to *promote* them by increasing awareness of rights among policymakers and other professionals, but also among the general public, i.e., among the rights-holders themselves. This includes, of course, those rights-holders who might not be fully aware of their rights because they belong to various groups at risk:

- Migrants and asylum seekers;
- Persons in prisons, in detention and in closed residential institutions (e.g., older persons);
- Persons with disabilities;
- Children;
- Women who are victims of domestic violence, etc.

Some of the misperceptions of states are linked to a static image of human rights where all problems can be resolved in the form of a box-ticking exercise. This error is at least partly based on the misunderstanding of the dynamically developing character of international human rights law. The understanding of historic Covenants and Conventions should develop over time, above all through the guidance of treaty monitoring bodies and special procedure mandate holders, but also through the nationally specific work of NHRIs themselves.

The narrative of human rights (and the development of our human rights consciousness) is an open-ended one. In the past, we have seen it progress from an automatic assumption that rights are presumed to be there only or mainly for the average citizens, to the explicit recognition of rights of categories of persons at risk. This development has been reflected in the creation of the individual instruments of international human rights law, from the Convention on the Elimination of All Forms of Racial Discrimination half a century ago through specific instruments dealing with discrimination against women, the rights of the child, and most recently, the rights of persons with disabilities.

Only in some cases are these rights specific, as in the case of children. Most often, what is at stake is rather the special attention to guarantee their effective equality, their enjoyment of the same rights the average citizen would take for granted, without any discrimination. This may require explicit attention and specific non-discrimination policies and measures, including – for instance – those concerning persons with disabilities. In such situations, as we all know, treating people equally does not mean treating them in the same way. In this context, NHRIs can play an important role in bringing the appropriate attention to various groups of persons at risk.

Moreover, the developmental narrative will surely remain open-ended in the years to come. For instance, the issue of rights of persons across two divides constitute newly recognised frontiers: the "cognitive divide" (involving persons with intellectual and psychosocial disabilities, including a growing number of older persons with dementia) and the "legal status divide" which involves migrants in various shades of irregularity, or else migrant domestic workers who are often barred from effective protection by their status (e.g., working in diplomatic families). Again, NHRIs are called upon to focus the attention of societies on those categories of problems.

Indeed, the 21st century has already brought new challenges:

- In the form of new security risks which appeared after 9 September 2001 and of the (sometimes disproportionate) reactions to these risks in the form of new security-focused policies;
- In the form of new technologies, from information technology and surveillance technologies to new biomedical technologies which challenge us to reconcile the right to health with the right to reject treatment etc;
- In the form of the not entirely new, but increasingly recognised role of business and human rights, given that some major multinational corporations are now more powerful than many states, yet they are not party to the instruments of international human rights law.

For all these issues to be addressed in a coherent and systematic manner, all states need a NHRI – an independent, official, state-funded body that is constitutionally or legally based, with authority to independently promote and protect human rights at the national level.

5. NHRIs AS NATIONAL AND INTERNATIONAL ACTORS

NHRIs refer to international human rights law while at the same time remaining *national* actors, relating to the domestic constitutional order. This is extremely important as states sometimes treat recommendations by international human rights mechanisms (treaty monitoring bodies, special procedure mandate holders) as coming "from abroad", from bodies which may have the authority and general expertise but "cannot possibly understand our specifics" etc. In fact, the "local knowledge argument" is usually unconvincing, given that treaty bodies and special rapporteurs tend to produce well-informed and objective recommendations and their positions are often quite closely aligned with that of the NHRIs (that is, if they are genuinely independent ones). However, it is clear that such accusations cannot possibly be made towards NHRIs who obviously do understand the specifics of the country where they live.

Thus NHRIs can be seen as a conduit between the national and international systems: they bring independent expertise and international experience to the concrete national level and convey the local perspective to regional and international forums. NHRIs also have an important role to play in monitoring compliance at the national level with states' obligations under international and regional treaties and with the UPR. It has been identified that this follow-up role has not been exploited significantly to date[20] and OHCHR would encourage NHRIs to play a more active role in this regard.

6. NHRIs IN EUROPE AND THE WORLD

OHCHR works closely with NHRIs worldwide. We regard them as the interface between national and international systems. We are lobbying the European Parliament to include in its resolution on fundamental rights a statement that it encourages EU Member States to establish NHRIs. In this context we welcome such a statement in the Council of Europe's Brighton Declaration on the reform of the European Court of Human Rights.[21]

Our headquarters in Palais Wilson, Geneva, provide office space for the secretariat of the NHRIs' International Coordinating Committee (ICC). However, it must be pointed out that the ICC remains strictly independent of OHCHR as well as its Subcommittee on Accreditation which decides about the A-, B- or C-status of particular NHRIs.[22]

At the global level, OHCHR is very interested in promoting knowledge transfer between NHRIs (between the global North and South) and in the strengthening of cross-regional networks. Of course, we recognise that there are regional differences around the world, particularly in terms of the form of NHRIs. In Latin America, constitutionally based ombudsman institutions dominate, while African countries tend to have constitutionally based commissions, and Asian countries mostly have statute-based commissions. Europe does not provide a single model for other parts of the world since due to its wealth of different

20 OHCHR 'Survey on National Human Rights Institutions: Report on the Findings and Recommendations of a Questionnaire Addressed to NHRIs Worldwide', Geneva, July 2009, p. 5.

21 Council of Europe, 'High Level Conference on the Future of the European Court of Human Rights, Brighton Declaration', 19 April 2012, available at: http://hub.coe.int/20120419-brighton-declaration, para. 9 (c) ii).

22 See G. De Beco, 'Assessment of the Paris Principles and the ICC Sub-Committee on Accreditation', Chapter 11 in this volume.

legal traditions, the types of NHRIs are quite varied, as is their relationship to the specific equality bodies created under the EU non-discrimination directives,[23] and to ombudspersons.[24] In some EU Member States, there is a range of specialised national institutions with different functions. In other EU countries, national institutions have been subject to fusion. In others still, there is what one would call a multi- functional ombudsperson acting on the one hand as a "classical" ombudsperson investigating administrative malpractice while simultaneously carrying out the roles of a NHRI and an equality body under EU non-discrimination directives. The multi-functional ombudsperson can also act as the national preventive mechanism (NPM) envisaged under the Optional Protocol to the Convention against Torture, or as the national monitoring mechanism under Article 33 of the Convention on the Rights of Persons with Disabilities. Poland has such a multi-functional ombudsperson.[25] What matters most for an NHRI is its independence, integrity and capacity to carry out its function. The OHCHR Regional Office for Europe, which has been based in Belgium for the last two years, has been involved in the process of the envisaged upgrade of the Netherland's NHRI to A-status,[26] and has also been involved, albeit to a lesser extent, in the case of Belgium.[27] OHCHR very much welcomes the commitment of these governments to this goal, in the case of Belgium both in its response to recommendations made under the UPR and in the programmes of the new government.

However, OHCHR has also been involved, together with experts from European NHRIs, in the discussions concerning the establishment of a NHRI in Turkey, aiming at effective knowledge transfer. It has been a difficult and to date not particularly encouraging process. After two seminars in the last quarter of 2011 – one organised by OHCHR and the other by the EU – the Turkish Government responded by re-submitting their previous proposal, which provides for a clearly non-independent institution, to the Turkish Grand National Assembly.[28] The fact that many EU Member States do not have A-status NHRIs either, or lack NHRIs

---

23 *Supra* notes 12, 13, 14.

24 For an extensive analysis of the different types of NHRIs in Europe and the EU, see M. Nowak, 'National Human Rights Institutions in Europe: Comparative, European and International Perspectives', Chapter 1 in this volume.

25 For an analysis of the Polish NHRI, see A. Gliszczyńska-Grabias & K. Sękowska-Kozłowska, 'NHRI in Poland: As Good As it Gets?', Chapter 3 in this volume.

26 For an analysis of the Dutch NHRI, see Y. Donners & M. Olde Monnikhof, 'The Newly Established Netherlands Institute for Human Rights: Integrating Human Rights and Equal Treatment', Chapter 4 in this volume.

27 For an analysis of the Belgian situation, see J. Vrielink & S. Sottiaux, 'Federalism, Equality Bodies and NHRIs: A Critical Analysis of the Belgian Debate on Equality Bodies and NHRIs', Chapter 5 in this volume.

28 The draft law establishing the institution was approved, without any changes being proposed, by the Parliamentary Human Rights Investigative Commission on June 13, 2012, and was passed by the General Assembly of Parliament on 22 June 2012.

altogether, has also not made our task to persuade our Turkish counterparts any easier. Still, our joint efforts have at least succeeded in establishing consistent cooperation with Turkish civil society, thus giving us hope that at least step-by-step progress might be achievable.

OHCHR encourages all – NHRIs, civil society organisations, and the academic world – to continue building similar cooperation in order to help make the open-ended development of human rights in the world into a narrative of continuous progress.

CONCLUSION: TOWARDS A BETTER UNDERSTANDING OF EUROPEAN NHRIs IN A MULTI-LAYERED HUMAN RIGHTS SYSTEM

Katrien MEUWISSEN and Jan WOUTERS

This publication is one of the academic outputs of COST Action IS0702 on the European Union (EU) and United Nations (UN) human rights reform. It presents a comparative, European and international perspective on the functioning of European NHRIs. It elucidates the opportunities and challenges that arise from the increasing emergence of NHRIs in Europe for the multiple levels of human rights promotion and protection. These chapters have touched upon many different aspects that are of relevance to the functioning of European NHRIs. This conclusion weaves together identified common threads and main findings and selected reflections are developed regarding future research.

1. UNDERSTANDING "NATIONAL HUMAN RIGHTS INSTITUTIONS" IN EUROPE

As pointed out in the book, there is an immense variety of national institutions promoting and protecting human rights, ranging from data protection authorities, to ombudsmen, national human rights commissions, and equality bodies. Thus the task of determining when such an institution can be considered to be a "National Human Rights Institution (NHRI)", and when not poses a formidable challenge. Kirsten Roberts observed in chapter 10 that 'the diversification in form and function means that viewing NHRIs as a block can be problematic'. This applies especially for Europe, the continent with the strongest diversity in domestic human rights institutions.

Manfred Nowak (chapter 1) described NHRIs as independent non-judicial national institutions with a pluralistic composition and a politically sensitive task to promote and protect human rights in a broad sense. This reflects the predominant definition of NHRIs as conceived by the UN and the ICC (together with its regional networks) and echoes the international standards laid down in the Paris Principles. The contributions to this book have revealed that identification of NHRIs on the basis of the Paris Principles excludes many of the European national institutions involved in human rights protection and promotion from the "NHRI category". Data protection authorities, sub-national institutions or thematic institutions, for example, do not fit the Paris Principles-compliant NHRI category.

The Paris Principles outline standards concerning the responsibilities, composition and working methods of NHRIs, but they remain vague and do not provide a definition of what an "NHRI" is. Interestingly, they have been further interpreted by NHRIs in the context of their accreditation procedure.[1] For example, while the Paris Principles originally seemed to exclude ombudsmen from the NHRI category,[2] the ICC currently accredits ombudsmen-type NHRIs as being in full compliance with the Paris Principles. In other words, the "NHRI"-denominator should not be seen as a rigorous categorisation and is subject to further refinement instead.

This book illustrated that the identification of "NHRIs" is important, since it determines which national institutions are granted access to the procedures of international and regional human rights organisations. ICC accreditation on the basis of the Paris Principles is increasingly used as *the* benchmark to assess the credibility and legitimacy of NHRIs at home and in the wider human rights system. Accordingly, the shortcomings of the ICC accreditation process – identified by Gauthier de Beco in chapter 11 – deserve more attention of the international community. Notably, the ICC both serves as promoter and regulator of NHRIs worldwide. The current accreditation process lacks transparency and includes stakeholders (such as independent UN human rights experts or civil society) only in a very limited manner. Moreover, the ICC accreditation focuses on institutional characteristics of NHRIs and does not consider the effectiveness of their functioning. Therefore, it is questionable whether the current ICC accreditation suffices as an accountability mechanism for NHRIs, which get an increasingly important role as independent participants in the international human rights system. Since the international support for and engagement with NHRIs provides these institutions with legitimacy, it is of vital importance that it can be accurately checked whether they are effectively carrying out their functions

1 The General Observations outlined by the ICC SCA complement the Paris Principles: Rules of Procedure for the ICC Sub-Committee on Accreditation, 14 September 2004 (amended 15 April 2008), Article 6.3 (c). See also G. De Beco, Chapter 11 in this volume.

2 See: Paris Principles, 'methods of operation', f): 'Within the framework of its operation, the national institution shall: […] f) Maintain consultation with the other bodies, whether jurisdictional or otherwise, responsible for the promotion and protection of human rights (in particular ombudsmen, mediators and similar institutions)'. See in this regard also: L. Reif, 'The Shifting Boundaries of NHRI Definition in the International System', in R. Goodman and Th. Pegram (eds.), *Human Rights, State Compliance and Social Change, Assessing National Human Rights Institutions*, Cambridge University Press, 2012, Chapter 2.

in an independent manner and whether they contribute to better human rights protection.[3]

While the ICC conception of NHRIs is the predominant one, it appears that the exact definitional boundaries of "NHRIs" can vary in specific contexts, depending on the interpretation adhered to by the organisational gatekeepers in question. The UN Human Rights Council adopts a very stringent approach with regard to NHRI identification and only accords participation rights to NHRIs which the ICC deems to fully comply with the Paris Principles. On the other hand, UN treaty bodies also promote the Paris Principles-compliance of NHRIs but adopt a wider approach towards NHRI identification when it comes to determining which "NHRIs" can participate in their procedures. 'Even if national institutions with a thematic mandate are not fully in compliance with the Paris Principles, these are considered to be important interlocutors by the UN treaty bodies, and can participate as "NHRIs" in the treaty body procedures (see Meuwissen, chapter 12). Furthermore, as indicated by Adamson in chapter 6, the Council of Europe engages with NHRIs in accordance with the broader notion of "National Human Rights Structures" (NHRSs). Next to NHRIs in the "ICC Paris Principles-compliant" sense, NHRSs encompass a range of other bodies such as national ombudsmen, thematic ombudsmen and equality bodies set up under EU legislation.[4] While these non-Paris Principles compliant NHRIs are integrated in human rights procedures of the UN treaty bodies and the Council of Europe, it is unclear how they are exactly identified and how their performance and reliability can be checked. Even if the participation of NHRIs in international and regional procedures is in a nascent state and is still further developing, their participation as "independent actors in their own right" seems only to be warranted if benchmarks and mechanisms are in place which allow the assessment that only reliable national institutions can participate in the procedures.

The Paris Principles do provide an internationally recognised yardstick to identify and assess "NHRIs". However, as different chapters have shown, the exact conception of an "NHRI" is influenced by a multiplicity of context-, policy- and time-specific variables. It is therefore important both for actors cooperating with NHRIs and academics (when analysing NHRIs) to be aware of the boundaries and evolutionary nature of the predominant NHRI concept. The Paris Principles have been described as 'minimum standards',[5] focusing on institutional NHRI

---

3 See in this regard P. Rosenblum, 'Tainted Origins and Uncertain Outcomes', in R. Goodman and Th. Pegram (eds.), *supra* note 2, Chapter 12.

4 Note that the Council of Europe Commissioner on Human Rights, however, describes NHRSs as 'national, regional, local or thematic institutions, which comply with the Paris Principles and abide by the Council of Europe's values'. See: Council of Europe Commissioner on Human Rights, *Cooperation with National Human Rights Structures*, available at http://www.coe.int/t/commissioner/activities/nhrs/default_EN.asp.

5 See for example: FRA, *National Human Rights Institutions in EU Member States, Strengthening the fundamental rights architecture in the EU*, Luxembourg, Publication Office of the European Union, 2010, p. 6.

characteristics. Consequently, it is essential that analysts look beyond the standards set out in the Paris Principles when assessing the functioning of NHRIs and the impact these institutions have on the human rights performance of states.[6]

2. TOWARDS A MORE COMPREHENSIVE NHRI LANDSCAPE IN EUROPE

In European countries, the picture emerges of a fragmented human rights scene populated with many domestic human rights institutions that have been accorded issue-specific mandates. While under the influence of UN promotion,[7] a broadly mandated NHRI has become the international standard, fundamental rights obligations in the EU have entailed the establishment of a variety of thematic institutions in EU Member States, such as equality bodies or data protection authorities. As indicated in chapters 4 and 5, the prior existence of various thematic institutions may hold back the willingness of European countries to establish a Paris Principles-compliant NHRI with a broad human rights mandate. In countries where several national bodies dealing with human rights already exist, the added value of such broadly mandated NHRIs is less obvious and triggers questions on how to consolidate existing specialised bodies in order to prevent duplications and inefficiencies.

With its large number of thematic institutions, Europe is the region in the world with the most B-status NHRIs that are deemed to be "not fully compliant" with the Paris Principles. Pressure is mounting on European governments to establish an NHRI that is in full compliance with the Paris Principles. At the international level, the B-status of many European NHRIs entails a more limited role and lower credibility of these domestic institutions. As has been pointed out in part III of this publication, in the context of UN human rights procedures (such as the Universal Periodic Review of the UN Human Rights Council or the reporting procedures of UN treaty bodies), governments are recommended consistently to establish or strengthen their NHRI in accordance with the Paris Principles. European governments that aim to be human rights "frontrunners" are prompted especially by international criticism of the lack of a Paris Principles-compliant NHRI to establish a domestic institution that complies with the international NHRI standards. Furthermore, the rejuvenated attention of the EU to develop a more comprehensive European human rights architecture (see chapter 9) triggers an increased attention from its side for domestic institutions active in the field of human rights. In a 2010 report, the EU Fundamental Rights Agency has called upon EU Member States to avoid fragmentation of the human rights landscape

6 See in this regard: R. Goodman and Th. Pegram (eds.), *supra* note 2.

7 For an elaborate overview, see: A. Pohjolainen, 'The Evolution of National Human Rights Institutions – The Role of the United Nations', Danish Institute for Human Rights, 2006, available at http://www.nhri.net/pdf/Evolution_of_NHRIs.pdf.

and to adopt a more comprehensive approach towards human rights promotion and protection, 'with efforts and resources focused on key institutions, such as a visible and effective NHRI in each Member State'[8]. In chapter 1, Manfred Nowak echoed the call of the FRA and submitted that 'it would be desirable for a well-functioning human rights architecture in Europe that the EU requests from all its Member States to create fully independent, professional and pluralistic NHRIs with a strong preference for National Human Rights Commissions with an overarching mandate, including the examination of individual complaints'.[9]

In a fragmented European human rights scenery, broadly mandated NHRIs have the potential to "fill the gaps" in domestic human rights protection systems. NHRIs can ensure that all human rights are covered within a country and that human rights receive due attention in their entirety, an argument that is of particular relevance in view of the universality and indivisibility of human rights.[10] NHRIs could function as structures overarching the various thematic institutions active in the field of human rights within EU Member States. Accordingly, A-status NHRIs can serve as national human rights focal points, providing comprehensive information and support for citizens, civil society, national governments but also supranational (European and UN) human rights institutions.[11] Also for reasons of cost-effectiveness, easy identification by the public and consistency in the application of standards, the establishment of broadly mandated NHRIs in EU Member States should be favoured.[12] However, this does not necessarily mean that the different existing domestic institutions need to be merged into one NHRI. As chapters 4 and 5 indicated, the conjunction of domestic human rights bodies can engender advantages but also disadvantages. Importantly, in each particular national context it needs to be assessed which form of cooperation among national institutions with a human rights mandate would engender the most effective and comprehensive domestic human rights system. This can be done through merging different institutions into one NHRI, but also through a joint planning of strategic action, the organisation of common

8 FRA, *supra* note 5, p. 7. To strengthen its argument, the FRA refers to a resolution of the EU Parliament: Resolution of 20 May 2008 on progress made in equal opportunities and non-discrimination in the EU, Recital E in *OJ* C 279E, 19 November 2009, para. 19.

9 See also: Cost Action IS0702 'The Role of the EU in UN Human Rights Reform, recommendations on National Human Rights Institutions (NHRIs)', included as an annex to this book [further: COST recommendations on NHRIs], recommendations 1 and 5.

10 See article 21(1) of the Treaty on European Union, *OJ* C 83/13, 30 March 2010: 'The Union's action on the international scene shall be guided by the principles which have inspired its own creation, development and enlargement, and which it seeks to advance in the wider world: democracy, the rule of law, *the universality and indivisibility of human rights and fundamental freedoms*, respect for human dignity, the principles of equality and solidarity, and respect for the principles of the United Nations Charter and international law.' [emphasis added].

11 See also: COST recommendations on NHRIs, recommendation 6.

12 See also: R. Carver, 'One NHRI or Many? How Many Institutions Does it Take to Protect Human Rights? – Lessons from the European Perspective', *Journal of Human Rights Practice*, vol. 3, no. 1, 2011, pp. 1–24 at p. 22.

initiatives or the mutual exchange of information.[13] Centralisation of different human rights mandates under the coordination of one "umbrella NHRI" is the current trend. However, several chapters in this book point to the problems that arise for NHRIs with a broad human rights mandate, which encompasses various thematic mandates. Especially the prioritisation of tasks and the allocation of resources seem to be increasingly challenging for broadly mandated – Paris Principles-compliant- NHRIs in Europe. As noted by some authors, in each specific context the question should be posed as to what the added value of Paris Principles-compliant NHRIs is in comparison to "other institutional initiatives", such as bodies developed to respond to specific human rights issues.[14]

3. UNDERSTANDING EUROPEAN NHRIs AS "MULTI-DIMENSIONAL" HUMAN RIGHTS ACTORS

Throughout this book it has been seen how NHRIs function on multiple levels of the human rights system. On each of these levels, NHRIs should engage in cooperative relations with a variety of actors, be it their government, civil society, other domestic human rights actors, or regional and international human rights institutions. The unique positioning of NHRIs as "bridges" between the diversity of actors and the multiple layers of the human rights system has led to the acceptance of NHRIs as actors occupying a distinct place in the human rights arena. Both in the context of UN and European human rights procedures, NHRIs get an increasingly important role to play. NHRIs are not only accepted but also widely promoted on the international human rights scene because of their potential to fill the gap between domestic implementation on the one hand and international or regional human rights standards and mechanisms on the other hand.

Being endowed with a mandate to promote and protect human rights, NHRIs can serve as a domestic human rights access point, both for national actors (such as citizens or civil society) as for international actors (such as UN special rapporteurs or the EU Fundamental Rights Agency). Since states retain the primary responsibility to implement human rights, the institutional link

---

13 See, in this regard: Equinet (European Network of Equality Bodies), *Equality Bodies and National Human Rights Institutions, Making the Link to Maximise Impact*, November 2011, p. 7, http://www.equineteurope.org/IMG//pdf/EN_-_Equality_Bodies_and_National_Human_Rights_Institutions.pdf.

14 C. Flinterman and M. Zwamborn, *From Development of Human Rights to Managing Human Rights Development, Global Review of the OHCHR Technical Cooperation Programme*, Utrecht, Netherlands Institute of Human Rights, 2003, available at http://www.ohchr.org/Documents/Countries/global-reviewsynthesis.pdf, p. 54; P. Rosenblum, 'Tainted Origins and Uncertain Outcomes', in R. Goodman and Th. Pegram (eds.), *supra* note 2, p. 303. In this book, see J. Vrielink and S. Sottiaux, chapter 5.

and cooperative relations between NHRIs and their government is especially important. NHRIs can advise or pressurise governments to comply with their human rights obligations, and often NHRIs serve as national implementing body under specific international treaties or EU Directives. Moreover, the engagement of NHRIs at one level of the human rights system can have a positive "spill-over" effect on their position at another level. The recommendations made to states to strengthen their NHRI in the context of the Universal Periodic Review of the UN Human Rights Council, for example, can lead to a stronger position of NHRIs towards their governments on the domestic level.

While the multi-dimensional engagement of NHRIs opens up many windows of opportunity, it also enhances the vulnerability of NHRIs. Being at the crossroads of cooperation with a variety of actors, it can be difficult for NHRIs to retain a balanced and independent position towards all these actors. As has been illustrated in various chapters, the institutional intertwinement and the financial dependence of NHRIs upon their government pose a risk to their independent functioning. Importantly, the question arises to what extent governments endow NHRIs with the necessary capacity and independence to fulfil their function, or whether they rather perceive NHRIs as a promotional tool and a convenient and cost-effective manner to enhance their human rights image on the international scene.[15]

NHRIs are confronted with many challenges. As this book has shown, the multiplication of the avenues for NHRI engagement goes together with an amplification of the aspirations related to their performance. As the roles of NHRIs continue to increase, the probability that they cannot live up to all expectations rises accordingly. Each additional task puts an extra burden on the staff and financial resources of NHRIs. The different case-studies in Part I illustrate that while the mandates of NHRIs expand exponentially, their additional tasks are most often not matched by extra investments. NHRIs thus lack the resources to fully carry out all their functions. Consequently, prioritisation and balancing of roles are increasingly proving challenging for NHRIs. The prioritisation of some roles logically entails that other dimensions of NHRIs' functioning could be underdeveloped or not represented at all in their work. As indicated in chapter 3, for example, the Polish Ombudsman does not consistently engage with UN human rights mechanisms and focuses his international engagement on cooperation with ombudsmen from the Eastern European region.

In view of their many areas of engagement, it also becomes increasingly challenging to measure the (direct and indirect)[16] impact of NHRIs on the

---

15 See in this regard, P. Rosenblum, 'Tainted Origins and Uncertain Outcomes', in R. Goodman and Th. Pegram (eds.) *supra* note 2.

16 As Christoffer Badse remarks in chapter two: 'It is obvious that an impact indicator cannot only be succeeding in changing and amending legislation. That would be to set the bar too high. Sometimes, the input of the DIHR has a direct impact, while on other occasions the DIHR joins with other human rights stakeholders to have an impact on policies and legislation'.

promotion and protection of human rights. Arguably, their impact should not only be measured in relation to the enhancement of national compliance with human rights, but also in relation to the more effective functioning of regional and international human rights mechanisms.

For now, we can conclude that any comprehensive assessment of NHRIs should take into account their multi-dimensional functioning. All actors should be aware that the engagement of NHRIs at the different levels of the human rights system entails both opportunities and risks, and that engagement at one particular level may impact the engagement at other levels. While the ICC Sub-Committee on Accreditation may guarantee that minimal requirements set by the Paris Principles are met, it will not consider the concrete role of NHRIs in the implementation of human rights, their potential engagement in critical issues nor their impact on the work of other actors.[17] Accordingly, an important task for analysts consists in elucidating how the impact of NHRIs on human rights protection can be assessed in a more comprehensive manner, which would better facilitate the identification and addressing of the shortcomings of NHRIs as bridge-builders in a multi-dimensional human rights reality.

4. TOWARDS A MORE STRATEGIC INTEGRATION OF EUROPEAN NHRIs IN THE MULTI-LAYERED HUMAN RIGHTS SYSTEM

European NHRIs operate on the continent with the widest variety of human rights mechanisms. Next to their engagement with national actors and international mechanisms, European NHRIs have opportunities to cooperate with EU institutions and agencies, Council of Europe mechanisms and OSCE bodies. From the different chapters it appears that, while many actors engage with NHRIs, there is scope for further integration and consolidation of the role of NHRIs in the multiple layers of the European human rights system. Human rights standards and mechanisms are in need of a better connection with national realities, and NHRIs have been hailed in the international arena as welcome actors needed to narrow this gap.

As NHRIs are relatively new actors on the human rights scene, they are still developing their relationship with the different international and supranational mechanisms at hand in Europe. Especially in view of the diversity of the European NHRI landscape it can be difficult for their counterparts to view European NHRIs as one block and to treat these institutions as independent actors in their own right. The Council of Europe's focus on NHRI interaction within the broader concept of 'National Human Rights Structures' illustrates this. When supranational and international human rights mechanisms engage with NHRIs

17 As noted by De Beco, chapter 11 in this volume.

they do not always do this consistently. The abundance of different procedures and standards complicates the involvement of NHRIs.

As Bruce Adamson indicates in chapter 7, setting up a permanent secretariat for the European Group of NHRIs is a significant step in further strengthening the position of NHRIs in Europe. Regional NHRI groups are better developed in other regions of the world than on the European continent. An enhanced coordination of NHRIs in Europe could prove to be important with a view to the different levels of engagement of such NHRIs. A more intense coordination among European NHRIs would better enable the latter to share best practices among each other and to find effective solutions to tackle common challenges. Additionally, more effective regional coordination has the potential of better integrating European NHRIs into the international human rights scene. The European Group is part of the international coordinating network of NHRIs, whose members engage in international initiatives and support each other to engage in UN human rights procedures.

Despite the great potential of strengthened European NHRI coordination, the European Group could only secure minimal funding for the establishment of a secretariat. This finding reflects the more general observation that, while opportunities increase for European NHRIs to operate at the multiple levels of the human rights system, they lack sufficient resources to fully engage in the system. Many chapters in this book come to the same conclusion. Accordingly, even if NHRIs are increasingly given their own position and role in the human rights system, it is unsure whether they will be able to live up to expectations.[18] One of the most important challenges for NHRIs in the near future thus appears to be to strengthen their capacity in order to be able to function as bridge-builders between the different layers of the human rights system. On the other hand, the various NHRI counterparts should also consider investing more in these actors and should explore new avenues to cooperate with NHRIs in a strategic way. This strategic engagement with NHRIs should include checks and balances that ensure that only reliable NHRIs get the opportunity to participate as "actors in their own right" in human rights procedures.

The EU does engage with NHRIs, but so far it has not included NHRIs in its human rights policy framework. Since the position of the EU towards NHRIs currently remains undefined in its policy documents, it is difficult to assess the EU's interaction with these actors.[19]

---

18 The OHCHR survey on NHRIs, for example, indicates that 'the level of NHRI engagement with international and regional human rights mechanisms – particularly in following up on recommendations – remains significantly underdeveloped overall and reflects a limited familiarity with these systems'. See: OHCHR, Survey on National Human Rights Institutions', Geneva, Switzerland, July 2009, available at http://www.nhri.net/2009/Questionnaire%20-%20Complete%20Report%20FINAL-edited.pdf, p. 5.

19 Note for example that interviews with EU officials conducted in the context of chapter 9 uncovered some aspects of EU engagement with NHRIs that could not be traced back in publicly accessible documents.

It appears that with regard to *third countries*, the EU consistently encourages the establishment and strengthening of NHRIs in accordance with the Paris Principles. *Internally*, though, emphasis is placed to a great extent on national institutions with a specific human rights mandate, and only 11 out of 27 EU Member States have an NHRI that fully complies with the Paris Principles. In order to strengthen its fundamental rights architecture internally, and to enhance the credibility of the EU's external human rights policy and action, the EU should also encourage and support its Member States to establish effectively functioning NHRIs, which are (at least) in compliance with the Paris Principles.[20]

The recommendations that were elaborated regarding NHRIs in the context of COST Action IS0702 on the role of the EU in UN human rights reform, reproduced in an annex to this book, can offer food for thought for EU policymakers in order to better integrate NHRIs in the EU's human rights policy and action. Within the EU, EU-NHRI cooperation bears special importance with a view to fostering a fundamental rights culture across Europe. The Council, Commission and European Parliament should consider the greater active involvement of European NHRIs and the European Group of NHRIs in fundamental rights initiatives, in areas including consultation and the development of fundamental rights policy.[21] Moreover, the EU should promote NHRIs to serve as a national focal point for EU citizens to obtain comprehensive information on the protection of their rights on the basis of the EU Charter of Fundamental Rights as well as international human rights treaties.[22] NHRIs can also function as partners in the EU's promotion of human rights across the globe.[23] Especially on common thematic human rights priorities (such as business and human rights, or the rights of persons with disabilities[24]), but also on specific country situations (e.g. the consultation of NHRIs in the context of the Universal Periodic Review of the UN Human Rights Council), more strategic EU-NHRI cooperation could entail important synergies.

5. SOME AREAS FOR FURTHER RESEARCH

Even if the presence of NHRIs in the multi-layered European human rights system becomes a settled fact, the academic focus on these institutions has been, so far, limited.

This book was a first endeavour to focus on the European NHRI landscape, touching upon each of the dimensions and levels of NHRI engagement.

20 See further chapter 9 in this volume.

21 COST recommendations on NHRIs, recommendation 8. See also chapter 9 in this volume.

22 COST recommendations on NHRIs, recommendation 6. See also chapter 9 in this volume.

23 COST recommendations on NHRIs, recommendation 13. See also chapter 9 in this volume.

24 See especially chapter 9 in this volume for more information on the potential of coherent EU-NHRI cooperation in the area of the rights of persons with disabilities across human rights fora.

Obviously, it does not provide a complete overview of the European NHRI scenery, and neither was it its purpose to do so. Four case-studies were conducted: the Danish Institute for Human Rights (chapter 2), the Polish Ombudsman (chapter 3), the Netherlands Institute for Human Rights (chapter 4), and the Belgian Centre for Equal Opportunities and Opposition to Racism (chapter 5). These case-studies provide insights into the functioning of European NHRIs of different types in varying national settings. Nevertheless, a broader comparative study encompassing the full spectrum of European NHRIs –including NHRIs from outside the EU – would be of great interest. Such a study would especially be relevant in view of the many context-specific variables that influence the conception, role, functioning and effectiveness of each of the European NHRIs. Clearly, the People's Advocate in Albania, the Russian Commissioner for Human Rights or the recently established Human Rights Institution in Turkey work in very different settings and face challenges of a different nature than those faced by the NHRIs discussed in this book.

In a European context, it is of particular relevance to assess whether NHRIs enhance the coherence and effectiveness of human rights promotion and protection, while preventing overlaps and inefficiencies because of the functioning of different human rights actors in the same geographical setting. In this regard, more attention should be paid to the interactions between NHRIs and other actors in the human rights field. This applies in particular to the multi-faceted relation of NHRIs with civil society, governments and regional/ international human rights organisations. In addition, the interaction of NHRIs among each other and with other domestic institutions with a human rights mandate – including in the framework of the coordinating groups of national institutions – needs further exploration. Christoffer Badse highlighted the functioning of the European Group of NHRIs in chapter 6. Other European networks of national institutions with a human rights competence (such as the European Network of Ombudspersons for Children and the European Network of Equality Bodies, Equinet), and possible synergies among the European networks did not so far receive enough attention.

NHRIs are established in all regions of the world as they have the potential to bridge international standards with local realities and can respond to the need to "localise" universal human rights.[25] Accordingly, it would be highly relevant to engage in a comparative study of NHRIs that function in countries and regions beyond Europe. Such a comparative study would not only allow for an identification of challenges and opportunities for NHRIs that function in regional and local settings where other interpretations of human rights are practiced,[26] but could also engender cross-regional learning on NHRIs. It can be noted for

---

25 See, for example: K. De Feyter, 'Localising Human Rights' in W. Benedek, K. De Feyter and F. Marrella (eds.), *Economic Globalisation and Human Rights*, EIUC Studies on Human Rights and Democratisation, Cambridge University Press, 2011, pp. 67–92.

26 E.g., the South-African NHRI faces considerable challenges when trying to explain the meaning and value of international human rights standards to local tribal communities.

example that the NHRI coordination network in the Asia-Pacific region is much more developed than the European Group of NHRIs. Since this book indicated that one of the most important shortcomings for NHRIs in Europe is the lack of sufficient resources, it would also be of great interest to analyse and assess the international and inter-regional flows of financial and technical cooperation that purport to strengthen the capacity of NHRIs, including in developing countries.[27]

The worldwide support for the establishment and strengthening of NHRIs is grounded in the belief that NHRIs play a vital role in transmitting and implementing international human rights norms at the domestic level. The growing recognition of NHRIs and their potential should however not preclude a critical assessment of these institutions. One could, for example, raise the question whether, twenty years after the adoption of the Paris Principles, the time has not come to update the 'minimal standards'[28] laid down in these Principles, which after all remain vague and need to be specified before they can be applied.[29] Furthermore, there is a lack of attention on the effectiveness of NHRIs with regard to the promotion and protection of human rights. As has been indicated, ICC accreditation – which is used as an international benchmark to assess the reliability of NHRIs – focuses mostly on institutional NHRI characteristics, rather than on the effectiveness of these institutions.

Multidisciplinary research is needed in order to assess NHRI performance, combining political and social sciences with legal or institutional approaches. Due account should be taken of the internal functioning and the governance of NHRIs. Attention should be paid to how decisions are taken within NHRIs and how and why priorities are set by them. While opportunities for NHRIs to engage with the wide variety of human rights mechanisms are multiplying, the question how NHRIs can be held accountable for their conduct becomes increasingly relevant. Research should therefore also consider the relations of NHRIs with parliaments and governments, the appointment processes for NHRI staff, as well as NHRI reporting obligations, and the control over NHRI expenditures.

Finally, in view of their many areas of engagement, it is imperative to study the (direct and indirect) impact of NHRIs on human rights promotion and protection. Further research should notably consider how NHRIs interact with

---

27 As indicated in chapter 9 of this volume, the EU does support the establishment and strengthening of Paris Principle compliant NHRIs through political and financial means, including the European Development Fund. On the international level, both UNDP and OHCHR support NHRIs. See for example: UNDP, UNDP-OHCHR Toolkit for Collaboration with National Human Rights Institutions, December 2010, available at http://www.ohchr.org/Documents/Countries/NHRI/1950-UNDP-UHCHR-Toolkit-LR.pdf.

28 FRA, for example, concluded that 'EU Member States should all benefit from NHRIs that go above and beyond the minimum standards laid down in the Paris Principles'. See: FRA, *supra* note 5, p. 6.

29 Note for example that the ICC Sub-Committee on Accreditation adopted general observations which guide the ICC in its determination of applications, and aim to provide a clarification of the Paris Principles. As noted by G. De Beco in chapter 11, further guidance on the Paris Principles is required, as reflected by the current review of the general observations by the ICC.

the various actors and mechanisms at the different levels of the human rights systems in order to enhance domestic human rights performance. Just one example: after providing information to UN treaty bodies on human rights violations within a country, NHRIs should follow up the ensuing international recommendations and use these in their lobby work towards the government. Since the international support for and engagement with NHRIs provides these institutions with legitimacy, it is of vital importance that it can be accurately checked whether they are effectively carrying out their functions and deserve a distinctive place as independent actors in the human rights arena.

ANNEX 1
COST ACTION IS0702

Recommendations on National Human Rights Institutions

1. The EU should encourage and support EU Member States to establish effectively functioning NHRIs, which are at least in compliance with the international minimum standards set forward in the Paris Principles, requiring: a broad human rights mandate clearly set forth in a constitutional or legislative document; a pluralistic composition with independent expert members, including from civil society; and sufficient resources, staff, and infrastructure enabling them to fulfill their mandates in an independent manner.
2. The EU should encourage European NHRIs to apply for accreditation by the International Coordinating Committee of NHRIs (ICC), which assesses whether NHRIs are in compliance with the Paris Principles (A-status).
3. At the same time, the EU should encourage the ICC to strengthen its accreditation procedure, particularly by involving independent experts to assess compliance with the Paris Principles. The EU could consider providing financial support for independent experts to be involved in the ICC accreditation procedure.
4. The EU might consider using the ICC accreditation as a benchmark for its own cooperation with NHRIs, similar to the practice of the UN Human Rights Council.
5. The EU should promote NHRIs as "overarching" human rights bodies which should include, as far as possible, cooperate with or serve as umbrella organizations for other national non-judicial bodies, such as equality bodies or special bodies for the rights of children, minorities, older persons, the sick, or persons with disabilities. Therefore, the EU institutions should refer to the Paris Principles and the need for a comprehensive approach to monitoring in the wording of relevant proposals for EU legislation, such as the proposed Horizontal Directive on Equal Treatment across All Grounds of Discrimination.
6. The EU should promote NHRIs to serve as national focal points for EU citizens to obtain comprehensive information on the protection of their rights on the basis of the EU Charter of Fundamental Rights as well as international human rights treaties. NHRIs should be encouraged to provide

country-specific information to treaty bodies on States parties' compliance with their respective treaty obligations. NHRIs should be promoted to serve as "one-stop-shops" directing EU citizens towards the competent human rights mechanisms (local, national, European, international) in case of a violation of their human rights.

7. The EU should strengthen the cooperation among European NHRIs, including through the delivery of financial support for the recently established Secretariat of the European Group of NHRIs.
8. The Council, Commission, and European Parliament should actively involve European NHRIs and the European Group of NHRIs in fundamental rights initiatives, including in consultations and in the development of fundamental rights policy, and provide financial support for these services.
9. In addition, EU institutions should consult NHRIs when assessing the impact of their legislative proposals upon the enjoyment of fundamental rights in EU member States.
10. The European Commission should consult the European NHRIs before the drafting of the Annual Report on the Application of the EU Charter of Fundamental Rights.
11. The EU Agency for Fundamental Rights (FRA) should continue its consistent cooperation with European NHRIs, while informing the EU institutions and EU member States of the state of affairs of NHRIs in the European Union, as it has done in a 2010 Report.
12. The EU is requested to take more seriously FRA's expertise and functioning as its own "NHRI". Accordingly, the EU should further develop the mandate and composition of FRA in order to ensure the full compliance of FRA with the Paris Principles. Especially, the mandate of FRA should include the competence to monitor the respect for human rights in the EU's internal and external policy and action.
13. The European institutions, and in particular the European External Action Service and the EU Special Representative for Human Rights should consistently integrate NHRIs as partners in the EU's promotion of human rights across the globe, especially on common thematic human rights priorities (such as business and human rights, or the rights of persons with disabilities), but also on specific country situations (e.g.: the consultation of NHRIs in the context of the Universal Periodic Review of the UN Human Rights Council).
14. The EU should consult NHRIs and their regional and international coordinating networks when determining its human rights priorities and action plans, and before drafting the annual EU report on human rights and democracy around the world.
15. The EU should organize annual special meetings with NHRIs and their regional and international coordinating networks in order to determine best practices and to discuss improvements in cooperation and further areas for interaction with the European Union.

ANNEX 2
PRINCIPLES RELATING TO THE STATUS OF NATIONAL INSTITUTIONS (THE PARIS PRINCIPLES)

Adopted by the UN General Assembly, Resolution 48/134 of 20 December 1993, in Annex:

COMPETENCE AND RESPONSIBILITIES

1. A national institution shall be vested with competence to promote and protect human rights.
2. A national institution shall be given as broad a mandate as possible, which shall be clearly set forth in a constitutional or legislative text, specifying its composition and its sphere of competence.
3. A national institution shall, inter alia, have the following responsibilities:
   a) To submit to the Government, Parliament and any other competent body, on an advisory basis either at the request of the authorities concerned or through the exercise of its power to hear a matter without higher referral, opinions, recommendations, proposals and reports on any matters concerning the promotion and protection of human rights; the national institution may decide to publicize them; these opinions, recommendations, proposals and reports, as well as any prerogative of the national institution, shall relate to the following areas:
   i. Any legislative or administrative provisions, as well as provisions relating to judicial organizations, intended to preserve and extend the protection of human rights; in that connection, the national institution shall examine the legislation and administrative provisions in force, as well as bills and proposals, and shall make such recommendations as it deems appropriate in order to ensure that these provisions conform to the fundamental principles of human rights; it shall, if necessary, recommend the adoption of new legislation, the amendment of legislation in force and the adoption or amendment of administrative measures;

ii. Any situation of violation of human rights which it decides to take up;
iii. The preparation of reports on the national situation with regard to human rights in general, and on more specific matters;
iv. Drawing the attention of the Government to situations in any part of the country where human rights are violated and making proposals to it for initiatives to put an end to such situations and, where necessary, expressing an opinion on the positions and reactions of the Government;

b) To promote and ensure the harmonization of national legislation regulations and practices with the international human rights instruments to which the State is a party, and their effective implementation;
c) To encourage ratification of the above-mentioned instruments or accession to those instruments, and to ensure their implementation;
d) To contribute to the reports which States are required to submit to United Nations bodies and committees, and to regional institutions, pursuant to their treaty obligations and, where necessary, to express an opinion on the subject, with due respect for their independence;
e) To cooperate with the United Nations and any other organization in the United Nations system, the regional institutions and the national institutions of other countries that are competent in the areas of the promotion and protection of human rights;
f) To assist in the formulation of programmes for the teaching of, and research into, human rights and to take part in their execution in schools, universities and professional circles;
g) To publicize human rights and efforts to combat all forms of discrimination, in particular racial discrimination, by increasing public awareness, especially through information and education and by making use of all press organs.

COMPOSITION AND GUARANTEES OF INDEPENDENCE AND PLURALISM

1. The composition of the national institution and the appointment of its members, whether by means of an election or otherwise, shall be established in accordance with a procedure which affords all necessary guarantees to ensure the pluralist representation of the social forces (of civilian society) involved in the promotion and protection of human rights, particularly by powers which will enable effective cooperation to be established with, or through the presence of, representatives of:
   a) Non-governmental organizations responsible for human rights and efforts to combat racial discrimination, trade unions, concerned social

and professional organizations, for example, associations of lawyers, doctors, journalists and eminent scientists;
b) Trends in philosophical or religious thought;
c) Universities and qualified experts;
d) Parliament;
e) Government departments (if these are included, their representatives should participate in the deliberations only in an advisory capacity).

2. The national institution shall have an infrastructure which is suited to the smooth conduct of its activities, in particular adequate funding. The purpose of this funding should be to enable it to have its own staff and premises, in order to be independent of the Government and not be subject to financial control which might affect its independence.
3. In order to ensure a stable mandate for the members of the national institution, without which there can be no real independence, their appointment shall be effected by an official act which shall establish the specific duration of the mandate. This mandate may be renewable, provided that the pluralism of the institution's membership is ensured.

METHODS OF OPERATION

Within the framework of its operation, the national institution shall:

a) Freely consider any questions falling within its competence, whether they are submitted by the Government or taken up by it without referral to a higher authority, on the proposal of its members or of any petitioner;
b) Hear any person and obtain any information and any documents necessary for assessing situations falling within its competence;
c) Address public opinion directly or through any press organ, particularly in order to publicize its opinions and recommendations;
d) Meet on a regular basis and whenever necessary in the presence of all its members after they have been duly convened;
e) Establish working groups from among its members as necessary, and set up local or regional sections to assist it in discharging its functions;
f) Maintain consultation with the other bodies, whether jurisdictional or otherwise, responsible for the promotion and protection of human rights (in particular ombudsmen, mediators and similar institutions);
g) In view of the fundamental role played by the non-governmental organizations in expanding the work of the national institutions, develop relations with the non-governmental organizations devoted to promoting and protecting human rights, to economic and social development, to combating racism, to protecting particularly vulnerable groups (especially children, migrant

workers, refugees, physically and mentally disabled persons) or to specialized areas.

ADDITIONAL PRINCIPLES CONCERNING THE STATUS OF COMMISSIONS WITH QUASI-JURISDICTIONAL COMPETENCE

A national institution may be authorized to hear and consider complaints and petitions concerning individual situations. Cases may be brought before it by individuals, their representatives, third parties, non-governmental organizations, associations of trade unions or any other representative organizations. In such circumstances, and without prejudice to the principles stated above concerning the other powers of the commissions, the functions entrusted to them may be based on the following principles:

a) Seeking an amicable settlement through conciliation or, within the limits prescribed by the law, through binding decisions or, where necessary, on the basis of confidentiality;
b) Informing the party who filed the petition of his rights, in particular the remedies available to him, and promoting his access to them;
c) Hearing any complaints or petitions or transmitting them to any other competent authority within the limits prescribed by the law;
d) Making recommendations to the competent authorities, especially by proposing amendments or reforms of the laws, regulations and administrative practices, especially if they have created the difficulties encountered by the persons filing the petitions in order to assert their rights.

ABOUT THE EDITORS AND THE AUTHORS

Bruce Adamson

Bruce Adamson has been the Legal Officer at the Scottish Human Rights Commission since its establishment in 2008. He is a lawyer qualified in three jurisdictions (Scotland, New Zealand, England & Wales). He is a member of the Edinburgh Children's Panel, a tribunal that makes decisions in relation to children who have committed offences or are in need of care and protection. He is also the chair of the Board of Trustees of the Scottish Child Law Centre. Bruce was an independent expert on Fundamental Rights for the European Commission's peer review missions to Turkey and Ukraine in 2011 and to Macedonia in 2012. He was the Coordinator of the European Group of National Human Rights Institutions. Since March 2013, he is the Permanent Representative of the International Coordinating Committee in Geneva.

Christoffer Badse

Christoffer Badse works as senior legal advisor at the Danish Institute for Human Rights. Mr. Badse graduated law school from the faculty of law, Copenhagen University in 2001 and has been affiliated with the Danish Institute since 2003. Mr. Badse is team leader/manager of the legal NHRI monitoring team responsible for the coordination of legal briefs to Parliament, international parallel reporting to UN treaty bodies and reports submitted during the Universal Periodic Review of Denmark. In addition Mr. Badse is responsible for the annual status report of DIHR presented in parliament. Mr. Badse has been assigned as national expert in the European Network of Legal Experts in the Non-discrimination Field and was project manager on the FRA-NET Research Network. He has been drafting reports for the FRA-Lex Network, the RAXEN and European Network of Experts on Fundamental Rights. Mr. Badse is member of the parliamentary special committee on police and legal cooperation as well as the editorial panel for the magazine of The Danish Bar and Law Society "the lawyer".

Ana Sofia Barros

Ana Sofia Barros is a Junior Member of the Leuven Centre for Global Governance Studies (GGS) and of the Institute for International Law of the University of Leuven since 2012. She obtained her Law degree from the Faculty of Law of the University of Lisbon as well as a Master's Degree in Human Rights and

Democratisation from the European Inter-University Centre for Human Rights and Democratisation. Prior to joining GGS, Ana Sofia worked for two years in a Portuguese Law Firm and became a qualified lawyer in 2012. She also undertook internships at an international NGO and the European Commission. Her PhD research at GGS focuses on the responsibility of member states for the acts of International Organisations. Ana Sofia is author of a book on international human rights law and international environmental law, published in 2012.

Antoine Buyse

Antoine Buyse is associate professor and senior researcher at the Netherlands Institute of Human Rights (SIM) of Utrecht University and a member of the Young Academy of the Royal Academy of Arts and Sciences. He is executive editor of the Netherlands Quarterly of Human Rights, member of the editorial board of the Dutch human rights review, and he hosts a weblog about the European Convention on Human Rights (echrblog.blogspot.com). He studied history and international law at Leiden University, where he also wrote his PhD on post-conflict housing restitution for refugees and displaced persons with a case study on Bosnia and Herzegovina. He was awarded the Max van der Stoel Prize, the Wiarda Prize, and the Erasmus Study Prize for his academic writings. Currently, he is conducting research on the links between freedom of expression and conflict escalation, funded by the Dutch Organisation for Scientific Research.

Gauthier de Beco

Gauthier de Beco holds a J.D. from the University of Leuven, an LL.M. (Master of Laws) from the University of Nottingham and a Ph.D. in Law from the University of Louvain. He is currently post-doctoral researcher at the Institute for Human Rights and Critical Studies of the University of Leuven. He was previously teaching assistant at the University of Louvain (2005–2009), legal advisor at the Belgian Ministry of Justice (2009–2011) and head of the CRPD Unit at the Belgian Centre for Equal Opportunities and Opposition to Racism (2012). He also taught human rights at University College London (2011–2012). He is a regular consultant to the Office of the UN High Commissioner for Human Rights (OHCHR) and several NGOs. Gauthier de Beco has worked extensively in the area of NHRIs and is the author of several publications on NHRIs.

Yvonne Donders

Prof. Dr. Yvonne Donders is Professor International Human Rights and Cultural Diversity and Executive Director of the Amsterdam Center for International Law at the Faculty of Law of the University of Amsterdam. She has graduated from Utrecht University in international relations and has done her PhD at the Law Faculty of Maastricht University on cultural human rights and the right to cultural identity. She teaches courses on international law and international human rights law and gives lectures on cultural rights and cultural diversity.

Yvonne Donders worked from March 2011 to October 2012 as project manager (1 day per week detachment) at the National Human Rights Institute of the Netherlands, assisting the transformation from Equal Treatment Commission to NHRI. Yvonne Donders is currently member of the National Commission for UNESCO, member of the European Expert Network on Culture (EENC) and Chair of the Dutch United Nations Association (*Nederlandse Vereniging voor de Verenigde Naties*, NVVN).

Aleksandra Gliszczyńska-Grabias

Aleksandra Gliszczyńska – Grabias holds a Ph.D. on counteracting anti-Semitism with instruments of international human rights law. She is a recipient of the 2012 Fellowship of the Foundation for Polish Science for outstanding achievements in science and research and 2010/2011 Graduate Fellow of the Yale University Initiative for the Interdisciplinary Study of Anti-Semitism. She is currently a senior researcher at the Poznan Human Rights Centre, Institute of Legal Studies of the Polish Academy of Sciences. Her main fields of research are: racial discrimination, freedom of speech vs. hate speech, defamation of religions and universal human rights protection.

Peter Hustinx

Peter Hustinx (1945) has been European Data Protection Supervisor since January 2004 and was re-appointed by the European Parliament and the Council in January 2009 for a second term of five years. He has been closely involved in the development of data protection law from the start, both at national and at international level. Before entering his office, Mr. Hustinx was President of the Dutch Data Protection Authority since 1991. From 1996 until 2000 he was Chairman of the Article 29 Working Party. He received law degrees in Nijmegen, the Netherlands, and in Ann Arbor, USA. Since 1986 he has been deputy judge in the Court of Appeal in Amsterdam.

Jan Jarab

Jan Jařab (1965) has been the Regional Representative for Europe of the UN High Commissioner for Human Rights since January 2010. The Regional Office for Europe deals with the human rights dimension of internal and external EU policies as well as with human rights challenges in EU Member States and Candidate Countries. Previously, Jan Jařab served as Member of Cabinet of Vladimír Špidla, European Commissioner for Employment, Social Affairs and Equal Opportunities (2004–2010). In this role, he was actively involved in preparing the European Commission's 2008 proposal for a horizontal non-discrimination directive as well as in launching the EU Platform for Roma Inclusion and the Ad Hoc Expert Group on Transition from Institutional to Community-Based Care (both 2009). For almost four years (2001–2004) he served the Government of the Czech Republic as its Commissioner for Human Rights and Director of the

Human Rights Division of the Office of Government. Jan Jařab holds a doctorate in medicine from Prague's Charles University (1990) and a MSc in anthropology from University College London (1997). He has published a book of essays, over 100 articles (mostly in the Czech press), and numerous translations.

Katrien Meuwissen

Katrien Meuwissen is a researcher at the Leuven Centre for Global Governance Studies and is teaching assistant at the Institute for International Law of the University of Leuven since 2010. She is pursuing a PhD in international law on the topic of European NHRIs in a multi-layered human rights system. Katrien studied law at the KU Leuven and completed a Master of European Policy and Politics at the KU Leuven and Université de Genève. Before joining the Institute, Katrien has done two internships at the Belgian Permanent Mission to the United Nations in Geneva, attending the UN Human Rights Council sessions.

Manfred Nowak

Born 1950 in Bad Aussee (Austria), 1973 conferral of doctorate (Dr. Iur.) University of Vienna, 1975 LL.M Columbia University (New York), since 1992 Director of the Ludwig Boltzmann Institute of Human Rights (Vienna), 1993–2001 Member of the UN Working Group on Enforced or Involuntary Disappearances, 1996–2003 Judge at the Human Rights Chamber of Bosnia-Herzegovina, 2004–2010 UN Special Rapporteur on Torture, 2000–2012 head of an independent human rights commission at the Austrian Ministry of Interior (under the Human Rights Advisory Board of the Ministry); since 2008 head of the interdisciplinary research platform "Human Rights in the European Context" (University of Vienna); Member of the Austrian Monitoring Body of the UN Convention on the Rights of Persons with Disabilities; Professor of International Law and Human Rights at the University of Vienna; since 2012 Member of the Management Board of the EU Agency for Fundamental Rights in Vienna; since 2012 Scientific Director of the Vienna Master of Arts in Human Rights (University of Vienna); since 2012 Head of Visiting Commission of the Austrian Ombudsman Board; author of more than 500 publications in the fields of constitutional, administrative and international law with a focus on fundamental and human rights.

Marjolijn Olde Monnikhof

Drs. M. Olde Monnikhof is Head of the department of Research, Advise and Communication of the Netherlands Institute of Human Rights (*het College voor de Rechten van de Mens*). In the period June 2010 to October 2012, she was the project manager NHRI responsible for the transformation from Equal Treatment Commission to NHRI.

Previously Marjolijn Olde Monnikhof worked as a business consultant at Kiwa Management Consultants and before that as a researcher at the Radboud

University and the Erasmus University. She has graduated from Leiden University in Social and Organisation Psychology.

Katarzyna Sękowska-Kozłowska

Katarzyna Sękowska-Kozłowska is senior researcher at the Poznan Human Rights Centre, Institute of Legal Studies of the Polish Academy of Sciences. She holds a PhD from the Institute of Legal Studies of the Polish Academy of Sciences (2011). Her thesis on the UN Committee on the Elimination of Discrimination against Women (CEDAW) was published in Polish (Komitet ONZ ds. Likwidacji Dyskryminacji Kobiet – ustrój, kompetencje, funkcjonowanie, Toruń 2011). Her main fields of research are discrimination issues with a special focus on gender discrimination and the UN human rights mechanisms.

Kirsten Roberts

Kirsten Roberts BCL, M.Litt. is Acting Deputy Chief Executive and Director of Research, Policy and Promotion in the Irish Human Rights Commission (IHRC), Ireland's A-status National Human Rights Institution (NHRI). From 2008–2011 she was also coordinator of the European Group of NHRIs. Prior to joining the IHRC, Ms Roberts worked as a legal officer in the United Nations International Criminal Tribunal for the former Yugoslavia. Her previous experience has included the Permanent Representation of Ireland to the Council of Europe, European Court of Human Rights, European Court of Justice, and Amnesty International. Ms Roberts has spoken widely and written on the topic of NHRIs and has acted as a resource person on NHRIs for OHCHR and UNDP. She has also undertaken a number of missions as an independent expert under the European Commission's TAIEX programme.

Stefan Sottiaux

Stefan Sottiaux (MJur Oxford 2000, PhD Antwerp 2006) is Assistant-Professor of Constitutional and Administrative law at the University of Leuven. He teaches courses in constitutional law and European and comparative discrimination law. He was a visiting fellow at the Harvard Law School Human Rights Program (2006). His research focuses on comparative human rights law, with a particular interest in freedom of expression, non-discrimination and methods of judicial decision-making in multilevel systems. He is the co-author of Handboek Discriminatierecht (Kluwer, 2006) and the author of Terrorism and the Limitation of Rights (Hart Publishing, 2008). Stefan Sottiaux is a member of the Brussels bar and has experience in defending clients before the European Court of Human Rights, the Belgian Constitutional Court and the highest Belgian administrative court.

Jogchum Vrielink

Jogchum Vrielink is a post-doctoral researcher, and coordinator of the Centre for Discrimination Law (Institute for Constitutional Law, University of Leuven, Belgium). He holds a PhD in law from the University of Leuven (2010) and also studied anthropology and public administration in Belgium, the Netherlands, and Sweden. His research areas include discrimination law, anthropology of law, hate speech, freedom of speech, religion and religious freedom. He has published widely on these topics.

Jan Wouters

Jan Wouters is full Professor of International Law and International Organizations, Jean Monnet Chair ad personam EU and Global Governance and Director of the Leuven Centre for Global Governance Studies and Institute for International Law at the University of Leuven (KU Leuven). In Leuven, he teaches public international law, international organizations, the law of the World Trade Organization and humanitarian and security law. As Visiting Professor at Sciences Po (Paris) and the College of Europe (Bruges) he teaches EU external relations law. He also teaches international law in the Master of Laws in International Economic Law (IELPO) at the University of Barcelona and international criminal law in the European Master's in Human Rights and Democratisation (EMA, Venice). He is President of the Flemish Foreign Affairs Council, which advises the Flemish Government, is President of the United Nations Association Flanders Belgium, and practises law as Of Counsel at Linklaters, Brussels. He is a Member of the Royal Flemish Academy of Belgium for Sciences and Arts. Jan Wouters has published widely on international, EU, corporate and financial law (over 500 publications including 46 books and 85 international journal articles). Apart from his participation in many international research networks, he advises various international organizations, trains international officials and is often asked to comment international events in the media. From June 2013 onwards he is coordinator of a large-scale FP7 Programme FRAME, "Fostering Human Rights Among European (External and Internal) Policies".

INDEX

M

N

O

P

R

S

T

U

www.ingramcontent.com/pod-product-compliance
Ingram Content Group UK Ltd.
Pitfield, Milton Keynes, MK11 3LW, UK
UKHW051920100926
8556IPUK00021B/1283